# TURBULENT EMPIRES

# TURBULENT EMPIRES

## A History of Global Capitalism since 1945

MIKE MASON

McGill-Queen's University Press
Montreal & Kingston • London • Chicago

ISBN 978-0-7735-5321-7 (cloth)
ISBN 978-0-7735-5435-1 (EPDF)
ISBN 978-0-7735-5436-8 (EPUB)

Legal deposit second quarter 2018
Bibliothèque nationale du Québec

Printed in Canada on acid-free paper that is 100% ancient forest free (100% post-consumer recycled), processed chlorine free.

This book has been published with the help of a grant from the Canadian Federation for the Humanities and Social Sciences, through the Awards to Scholarly Publications Program, using funds provided by the Social Sciences and Humanities Research Council of Canada.

Funded by the Government of Canada | Financé par le gouvernement du Canada | Canada | Canada Council for the Arts | Conseil des arts du Canada

We acknowledge the support of the Canada Council for the Arts, which last year invested $153 million to bring the arts to Canadians throughout the country. Nous remercions le Conseil des arts du Canada de son soutien. L'an dernier, le Conseil a investi 153 millions de dollars pour mettre de l'art dans la vie des Canadiennes et des Canadiens de tout le pays.

**Library and Archives Canada Cataloguing in Publication**

Mason, Mike, 1938–, author
Turbulent empires : a history of global capitalism since 1945 / Mike Mason.

Includes bibliographical references and index.
Issued in print and electronic formats.
ISBN 978-0-7735-5321-7 (cloth). – ISBN 978-0-7735-5435-1 (EPDF). – ISBN 978-0-7735-5436-8 (EPUB)

1. Capitalism – History – 20th century. 2. Capitalism – History – 21st century. 3. History, Modern – 20th century. 4. History, Modern – 21st century. 5. Imperialism. I. Title.

HB501.M52 2018 330.12'20904 C2017-907846-1
C2017-907847-X

This book was typeset by True to Type in 10.5/13 Sabon

# Contents

# Acknowledgments

Due to my faulty memory, not all of those to whom I am indebted for ideas and interpretations am I able to acknowledge. But of those whose influence has remained indelible even over fifty years, I would like to remember those who taught me at UBC: Ronald Dore, Ping-ti Ho, and James Shirley in Asian studies; Fredrick Soward, John Norris, and Alf Cooke in history; and Stanley Z. Pech and Tadeusz Halpert Scanderbeg in Slavonic studies. Wayne Suttles introduced me to anthropology, a subject I subsequently studied at the University of Birmingham with R.E. Bradbury.

Among my colleagues and friends at universities in Canada, Britain, and Nigeria, I recall with great relish Robin Porter, sometime mandarin at the British embassy in Beijing, with whom I shared an early, and likely unjustified, enthusiasm for revolutionary China, and Emily Hill who supported me in more ways than one at Queen's. David Parker, also at Queen's, guided me in Latin American history. Much of my limited grasp of Indian history I owe to John Hill, who supplied me with inexpensive texts bought in India, Depunkar Gupta of JNU, and to Paritosh Kumar of Queen's who has tried to keep me up to date on Indian politics and Bollywood movies. Keith Meadowcroft was my first dragoman in India and Anthony Harris introduced me to further readings in development.

The expansion of my interest in the Middle East and Maghreb I owe to having taught mainly Muslim students in secondary school and university in Nigeria. At the Centre of West African Studies of the University of Birmingham I wrote a thesis on a nineteenth-century Muslim emirate in what is today Nigeria. At Ahmadu Bello University, where I was a Commonwealth scholar and then a lecturer, I was encouraged to think of the African Sahel and Sudan regions not so much as parts of a generalized and ethnicized Africa, as is conventional, but as a regions within the wide and cosmopolitan *dar al-islam.* The Nigerians and others with whom I studied West African history are too numerous to mention although I would like to recall especially the late John Lavers of Kano, Murray Last, latterly editor of *Africa*, and 'Remi Adeleye my host in Ibadan. Bill Freund, latterly of Durban, who seems to have read almost everything of interest to me, has helped keep me up to speed over the years. My enthusiasm for the rich arts of Nigeria I owe to Michael Cardew who introduced me to Kenneth Murray of the Lagos Museum and to Bernard Fagg of the Nigerian Department of Antiquities and later of the Ashmolean Museum, Oxford. John Picton at the School of Oriental and African Studies has sustained my interest in African arts over several decades and Kent Benson, has reminded me of an African aesthetic that both of us have discussed for half a century.

Of my Canadian colleagues in the field of African studies, several stand out for their sustaining support; Linda Freeman, Myron Echenberg, Bob Shenton, Dan O'Meara, Bruce Berman, and Barry Riddell.

To the anonymous readers for McGill-Queen's University Press, my thanks for a meticulous job and especially for encouraging comments. I would like to acknowledge and thank the three editors who have guided this book from submission to completion: Jacqueline Mason, Kathleen Kearns, and Shelagh Plunkett.

None of the above is responsible in any way for the omissions and travesties in the story that follows.

This book is for Mary with love and a most particular gratitude and for Amina, Hannah, and Sam who may discover whether I have been right or wrong.

PREFACE

# On with the Show

Even if the crises that are looming up are overcome and a new run of prosperity lies ahead, deeper problems will still remain. Modern capitalism has no purpose except to keep the show going.[1]

Joan Robinson

But never forget that what it's really about is top-down class warfare. That may sound simplistic, but it's the way the world works.[2]

Paul Krugman

This study deals with the recent origins of the globalized world that we inhabit. It is a coda to Eric Hobsbawm's *Age of Extremes* (1994), an unmatched history of the "short twentieth century" that began with the outbreak of the Great War and ended with the dissolution of the Soviet Union and the abandonment of communism throughout most of the world.[3] Adding a quarter century of recent history to Hobsbawm's "view into obscurity" has led me to shift my focus away from Europe towards Asia. It is here, and especially in China, that we shall very probably witness the most dramatic events of the twenty-first century. Eurocentrism is thus likely to be a costly vice. Likewise America Firstism.

The present study was originally to be called *When the Music Stopped*, but as time went by, and the band struck up again, that seemed inappropriately pessimistic. So as the banks were recapitalized, the market revived, the colossal Chinese economy boomed, the show went on, and the title was changed. The present title has been adopted to recognize not only the crisis of 2008 but all those crises, national and international, that have been the corollaries of the expansion and consolidation of post-war global capitalism, the seventy years that we might call, so far at least, "the short American century." This process of expansion in earlier times had been dubbed "free-trade imperialism," but now we give it a more tender description, "globalization." As I compose this preface in the aftermath of the "Brexit" vote of 23 June 2016, however, this globalization that engendered novel blocs of political and economic influence seems to have lost some of its mojo.

Capitalism is by nature turbulent and destructive; its episodic shifts have inevitably been marked by convolutions and even revolutions. We see this in the decades after 1945, years that still bore the scars of the wartime violence that had been manifest from one end of Eurasia to the other – civil wars, wars of imperial and neo-imperial contraction and expansion, of ethnic cleansing, and of massive human displacement and suffering with new blocs coalesced, older states stripped of territories, new dictatorships emergent, revolutions and counterrevolutions raging, and economies variously collapsing and vaulting. Guiding and structuring this change for several decades in the postwar era, in both the capitalist world and the communist bloc, planning reigned. Keynesianism and, to a large extent, import substitution industrialization (ISI) ruled in the world of capitalism. Then, slowly from the 1970s, neoliberalism and its prescriptions like the Washington Consensus, elbowed their way into credibility among politicians and professors. From circa 1990, with the demolition of the Berlin Wall, came a different set of convulsions, still evident in the Ukraine and the eastern realms of the EU.

To make my point about the turbulence of postwar capitalism, I have shifted my gaze from a single focus, let us say "American hegemony," to look at particular states and blocks of states from western Europe east to Japan and south to Latin America. In doing this it is possible to see that the ruling elites of states make, or try to make, their own histories, not, of course, under conditions that they might prefer but in the circumstances forced upon them. In the process they often shift their ideologies, their politics and their purposes quite radically; think about China, Russia, and Germany, which I discuss, and Vietnam and Cuba which I do not. Usually inadvertency dominates. No one could predict the breakup of the Soviet bloc, the outcome of the end of apartheid, the destruction of Iraq, the stagnation of the economy of Japan, the political crisis of Brazil, or even Brexit. To understand a little more that the world is not actually "made in America," I have sketched the national histories of several states.

There is nothing new I can say about capitalism nor anything novel about globalization; in different forms both have existed since at least the seventeenth century. Contemporary globalization, driven by the economic explosion of postwar America, has appropriated older forms of trade and commerce and affixed them to the new; French bankers still squeeze foreign borrowers, as they did the Egyptians in the nineteenth century, but social media transforms political possibility, as in Syntagma and Tahrir Squares. And, like its ancestor, contemporary globalization is both martial and commercial – it requires fleets and armies and huge defence and security expenditure as well as a web of banks and transnational corporations and an electronic net to sustain itself. American-dominated financial practices and institutions – the dollar, the IMF, the debt rating services, the Office of Foreign Assets Control – serve to channel the entire system. Not to exaggerate globalization, although the American version of English is the world's Latin in the marketplaces and counting houses, the airports, and at Davos, it will never be the lingua franca of the world's towns, and at the world's movies one is just as likely to hear Hindi or Brazilian Portuguese.

The overarching, ubiquitous, postwar imperial centre is still America. The practice that America engages in economically, militarily, and culturally to assure its dominance is called "hegemony," a relatively contemporary word revived and popularized, as I note in chapter 1, in the 1970s. Often American writers call hegemony by the bashful term "leadership," but the two refer to a similar practice. With the dissolution of the Soviet empire circa 1990 it appeared that hegemonic competition had ceased to exist; the "bipolar" world was toast. So for a brief, giddy, moment at the end of the twentieth century it looked like history had run out of road and we were now safely in McDonald's parking lot. Then, a convulsion. To the shock and horror of the world, 9/11 proved that the "end of history" view was premature. Then came a second convulsion, the crash of 2008 and within the following years a growing popular reaction to the assumptions and inequalities of the boom and bubble years. Among these reactions was the Brexit of June 2016 and the election of Donald Trump to the presidency of the US.

In sum, in the snapshots that follow I hope to consider several national developmental histories, most of which have shown themselves to be remarkable and all of which are distinctive. Yet, globally, America remains as *the* hegemon. The slogan "Bring America Back" is therefore otiose; America never went anywhere to come back from. Meanwhile, we are turning the pages of the American century and, to quote Joan Robinson, the show still goes on.

I started reading contemporary history in the autumn of 1956; my first undergraduate months coincided with the Suez crisis and the Hungarian Revolution. I launched the present essay just before Christmas 2011, in a week after the spokesman for the Canadian government said that we would be leaving the Kyoto agreement (12 December), Britain refused to accept changes to the EU constitution (16 December), and the last military convoy drove out of Iraq to Kuwait (17 December). On Thursday of the same week the Anglo-American essayist and polemicist Christopher Hitchens died and on Saturday, the Czech playwright and politician, Vaclav Havel. The Dow Jones Industrial Average exhibited skittishness, and Canadian government ten-year bonds sold at 1.862 per cent. Rich Greeks continued to flee their country, the West's most ancient, with suitcases full of euros – on average €4 to 5 billion a month. In China, the Guangdong village of Wukan remained besieged by police after a land dispute that led to the murder of one of the protests' leaders. Clashes continued on the streets of Cairo; the Arab Spring had morphed into a winter of discontent. On 25 December, St Theresa's Catholic Church in Jos State, Nigeria, was destroyed by a suicide bomber associated with a previously little known jihadi group called Boko Haram. In many quarters there was worry; it seemed that not only was the Muslim world once more in ferment but that several of the West's most favoured Arab tyrants were heading for Ozymandian fates. There was really little room for optimism about global economic recovery, either, although the pages of the financial press managed to turn out opinions by otherwise unknown fund managers who for the most part were bullish. There was always wealth to be increased for the prudent investor, they said reassuringly. It went without saying that this wealth might have to be managed and stored "offshore" – a word, like "privatization" in an earlier decade, that suddenly became common right across the capitalist world. "Inequality," the word and the concern, was on the rise in the media but, presumably, little mentioned in corporate dining rooms.

Yet, only a year earlier a successor to Joan Robinson at Cambridge, the economist Ha-Joon Chang, had commented: "The global economy lies in tatters" and in October 2013, Nouriel Roubini of New York University, known as "Dr Doom" for his prediction of the 2007–08 meltdown, claimed "this 'recovery' feels temporary." "We now live in an unambiguous age of crisis" announced the British political scientist and philosopher, David Runciman, in the same year. And at the time of the Greek crisis in mid-2015, Paul Krugman, an eminent Euro- and Sino-pessimist, wrote despairingly of "Europe's Impossible Dream."[4] Still the light of hope shone in the eyes of some. By mid-September 2015, "Dr Doom" had stunned his listeners with his change of heart. Others joined in the rising chorus of optimism. "Doomsday predictions of the Anglo-American media notwithstanding," wrote Konrad H. Jarausch, the historian of Germany, "the ghosts of Europe's bloody past are not returning and repeating previous catastrophes."[5]

# TURBULENT EMPIRES

# 1

# The American Leviathan

In 1981, the Harvard political scientist, Samuel Huntington, then at the apogee of his influence in a subject that was virtually owned in America, wrote "[I]t is possible to speak of a body of political ideas that constitutes 'Americanism' in a sense in which one can never speak of 'Britishism,' 'Frenchism,' 'Germanism,' or 'Japaneseism.' Americanism in this sense is comparable to other ideologies and religions ... To reject the central ideas of that doctrine is to be un-American ... This identification of nationality with political creed or values makes the United States virtually unique."

To go back a step is to see that American uniqueness has been often expressed as American "exceptionalism." This exceptionalism, it is argued, is an essential element in America greatness. In his book *No Apology: The Case For American Greatness*, for instance, former governor and later presidential hopeful, Mitt Romney, made the connection and dismissed those who might think otherwise: "This reorientation away from a celebration of American exceptionalism is misguided and bankrupt."[1] In what some Republicans called the "New American Century," a phrase that emerged at the end of the twentieth century, there was thus talk of exceptionalism and leadership but, perhaps not surprisingly, avoidance of any mention of "empire." Talk of empire was reserved for the critics of US foreign policy.

In February 1998, the Democratic secretary of state, Madeleine Albright, had added her weight to the exceptionalist view when, justifying the use of cruise missiles against Iraq, she admitted with a striking stridency: "If we have to use force, it is because we are America. We are the indispensable nation. We stand tall. We see farther into the future."[2] This idea of indispensability thus stands alongside Samuel

Huntington's "Americanism" and Mitt Romney's "exceptionalism." Later, however, there would be talk of making America "great *again*," as though, worryingly, greatness had, at some time in the recent past, slipped away.

Like all national ideologies, the triad comprising the singularity of Americanism, the claim of exceptionalism, and the assurance of indispensability has shifted and mutated like the coloured fragments in a kaleidoscope. It had also acquired other elements, like economism, which I shall mention below, and evangelism. The rich combination of elements thus assembled produced the view that America, more than any of its western allies, has developed to become a bastion of God-given economic freedom and political liberty, a universal ideal, and a Biblical city shining on a hill.

For many, Americans as well as others, the view that God had made America great may be justified retrospectively by the simple fact that with the fall of communism, it was unmistakably and singularly triumphant. For a decade, from 1991, America had no rivals, nor were there even any threats on the horizon. With the disappearance of the Soviet Empire and the decline of Japan, it was the sole superpower, the preponderant power, and the leader of the "New World Order." Almost all other major capitalist democracies, large and small (the EU, India, Canada), were sustained by and deferred to American power, as they had been since the end of World War Two.

Besides the other major democracies were other states that were viewed as being an American responsibility. These included, according to different definitions, dependencies, protectorates, and clients. From Central America to Central Asia, these welcomed American firms and often accepted American air and naval bases. Most housed conspicuous American embassies, while the majority trained their militaries with the American army, bought American arms, and wore American gear. They learned to think, consume, and even to speak American. Yet, we will come to the awkward fact that in the background to this American triumph was the unmentioned fact that by the 1980s the advanced capitalist world that America had dominated had entered an economic downturn. The view that this downturn had replaced triumph was called "declinism."

## ASCENSION: THE PRIVILEGE OF POSSESSION

The ascending arc of American power in the twentieth century – "the American Century" – has conventionally been seen as the most recent chapter of an epic known as "the rise of the West." This rise began around 1500 and lasted for half a millennium. In that half millennium, and especially in the early nineteenth century, a great divergence took place between the West and Asia with western Europe and America pulling away from the advanced parts of the East. And in the same century, and well before the Great War of 1914–18, America had superseded, in practically all terms, its European rivals. By the end of the 1939–45 war, a war that had devastated the European competition and wasted Japan, America stood out as the number one capitalist state.

Even before the war ended America had a hammerlock on practically everything that was worth having, including more than half the world's gold used to settle payments for international trade. It also had the dollar, the world's reserve currency; possession of which was "an exorbitant privilege" according to one indignant French commentator.[3] From its relatively high level of per capita GDP growth as well as these two advantages (not to mention the industry behind a massive and modern military) came the new global order, expressed in confident terms as "American leadership" or, less frequently, "American primacy."[4] But leadership and primacy did not imply the beggaring of neighbours. While US planners were obviously preoccupied with US postwar prosperity, they also supported the future development of poorer nations, first the Western Europeans and then Japan. Actually, the two went together. In a booklet produced for the public, American delegates to the conference at Bretton Woods told representatives from what was to become the Third World: "If we help you to become prosperous, *you will be able to buy more things from us.*"[5]

It followed from the faith of the Allies in American leadership that the headquarters of the newly formed United Nations would rise in New York, the centre of the New World. The UN building itself was to stand on property donated by the richest of Americans, the Rockefellers, whose fortune came from coal, oil, and banking, the greatest assets of the twentieth century. Right from the beginning, Washington not only had a seat on the Security Council of the UN but, as well, held the franchises for a number of the votes of its Third World dependencies in the General Assembly. At the end of the twentieth century, the ten commandments for globalization including deregulation, privatization, and an encouragement of external debt became known as the "Washington Consensus."[6]

Essential to its hegemony was not merely its gold and its guns but the matter of America possessing the world's dominant culture, its language, and its economic theory – which has been called "economism."[7] Culture was part of America's "soft power"; it took the form of "the American way of life" for all to emulate. (We will see more of American culture and language in the next chapter.) Even before World War Two much popular music in the Western world had been either invented or was dominated by Americans – blues, jazz, folk, musicals, country, bluegrass. Although certain field sports remained unAmericanized, Americans were usually dominant right across the board in the Olympic Games and in such sports as golf and tennis. Religion, however, did not recross the Atlantic from which it had originally come to the New World. European politicians rarely invoked any god.

It was in the Europe countries in which its armies had fought and later occupied that American culture first turned on its charms. Victoria De Grazia:

> The Old World was where the United States turned its power as the premier consumer society into the dominion that came from being universally recognized as the fountainhead of modern consumer practices ... [T]he Market Empire pressed its advantage from the outset of the Cold War. Once the pillars of the old regime of consumption had been knocked from under it and western European societies resolved to build anew on the basis of the right to a decent standard of living, all forces grasped the stakes. And all sides played the card of consumer desire. Starting in 1948 with the Marshall Plan, the Market Empire acknowledged as much, both by trying to bind western Europe to its own consumer democracy and by warring to overturn the Soviet bloc's state socialism.[8]

Not even the French, whose intellectuals and political masters were often indignant about threats to their own cultural superiority, were immune to the attractions of American culture. Sarah Bakewell, in her survey of the masters of postwar existentialism in France, has underlined this:

> The existentialist culture of the late 1940s seemed very Parisian to anyone looking in from the outside, but it was also driven by a love, or at least a fascination, for all things American ... Few young Parisians could resist American clothes, American films or American music ... In the cinemas ... people devoured American crime movies and, from the *bouqinistes* along the Seine, they bought American fiction ... Many American books were translated by French publishers: "traduit de l'americain," became a favourite phrase on covers.[9]

And not just Europe: Elvis Presley's "Love Me Tender" played in distant Kabul in 1962, and "Elvis' songs became a staple of youth performances."[10] Young men everywhere wore baseball caps, jeans, and t-shirts; in the army they wore uniforms, haircuts, and name tags in the style of the ubiquitous GIs. There were other aspects of American cultural hegemony, as well: I will mention the haunting fear of hamburger hegemony in the next chapter.

And how can we factor in the immeasurable advantage of Americans owning the English language and communicating in it natively? At Deutsche Bank, Germany's largest commercial bank, in the 1990s English became the language of choice. Before that, in 1965, the *Swedish Journal of Economics* changed its language from Swedish to English.[11] Virtually all economic neologisms from "asset price inflation" and "toxic assets" to "Greenspan put," "zombie banks," and "offshore" were coined or circulated in American English, which became the Latin of the American Century. Even "arbitrage" had an American ring. And even now (2017) there is in Paris a prominent language school that teaches "Wall Street English."[12] While the British Broadcasting Corporation (BBC) served listeners throughout the world, and was viewed by one British commentator as being "more important in keeping these islands glued together than any political party," its distinctive spirit began to diminish in the late 1970s after which more of its content and advertising became Americanized.[13]

In his postscript, in which he offers a perspective on American economic performance, not to say decline, Robert J. Gordon consoles us with a kind of complacency. "American inventions have established a new phase of dominance," he stresses, and continues:

> Though few computers and smart devices are being manufactured in the United States, almost all the software and organiza-

> tional creativity of the modern digital age has originated within US borders. Of the ten most valuable companies in the world, eight are located in the United States ... Research and development is at an all-time high as a percent of GDP, and the development of new drugs by the pharmaceutical industry is also dominated by American firms. Innovations in the exploration and production of shale oil and gas have reduced America's import dependence faster than was predicted only a few years ago. America's private and public research universities have a near monopoly in the league table of the world's top thirty institutions of higher education.[14]

So if America declines, he implies, it will be a relative decline, a slowing down but hardly a defeat.

### TAKING CARE OF BUSINESS

The foundations of the postwar economic order were laid at the Bretton Woods conference in New Hampshire in 1944. There forty-four official delegates met and talked about the future that they vowed would be unlike the past. The leading voices at the conference were J.M. Keynes and Harry Dexter White. While Keynes was by far the most celebrated economist at the gathering, White had all the economic clout of Wall Street behind him.[15] Jeffrey A. Frieden:

> The United States was now unchallenged in world trade, finance, and investment. The dollar no longer shared monetary leadership with the pound sterling and the French franc; most British and French overseas investments had been liquidated. Europe seemed to have an insatiable hunger for the products of America's manufacturing powerhouse, rather than compete with American industry. Exports at war's end were twice as important to American industry as they had been in the 1930s, while import competition was much weaker.[16]

During the conference, US officials "kept tight control of the proceedings and sought to avoid votes on issues where US goals might not be served."[17]

More was to come. On 5 June 1947 the US secretary of state, George Marshall, launched the eponymous Marshall Plan, officially known as the "European Recovery Program" (ERP), which saw a total of $12.5 billion being sent to Europe over the next several years. In April 1948 the Americans established the Economic Cooperation Administration and the Organization for European Economic Co-Operation (OEEC). The OEEC was later to become the Organization for Economic Co-operation and Development (OECD). One of the most significant effects of the Marshall Plan was to integrate the western sector of the defeated Germany into the overall economy of Europe. It therefore must be seen as the ancestor of the European Union – an organization behind which Washington stood solidly. A unified European market, yearning for American goods, was a dream come true for American business. And Europe, even its communist states, did recover. Here is Eric Hobsbawm on what he called the "Golden Age" and the French, *les Trente Glorieuses*:

> It is now evident that the Golden Age essentially belonged to the developed capitalist countries, which, throughout these decades, represented about three quarters of the world's production and over 80 per cent of its manufacturing exports ... The world economy was ... growing at an explosive rate. By the 1960s it was plain that there had never been anything like it. World output of manufactures quadrupled between the early 1950s and the early 1970s and, what is even more impressive, world trade in manufactured products grew tenfold ... Initially this astonishing explosion of the economy seemed merely a gigantic version of what had gone before; as it were, a globalization of the state of the pre-1945 USA, taking that country as the model of a capitalist industrial society. So, to some extent it was ... Much of the great world boom was thus a catching up, or in the USA, a continuation of old trends.[18]

From the time of the Marshall Plan, most influential European corporations emulated American practices while the City of London, Europe's financial Vatican for most of the nineteenth century and even into the twentieth, became progressively diminished in importance and Americanized, especially from the 1960s onward. By mid-2015, the last British bank to compete with Wall Street in the securities market folded. Goodbye, then, to the idea that London might continue to flourish as an autonomous financial services capital.[19]

Previously, at Bretton Woods, it had been accepted that the head of the World Bank, located in Washington, was to be an American. J.M.

Keynes tried to prevent this, arguing that it would put an ineradicable American stamp on postwar capitalism, but he was overridden.[20] The IMF, too, was located in Washington. Although sometimes led by a French person he or, later, she, was never one out of step with the dominant orthodoxy. One official in the US treasury referred to it as a "convenient conduit for US influence."[21] It was useful in advocating the new neoliberal orthodoxy when its time came.

Later, from 1975, three American private agencies emerged that were licensed to rate the quality of global bonds.[22] Until the present, their influence has remained unshaken; so, during the crisis of the euro in 2010, the rate for Greek sovereign bonds and even German *bunds* was decided in offices on Wall Street. The Germans may have accepted this with a strained stoicism although the Greeks became outraged at the whole arrangement.[23] International law on investment was also according to American rules.

Up to the 1960s, during the administrations of presidents John F. Kennedy and Lyndon B. Johnson (together 1961–69), Keynesianism reached its peak. Even Johnson's successor, Richard Nixon, announced in 1971, "I am a Keynesian in economics."[24] But then, with the alarming decline of the rate of profit for American businesses, Keynesianism went out of popularity. In the next decades, a new ideology that had come to be called "neoliberalism," sometimes "market fundamentalism," became the governing economic theory adopted by governments, businesses, banks, and international institutions like the World Bank and the IMF. The tenets, like globalization, of economics departments and business schools, of which that of Harvard was the Mecca, were broadcast by financial journals as if they were Gospel. In the form of austerity programs adopted after the 2008 recession, both Germany and Britain followed the US neoliberal lead with unflinching enthusiasm.[25] Although Keynesians continued to exist, and their spokespeople continued to command respect (all the more during times of crisis, as after the 2008 recession), neoliberalism was beginning to dominate the ruling heights of economics.

So in spite of its gunboats and "full spectrum dominance," subjects that we will touch on below, the American empire was not secured by foreign policy or by bases and bombers but by global economic influence, that is, by ideas. Alongside the schools of business that often dominate the campuses of Western universities and the think tanks mentioned below, there were other institutions, some of hoary antiquity, that echoed a similar ethos. One such was the constellation of

Rotary clubs, the first being founded in Chicago in 1905 and by 1939 reaching almost everywhere in Europe. These clubs were associations of small businessmen whose solidarity helped protect them from big capital and who thrived in the lower-middle class culture that de Grazia refers to, unkindly, as "Babbitry." Rotary International was to become the world's largest service club with 30,000 branches. In origin and inspiration it was as American as apple pie or, later, Happy Meals. "He profits most who serves best" was its motto.[26]

## AMERICA AND NEOLIBERALISM

In the world of economic ideologies, the time for a new revelation had finally come. "The market is always right," market fundamentalists had professed even in the 1960s. Trade unions and the minimum wage caused distortions, they claimed. Welfare systems had to be cut back: "There is no alternative," insisted Margaret Thatcher, then British prime minister (1979–90) and doyenne of the new economic philosophy.

The Adam Smith of neoliberal thought was the Austrian Friedrich von Hayek who migrated to America via the London School of Economics at the end of the war. The main argument of his radical book *The Road to Serfdom,* published in 1944, was that the role of the state in managing the economy, the central advocacy of Keynesianism, could only lead to serfdom. The regulation of economies by the state, such as Keynesian demand management, was disastrous. Only the market knew the way forward; in the writings of his followers, in fact, markets often became reified, that is, given life, and were assumed to be omniscient.

Initially Hayek's ideas fell on stony ground. Then, from the 1970s, leading economists and managers, conscious of the decline of profits and prompted by generous contributions from big business in America, organized around the advocacy group Business Roundtable, swarmed to his arguments.[27] The American economist, Milton Friedman, who was to become the Messiah of the neoliberal school, made Hayek's message clear in 1978, two years after he had won the Swedish banks' Nobel Prize in Economics:

> The tide is turning ... not because people like myself have preached the fallacy of the erroneous elements in Keynesian thinking, but because demand management has obviously been a failure. Because, far from achieving a nirvana of steady high

> levels of employment with stable prices, it has managed to achieve the worst of both worlds; high inflation and high employment ... The role of thinkers I believe is primarily to keep options open, to have available alternatives, so when the brute force of events make a change inevitable, there is an alternative to change it.[28]

Elsewhere, he wrote, soaringly: "A society that puts equality – in the sense of equality of outcome – ahead of freedom will end up with neither equality nor freedom ... On the other hand, a society that puts freedom first will, as a happy by-product, end up with both greater freedom and greater equality."[29]

By the late 1970s, then, sustained by the sudden flowering of think tanks supported by rich businessmen and firms like Shell Oil and Citicorp, neoliberalism was about to begin its victory lap.[30] The carrier of the neoliberal torch was Alan Greenspan, head of the US Federal Reserve Bank Board from 1987 to 2006. A few meters behind him was his protegé, Ben Bernanke, who ran the Federal Reserve Bank Board from 2006–13. Greenspan was called "the Maestro"; from the late 1980s through the 1990s he appeared on the cover of *Time Magazine* on numerous occasions, smiling augustly and contentedly. Few economists have enjoyed such adulation or influence. It was under him that the Washington Consensus, was launched.

Then, suddenly, it stumbled. The worst moment for neoliberalism (so far) came at the end of 2007 and extended throughout 2008 when much of the capitalist world, the world that had been governed by the apparently irrefutable laws of economism, looked like it might collapse. The US economy hit bottom in June 2009. Recovery began in July of the same year but, unlike previous recessions in 1974–75 and 1981–82, it was sluggish. By 2015 GDP growth had reached 2.4 per cent. From 1948 to 2016 it had averaged 3.20.

Greenspan's successor, Bernanke, an unapologetic Friedmanite, supported the idea that the age of "Great Moderation," had arrived. Bernanke claimed that in his day there would be no more ups and downs of the capitalist world economy; national economies might go up and down with business cycles but the world economy would tick away rhythmically and as predictable as a heartbeat. Indigestion with a little gas, perhaps, but without heartburn. In fact, this belief was not entirely unreasonable; most G7 economies, as well as others on the periphery like Russia and Australia at least up to the crisis that began in 2007, had enjoyed exceptional growth. In the UK, for instance, this had lasted a record of sixty-three quarters from 1993 to 2007. So, for its many believers, the Great Moderation did signal the end of history. Some economists predicted 3 per cent growth forever.[31]

It was on the very cusp of the Great Recession of 2008, that Bernanke, possessed of an ardent faith in unregulated finance markets, let it be known that, "The increasing sophistication and depth of financial markets promote economic growth by allocating capital where it can be most productive. And the dispersion of risk more broadly across the financial system, thus far, increased the resilience of the system and the economy to shocks."[32] So then, to his dismay, 2008 hit and tears resulted. While some economists accused others of being unduly credulous, and many may have suffered acute remorse, none accepted blame.[33] In Britain, Queen Elizabeth, on a visit to the London School of Economics, asked why nobody had predicted the credit crunch, the answer came back in a letter from the professors: "In summary, Your Majesty, the failure to foresee the timing, extent and severity of the crisis and to head it off ... was principally a failure of the collective imagination of many bright people, both in this country and internationally, to understand the risks to the system as a whole." At the end of the letter they noted, unblushingly, "We hope Her Majesty – and indeed others – will find our letter informative."[34] It seems that they thought they had looked at the problem right in the eye.

## THE IMPORTANCE OF GUNBOATS

Quite unsurprisingly, from 1947 when the British, still clinging to the illusion they had a role, if no longer a dominant one, in the eastern Mediterranean, admitted that the civil war that had erupted between monarchists and communists in Greece was beyond their control, the United States took military charge of the postwar West. NATO, founded in 1949, was its invention. The supreme commander of NATO was always to be an American. Why not? The lion's share of the cost of NATO was borne by Washington.[35]

NATO at its inception was supported by Britain, France, Canada, and ten other nations including Turkey. Never before, at least since the time of the Roman Empire, had there been multinational legionnaires assigned to defending and even extending an empire like NATO.

For the forty years of the Cold War (1949–90) NATO's managers justified NATO's existence essentially as Western Europe's protection against its communist equivalent: the Warsaw Pact. It provoked much discussion, staggering expenditure, and many pointless military exercises based on armies of Warsaw Pact tanks roaring through the Fulda Gap and across the North German Plain. "For decades, the [NATO] alliance had formed the cornerstone of Washington's claim to European leadership," Andrew Bacevich has noted.[36]

Profits seem to have been hardly mentioned in security circles. In any case, what Washington and Wall Street both wanted above all else was a peaceful and affluent world that their sprawling transnational firms and their spreading international banks could dominate and lay down the rules for business. NATO thus became the mailed glove within which lay the businessman's soft hand but which between the Korean War (1950–53) and the assault on Serbia (1989) never struck in anger. Jackson Lears explains that the phrase "global leadership" "has served as a euphemism for military intervention – multilateral if possible, unilateral if necessary."[37] Most of the time between the Korean War and the new Middle East Crusades (which began with a blitzkrieg of Libya in 2011) it was "multilateral lite" or "unilateral plus." Not everyone was keen on military sacrifice. In Vietnam, the most furiously hot war of the Cold War era, although there was a substantial Korean contingent and a token representation of hoplites from Australian and New Zealander, there were no Brits or Canadians or Germans. The French, having been burned more than once in Indochina, not to mention Suez and Algeria, were twice shy. In Libya, however, the Brits, Canadians, and French took part though at a safe distance – in the air or at sea – and certainly not in any "boots on the ground" roles. In the 2015 war against ISIS, the Canadian air force bombed fitfully before the government changed and withdrew it altogether. Still, one of its warships patrolled the Black Sea as part of the NATO strategy of containment of Russia.[38] Increasingly as the twenty-first century progressed, drones became the assassins' weapon of choice, the rich man's car bombs. Andrew Cockburn has called them, or at least their technicians, "high-tech assassins." Bacevich indicates that "during the Obama presidency drones operating over Pakistan killed at least two thousand and perhaps more than three thousand people." Drone strikes in Yemen killed at least 450 and perhaps 1,000.[39] NATO theory spoke of "Atlantic defence," that is, the defence of Western Europe, the eastern Mediterranean, and even the Black Sea. Of course keeping Soviet armies out of the West and the communist parties of Western Europe out of power was vital to the future of capitalism: that the Americans should benefit from using NATO to maintain their own dominance in Europe seemed quite obvious.

American leadership in the West was half the equation of "bipolarity," a term favoured by political scientists to describe the Cold War division of the world. To support American leadership, the members of NATO kept troops and airmen in West Germany, doing nothing dangerous for decades at a time. Submarines loaded with intercontinental missiles patrolled the briny deep although few, other than the British, could afford nuclear subs and the missiles that they packed. Then in November 1989, the wall that separated Berliners was breached and communism and the protectionism of the Soviet bloc collapsed with it. Globalization surged through Checkpoint Charlie. Communist leaders took flight as had Nazi leaders in 1945. The world watched with astonishment. There was talk of a peace dividend. Mikhail Gorbachev had done what no leader of the Western world had come near to accomplishing. What next?

The disappearance of the Berlin Wall and the dismemberment of the Soviet bloc may have seemed like NATO's death knell, but not so: it became immediately apparent that the EU could hardly look after itself militarily. In 1991, at the time of the Yugoslav wars, the head of the European Council, Jacques Poos, exclaimed: "The hour of Europe has dawned." But it hadn't; not really. The European army, for instance, was useless, and the Dutch contingent in Bosnia had shown itself to be utterly pusillanimous – walking away to let Serbs slaughter unarmed Bosnians. The West prevailed over the Bosnian Serbs only after the Americans took command of NATO, and the Russians stepped out of the fray (by withdrawing support for the Serbs). Later, the British proved the same point. They had marched with the Americans in the invasion of Iraq and were heard to talk the talk, although, as it turned out, they failed to walk the walk.[40]

In fact, the Europeans and even the Canadians had, until the rise of ISIS, preferred to contemplate not defence spending but other subjects, such as debt, employment, and the anaemic state of their economies. A cartoon in *The Globe and Mail* in September 2013 showed President Obama standing on a plinth next to a missile and urging a small crowd of people forward. Inscribed on the plinth are the words: "Syrian Campaign. Charge." Members of the crowd are stepping off in the opposite direction.[41] The Europeans remained inert. Konrad Jarausch: "The inconclusive war against terrorism suggested that simply substituting Islam for communism as the new threat [to the Western powers] did not provide sufficient motivation to hold the disparate sides [ie. the US and the Europeans] together."[42]

Almost the last thing many Europeans had wanted during the Cold War was a rival in the form of a united and reborn Germany. As Lord Ismay, the first secretary of NATO had quipped, the main purpose of the organization was "to keep the Russians out, the Americans in, and the Germans down." When the Berlin wall came down, the British prime minister, Margaret Thatcher, panicked. She had tried to obstruct German unification. When Germany did become unified she phoned the American president and suggested that relations with the Soviet Union should be repaired as a counterweight to the Germans. It was the turn of the State Department to panic.[43]

As long as the Soviet Union existed almost all Europeans, but especially the British, had accepted American postwar hegemony. This was the essence of "Atlanticism," in the British case known as the "special relationship." But it became increasingly obvious that the relationship was one of patron to client, not one of equals. As Christopher Layne has suggested: "The British were forced to accept Washington's terms, because Britain desperately needed the money and lacked the power to resist US demands." Yet it is difficult to believe Layne's argument that "London entertained few illusions about US intentions."[44] London did entertain illusions: indeed it continued to entertain them right into the early twenty-first century, the era of Prime Minister Blair and President Bush, when Blair turned his back on his European partners in order to cement his ties with Washington by participating with the Americans in the invasion of Iraq. Later, as we shall see, one of Blair's successors, Theresa May, sought to extricate Britain from the EU as painlessly as possible. Many were appalled. Backpedalling began almost immediately.

The French did not share the British affection for America. When Charles de Gaulle was elected president of France in 1958 he initiated concrete measures to counterbalance American hegemony by embracing West Germany and freezing out the British. Slowly, as the Europeans became more prosperous and less worried about communism, the attempt to escape from the embrace of "America's power and purpose" continued. Not only did de Gaulle reject American hegemony in western Europe in principle but the German's supported an *Ostpolitik*, which accepted rapprochement with the Soviet Union and its subordinates. Van Der Pijl calls this shift away from American leadership "the crisis of Atlantic integration." This crisis approached full flood when Germany and France refused to join the US in the invasion of Iraq.

So while the Europeans, with declining enthusiasm after the mid-1960s, accepted the American-dominated NATO shield, actual sword-swinging in the Atomic Age was the last thing they wanted. Thus Denis Healey, the Atlanticist British defence minister of the late 1960s: "[F]or most Europeans, NATO was worthless unless it could prevent another war; they were not interested in fighting one."[45] Of course, Washington was hardly indifferent to the European disinclination to spend money on the military. A piqued Dean Rusk, the American secretary of state for most of the 1960s, had once growled at a British journalist, "when the Russians invade Sussex, don't expect us to come and help you."[46]

## PATROLLING ASIA

Obviously, East Asia was always going to be a different matter than Europe. At a higher pitch than the restrained and even ritualized manoeuvrings of NATO in Europe was the noisy and flamboyant exercise of militarily guaranteed security that continued to be evident in the skies over Central Asia and the seas of Japan. This included a contingent of ten roaming aircraft carrier groups churning back and forth across the Pacific and Indian Oceans and adjacent seas. The US navy actually had twenty commissioned carriers, one in reserve, three under construction, and one on order. Besides the largest navy, the US also possessed the world's biggest air force. The US navy had the world's second largest air force. The carriers served as the centre of large battle fleets comprising surface ships of all kinds as well as submarines. In addition, the US navy had fifty-four nuclear-powered attack submarines, more than the rest of the world put together. When Iraq was bombarded by cruise missiles in 1996, the missiles were launched from one of those submarines on picket in the Red Sea.

The nearest rival to the American fleets was the Chinese navy, that had, before a second was launched in early 2017, only one carrier, a refitted hand-me-down. "The annual Pentagon budget of $700 billion was equivalent to the *combined spending* of the next twenty largest military powers," commented David E. Sanger of *The New York Times*.[47] Then there was the matter not just of security in the seas and the air but of actual fortifications; the US embassy in Baghdad, completed in 2007, was as sprawling as the Vatican. The world's largest embassy, it cost $600 million and could shelter thousands of US citizens, some in bomb-proof apartments.[48] For all analysts on US foreign policy, "without exception," notes historian and political essayist Perry Anderson, "military control of the Gulf is a *sine qua non* of US global power.[49] Then there was Okinawa, like Guantanamo an unpopular military base on someone else's sovereign territory but even more controversial. One report, explaining how 9,000 Marines were being moved from Okinawa to Guam, leaving 9,000–10,000 on Okinawa, pointed out that this was "part of a much larger military build-up in Asia, a realignment that comes amid China's rapid growth as a major economic and military power."[50]

To a large extent, bases, arms, and civilian sales inventories marched around the world shoulder to shoulder behind the flag. It is hardly a secret that the real, and even avowed, purpose of the deployment of Terminator drones and Bradley Fighting Vehicles was to pry and keep open foreign markets; this, incidentally, had been the purpose of British gunboats during the Opium Wars (1839–42) against China. "[T]he whole defense business is predicated on selling," explained Andrew Cockburn, the historian of drones, the hottest military commodity in recent times.[51] Here is Thomas Friedman, the American Pangloss of globalism, hymning his "almighty superpower" manifesto that underlines how essential firepower was to sales:

> For globalization to work, America can't be afraid to act like the almighty superpower that it is. The hidden hand of the market will not work without a hidden fist. McDonald's cannot flourish without McDonnell-Douglas, the designer of the F-15, and the hidden fist that keeps the world safe for Silicon Valley's technology is called the United States Army, Air Force, Navy, and Marine Corps.[52]

In Friedman's quite plausible explanation, the invasions of Iraq and, just a little later, Afghanistan and interventions elsewhere from Central America and the Caribbean to Central Asia were essentially driven by the same purpose that the Opium Wars and the "Open

Door Policy" of the early nineteenth century were – that is, to open global channels to free trade and to ensure American access to markets, raw materials, and investment opportunities. The Americans did sometimes invade for reasons that were not even remotely commercial. Under President Reagan, for instance, the independence of the tiny Caribbean island of Grenada was snuffed out by an airborne and seaborne invasion.[53] The object of that invasion seems simply to have been a demonstration of power – "see what happens if you toy with socialism in our lake."

Besides ensuring security, the production of arms had another purpose; the US was the world's greatest arms bazaar. In 2001, the year of 9/11, the US sold nearly $60 billion worth of arms. Its nearest competitor, Russia, sold just $340 million. Most of US arms went to allies and client states, some of them quite prosperous, which may have exaggerated their insecurity: Taiwan, Singapore, and Japan were among the richest while other eager buyers included several Middle Eastern and Gulf States – Egypt, Israel, Kuwait, Saudi Arabia, and the United Arab Emirates. War zones like the Middle East were especially good for sales. "Arms sales are important ... because they create the very violence that the United States uses as an excuse to step into a conflict. Of the twenty-four countries that experienced at least one armed conflict ... the United States sold weapons and/or provided military training for twenty-one of them at some point during the 1990s."[54] US arms sales by 2012 had once more reached $60 billion of which the Saudis, nervous about the war whoops of the circling Shi'as, paid $29.4 billion.[55] The Japanese, prone to offending the Chinese by celebrating their war criminals, in spite of their economic woes, spent $10 billion.[56] In 2014, Russian arms sales skyrocketed to $15 billion with China holding on to third place.

## THE END OF HISTORY AND OTHER DREAMS

Few literary events, other than works of fiction, have had the same gobsmacking reception as Francis Fukayama's provocative and widely read article, "The End of History," of 1989. Of course timing was everything; "The End of History" came just as America's two great rivals, the Soviet Union and Japan, were being left behind in the great game of global rivalry. This combination of positive certitude and comforting dominance entitled it to be cast as the most forthright philosophic celebration of postwar American triumphalism. In the article, Fukayama, hitherto a little known commentator on global affairs, claimed unhesitatingly that the US possessed "the world's only viable economic system." His boast that "we cannot picture ourselves a world that is *essentially* different than the present one and at the same time better." Liberal democracy, perfected in America, was the only political idea that had a plausible future ahead of it. The declinist, Paul Kennedy, whom we shall meet below, had, therefore, been wrong; material circumstances, even fiscal overstretch, would not be the cause of America's decline. Democracy, explained Fukayama, would not be doomed unless people believed it was doomed. Beliefs mattered. America, thus, still had a future. Its rivals: only the past. "Europe was a nice place to live in which there was nothing significant to do," he explained.

In spite of his many critics, for a while Fukayama was the most famous intellectual in the world. In 1992 he published the book-length version of his 1989 article. It was called *The End of History and the Last Man*, and in the late 1990s he had become an adherent of the Project for the New American Century, a hooray America think tank that counted among its members many of the hawks who had advocated the disastrous invasions of Afghanistan and Iran. After that Fukayama began to have second thoughts about his predictions and turned against his erstwhile neoconservative comrades.[57] But Fukayama was not alone in celebrating the wonder of the 1990s. Decades later a German journalist was to write that, "[t]he 1990s were the happiest time for the West. The democratic world had grown and the fear for our freedom seemed to have been dispelled once and for all."[58]

Unlike most of the citizens in other advanced capitalist countries, Americans, especially from the Eisenhower era of the 1950s, held firm to a belief in a god that was quite obviously very much like them, especially if they were western European in origin. Many Americans, in common with the Salafists, believed their scriptures held immortal truths. They announced their faith in their god even on their money and postage stamps: "In God We Trust," they professed. Perhaps surprisingly, they had not always been so pious, at least not before the leaders of American capitalism rallied around their showbiz pastors to fight against President Roosevelt's social democratic reforms of the 1930s. Their champion was Billy Graham (1918–present) and their campaign was called "Spiritual Mobilization."[59] More than fifty years later it, and he, was still going strong. Supported by General Dwight D. Eisenhower, the great wartime leader who became president in 1953, official evangelicalism spread broadly and deeply within the American state. In a famous speech at Christmastime, 1952. Eisenhower proclaimed his faith in "Whatever Monotheism": "our form of government has no sense unless it is founded in a deeply-felt religious faith, and I don't care what it is."[60]

Ronald Reagan (in office 1981–89), Eisenhower's political descendant, became a further key figure in the relaunch of a new political–religious dynamic announcing, in his presidential nomination speech, that, "only a divine providence could have created the United States." "The strength of our nation is our faith," echoed his vice president and successor George H.W. Bush (in office 1989–93). George W.'s son, a George and a president also (2001–09), claimed in a 1999 debate that Christ was his favourite philosopher, "because He changed my heart." And when Lloyd Blankfein, chairman and chief executive of Goldman Sachs, was called upon to manage the US treasury after the 2008 meltdown he claimed that he was "doing God's work."[61]

Yet in spite of professions of piety on the part of America's political elite, according to a Pew poll, by the second decade of the twenty-first century, "irreligion" had become the fastest growing profession of faith in the country.[62]

## END TIMES?

Of course, there were bound to be naysayers, Cassandras, who warned about American over-extension and the possibility of decline. The end, at sometime or other, was bound to come; as it had for the Roman Empire and even, more recently, the British Empire, both subjects, unlike, say, the history of China, which most Americans had studied. Even by the late 1970s, Thomas Piketty, the celebrated French economist who had been a student in the US noted, "US magazine covers often denounced the decline of the United States and the success of German and Japanese industry."[63] A decade before, the liberal historian, Paul Kennedy, drew up his charter for US decline that was centered on imperial overextension; empires, he explained, using examples from European history, stretched until they snapped. In his own lifetime, Kennedy had watched the sun set on the British empire and on the British economy. Obviously, he made it clear, there was a lesson here for America.

Kennedy's prediction inevitably provoked rebuttal. Joseph Nye Jr., Washington mandarin, Harvard professor, and public intellectual, led the countercharge. The title of his book advertised his message; it was called *Bound to Lead*. This confirmed the understanding by students of international relations and diplomatic history that in the postwar period, and probably since the Great War, America had become the leader of the Western pack. There was little doubt, therefore, that the twentieth was America's century, and why not the twenty-first as well? Samuel Huntington, writing in the 1990s, stood out among the doubters.[64]

The formula for leadership was significant. While some writers held that as hegemon America did not have to follow the rules that governed its subordinates, Nye himself repudiated unilateralism in foreign policy and celebrated cooperation between America and her allies. *Why the World's Only Superpower Can't Go It Alone* was the subtitle of his next book. So leaders needed followers and, conversely, followers required strong leadership. And they got it, right up to the end of the twentieth century. From the time of the Washington-led Dayton Accords (1995), which put an end to the Bosnian War, "American foreign policy seemed more assertive, more muscular," claimed Richard Holbrooke, the main architect of the accords. "America was back," he insisted.[65] And in the years that immediately followed, American leadership may have seemed beyond doubt.

Yet within a few years, as though fulfilling the prophesy of "end times," came the horror of 9/11. "Everything changed" thereafter, and the debate about American leadership was tracked by discussions about the American empire. On top of 9/11 and the Middle East imbroglio that followed came the bursting in 2008 of the subprime mortgage bubble and the economic stagnation that continued. This became more apparent from 2010 onward.

Other unsettling questions were sensed, like miasmas rising from what was later imagined to be a swamp of malfeasance. Some of these, like racism, had been around since at least the nineteenth century. Others, like the increase of inequality, appeared to be relatively novel; they seemed not to be evident in the immediate postwar years but then became apparent in the 1970s. Not everyone cared; in the 1980s one heard that greed was good. Goldman Sachs and other leading banks continued to distribute almost unbelievable bonuses in a celebration of rule by plutocracy.

Some of America's problems involved more than the economic renaissance of China (which we will come to below) but new threats, like the Taliban and ISIS. So books were written, no longer trumpeting American exceptionalism or its redemption following the defeat in Vietnam[66] but about military muddles and their cost and the inequalities that were a visible part of neoliberalism. Blame was apportioned, neoliberalism and globalization were interrogated, and Paul Kennedy's prediction came back in the new century. In 2003, Immanuel Wallerstein, celebrated tracker of "world systems," published his prophetic *The Decline of American Power: The US in a Chaotic World.* In fact, not just America but the whole world of capitalism had become more chaotic. The prolific geographer, David Harvey, wrote of the end of capitalism[67] and so did Wolfgang Streek; *How Will Capitalism End?* Streek asked in a book published in 2016. Streek, moved by the chaos in the EU, stressed the fiscal crisis of the contemporary state due to persistent decline in the rate of economic growth. This growth, it became clear from Thomas Piketty's 2014 monumental study of twentieth-century capitalism, had slowed from 3 to 2 per cent between 1950 and 1990, "notably thanks to European catch-up," and again between 1990 and 2012, "thanks to Asian and especially Chinese catch-up." He anticipated that the economic growth of the richest countries might be at a rate of 1.2 per cent from 2012, and that by 2050 the growth rate of many of the poorer countries will converge with the richer ones. Meanwhile, the war in Afghanistan sputtered on.[68]

Streek's focus was exclusively on the West. He ignored the rise of Japanese, Chinese, and Vietnamese capitalism although it was obvious that capitalism everywhere was a single, globalized, phenomenon. The sole beneficiary of the crisis in the West, Streek wrote, was the financial industry, with Goldman Sachs, the patron and benefactor of so many of the world's leaders, rubbing its collective hands together most conspicuously. "There would seem to be little reason indeed to be optimistic," Streek warned his readers. The election of Donald Trump, mused another German writer in late 2016, was the seal on American decline and was part of the larger question of "world disorder."

When Robert Gordon published *The Rise and Fall of American Growth* (2016) it was greeted with serious respect but a certain alarm by his colleagues and the financial press. He predicted that the US GDP growth rate for the period of 2015–40 would be even lower than what Piketty had predicted, deflating to a mere 0.8 per cent per year. The past had certainly been more satisfying. In the two decades following World War Two, per capita growth in the US had been at 2.3 per cent per year; in the 1960s, it had increased to 3.0 per cent, but then, in the 1970s dropping to 2.1 per cent. In the 1980s it had slipped to 2.0 and in the 1990s to 1.9 per cent. In the first decade of the present century it was at 0.7 per cent or 1.6 per cent excluding 2008–09. EU GDP growth for 2016 was foreseen at 0.3 per cent. (There was headlined relief when the French economy grew at 0.2 per cent in Q3 of 2016.) Thus there seemed to be a deceleration from 2.3 per cent in the 1950s in the area of 0.2 per cent in the mid second decade of the twenty-first century. Although greatness is usually relative, it is difficult to imagine any country being truly great with a GDP growth rate of 0.2 or even 0.5 per cent.

Nor in foreign affairs did the news after 9/11 inspire optimism. In spite of security precautions of hitherto unthinkable technological sophistication and even a fleet of titanic new aircraft carriers (at $15 billion a pop) uncertainty shivered like a diabolical mirage all the way from the South China Sea across the Hindu Kush to the Sahel of West Africa. The real problem for American confidence may have been economic stagnation but the most sensational problem was a new jihadi virus, variously called "ISIS," "IS," "ISIL," or "Daesh," which manifested itself in 2014 in a monster called "the Islamic State of Iraq and the Levant." In short order, as we shall see, this metastasized uncontrollably. Was it a political party, an ideology, or merely an "evil death cult"? "Today al-Qaeda-type movements rule a vast area in northern and western Iraq and eastern and northern Syria, several hundred times larger than any territory ever controlled by Osama bin Laden," the journalist Patrick Cockburn observed in 2014. Right across the Middle East and Maghreb – in Damascus, Benghazi, Mogadishu, and Sana'a – American embassies felt it prudent to close. The American ambassador in Benghazi had actually been gunned down. The "War on Terror," the attempt to extirpate radical Islam after 9/11, seems to have failed "catastrophically"; a new Islamic empire, ruled by Caliph Abu Bakr al-Baghdadi, had manifested itself.[69] Both within this empire and on its peripheries there was war – in Syria, Iraq, and Yemen, and, potentially, between Saudi Arabia and Iran. In Syria alone in late 2015 there were an estimated 250,000 dead, 11 million homeless, four million refugees. No one even counted the death toll caused by Boko Haram in Nigeria. Would Africa become "tomorrow's battlefield," as Nick Turse had predicted? By 2015 there were eight wars being fought in Muslim countries in the Middle East and northern Africa.[70]

Then there was China again with a different threat; wasn't its expansion in the South China Sea by turning reclaimed atolls into unsinkable warships likely to be a problem for American hegemony in the Pacific? And what about the "carrier killer" missiles, admittedly still entubed, paraded first on 3 September 2015? "Why is China Parading Missiles on TV?" asked Evan Osnos in the *New Yorker.* A couple of months later in November China established its first overseas outpost, located on the former French colony of Djibouti at the mouth of the Red Sea. Djibouti was strategically located between Egypt and Aden, both former British bases in the Canal Zone and both abandoned during the postwar period of decolonization. The United States also had a base there, Camp Lemonnier, one of the Pentagon's largest and most important foreign installations. From there it flew drones. Almost alongside the American base was that of the Chinese who were also building a railway from Djibouti to Addis Ababa. So maritime Asia was now bracketed by the Chinese from the Yellow to the Red Sea while terrestrial Asia was pierced by the Chinese-refurbished Silk Road (known as the "Belt and Road" initiative). As businessmen and settlers, the Chinese were, in their tens of thousands, all over Africa and Latin America and alarmingly busy in the Middle East.[71]

Even after the demise of communism there were uncertainties on the European frontier. In mid-2013, in the aftermath of the Russian defeat of Georgia in the summer of 2008, came the Russian take-over of Crimea and Moscow's move on the Donetz area of Ukraine. Further lessons in the failure of American leadership and NATO indecision were now evident.[72] In 2008, the British journalist Neal Ascherson, describing the Russian tank columns grinding along Georgian roads had written: "Russia has called our bluff over countries we can't defend." The "we" here would be NATO, the sword of the West. "[The Russians] wanted to show the world the sort of price which would be paid for taking Georgia into NATO and also to suggest that Georgia is too erratic to be a NATO partner."[73] In 2014 Russia would strengthen its airbases in Syria and refurbish its warmwater anchorage at Tartus on the Mediterranean for its Black Sea fleet. It even tried to get a naval base going in Montenegro on the Adriatic coast. In February 2016, the Russian prime minister, Dmitry Medvedev, warned of a new Cold War. With Chancellor Merkel of Germany saying "no" to campaigning in Syria and the British parliament also voting against engaging there, President Obama was bound to become increasingly frustrated with his NATO allies: "Free riders aggravate me," he complained.[74]

Elsewhere in the globalized world trouble brewed and gloom spread. Economic and political crises that had unsettled the Eurozone in 2008 continued with the bitter matter of Greece's external debt and economic dissolution remaining without an apparently equitable solution. After years of stoking, Germany's international credibility, its hegemonic role within the EU, came to the verge of collapse. Its role as the home of Christian democracy, Europe's, not just Germany's, natural party of government, was cast into serious doubt. In other quarters there were nasty surprises, too. Sunday, 25 October 2015, "proved a political turning point in Poland." The right-wing Law and Justice party had surprisingly won an absolute majority in parliament and a near two-third majority in the senate. "[F]ew if any imagined the magnitude of the bombshell."[75]

In Asia, by late 2014, after a brief remission, Japan's economy continued to wobble. Its GDP growth for 2015 was forecast at less than 1 per cent, a twenty-five year low. In Argentina and Brazil, countries conveniently ignored since the fall of their dictatorships in the 1980s, economies seemed to be decelerating as the commodities boom ended.

Only a little less worrying was the Chinese economy. According to one study, imports from China to the US resulted in the loss of 1.5 million American manufacturing jobs since the early 1990s. "In total," it notes under the heading "Clear Losers of Globalization," "[S]ome 6.9 million industry jobs were lost in the US between the early 1990s and 2011."[76] But even more worrying perhaps was that China's rate of GDP growth had fallen, by official admission, from more than 10 per cent to under 7 per cent in November 2015. Real estate and stock market values had been slashed. Some economists argued that China's growth was even more feeble than has been admitted. China's expenditure on arms continued to increase parallel with its claims on the South China Sea. Worrying to investors, its banks were faced with billions of irrecoverable loans.[77] Thus the several pillars of postwar economic and military strength that had risen to sustain American hegemony, including a close relationship to Chinese growth, now looked insecure. In an analysis early in 2016, Yuan Yang reported that the Chinese growth had reached the lowest rate in twenty-five years.[78]

According to Geoff Dyer, the Washington correspondent for the *Financial Times*, in a new national security document, "Mr Obama made the case that the US remains the dominant global power but also needs to recognize limitations on its ability to influence complex events and crises around the world."[79] Circumspect primacy, we might say. Or putting a brave face on bad news. Would disillusion come in the following years? Would Vladimir Putin or Abu Bakr al-Baghdadi replace Osama bin Laden? Would the Chinese reclaim hegemony in East Asia? Would the EU decline into impotence and irrelevance? Would the cenotaph marking the end of the American Century stand like the statue of Ozymandias somewhere in the desert near Raqqa, the ISIS capital? Or is the present crisis merely a manifestation common to all healthy democracies?

# 2

# European Uncertainties

The "Long nineteenth century" (1815–1914) was western Europe's most glorious modern epoch. By the end of that century the western states of the continent, led by Britain, France, and Germany, stood above the rest of the world for their achievements in practically all major spheres – science, culture, political influence, and economic strength. Virtually all of Asia, Africa, and Latin America looked to these great powers for inspiration. Even colonial peoples who were quite aware of the exploitative nature of imperialism stood in awe of the majesty of Europe's accomplishments.

Then came the second "Thirty Years War" (1914–45) at the end of which, on 8 May 1945, much that Europe had accomplished was laid low and much of the continent was reduced to poverty and ruin. The European nation-state, centuries in the building, seemed to have utterly failed. Alan Milward:

> Between 1938 and the end of 1940 most of [Europe's nations] proved incapable of fulfilling even their oldest and primary duty, the defence of the national territory and the protection of their citizens. Of the twenty-six European nation-states in 1938, by the close of 1940 three had been annexed, ten occupied by hostile powers, one occupied against it wishes by friendly powers, and four partially occupied and divided by hostile powers. Two others had been reduced to a satellite status which would eventually result in their occupation. The only one which had extended its power and triumphantly dominated the continent offered as little hope to mankind as any political organization which had existed.[1]

But after all, Europe revived, not entirely intact, to be sure, but more or less so. In the immediate postwar years, in fact, there emerged two distinct Europes, West and East, separated by what Western leaders called an "Iron Curtain." One Europe, soon to become the "European Union," was unevenly capitalist and increasingly liberal and the other, somewhat unhappily, communist.[2] Between the Treaty of Paris in 1951 and the "Brexit" referendum of 23 June 2016, capitalist Europe remained unified, expansionist, and prosperous. [3]

During World War Two, Eastern Europe had been reduced to a palace of horrors. In the short span between 1939 and 1945, most of the 36.5 million Europeans slaughtered by other Europeans had been killed there.[4] No war in history had seen so many people killed in such a short space of time, so many cities pulverized, so many countries desolated, or so many people driven from killing ground to wasteland. In North America, we forget that over the whole of the twentieth century, not a city was destroyed, no civil or class wars were fought and, indeed, not a single bomb was dropped on this continent. This partly explains the shock of 9/11. In the years after the World War Two, as before, for much of the West, Eastern Europe was viewed as a troubled backwater, a dead zone of shadows, urban ugliness, and repression.

The three pillars of postwar Western Europe, as before the war, were Britain, France, and Germany, the latter reduced to less than half of its prewar size and the home to 10 million refugees. From 1961 Berlin, the German capital, had been divided into two sectors by a concrete wall topped with barbed wire. The main crossing point was the celebrated "Checkpoint Charlie." The Berlin wall was a symbol of Europe's division. When it came down in November 1989, East and West Germany were unified, and the Soviet empire fell apart.

In spite of the amputation of its eastern half, Germany rose from defeat and obloquy to dominate the continent through the European Union (EU). With monetary union in 1990, the Stability Pact of 1997, and the Single Market Act of 2011, German hegemony advanced at a quickened pace. Britain had started the postwar period in the lead but then was to stall after victory to become the most dissonant player in the European concert. France was to rise from defeat and the bitterness of collaboration and lost colonial wars to a cultural efflorescence and political significance that lasted for two decades before, as in the 1930s, falling into division and political lassitude.

To most observers, it might not have been surprising that soon after West and East Germany were unified, the new federal republic rose above continental Europe with a new old capital, Berlin, that became economically powerful and culturally vibrant, if not altogether attractive.[5] It would have been more than a slight shock to be told that in the late 1980s, Italy's GDP would surpass that of Britain or that, into the second decade of the twenty-first century, (2015) Britain would be debating "Brexit," that is, whether it should continue its membership in the EU or go with the surge of national anti-European sentiment and attempt to reassert its independence as an offshore archipelago, one with an unspecified but subordinate relationship with the US. (And if it separated, what form would Britain itself take? Would it be with or without a Scotland, which might walk out on continued membership in the United Kingdom?[6] Recall that just under four decades earlier Tom Nairn had written a prophetic study of "Ukanian" nationalism titled *The Break-Up of Britain*.[7])

It would certainly be a source of dismay to hear that by 2015 the brilliant France of *les trente glorieuses culturelles* (1980–2010) would become the home of murderous resentments: its society irreparably fissured between haves and have-nots, "insiders" and "outsiders" (youth/elders, employed/unemployed, emigrants/natives, unionized/nonunionized workers); its politicians, left and right, execrated (and none more so than the president); and a quarter of its electorate willing to flirt in the 2014 EU elections with the right-wing anti-EU Front National, a party said to be, inexactly, "Camembert fascist."[8]

Europe seemed in the new century to have become a continent barely able to contain a maelstrom of divisions, dismayingly echoing the furious and intolerant world of the 1930s; the major difference being that it was now more or less united into a more or less single polity and that it was minus the two most poisonous European ideologies of the twentieth century: communism and fascism. Yet in common with the 1930s, from about 2010 Europe was buffeted by the headwinds of economic crisis and, like America, renewed warnings of declinism. In early 2016 Martin Wolf, resident guru of the *Financial Times* had written: "What are the chances of a significant recession in the UK before 2025? Very high indeed. The same surely applies to the US, Eurozone and Japan."[9]

In the rest of this chapter I shall first outline the postwar history of Western Europe, mentioning particularly American penetration and the rise, triumph, and trials of the European Union (EU), before briefly outlining the flow of events in the early twenty-first century. We might note that the landmark meltdown of 2007–08, a consequence of the spread of financial deregulation, a central tenet of neoliberalism, as well as the sovereign debt crisis of 2010, had a depressing effect on the EU, although more on the periphery than in the centre. Many, like Martin Wolf, doubted that there would be recovery within a decade; some, like Robert Gordon, writing about the US, thought growth was over.

Yet the shock of the financial crisis may have been exaggerated; many older Europeans seem to have become habituated to living under the volcano; less than two decades before the 2007–08 economic turmoil they had witnessed the final spasm of communism, the governing ideology of half of the continent for nearly half a century, and before that, in 1986, a manmade volcano of sorts, Chernobyl, and before that the uncertainties of decolonization and post-imperial redemption. Yet, in mitigation, a soothing bromide: for more than half a century, Western Europeans had stopped shooting and bombing one another and, in fact, had never had it so good.

## PHOENIX

Postwar Europe can be seen thus as a distinctive epoch lasting between two capitulations; the first in May 1945 marked by the surrender of Germany and the demise of Nazism, the second in December 1989 celebrated by the breaching of the Berlin Wall and the demise of communism. Within that period, Europe had been divided into two hemispheres; from January 1990 it was once again largely united. In the period of its division it had been transformed by several radical shifts that were a direct consequence of one or both of the world wars. First, between 1945 and 1947 came the division into a capitalist West (Ireland, Britain, France, West Germany, the Benelux countries, Scandinavia, Spain, Portugal, Italy, Switzerland, Austria, Greece) and a communist East (Soviet Union, East Germany, Poland, the Baltic countries, Czechoslovakia, Hungary, Bulgaria, Romania, Yugoslavia, Albania). For several decades after 1945 – let us say until some time in the 1980s – the effective capital of the West in most key respects hovered between New York ("the capital of the twentieth century") and Washington; it was there that money and power were to be found and it was there that the agenda for the Bretton Woods conference and the European Recovery Plan, the ERP, known as the Marshall Plan, were formulated.

When the Marshall Plan was wound up, Western Europe appeared confidently on its way to postwar recovery. Indeed, even before the last dollar had been shelled out, it was back in the game not as a collection of rival states but as an integrated and liberalized economic union that emerged in 1952 and was known, colloquially, as "the Six."[10] Yet although the Marshall Plan has in some arguments been seen as the indispensible starting point of Western Europe's postwar recovery, this view may be unwarranted. An alternate view is that Western Europe was already on the road to recovery from 1945, thus independently of the American Marshall Plan.[11]

Besides the formal aid of the Marshall Plan, there was private investment that flowed across the North Atlantic in waves. Between the wars, US overseas investment in Europe was about half in Britain and a quarter each in France and Germany, but the Americans invested three times as much in Latin America as in Europe. After the war, this reversed and the flow to Europe exceeded that to Latin America. American investment in Europe, its buying into the industries and agencies of the continent, is one of the main stories of this period. "Living in the American Age" is how one author has seen postwar Britain.

The Bretton Woods agreements and the Marshall Plan were sold to the American public in a wrapping of "security," that is, with the claim that if American loans (and debt forgiveness) were not made, Europe would succumb to autarky and anarchy and, divided and weakened, be ripe for communism. American isolationists could not be persuaded with the idea that European recovery was a good thing in itself so security became the lynchpin of American foreign policy in Western Europe and elsewhere during the Cold War, that is, from 1946 to 1990. Robert Gilpin, writing in the field of international political economy, echoes this view: "Emphasis on security interests and alliance cohesion provided the political glue that held the world economy together and facilitated compromises of important national differences over economic issues."[12]

Gilpin's emphasis differs from mine only in emphasis. My argument is that the principal, if simplified, object of American foreign policy in Western Europe (and elsewhere) was less security than trade liberalization that would be, as far as was feasible, dominated by the US. Domination meant integration: Western Europe was meant to be integrated into a North Atlantic system directed from New York and Washington. Financial power would be transferred from London; the City of London would be a gibbous moon weakly reflecting the dazzling Wall Street sun. The Cold War, a war that never happened, and NATO, a force that seldom fought (after the truce in Korea in 1953), were the military means to an economic end. The Americans won the cold war in Europe. This victory took the form of the dissolution of the communist system and, it was expected, the extension of American economic penetration eastwards all the way to the western frontiers of Russia. It was expected that NATO would move eastward, too. By 2015, when this essay ends, neither had eventuated.

Of course, it would be unwise to suggest that the fundamental purpose of American militarism was simply economic; this would be akin to saying that the purpose of British imperial policy in the eighteenth and nineteenth centuries was simply commercial. No: the Americans and the British had many purposes, some large, some small, some material, some not, and many not entirely cogent from any reasonable point of view. In most cases, the economic purpose was simply the most consistently important; the Marshall Plan had as its main object the rehabilitation and American commercial penetration of Europe. Thereafter other agencies took up the cause: for instance, the IMF and GATT.[13] In some cases, true, the strategic trumped the economic; this is the case with Japan where the Americans accepted closed markets in return for strategic subordination. Japan was to guard the gate to China with Okinawa, a Japanese island commandeered by Washington, the Asian equivalent to Berlin's "Checkpoint Charlie." Up to a point American policies were successful.

The genius of the Marshall Plan was revealed in the fact that it worked, perhaps even more than expected. Taking off slowly right after the end of the war, European and Japanese exports to America shot up suddenly with the outbreak of the Korean War in mid-1950. Jeffry Frieden: "Europe and Japan embarked on an American-based export boom that continued through the 1950s. Western Europe's exports in 1946 were ... eight billion dollars. By 1948 they had doubled, and by 1951 they had risen to twenty-seven billion ... The three biggest economies, Britain, France, and Germany had by 1951 ... surpassed their record of recovery during the entire period from the end of World War One through the Depression of the 1930s."[14] European exports to America earned the foreign exchange to pay for European imports from America.

Still, the imports by the individual economies of Western Europe were for the most part European in origin, not American (or Japanese). Trade between Europe and America was always less than half the trade within Europe, and by the twenty-first century some European countries were importing more from China than America. Beside financial aid, there was forgiveness. West Germany not only got dollars but also benefitted from the London Agreement on German External Debts of 1953. By this means, some 60 per cent of Germany's external debt was restructured. Thus, where 13.5 billion Deutschmarks were owed, this was reduced to 7.5 billion. At the time of the debate over the Greek debt, which I will discuss at the end of this chapter, this became a bitter issue. After all, the Greeks did not get into debt while attempting to dominate Europe.

The recovering economies in France, Britain, and Italy were, to varying degrees, guided by Keynesian precepts. The state, planning, the public sector, protectionism, bureaucratization, and dirigisme were everywhere expanding, guided by parties, often quite stiffly conservative (like that of Adenauer in West Germany, de Gaulle in France, or Macmillan in Britain), that accepted that in the future public ownership should be manifest. Tony Judt: "Between 1950 and 1973, government spending rose from 27.6 per cent to 38.8 per cent of the gross domestic product in France, from 30.4 per cent to 42 per cent in West Germany, from 34.2 per cent to 41.5 per cent in the UK and from 26.8 per cent to 45.5 per cent in the Netherlands – at a time when that domestic product was itself growing faster than ever before or since. The overwhelming bulk of the increase in spending went on insurance, pensions, health, education and housing." The Western countries spent 40 to 50 per cent of GDP on welfare.[15]

Of course, even after they had entered the *Trente Glorieuses*, the Europeans were not yet out of the woods. The Germans were still divided, and their urban landscape was still battered. The French had not yet sorted out their imperial yearnings; this was to be a drain on their economy until the early 1960s. (The savage war in Algeria, which was fought to keep that colony within the French Empire and which lasted from 1954 to 1962, saw a desolation inflicted on the Algerians that may be compared to that inflicted by the Americans in Vietnam between 1954 and 1974. It almost led to civil war in France.)

And then there was the perennial problem of the business cycles of capitalist economies – upturn followed by downturn, boom by stagnation, deflation by inflation. The cost of high levels of social expenditure and skyrocketing consumption was unsustainable and led to crisis that became manifest in the autumn of 1973, the moment of the October War with Egypt and Syria on one side and Israel on the other. This led to crude oil prices rising from $2.70 per barrel in 1973 to $9.76 in 1974. After that came the 1979 revolution in Iran that pushed oil prices up even higher. "From that time on, nothing worked as usual."[16] By 1981 stagnation had combined with inflation to produce "stagflation." Slow growth, high unemployment and inflation now ruled while interest rates had gone up by 1981 to over 13 per cent. Consumer prices doubled in western countries; in the Mediterranean they quadrupled. The advanced industrial countries of western Europe entered into deep recession with their traditional industries such as coal and steel production, textiles, and shipbuilding falling into irreversible decline.

By the early 1980s problems, not the least of which were European and Japanese economic prosperity, were evident. Initially, the Plaza Accord of 1985, which devalued the dollar and shifted the problems of overcapacity to Germany and Japan, sought to assure continued American leadership economically as well as politically.[17] But this was at best a stop-gap measure – one that lasted, nonetheless, for two decades.

## LE DÉFI AMÉRICAIN: MCDO AND CO.

Investment was one of the keys to postwar success not only in Western Europe but also, later, in Asia. Before the war, foreign investment tended to be in mines and plantations – that is, in colonies that could produce minerals, rubber, rice, vegetable oils, or tea or in semicolonies that could produce bananas or petroleum, or in developing economies like Russia and Argentina that needed investment in railways. After the war this changed: by the late twentieth century, most American investment abroad was *in* OECD countries, and most investment in America was *by* OECD countries. Relatively less American foreign direct investment (FDI) was in Third World countries.

By 1973, according to Frieden, half of FDI, that is, about $100 billion around the world, was of US origin.[18] But here too, the economic situation was unstable. Although in the postwar period overall American transnational corporations (TNCs) were credited with half or more of the manufacturing sales in most European countries,[19] by mid-2006 the situation seems to have been reversed. According to Andrew Glyn writing in that year, "income from US investments abroad fell short of interest and profits paid on overseas assets held in the USA, compounding instead of offsetting the long-running trade deficit." And a report by the US Congressional Research Service dated December 2013, noted that while "(t)he United States is the largest investor abroad and the largest recipient of direct investment in the world," US net investment abroad fell from $409 billion in 2011 to $388 billion in 2012, and FDI in the US fell by $66 billion in 2012, a drop of 28 per cent compared with the $230 billion invested in 2011.[20]

Even before World War Two the Americans, quite distinctly from the Europeans, had invested in "branch plants" and retail outlets that produced and marketed cars and trucks; Ford was everywhere. After the war other goods produced by American factories and movie studios reached eager European consumers. Not just driveables produced by branch plants and watchables distributed from Hollywood movie studios but edibles as well: the Americans established McDonald's, arriving in Europe in 1971 and known in France as "Chez McDo," wherever they went. And then there were KFC franchises everywhere and even a EuroDisney on the outskirts of Paris.

In 1909 the first overseas branch of Woolworth stores was established in Liverpool, Britain's great entrepôt on the Irish Sea (and the centre in earlier centuries of the Atlantic slave trade). "Frank Woolworth's giant chain was to the invention of the five-and-dime what the Model T [Ford] was to mass mobility, Rotary was to men's service clubs, Coca-Cola to soft drinks, and McDonald's to fast food." Soon "Woolies" was ubiquitous; in 1928, twenty-three branches of Woolworth's were opened in Germany. Although most Woolworth stores in Europe closed in 1997 and were replace by other stores, all of the replacements were to use American supermarket methods, ultimately perfected by Walmart, which combined nonunionized labour and cheap Asian goods.[21] Besides retail chains, the Americans were the main force behind the spread of postwar TNCs and banks in Western Europe. Business schools, like the prestigious INSEAD near Paris (considered the "Harvard in Europe") were ubiquitous.[22] INSEAD itself was supported by the Ford Foundation.

Americans remained in the passing lane in the new and profitable area of information technology. Computers were central to the information revolution that began in the 1980s. Jeffry Frieden:

> The computer industry was small, especially relative to auto, but by the early 1960s it was clear that it would be key to a host of new technologies. And although many early innovations were European, by the late 1960s the industry was controlled by American multinationals. American companies made over 80 per cent of Europe's computers, and another 10 per cent were made on licenses from American firms. IBM alone had 82 per cent of the German market and 63 per cent of the French. The American firms dwarfed European competitors – IBM employed four times as many people in data processing than the eight largest European companies combined ... The global computer industry was dominated by American multinational corporations."[23]

And, at least before the Europeans got it together to produce passenger jets jointly, it looked as if the Americans would dominate the world's skies with Boeing.

Unsurprisingly, when France became inundated by American consumer goods (one of the conditions of US aid) a 1948 study asked, "Will France become an American colony?" Fretfulness, which never died, spiked again in 1967, when the French journalist and politician Jean-Jacques Servan-Schreiber published *Le défi americain* in which he claimed that the Common Market was an American Trojan horse: Europe would welcome it in, only to have it conquer the European market. His tract became the fastest selling book in modern French history. Thirty-five years later another best seller emphasized a similar theme; Emmanuel Todd's *Après l'Empire* argued that "The American social model threatens Europe ... the exportation by the United States of its distinct model of deregulated capitalism constitutes a threat to European nations,"[24] and, at a more gustatory level, "Resistance to the hegemonic pretences of hamburgers is, above all, a cultural imperative." At Millau, in the Midi-Pyrénées, also fighting the insidious invasion of American hamburgers, the farmer José Bové demolished a McDonald's with his tractor, becoming a Jeanne d'Arc figure for the antiglobalization movement.[25] Globalization, neoliberalism, and genetically modified foods had become the *bêtes noires* for a broad range of protests against threats to the France that was, it was believed, profound, eternal, and burgerless. On the whole, however, most Europeans, and especially the youth, accepted the American "empire by invitation" to any alternative that they themselves had been able to conceive in the twentieth century. Even the French learned to say *frappé* ("milkshake") and *hamburger* while between 4,500 and 20,000 Americanisms spread into the German language.[26]

In West Germany, most, especially youth, seemed to gravitate towards American culture rather than return to the culture of prewar and wartime Germany. Wartime films had been suffused with Nazi propaganda, and so the German film industry had discredited itself and never returned to its prewar eminence. Postwar German culture had to compete with American imports, which were diffused through a dozen "American Houses" and the Armed Forces Network, which provided a regular diet of swing and rock. The SED, the East German communist party, denounced rock as "decadent amusement" and disparaged it as the "cultural rubbish of a decaying social order."[27] But to little avail; for decades after the Americans had moved into Germany as victors in the war, their material affluence impressed the Germans as tangible evidence of an inherently superior culture "although [predictably] the representatives of German intellectual culture maintained a considerable reserve toward American mass civilization."[28]

So it was, in a complementary argument, that New York stole the idea of modern art from Paris at the end of World War Two.[29] Museums, storehouses of past glory (and larceny), rose in America as reflections of buying power and political domination. Hollywood became the Paris of the new global media, the template for the Bollywoods elsewhere in the world. Victoria de Grazia quotes Jack Valenti, president of the Motion Picture Association of America: "We dominate world screens not because of armies, bayonets, or nuclear bombs, because what we are exhibiting on foreign screens is what the people of those countries want to see." In the case of Germany, "[t]he US [film] marketing cartel's offensive to carve up the ... media market, actually financed by Washington as part of its information policy, contributed to the quashing of German competition."[30] Thus the war for the movies was lost. Ivan T. Berend comments on the story of the Hollywoodization of TV programs and film theatres:

> Traditional postwar European art movies, mostly Italian and French, lost ground and mostly collapsed because of competition from the American film industry. Distribution and film theatres were also taken over by American companies, and Hollywood ac-

tion movies produced with the latest technology now attracted many more Europeans than domestic films ... The best illustration of what some critics call "cultural colonization" via Hollywood firms is that in 1960, only 35 per cent of box office revenues came from American films, but at the turn of the century, it jumped to 80 to 90 per cent in continental Europe.[31]

At the beginning of the twenty-first century, the American neoconservative Robert Kagan published an essay titled "Power and Weakness." Considering the difference between US and EU foreign policies he argued that "on major strategic and international questions today, Americans are from Mars and Europeans are from Venus." Not everyone was convinced. "Though intended to stimulate reflection about the structural sources of conflicts within NATO," wrote Konrad Jarausch, "the article ironically had the opposite effect of reinforcing stereotypes by stirring a passionate debate. The American attack on Iraq to overthrow Saddam Hussein made Kagan's subsequent book look like a power-political justification of neoconservative adventurism."[32]

At any rate, did anyone outside of the chattering classes in a postwar France struggling with austerity or worrying about Algeria really care about American foreign policy or the threat of US hamburgers? From the mid-1960s when France's GDP overtook that of Britain there was every reason for contentment, at least for the white, employed majority. Maybe not so much for unemployed youth and emigrants.[33]

## CITIZENS, THE UNEMPLOYED, MIGRANTS

Postwar prosperity in Western Europe was based on a combination of renovation, revived industrialization, lowered tariffs, and increased regional and international trade. Liberalization replaced protectionism. Cities, where they had been destroyed, were rebuilt and autobahns and railway lines extended. Traffic in cars went from a trickle to a jam. Employment was transformed; more women worked, and worked more hours, and emigrants, called in Germany *gastarbeiter* ("guest workers"), took up jobs that citizens shunned. Unemployment during the 1950s and '60s dropped. During the golden years it had fallen to a level lower than the previous or the succeeding two decades. Unemployment in France had been around 3.3 per cent in the 1930s; in 1950–69 it dropped to 1.4 per cent. In Britain the drop was especially dramatic: 11.5 per cent unemployed in the thirties, 1.4 per cent in the 1950s and '60s.[34] But for young people entering the workforce from around 1980, the situation was again frustrating: in 1984 in Italy where unemployment had been about 5 per cent in the 1930s, it rose to 19.6 per cent of the fifteen to twenty-nine age group. In France around 2000, youth unemployment reached 30 per cent and underemployment 75 per cent. By 2014 the situation had worsened; Eurozone youth unemployment was at 12 per cent, Britain's at 21 per cent, France's 23 per cent, Germany's 7.5 per cent, and Greece at around 58 per cent. Canada's was 13.5 per cent.[35]

Many major European countries, in common with the US, showed a tendency towards greater equality up to about 1980 and thereafter a slide towards relatively greater inequality with the top 10 per cent, and especially the top 1 per cent of the population, coming to possess an increasing percentage of the national wealth.[36] Alongside inequality came corruptibility. European political corruption, in both its breadth – right across the continent – and its depth takes your breath away. According to the European Commission the cost of corruption remained at more than €120 billion annually. Swedes were the least corrupt and Spaniards, Poles, Slovakians, Hungarians, and Greeks, the most. The EU police agency, Europol, has testified that there were at least 3,000 criminal gangs operating across Europe.[37] Financial corruption was monumental. "Offshore" became a familiar word in all European languages. Britain with its laundromat archipelagos from Guernsey to the Virgin Islands became the European centre for hot money.[38]

While regional, if not global, prosperity was remarkable over the whole postwar period, it was obviously uneven. Uneven development led to a great flow of migration from the less prosperous (and often colonial or at least historically deprived), to the more prosperous – that is, from Ireland to England, from Portugal to France, and from the DDR to the *Bundesrepublik*. There was also migration from outside of Europe – from the Maghreb (especially Algeria) to France, from Turkey to Germany, and from Jamaica and Nigeria to Britain. According to Tony Judt: "By 1973 in West Germany alone there were nearly half a million Italians, 535,000 Yugoslavs and 605,000 Turks." In France by 1969 there were 600,000 Algerians and more on the way.[39] This was to lead to wild right-wing fantasies about a Muslim take over of the European *heimat* and the creation of "Eurabia"; anti-Semitism in a different register. This reached its most deadly extreme in Norway in 2011 when a fanatic massacred nearly seventy children to draw attention to emigration from Asia, especially of Muslims.[40] With the spread of Islam in France we have an example of the empire striking back since many French Muslims were fugitives or descendants of fugitives from the colonial war in Algeria that devastated the colony from 1954 to 1972 and uprooted nearly two million people. The founder of the most right-wing anti-immigrant party in France, Jean-Marie Le Pen of the National Front, had fought with the Foreign Legion in colonial rear guards in Indochina, Suez, and Algeria.

Migration, like its subjects, was to a large extent coloured by imperialism, the end of which was the third major change that affected the larger states of Europe, especially Britain, France, the Netherlands, Belgium, and Portugal. From even before the era of colonial independence (which began in 1947 with the freeing of India and Pakistan), migrants moved out of formerly colonized countries (India, Algeria, Indonesia) to countries that had once dominated them, but which in many cases their soldiers had fought not against but *for*.[41] This pattern continued over our whole period, both while empires still existed, that is up to 1975 when the last of the great African empires, the Portuguese, was closed down. Imperialism, defined as the extension, protection, and exploitation of empires, one of the most defining characteristics of the states of Western Europe and the source of competitive self-glorification, was thus of diminished concern just a couple of decades into the postwar period; in Britain between the Suez Crisis (1956) and the independence of Nigeria (1960) and in France between the defeat at Dienbienphu (1954) and the independence of Algeria (1962). But two long-term effects of empire continued to be felt: first, migration, as we have mentioned, and second, neocolonialism, which I will discuss further in chapter 8.

## EUROPEAN UNION

In Western Europe in the post-1945 decades, a new world of managed capitalism had risen from the ashes of the old. Rather than confronting, and where necessary battling, the working class, Europe's far-seeing capitalists in several countries had come round to the idea that the workers should be included as minority profit-sharers and incorporated: "corporatism" was the word that described the cooperation, ideally at least, of the state, capital, and the working class. But there were different forms of corporatism. Generally, the postwar era saw more welfare and less class warfare and, with more globalism, the end of nationalist rivalries.

At the heart of this new Europe emerged a new, forgiving, economic alliance known as the "Common Market." The original common market (in the form of the European Coal, Iron, and Steel Community) blossomed into the European Economic Community (EEC) at the beginning of 1958. In 1973, the UK, Ireland, and Denmark joined and in 1981, Greece and in 1986 Spain and Portugal. The benefits of the wider economic market were in some cases immediately obvious. Take the case of Ireland, one of the poorest countries in Western Europe, which had a standard of living per person less than half that of France and Germany in the 1950s. In the 1970s, waves of foreign capital flooded the country, and by 1980 "fifty-five large foreign firms produced almost one-fifth of the industrial output, but they delivered nearly two-thirds of industrial exports ... The rate of export growth was the second fastest in the world behind Japan." By the next decade, Ireland was spoken of as a "Celtic Tiger" and produced, thanks to Apple and other, mainly American transnationals, the computers for half of Europe.[42]

In 1959 the first concessions had been made by the EEC to Spain, still under the repressive and backward Franco dictatorship. Because of its pariah political status, Spain had been kept out of the EEC, but gradually it was accorded Common Market privileges such as lower tariffs and increased investment. As a consequence of the opening up of Spain's economy, a kind of economic miracle took place; industrialization increased, exports boomed, and economic growth shot up to 5.8 per cent. Tourists flooded into Spain pushing the profits from tourism up to $3 billion by the 1970s. Still, as long as the *caudillo* and his cronies clung to power, Spain remained an embarrassment to the democracies of Western Europe. When the *caudillo* died in 1975, Spain was released from the grip of is sclerotic dictatorship. It applied to join the EU in 1977 and was admitted in 1986, alongside Portugal, during the third enlargement of the community.

With its new members, the European Union became an economic unit even larger than the US. By 2014, its twenty-eight member states were home to half a billion people who now had "European" stamped on their passports. Europe had expanded to the very edges of the historic continent to include Malta and Cyprus in the Mediterranean and Bulgaria, Romania, Croatia, and Slovenia in the Balkans. But by then the optimism of the early period had been undermined by slow growth, debt, bureaucratic constipation, and political friction.

As the EU expanded, several conspicuous features stood out: first, its relative cultural and consumerist homogeneity, a product of increased levels of internal trade and an improved standard of living. More than anything, it was industrialization that accounted for improved standards of living with workers shifting from agriculture to industry. In Germany agricultural employment dropped from 23 to 8 per cent, in France from 28 to 13 per cent, and in Italy from 40 to 19 per cent. With growth rates as high as 5 per cent (up to 1973, at least) nearly everyone in the Union "had it good."[43]

With improvements in standards of material well-being, organized religion collapsed; everywhere, as one generation succeeded another, churches became empty and the role of the clergy, as for instance in education in France and Ireland, evaporated. Only in communist states like Poland and the DDR did religion have any political role and even this was offset, as in Ireland, by the sins of the church itself. The Protestant charismatics who became a feature in the politics of America and Latin American were largely absent from Europe. Thus as Rome was forced to retreat from cultural spaces, in western Europe consumerism, not evangelicalism, swept in. And in the dark corners of those spaces, nationalism, barely acknowledged until the early 1990s, survived.

A second conspicuous feature of the European Union was its high level of welfarism and its avowed commitment to social improvement. The commitment to welfarism became regarded as an essential feature of the European social model but even before the 2008 economic crisis, as the EU increasingly adopted forms of neoliberalism, this came under threat. In Britain, welfarism (in the form of the "welfare state") suffered a frontal assault by the Conservatives under Margaret Thatcher in the 1980s and then by the same party after it returned to power in 2010 and propounded the doctrine of austerity. In France, welfarism came under pressure when the socialist François Mitterand (in office 1981–93) retreated from his "break with capitalism" in 1983. In Germany, a program of retrenchment initiated in 2011, has been called "one of the biggest austerity plans in the history of the Federal Republic."[44] One writer has noted:

> This quarter-century [ie.1980 to 2005] has seen a wave of enthusiasm for cutting taxes and transfers [tax-based government spending], privatizing state industries and trimming union power … [However] the welfare state is not an endangered species among the industrialized OECD countries. While its growth clearly slackened after 1980, social transfers continue to take a slowly rising share of GDP … there is no sign of a global "race to the bottom," either in the 1980s or since 1990. There is nothing even faintly suggesting that countries are scrambling to reduce tax rates implied by their social budget.[45]

We shall see below how this evaluation has to be modified in the light of the programs of austerity imposed, or at least attempted, by conservative and social democratic governments of Germany and Britain.

And so what the members of the Union had in common, besides a social model and currency, were the social and material elements of cultural modernity: greater opportunities for women, technology (televisions, cars, washing machines, phones), travel, cuisine, social practices (including tolerance for different forms of marriage, nonmarriage, and sexuality), atheism, and so on. Even university education, in many institutions quite impoverished, became commonplace.

A third feature of the European Union, and a concession especially to France, was the commitment to agriculture in the form of guarantees to farmers that their prices would be upheld by a wide range of subsidies and support prices (costing the EU about a third of its budget). The common agricultural policy was a bone of contention since it consumed so much of the budget of the EU and kept consumer prices so high – while keeping the products of poorer countries at a disadvantage. Thus the commitment to "aid" and "development" were offset by the practice of protectionism. But the EU agricultural policies made French farmers rich, so by the 1980s France had become the second largest exporter of farm products in the world with around a quarter of the EUs total agricultural exports. However, gradually laws were introduced that had the effect of diminishing farm subsidies and price supports and diminishing the number of family farms. The rural population thus continued to decline while some of the most attractive parts of southern France became dependent on resident emigrants from northern Europe.

All the while, then, the map of the Union within postwar Europe was continuously redrawn, starting with the Six becoming the Twenty-Eight. Thus emerged a different Europe, prosperous beyond anyone's imagination, overweight, standardized, high speed, and modernized (think IKEA),[46] manipulated by bureaucrats, army-less, empire-less, and even largely prayer-less for the first time in centuries.

But it was with the unification of Germany in 1990 that came the most jolting and unbalancing internal change. Germany became not just the most productive and the most populous state within the union but also the one with the deepest pockets. In fact it became, almost immediately upon unification, the first among unequals, since no other state had quite as much economic and political clout. Soon the question was asked, "Was there to be a European Germany or a German Europe"? According to Conor Cruise O'Brien, the Irish politician, journalist, and editor with half a century of experience in both Europe and Africa, writing in early 1992, the answer was clear:

> Germany was in favour of the recognition of [Croatia and Slovenia, after the breakup of Yugoslavia]. The rest of the Community was against, and the United States strongly so. Faced with such an apparently powerful "Western consensus," on any such matter, the old pre-1990 Bundesrepublik would have respectfully backed away. The new united Germany simply ignored the United States, and turned the Community around. Germany recognized the independence of Croatia and Slovenia, and the rest of the Community followed suit within a few days. The reversal of the Community position was particularly humbling to the French … The two new republics are now part of a vast German sphere of interest … German economic hegemony in Europe is now a fact of life.[47]

Twenty-two years later, Ulrich Beck was to confirm O'Brien's analysis and answer the question about German Europe: "The fact is that Europe has become German. Nobody intended this to happen, but Germany has 'slipped' into the role of the decisive political power in Europe."[48] At an SPD conference at the end of December 2011, the German politician and publisher Helmut Schmidt had warned of this: "Germany should not try to lead the EU, it should work co-operatively with its neighbours, especially Poland and France."[49] This advice was disregarded by Germany's political rulers.

## THE DEBT OF EUROPE

The European crisis began a year after the global meltdown of 2008. On 16 October 2009, the newly elected Greek government of Georges Papandreou announced that the figures transmitted by his predecessor, Kostas Karamanlis, were in error; in fact, with the help of Goldman Sachs, they had been fabricated. Worse: it became apparent that Greek public debt had reached 12.7 per cent of GDP although earlier claims put it at a mere 6.5 per cent, itself more than double the level agreed upon in the Maastricht Treaty of February 1992, which had created the European Union.[50] Greek GDP had declined by nearly a quarter since 2007. In December all three of the American debt-rating agencies downgraded Greece's sovereign credit rating. This meant that the cost of borrowing would increase, since Greek sovereign bonds would have to pay their buyers a higher interest rate. By late April (2010) Greece's ten-year bond rate had reached 8.7 per cent. Canada's rate was around 1.8 per cent.

In March (2010) European leaders, together with the IMF, announced that they would bail out the Greeks – to the tune of €110 billion. The German share was €22.4 billion, and the Greeks had to agree to €30 billion in austerity cuts. Then debt contagion spread. In November the Union agreed to grant an €85 billion assistance package to Ireland. Yields (i.e. interest rates) on ten-year Irish government bonds soared to more than 9 per cent. In May (2011) the European council agreed that a financial assistance package totalling €78 billion would be provided to Portugal. The Italians and Spanish, respectively responsible for 11 and 17 per cent of Euro-area GDP and also in the midst of economic crises, were also brought around to the disciplinary measures of the European leaders. By October the credit rating of both those countries had been downgraded; they, too, would have to offer higher interest rates on their bonds. Spain, having seen its property bubble burst and burdened with high levels of personal and sovereign debt, also seemed financially dodgy. By the end of the year, capital was being withdrawn from southern Europe on a massive scale. Predictions were rife that the end of the EU was imminent. In January 2012, sovereign debt was further downgraded – even Austria and France lost their top (triple A) status. In February, 2012, Jürgen Stark of the European Central Bank (ECB) resigned in disagreement with the bank's policy.

The crisis then seemed to have reached its highest point; over the next months resignations of more officials and politicians were submitted, governments changed, austerity ravaged consumers, money packed up and moved, and interest rates rose. In May 2012, President Nicolas Sarkozy was defeated in French elections and in Greece in June the right-wing New Democracy formed the government. Greece's souvlaki-fascist Golden Dawn party surged in popularity. Cyprus joined the queue of southern countries requiring financial assistance. In late October there was rioting in Greece over the austerity package agreed to by the government, and on 11 November a new technocratic government was formed. In November the right-wing People's Party of Mariano Rajoy defeated the Socialist Party in Spain. In December there was uncertainty in Italy. The former prime minister Silvio Berlusconi, a sleek cad infamous for his debauchery who dominated Italian politics in the 1990s and whose policies devastated the Italian economy, indicated that his party would not support the budgetary measures of the prime minister, Mario Monti. Germany's international credibility meanwhile faltered. Its role as the home of Christian Democracy, which aspired to be Europe's (not just Germany's) natural party of government, was cast into serious doubt. But then there were also doubters as to whether the euro, the EU currency, or even the EU itself would survive.

Gradually the misery appeared to abate. In April (2012) the IMF received $430 billion in pledges from its members, increasing its lending capacity to €700 billion from €500 billion. By midsummer, Ireland's recovery appeared to be on track. At the end of 2012 European ministers of finance agreed upon further steps towards a European economic and banking union. According to one writer, this was a watershed.[51] Yet even into early 2013 uncertainty continued with some EU member states like Greece showing huge stress and others exhibiting apparently insuperable difficulty in fulfilling their undertakings. In Italy in February, the government of Mario Monti, fell. By the end of October, however, statistics showed that the Spanish economy had emerged from recession after nine quarters of negative growth. In late November Berlusconi was expelled from the Italian senate, opening the door for further reforms in Italy. In December, Ireland become the first euro-area country to successfully exit from its financial assistance program. Just before Christmas (2013) finance ministers of the EU announced that they had reached an agreement on how to deal with ailing banks. While the position of Angela Merkel and her government had been against bailouts and shared debts – and in some cases even against any support for

Greece – this had shifted so that by the end of May 2014, in the words of Peter Spiegel, "she struck a deal that would mark the biggest shift in sovereignty since the euro's creation; in exchange for allowing common eurozone funds to rescue failing European banks, oversight and liquidation of those institutions would move from national to EU control."[52]

Negotiations between debtors and the creditors, represented by the troika of the European Commission, the European Central Bank and the IMF, stalled. No debt relief was offered. A report by the IMF explaining that Greece's debt was unsustainable was suppressed by the Europeans. The IMF had argued that all Greece needed was for the creditors to take a 30 per cent "haircut" and for Greece to be loaned another €52 billion. No dice. In elections in January 2015 the ruling right-wing New Democracy fell from power, to be replaced by Syriza, a party of social democrats and communists, antiausterity, and more radical than anything seen in contemporary Europe. The leader of Syriza was Alexis Tsipras. Six months later Syrzia's resistance collapsed, and the party forced through the most severe austerity package the Greeks had ever seen.

With Syriza in power, the stalemate with the troika had deepened. Blame flew in all directions and steadily became more vitriolic and even more global; critics of austerity, the policy favoured by most European governments, said that the creditors, German and French banks and the IMF, had mismanaged the Greek dossier. The troika, they pointed out, was profoundly antipathetic to democracy. Its leaders in the European Central Bank and the European Commission were, none of them, after all, elected. Embracing the principles of neoliberalism, they were unforgiving. Their only concern, it was argued, was the bottom line of the lenders. The major advocate of this line of argument was Wolfgang Schäuble, the powerful conservative (CDU) finance minister. It was stressed that the terms of repayment would keep the Greek economy in poverty for decades. Among others, poor pensioners, sustained by welfare, would become paupers. Welfarism, accepted by most members of the EU as essential to European civilization, would wither and die.

The exit of Greece from the EU, known as "Grexit," would have a daunting symbolic value for Europe it was feared; Greece was, it was widely accepted, where European democracy had begun. Greece had been under a military dictatorship until the 1970s, the last noncommunist European country to have surrendered democracy to quasifascist rule, and the return of democratic government to Greece, at the same moment that Europe was going from glory to glory, was seen as a final escape from the political darkness that had enshrouded the continent for most of the first half of the twentieth century.

So Grexit would be the end of the European experiment, the death of the dream. "A Greek exit from the EU is an outcome no one should want. Whatever the result of the Greek referendum, Europe must not be allowed to self-destruct," wrote one. Manuel Valls, socialist prime minister of France, made it clear: "We cannot let Greece leave the eurozone. Nobody can say what the political consequences would be, what would be the reaction of the Greek people."[53]

The talking heads were divided; Keynesians and social democrats on the side of Greece, neoliberals and conservatives on the side of the troika and the banks. From Britain one editorial in the left-leaning *Guardian* spoke to the case of the Greek exit from the Euro. "It would," the editorial argued, "pile disaster upon disaster ... Europe must stare into this abyss to prevent itself from falling into it." Referring to the "Creditors," even Ambrose Evans-Pritchard, international business editor of the right-wing *Daily Telegraph*, a paper which had little time for the EU anyway, pointed out that, "They stuck rigidly to their script, refusing to recognize in any way that their own Dickensian prescriptions have been discredited by economists from across the world." "Like a tragedy from Euripides," he concluded, "the long struggle between Greece and Europe's creditor powers is reaching a cataclysmic end that nobody planned, nobody seems able to escape, and that threatens the greater European order in the process."[54] Nobody spoke of *le défi americaine.*

In a pair of forceful interventions, an open letter and an interview in *Die Zeit*, Thomas Piketty, by then Europe's hottest economist, stressed that austerity had failed and Germany, whose conservative leaders had insistently proclaimed the righteousness of debt repayment, was in no position to lecture Greece as Germany, "is really the single best example of a country that, throughout its history, has never repaid its external debt." Together with economists Jeffrey Sachs, Dani Rodrik, and others he appealed to Chancellor Merkel and the troika. Unless they abandoned their insistence on further austerity for Greece and prevent the Greek exit from the EU, they said, "(t)he collateral damage will kill the Eurozone as a beacon of hope, democracy, and prosperity, and could lead to far-reaching economic consequences across the world." In *Die Zeit*, Piketty made the point, heard by now quite frequently, that the Germans themselves had escaped the burden of external debt after World War Two. Had this not been the case there would have been no *Wirtschaftswunder*.[55]

Still, the "brutal creditors" pushed on. At the end of the weekend of 11–12 July (2015), the Eurozone project was on life support. In the *Financial Times*, the paper that had regularly criticized Thomas Piketty, columnist Wolfgang Munchau denounced Greece's creditors and especially the unforgiving Wolfgang Schäuble.[56] Greece's creditors, he wrote, had "destroyed the eurozone as we know it and demolished the idea of a monetary union as a step towards a democratic political union." The editors of *The Guardian*, introduced a novel concept, the "debt colony." Unlike the Germans, France's proposals "did not envisage Greece's reduction to the status of a debt colony, not too different from the conditions once imposed on Egypt and China in the imperial era, with foreigners in controlling positions in the economy." Paul Krugman, giving his view in an opinion piece in *The New York Times* quoted the hashtag "ThisIsACoup." The creditors demands ("madness") go "beyond harsh into pure vindictiveness, complete destruction of national sovereignty, and no hope of relief." It was "a grotesque betrayal of everything the European project was supposed to stand for." By 2017 *The Financial Times* reported, 15 per cent of Greeks were living in extreme poverty. The *Chania Post* reported that the figure was four out of ten.[57]

Then came the refugee crisis. By August 2015 the German chancellor, Angela Merkel, was speculating that refugees would preoccupy Europe more than the Greek crisis that had taken up headlines since 2010. The issue of asylum "could be the next European project." The Germans along with the Swedes had welcomed the largest number of asylum seekers. A record of more than 800,000 were expected to apply for residence in Germany in 2015, three times more than in previous years. Washington announced it would accept 100,000. Canada had taken in some 25,000 refugees in 2014 and anticipated more in the future. The Conservative Canadian government announced that it was considering the emigration of Middle Eastern Christians as a priority. Then the government changed and so did its policy. Meanwhile in Berlin, Muslim refugees were converting to Christianity "in droves." The United Nations refugee agency, UNHCR, referred to the situation as a "colossal humanitarian catastrophe."[58]

In a single page essay in *The New York Review of Books*, Thomas Piketty took up his pen concerning recent French elections and what they tell us about the fate of Europe:

> The far right has surged in just a few years from 15 percent to 30 percent of the vote in France, and now has the support of up to 40 percent in a number of districts. Many factors conspired to produce this result: rising unemployment and xenophobia, a deep disappointment over the left's record in running the government, the feeling that we've tried everything and it's time to experiment with something new. These are the consequences of the disastrous handling of the financial meltdown that began in the United States in 2008, a meltdown that we in Europe transformed by our own actions into a lasting European crisis. The blame for that belongs to institutions and policies that proved wholly inadequate, particularly in the eurozone, consisting of nineteen countries … Only a genuine social and democratic refounding of the eurozone, designed to encourage growth and employment, arrayed around a small core of countries willing to lead by example and develop their own new political institutions, will be sufficient to counter the hateful nationalistic impulses than now threaten all of Europe.[59]

Nor was Germany, Europe's economic motor, flourishing. Its growth rate since the turn of the century was below the EU average, while wage growth had stagnated. Poverty and wealth inequalities had become among the highest in on the continent.[60]

## BREXIT

On 23 June 2016, by a vote of 52:48 came the UK vote to leave the European Union after being a member since 1973. "Brexit," this was called. "[T]he event was cast in epochal terms," Susan Watkins wrote.[61] The surprise of the vote provoked a gloomy range of interpretations including a revolt against globalization, the yearning of oldies for Empire, the dissatisfaction of youth, xenophobia, regional protest against the London elite, the disenchantment with the ruling Conservatives, the feebleness of the "Remain" campaign. Nearly two-thirds of the working class, which made up some 46 per cent of the British population, voted to leave. So did 60 per cent of the people in the Midlands, the North, and Wales. Young people, intellectuals, and the middle class voted in favour of "Remain"; these groups, represented in papers like *The Guardian, The Financial Times*, and *The Economist* and supported by voices from overseas like *The New York Times*, were shocked by the outcome of the referendum, no more so than the ruling prime minister at the time, David Cameron, who, apparently dismayed, resigned almost immediately upon hearing news of the vote. After three weeks a new prime minister, Theresa May, was sworn in. She made it plain that she was unwavering in her support of the exit vote.

There was universal fear that the Brexit vote was just another sign of the senescence of the EU or, more generally, the decline of capitalism. "The departure of the EU's second-largest state is a ... serious blow. At a stroke, it loses an eighth of its population, a sixth of its GDP, half of its nuclear-arms cache and a seat on the UN Security Council – its diminution mocked in the Chinese media as the decline of the West."[62]

But Adam Tooze had a less disquieting interpretation. Alluding to the disaster of Imperial Germany in 1918 and the rise of Weimar and Nazism that followed, he signalled his dissent from disillusionment and his faith in the democratic solidity of Germany, the keystone in the EU Lego:

> [W]e are not in the early Weimar Republic, nor are we living through the decline of the Roman Empire. We have our own problems and they are bad enough. The shocks of the financial crisis, the Eurozone crisis, Ukraine and the refugee crisis goes deep. The Trump presidency may unleash even worse ... The rallying of nationalism across Europe is undeniable and dangerous ... [But] ... In Germany, the solidity of the checks and balances in its constitution and the sophistication of its democratic culture mean there is no real risk of a Trump, Le Pen, Brexit-style swerve to the right."[63]

Throughout 2016 and into 2017, the debate over Brexit continued with the Conservative prime minister, Theresa May, at first defending it, then waffling, and finally being put on the defensive while the Labour Party, at the time of Brexit in apparently terminal decline, springing back to life and with it, the possibility of a renewed membership in the EU.

# 3

# Russian Alternatives

There were two revolutions in Russia or, rather, a revolution and a counterrevolution. The revolution of 1917, led by a small vanguard party under V.I. Lenin known as the Bolsheviks and normally called the Russian Revolution, yielded the communist regimes that ultimately dominated most of Eurasia for the majority of the twentieth century. "Russia" became the heartland of the "Union of Soviet Socialist Republics" (USSR), a sprawling empire that stretched 6,000 miles from the Baltic across the endless boreal forest to the Pacific and included much of Central Asia. The USSR was twice the size of Canada. Of its population, the Russians themselves, the "ethnic Russians," comprised just more than half of the 280 million total in the 1980s. Others included Ukrainians and Belarusians (Belorussians), Latvians, Lithuanians, Estonians, Armenians, Georgians, Azeris, Moldavians, Jews in Europe, and Chechens, Tatars, Kazakhs, Kyrgyz, Tajiks, and Turkmen, and several other groups in the Caucasus and in Asia.

The Bolsheviks came to power in November 1917, after an invasion by western countries and Japan. They banished rival parties, thereby creating a one-party state. Joseph Stalin succeeded Lenin in 1929 and ruled dictatorially until 1953. In June 1940 the Soviet Union was invaded by Germany. In the following years of the "Great Patriotic War" the Soviets suffered from the German occupation of Ukraine, Belorussia, and Crimea, and even as far east as the oil-rich Caucasus before they drove the Germans westwards all the way to Berlin. This victorious advance had been largely completed by the time the Americans, British, and Canadians landed in Normandy on 6 June 1944 (D-Day).

Following from the destruction of the German armies in the Soviet Union came the liberation of Poland, Hungary, Czechoslovakia, Bulgaria, and Romania and ultimately the occupation of eastern Germany, forcing the German surrender in May 1945. The Red Army thus came to occupy the whole of eastern Europe and most of the Balkans (but not Greece or Yugoslavia). From 1945 until 1990 this area became known as the Communist (or Eastern) Bloc. Western Europe was considered part of the Free World, a bloc that included the right-wing dictatorships in Spain, Portugal, and Greece. The Communist Bloc was separated from the Free World by an ideological construction known as the Iron Curtain. The bloc was the most singular geopolitical innovation of the twentieth century; no communist states existed at the beginning of that century and none of significance remained by the start of the twenty-first. While it existed, however, the Soviet empire was the polar opposite of America: both claimed possession of the future and had the capacity to annihilate the present, and both claimed the mandate to transform the rest of the world. Moscow had become one of the world's great imperial capitals and, alongside Washington, head of one of the two "Great Powers."

Allied to the Communist Bloc was China from 1949 and North Korea from 1953. Thus came into existence the adversarial world of the Cold War. Soviet communism itself died at the end of 1991, predeceased, in all but name, by Chinese communism. Only North Korea, totalitarian and autarkic, has remained faithful to the kind of Stalinist–Maoist dictatorship that had disappeared all around it.

The defeat of Germany by the Red Army was the guarantee of communist hegemony over the whole of eastern Europe. Europe was now divided: the West, including most of Germany, was under control of the capitalist democracies; the East, including the eastern provinces of Germany, under the communists. Significant parts of what had been Baltic Germany east of the Oder River were permanently redistributed to the Soviet Union and Poland and their German populations driven westwards in their millions.

Even in the postwar West the communists remained a formidable political force, especially in Italy and France. Although they were normally excluded from power, their influence remained significant as late as the 1980s. Communism was strengthened by the fidelity of its members, the intellectuals that were associated with it, and a certain resilience that allowed communists not only to accept alliance with socialists, as they did under François Mitterrand as late as the 1980s, but to formulate more flexible doctrines, such as the Italian-made "Eurocommunism."[1] What was more, throughout most of the postwar era, communism was palpably spreading, to China and North Korea, to Cuba in 1959, South Vietnam and Laos in 1975, Ethiopia, and Angola and Mozambique in the 1970s. Communist parties ruled at a lower level as well, as in a couple of states, Kerala and West Bengal, on opposite ends of India. And, better late than never, a communist party seized power in Nepal in 2006. Although a split had divided Moscow and Beijing from the early 1960s, few informed people in the 1980s would have thought that both European and Chinese communism were approaching the end of the road.

## COLD WAR

In Winston Churchill's widely cited "Iron Curtain" speech in Fulton, Missouri, of early 1946, he warned his American hosts: "If the Western Democracies stand together ... no one is likely to molest them. If however they become divided or falter in their duty and if these all-important years are allowed to slip away, then indeed catastrophe may overwhelm us all."[2] Here was "Atlanticism" in healthy bud; by "Western Democracies," Churchill, son of an American mother and author of a history of the English-speaking (white) peoples, really meant Britain and the US.[3] To the extent that Churchill was one of the greatest of twentieth-century imperialists, his worry about communism was that it might threaten the empire and thus the recovery of Britain as a world power securely attached to America's side.

A year after Churchill's Fulton speech, on 12 March (1947) President Harry Truman proclaimed "the Truman Doctrine" calling for military aid to Greece and Turkey to counteract the "totalitarian" threat of communism. Thus commenced the Cold War.[4] The tenor of these early Cold War proclamations of Churchill and Truman was always as moralistic and even metaphysical as economic. Even more than Churchill, no amateur rhetorician, the American view was enunciated by George Kennan (celebrated as the greatest of his country's postwar diplomats and the "father of containment").[5] Gratitude was owed to providence, Kennan intoned in what was to become "the Kennan Doctrine," for providing the American people "with this implacable challenge [ie. confrontation with the communism in Greece] that has made their entire security as a nation dependent on their pulling themselves together and accepting the responsibility of moral and political leadership that history plainly intended them to bear." Again, nothing was mentioned about the need on the part of American capital for investment opportunities abroad and for markets and cheap labour and raw materials. The Marshall Plan, discussed in chapter 2, was an aspect of containment policy. At the Paris peace conference in June 1947 economic assistance was offered to East European governments. When Czechoslovakia and Poland seemed tempted by it, Moscow put on the brakes and withdrew from the conference. The Czechs and Poles were thus deprived of needed dollars and condemned to a slow and exhausting recovery from the effects of war. Their only choice was to join the Soviet equivalent of the Marshall Plan, COMECON, the "Council of Mutual Economic Assistance." Nonetheless, the communist states of the East did make marked progress, especially in the 1950s and '60s.

For the West, the Cold War took an alarming turn when the Soviets successfully tested an atomic bomb in August 1949. Less than a year later, in June 1950, the first and only hot war of the Cold War era broke out, with communist North Korea invading the American-supported south. Stalin was uncertain about supporting the communists of Pyongyang although he did supply military aid including jets and pilots. It was the Chinese communists who defeated the Western armies that fought under the auspices of the UN.

The Korean War had already reached an impasse when Joseph Stalin died in March 1953. The question of succession now rose. Nikita Khrushchev, the least likely of the contenders, defeated his rivals who were then sidelined. But they survived. The head of the NKVD, the dreaded secret police, did not. He was shot as a "capitalist agent" and an "enemy of the people." Khruschev himself became, like Stalin before him, both prime minister and general secretary.

In Khrushchev's day while key elements in Soviet domestic policy remained the same, there was a radical shift aimed at winning over the consuming public. The Soviet Union, boasted the Soviet leader, would soon outproduce the United States in milk, meat, and butter. This was to happen in spite of massive investments in the military and space technology. On top of this there was also to be an end to mass terror, no more sweeping purges or wholesale deportations or forced labour or other industrial-scale human rights travesties. In fact, 1.5 million out of a total of 5.5 million people living in labour camps, colonies, and penal colonies were amnestied. Even the crime of "counterrevolutionary crimes" disappeared from the criminal code, to be replaced by "crimes against the state."

Right from the beginning of Khrushchev's reign, there was a degree of détente with the West including an armistice in the Korean War signed in July 1953 and a conference over the fate of Indochina arranged for the next year. In 1955 the four-power occupation of Austria came to an end; so the Soviet Union was now out of Western Europe, and the Austrians could begin to roll out their campaign to exempt themselves from the devastations caused by the Nazis (whose leader, of course, had been an Austrian). Still, Europe remained divided, and the Soviet glacier seemed permanent. In 1956 came the Hungarian Uprising and in 1968 the Prague Spring; both uprisings against communist dictatorship underlined the apparent truth that there could be no such thing as a "Third Way" of democratic communism. There could be reform, as Khrushchev pointed out, but only *within* a system ruled from Moscow.[6]

In the years that followed the advent of Khrushchev, there was little more domestic drama and certainly less terror, just year in and year out of slowly abating struggle, kept alive by a residual optimism that put faith in a Communist utopia and was enlivened by some remarkable military and scientific triumphs and an inching upward of the standard of living. As one East German journalist explained to his British homologue:

> At [the newspaper] *Neues Deutschland* we told each other jokes in the canteen. We weren't blind to the failings of the system, but we convinced ourselves that this was only because it was early days and the class enemy was perpetuating sabotage wherever he could. One day, we thought, all problems would be solved and there wouldn't be any more jokes because there wouldn't be anything left to joke about.[7]

In the West, despite immense material advances, fears that communism might, in the long run, prevail were kept alive by a combination of regular media scares and Soviet grandstanding. In 1956 Party Secretary Khrushchev had explained confidently to a Western audience: "Whether you like it or not, history is on our side. We will bury you." There was no reason *not* to believe him since, after all, in the same year the Soviets had launched the *Sputnik*, the first orbiting satellite. Soon they would put a dog and then a man in space. The confidence of Americans, their main rivals, was shaken. Those who took the threat of communism seriously were encouraged to dig bomb shelters in their backyards, and for several years in the 1950s and again during the Cuban missile crisis of 1962 they were gripped by a deep fear of nuclear annihilation. Novels were written and movies made featuring the consequences of nuclear war. Right across northern Canada three lines of radar stations were built to search the skies for invading Soviet bombers, better to shoot them down over the Northwest Territories than over New England. In Ottawa there were bomb drills and air raid shelters. (The Hilton of bomb shelters in Canada's capital was meant to hold a mere 500 civil servants, perhaps an indication of taciturnity. Designed and built in secrecy, it was known as the "Diefenbunker" after Canadian prime minister John Diefenbaker, in office 1957–63). In early 1960 Khrushchev boasted: "We now have a broad range of rockets and in such quantity that we can virtually shatter the world."[8]

Certainly, the idea of communism was potent. To many in the West, it was seen as a frightful virus likely to spread to the minds of the uninoculated citizenry. Thus the Daughters of the American Revolution, the all-white and middle class ancestor of the Tea Party, in 1959 passed a resolution opposing cultural exchanges with Communist countries because the "underlying purpose [is] the softening of Americans towards communism."[9] "Soft on communism" was a form of moral and political turpitude. Few realized, in large part because of the propaganda of American spying agencies like the CIA, that in spite of Soviet advances in certain technologies, and the glories of their physics and mathematics, the Russians and their allies were technologically decades behind the Americans. Still, Soviet accomplishments were undeniable. In the forty years since the launch of the first Five-Year Plan in 1928, the GDP of the Soviet Union had increased at least seven times, and the average annual growth rate had been a substantial 6 to 7 per cent per year. By 1970 the population of the Soviet Union enjoyed a higher standard of living than ever before. And because of its profuse natural resources, especially oil, gas, minerals, and timber, even in spite of chaotic economic planning and a dogmatic adherence to antimarket ideology, it was able to forge ahead and maintain the massive military that had become the leading element in its economy. So, while the reforms of Nikita Khrushchev continued to improve the standard of living for the mass of the people, the orbiting *Sputnik* gave the Soviet Union (and communism) a terrific boost of credibility.

## KHRUSHCHEV, BREZHNEV

Nikita Khrushchev held on to power for nearly a decade. The Khrushchev years were the apogee of Soviet history. Probably for more than any other reason, his tenure is recalled for having revealed the truth of Stalin's terror in what has been called his "secret speech" at the Twentieth Congress of the Soviet Communist Party on 14 February 1956 in the Great Kremlin Palace.[10] This was the most spectacular political assassination of the whole of the twentieth century; the denunciation of Mao Zedong by Deng Xiaoping and the terminators of Chinese communism never went nearly so far. When Khrushchev's speech was aired, shock, horror, confusion, and a great measure of disbelief transfixed communists all over the world. In the Soviet Union the party leadership reacted disingenuously, pretending that they had only heard about the terror recently – in fact most knew about it and many had actually participated in it and benefited from it. Khrushchev himself wobbled, retreating from his own denunciation of Stalin, before plunging on. It is suggested he made the speech as a matter of repentance – which we may or may not believe. At any rate, with the speech the traffic light of dogma turned from the red of absolutism to the amber of revisionism. Some mistakes had been made, it was admitted, and some changes could be considered, it hinted. Communism, however, was still the future of mankind.

The consequences of Khrushchev's speech were immediate; there were protests and strikes in Poznan in Poland in June (1956), which were put down with bloodshed although they led to certain reforms managed by the communist head of the Polish state, Wladyslaw Gomulka. A more widely felt crisis was the Hungarian Revolution, the uprising in October of the same year in Budapest, ignited by student protests and leading to the repudiation of Soviet rule. An immense statue of Stalin, like that of Saddam Hussein in Baghdad decades later, was toppled. Little time was wasted in calling in Soviet tanks. As many as 20,000 were killed and thousands fled the country. The leader of the Hungarian reformers, Imre Nagy, was arrested, tried in secret, and shot. The world might have been even more appalled had it not been that at almost the same moment the British, French, and Israelis invaded Egypt. While the Suez Crisis signalled the end of the British and French empires, the Soviet empire seemed to be good to go on and on.

Khrushchev's tenancy as general secretary spanned the middle years of the West's golden age and put Khrushchev on the same stage as US presidents Eisenhower, Kennedy, and Johnson (collectively, 1953–69). The Soviet Union had become a secure fixture in the apparently permanently bipolar world. There were, however, problems and one was that even in Khrushchev's time there was a lack of firm conviction among young people, especially in Eastern Europe, that the Soviet Union was part of the best of all possible worlds. When he backed down from the threat of global nuclear war over Cuba and agreed to withdraw Soviet missiles from the island in October 1962, Khrushchev lost face. Two years later, in October 1964, while he was on vacation in Georgia, he was summonsed back to the Kremlin to an emergency meeting where he was voted out of office. He left quietly.

Times had changed and with them the nature of communism itself. The fate of many of those who under Stalin had been imprisoned, shot, and sent to concentration camps in Siberia had been a matter of caprice. Under Khrushchev, between 1953 and 1960, two million of Stalinism's victims had been released, although millions more never returned. Taken as a whole, the 1960s were a time of rehabilitation, the release of tensions after the Cuban missile crisis, frustrated détente, and grinding economic progress, at least in the centres. Perhaps the most shocking break with the Stalinist past and the more tolerant future was the publication in 1962 of Aleksandr Solzhenitsyn's *One Day in the Life of Ivan Denisovich*, a novel that lifted the lid on Stalin's labour camps. A million copies were sold in the first six months with many copies having several readers. Another solvent was American culture that seeped into the Soviet conscience from as early as the mid-1950s. "Rock and roll and its attendant fashions captured the imagination of a generation of Soviet students who were too educated and sophisticated to be satisfied by the boring and conformist [official] culture. On their short wave radios they listened to the Voice of America and Radio Free Europe where rock and jazz were the draw for news and information of the freedoms of the West." Even Tarzan movies worked their magic. The poet Joseph Brodsky commented that these, "did more for de-Stalinization than all Khrushchev's speeches at the Twentieth Party Congress and after." [11]

Then, decline and the Brezhnev era,[12] its eponymous head being Khrushchev's successor, Leonid Brezhnev (in power 1964–82), a caricature of post-Stalin *Homo Sovieticus*, an old-fashioned *apparatchik*, pasty, mediocre, unrevolutionary, hostile to reform, but, at least compared to Stalin, fangless. Brezhnev was nonetheless an excellent networker, building alliances with regional party bosses and with his fellow members of the politburo, the cabinet, comprises the country's oligarchs. Although there was obviously more than a little of the usual sliding of favours under the table (notably to relatives), none of the *apparatchiks*, at least compared to their descendants at the end of the century, were spectacularly rich. Most had *dachas*, usually in the form of modest cottages in the country, none had opulent properties in the South of France, Spain, or London or owned Western football teams or newspapers, as did Putin's courtiers (or, indeed, the ruling class of contemporary communist China). All travelled in cars built in the Soviet Union and had their kids enrolled in schools in the Soviet Union. Above all, they wanted stability and most wanted détente. An army with massive troops of tanks; an air force with squadrons of supersonic jets, and missiles; and a navy with fleets of submarines was the price they were willing to pay. "This was a gerontocracy," writes Orlando Figes, "whose only ideology was to make things stay the same. Brezhnev gave a name to this conservative idea, "Mature Socialism"; the absurd doctrine that a socialist society had been successfully created and that all that was now needed to consolidate its gains … But at sixty years Soviet socialism was older than mature. It was at retirement age." And it needed outside support to keep it on its feet, depending on exports of oil and gas to finance imports of machinery and food. In this explanation, then, it had failed to become a "great power" but was instead a "semiperiphery," that is, a dependent annex of the global capitalist system. By the 1970s, the Soviet Union was also beset by the problem of faith. The Russians told jokes about their condition:

"Why isn't there any flour in the shops?"

"Because they've started adding it to bread."

"What would happen if they introduced a Five-Year Plan in the Sahara Desert?"

"Nothing at first, but in a few years there would be a shortage of sand."[13]

Whereas the Soviet rate of growth had been 5.2 per cent in the 1960s, it dropped to 3.7 per cent in the first half of the 1970s and 2 per cent in 1980–85. In response to the reformers' complaint that the Soviet economy was lagging in practically all departments, the conservatives claimed that the simple problem was waste, which could be solved by more prudent management. There was nothing wrong with communism *qua* communism, they insisted. More of the same was the sovereign remedy: the elderly would not change their diets.

Few anticipated that this "Era of Stagnation" was the penultimate act in the drama of communism. The temper of the times was partly determined by the aging of the actual rulers of the Soviet Union, the *nomenklatura* of the politburo, who collectively continued to shuffle towards their graves; at the end of the Khrushchev era their average age was sixty; at the end of the Brezhnev era it was seventy. Marshall Goldman recounts but one story from this dismal and disillusioning epoch:

> [F]or a time in the late 1970s to early 1980s, crime and by extension, corruption, seemed to pervade the Soviet society. Under Leonid Brezhnev communist morality all but disappeared. It did not help that Brezhnev's daughter was having an affair with a circus clown who was also a diamond smuggler while her husband, Deputy Head of the National Police, was on the payroll of the Uzbek Mafia.[14]

It was in the Brezhnev era that the Soviet Union stood out, at great expense to the development of other aspects of its economy, as a military superpower. Under him, the military budget increased eightfold and consumed about 15 per cent of the total. This was mainly financed by the bubble in oil prices, a consequence of the 1973 Arab–Israeli war; in fact, no non-OPEC country benefitted as much as the Soviet Union in the price inflation of oil. Yet in the Soviet Union itself these years were defined by the "shortage economy" during which citizens spent a remarkable amount of time queuing for food and other essentials, much of which was highly subsidized but inefficiently produced. The classic story was of potatoes rotting in the fields due to a lack of machinery to harvest them. Queues were justified by communists with the claim that they were a form of democratic distribution; the rich queued like everyone else. This wasn't true for two reasons: first, by contemporary standards there were no rich (yet) in the USSR and secondly, the *nomenklatura*, the Communist Party aristocracy, had special stores where they could buy Western delicacies.

Alas, mortality was inescapable. Brezhnev's health declined after a major stroke in 1975. Power passed to a troika of Yuri Andropov (1982–84), the Soviet Union's leading spook, Andrei Gromyko, the head of the Soviet foreign office, and Dmitry Ustinov, a general who had become head of the defence ministry. It was these three that marched the Red Army into Afghanistan in December 1979.

## GORBACHEV

Andropov's successor, Mikhail Gorbachev (1985–91), flourished in the era of Ronald Reagan and Margaret Thatcher (jointly 1979–91), the take-off years of neoliberalism. Generally admired in the West, we might imagine him as the Russian equivalent of François Mitterand (1981–95) – both late-century reformers, both swept up by currents set in motion by the neoliberal revolution, which they attempted to divert or at least shape, and both colossal yet tragic figures in the last epoch of the Cold War. Standing out for his relative youth and energy, in March 1985 Gorbachev was promoted to general secretary of the CPSU.[15] From the beginning he was a political reformer although this was not apparent immediately. It was widely hoped that he could put an end to Cold War and get the economically stalled country moving again. Nobody suspected that he might dismantle the Soviet system, that he would in fact be the last leader of the Soviet Union.

After the corruptions and disappointments of the Brezhnev era it was hoped that a reformer like Gorbachev might put the Soviet Union back on the path of economic expansion and even stimulate some sort of moral reawakening. Relations with the West could only improve. Gorbachev was acutely aware of how far behind the West the Soviet Union had fallen in terms of economic development and, especially, technology.

Gorbachev was unusual among Soviet leaders in that he had himself been to the West on several occasions since the 1970s and witnessed not just its rich material life but also its productive superiority. None of his visits impressed him more than that to Canada – like the Soviet Union in such key respects as location, climate, and resources, not to mention landmass and a devotion to hockey, but light years ahead in efficiency. Gorbachev was lucky in that his visit to the Soviet Union's northern neighbour coincided with the heyday of Prime Minister Pierre Trudeau (in office 1968–84) who, unlike certain of his predecessors and successors, and many of his colleagues in NATO, was anything but a dogmatic anticommunist. Trudeau was as sympathetic to Gorbachev as he had been to Fidel Castro, the neighbourhood communist leader. It was he who introduced Gorbachev to the British Prime Minister Margaret Thatcher who said, memorably, that the British could do business with him. Because of her close ties with President Reagan, Thatcher had the global clout to lead the way with a more open policy towards both the Soviet Union and the communist-ruled states of Eastern Europe. Quite obviously, détente was in the cards. It remained to Gorbachev to carry out the reforms within the Soviet Union to bring the Cold War to an end and bring the country's citizenry up to speed as producers and consumers.

During Gorbachev's tenure as general secretary, reforms one after another swept the Soviet Union. These were associated with the concepts of *perestroika* (openness) and *glasnost* (restructuring). *Perestroika* was about the economy. The market would be allowed to work its magic but alongside a planned economy; there are hints here of the German *ordoliberalism* and of the early stages of the Chinese road to capitalism. *Glasnost* was about socialist thinking: it emphasized "universal human values" and put aside class struggle. The Communist leaders of Eastern Europe, of course, would have to be on their own. Soviet tanks would no longer be idling in the side streets waiting for trouble. A collateral benefit: disarmament would reduce the crushing burden of military expenditure. In the West there was widespread approval, even excitement, at the policies of "Gorby."

Gorbachev's faith in communism was unshakeable. With the Soviet standard of living deteriorating steadily, he spoke of a "democratic market system" and of Russia becoming "a socialist beacon for all mankind." His first step upon having become general secretary was to shift the balance of advisors that stood behind him, dispatching the geriatric old guard and bringing in the new. Then, at a Council of Europe meeting at Strasbourg on 6 July 1989, he informed his audience that the Soviet Union would not stand in the way of Eastern European reform; that was "entirely a matter for the people themselves." In July in Bucharest he assured the leaders of other communist states that each state had a right to follow its own destiny into the future.[16] But the orderly and gradual transition from authoritarianism to reformed socialism that he had hoped for was swept away in the rush for change. The Berlin Wall came down in November (1989) and within the year Germany was unified – to the dismay of both Britain and France. Thus came the "end of empire" moment in the Soviet Union, a mere three decades behind the same moment in Western Europe.

In May 1990, the parliaments of all three Baltic republics declared their sovereignty almost without incident. By the end of the year Ukraine, Belarus, Moldova, Azerbaijan, Kyrgyzstan, Uzbekistan, Georgia, Tajikistan, and Armenia had exited the Soviet Union. As social and economic conditions deteriorated, Boris Yeltsin, who had been head of the Moscow Party, became president. He used his position to suspend the Russian Communist Party and to seize its assets and had imperceptibly come to eclipse Gorbachev as Russia's leading political figure. He denounced Gorbachev in March 1991. Gorbachev's enemies ground their teeth and waited (until he had gone on holidays to Crimea) and then fomented a coup in August 1991. But they proved to be divided, Yeltsin stood by Gorbachev, and the coup failed. Still, the Soviet Union was in its death throes.

On 17 December, Gorbachev agreed that the Soviet Union should be formally abolished. He then resigned as president. On Christmas Day 1991 the Russian flag replaced that of the Soviet Union on top of the Kremlin, once the seat of Soviet power. At midnight on 31 December 1991, the USSR ceased to exist. Yeltsin now became president of "Russia," a renovated old country. This Russia, however, was no broken remnant of a great empire. Even separated from its independent neighbours like Ukraine, which we shall discuss below, it was still the world's largest state in area, and its population was as great as Germany and Britain combined.[17] Still, it was feeble in many respects, running on its oil and gas reserves rather, unlike a number of Asian economies, than on the export of manufactures.

In the West there was barely contained euphoria at the end of the Soviet Union and its empire. No one was more upbeat than the US president George H.W. Bush, chief of what had become the world's sole superpower. In congress in March Bush had announced that "[W]e can see a new world coming into view. A world in which there is the very real prospect of a new world order."[18] It was at this point that the philosopher Francis Fukayama announced that history had come to an end – there was now only a single, unified, potentially democratic system, mentored, of course, by the United States, which stood at its head.

## YELTSIN, PUTIN I, MEDVEDEV, PUTIN II

The second Russian revolution, formally launched on the last day of 1991, had brought the Union of Soviet Socialist Republics (USSR), the communist fatherland, to its end. In the place of the Soviet Union, effective from 1992, "Russia" was thus reconstituted. This new Russia was not, like China or Vietnam in the same epoch, guided by native, excommunist reformers determined to keep some form of dictatorship and *dirigisme* alive but a Russia guided by a class of *nouveaux riches* like the billionaire neoliberals Anatoly Chubais and Mikhail Khodorkovsky. When the Soviet economy was liberated for capitalism in the 1990s, they were able to buy up, with borrowed money, huge assets including oil and other minerals. Besides owning a 36 per cent bloc of the oil company, Yukos, Khodorkovsky had established a private bank, Menatep, in 1992. He wrote: "MENATEP is the realization of the right to riches ... Our goals are clear, our tasks are defined – we aspire to be billionaires ... Membership in the Communist Party was a good school for us ... The Party took away a lot, but it also gave us a lot; experience, connections, life status."[19] Chrystia Freeland, the bureau chief of the *Financial Times* in Moscow in the 1990s, gave a polite name to the new Russian ruling class in the title of her 2012 book: *Plutocrats.* Karen Dawisha and others, more bluntly, have used the common term "kleptocrats"; she has compared them unfavourably with the Nigerian elite who have plundered that country recklessly for more than half a century.[20]

The plutocrats and kleptocrats did not rise unaided or untutored. Under Yeltsin, management of the Russian economy was coached by American experts, the most famous of who was the Harvard economist Jeffrey Sachs, later to pop up as an antipoverty campaigner.[21] Harvard in Russia in the 1990s was as the University of Chicago had been in Chile in the 1970s, in the thick of the "reform," that is, the destruction of *dirigisme* and the installation of neoliberalism. Later it was sued by the US Justice Department for alleged improprieties and its Institute for International Development, funded by the US Agency for International Development, was shut down. Offer and Söderberg explain:

> Among prominent [Harvard] economists, it was publicly alleged in 2006 that Andrew [sic] Shleifer, a Harvard economist and protégé of Larry Summers (himself chief economist at the World

> Bank, and later secretary of the Treasury), used his position on a government-funded Harvard advisory mission in Russia to facilitate insider trading by his wife, making use of mission premises. Harvard paid the US government more than twenty million dollars in exculpation. Summers, by then president of Harvard, resigned shortly after the exposé.[22]

Sachs and his colleagues worked with a number of institutions like the World Bank, prescribing the same "shock therapy" (also known as the "big bang approach") for Russia as the Americans had for Chile and postcommunist Poland.[23] The parallel Russian team, led by Anatoly Chubais and Yegor Gaidar, the "shock doctor" and acting prime minister under Yeltsin, were admirers of the Chilean dictator, Pinochet. "Let him be a dictator," they said of Boris Yeltsin who implemented the therapy on 2 January 1992, two days after the dissolution of the Soviet Union.[24]

Yeltsin had been elected as president in June 1991 and was reelected for a second term in 1996, thanks in large part to Anatoly Chubais. Important American voices were enthusiastic about his rule. In the early 1990s a Yeltsin cult had emerged: "as Yeltsin goes, so goes the nation." As late as 1999 *The New York Times* announced that he was a "key defender of Russia's hard-won democratic reforms" and "an enormous asset for the US."[25] In fact, Yeltsin's second electoral victory was a close run thing. Widely despised for his drunkenness and shambolic rule and with the Russian economy in shreds, Yeltsin's popularity had bottomed out. By late 1999, half of the population wanted him put on trial. What to do? Several of the leading oligarchs, schmoozing at the World Economic Forum in Davos in January 1996, had decided on a bailout. In return for bankrolling Yeltsin's reelection, an uphill struggle since his approval rating in 1995 languished at 5.6 per cent, they would be given another shot at Russia's state-owned industries. Thus emerged the "Davos Pact" and the win-win–lose-lose situation that followed: Yeltsin won, the oligarchs won, and the Russians in general and any prospect of democracy in Russia was lost.[26] The communists under Gennady Zyuganov also lost. The British journalist Angus Roxburgh: "[t]here is little doubt that the communist leader Gennady Zyuganov could have been elected president … if [the election] had been fair. Instead, the country's new oligarchs – billionaire businessmen who feared losing their new-found wealth if the communists came back – banded together to ensure a miracle."[27]

Many of the oligarchs had had close connections with the *nomenklatura*. In remarkable order they transformed themselves into a new class and joined the foreign legion of asset-stripping plutocrats from elsewhere in the emerging world. Like their homologues, not only in Mexico and Indonesia but also in the West, the Russian oligarchs made their fortunes by manipulating the laws in order to plunder the national economy. A large part of their loot they secreted in offshore accounts in small, British protected, Caribbean islands. They spent it conspicuously in the world's glamorous cities and sunny places, in particular, unsunny London, their Sodom of choice on account of its bright lights, Britain's lax tax laws, and supple justice system. Spain may have had the climate, but London had the addresses, the shopping, and the lawyers. It was here, among the "new class" of rentiers and kleptocrats from the Gulf, China, and even Africa that they squandered their loot, driving up the price of property in the richer parts of the British metropolis as well as the choicest parts of the Mediterranean (Provence, Sardinia, Costa del Sol, Corfu). In a common view, soon after he acquired power Vladimir Putin acquired wealth and properties abroad too. But either he feared his security abroad or he was a born homebody; his wealth was in the billions but his main residence was in Russia. He built a Downton Abbey lookalike for himself at Gelenzhik in Crimea, on the Black Sea, which cost Russia at least $1 billion.[28]

Privatization, especially of strategic industries like oil, was unpopular among the Russians themselves. This was not without justification, as the social cost to Russia was immense. Angus Roxburgh, in his discussion of Russia two decades later, noted, "Within a few years millions of Russians were reduced to extreme poverty, while a handful of go-getters and former communist officials turned themselves into billionaire oligarchs, snapping up the country's resources for a fraction of their value." Thus emerged the rationalization of Anatoly Chubais: "They steal and steal and steal. They are stealing absolutely everything and it is impossible to stop them. But let them steal and take their property. They will become owners and decent administrators of this property."[29]

Even given the assaults on them and their fortunes that began with the Putin era, that is, from about 2000, the number of Russian billionaires climbed from zero to 87 by 2012. As Ostrovsky explains, "The economic foundation of the Soviet system was destroyed not by an external enemy or by dissidents but by the proprietor's instinct of members of the *nomenklatura* who gladly exchanged their petty privileges for something far bigger – a piece of the pie. It was the *nomenklatura* who undermined the core principle of socialism." Quoting Yegor Gaidar, he goes on: "'The *nomenklatura* moved forward, testing its way through, step by step – not according to some thought-through plan but by submitting to its deep instinct. It followed the scent of property as a predator follows its prey.' Everything was done by trial and error. The benefits of the trials went into the pockets of the bureaucracy. The costs of the errors stayed with the state."[30]

Among the billionaires several stood out. Roman Abramovich, who owned the oil company Sibneft and bought London's Chelsea football club (thereafter nicknamed "Chelski"), was one of them. He sold Sibneft to Gazprom, the world's biggest gas company, for $13 billion. In the autumn of 1996 Boris Berezovsky, Putin's benefactor as we shall see, boasted that he and six of his cronies controlled 50 per cent of the Russian economy. In 2001 he fled to London where he spent his time tending his investments and calling for the overthrow of Vladimir Putin. "This regime will never permit a fair election to be held, so there is only one solution: taking power by force. It's important for people in Russia to understand that the time for empty talk has passed, and what we need now is action," he proclaimed. He was found in early April 2013, hanged in his bathroom. Foul play was hinted.[31]

## PUTIN RISING

As the new millennium approached, after a crisis that hit bottom around 1998, the Russian GDP, buoyed up by oil prices, grew at an impressive 7 per cent per year. In the 2000 election, just as the economy was beginning its rapid recovery, Vladimir Putin ran for president. The emergent middle class viewed him as a Russian Pinochet, the Chilean dictator who, in a military coup backed by the CIA, overthrew the reformist government of Salvador Allende on 11 September 1973.[32] He got nearly 53 per cent of the vote. When he ran for reelection in 2004, with world oil prices lubricating his popularity, he got 71 per cent. At the head of Putin's election team had been the oligarch Boris Berezovsky, owner of, among other assets, Russia's main, former state, television station that had been privatized. To support Putin, Berezovsky and his allies formed a new political party, "United Russia." "It had no roots, no philosophy, practically no policy other than its support for Putin," writes Angus Roxburgh.

"For most Russians, the decade of the 2000s was the best they had ever known, if only because it was such a welcome contrast to the 1990s, which had been one of the worst." Still, the American media on the whole had become disenchanted with the Putin regime. In Europe there seemed to be more tolerance or at least illusions. Of course there were profits to be made – hedge funds, banks, and cowboy entrepreneurs, alongside the more staid Dresdner Bank and Siemens AG, made good money. "In the end, they'll all become like us," claimed one senior German official of the Russians, echoing Anatoly Chubais.[33]

Putin was inaugurated as president on 7 May 2000. Under him, the private sector increased from 45 to 60 per cent of the economy. "We are not building state capitalism," he affirmed.[34] After paying his debts to Yeltsin and laying down the rules to the oligarchs, Putin moved to ensure that his rivals in politics and the media were neutralized. A handful of these seem to have been simply murdered. In 2003 he moved to take over the giant oil company, Yukos, of which Mikhail Khodorkovsky was the majority shareholder.

Khodorkovsky had got control of Yukos after the crash of the economies of East Asia and Russia in 1998, just as Vladimir Putin was appointed as prime minister. Oil prices had been low for more than a decade. In early 1999 they began to rise. Khodorkovsky bought Yukos in late 1995 for $309 million. Within a few months Yukos was worth $8 billion and Khodorkovsky became quite suddenly one of the richest men in the world. One of his partners was Vladimir Guzinsky who was also one of the stars of the Russian oligarchy, at least until he fled to Spain in 2000. Both backed Putin, at least for a while, and were considered the "winners of the 1990s."[35] His success gave Khodorkovsky a false sense of invulnerability and tempted him to challenge Vladimir Putin imprudently from within Russia. In October 2003 he was arrested for fraud and tax evasion and then slapped behind bars. He was to spend a decade in prison. His money, however, had found a safe haven in Gibraltar.

The Soviet oil industry had been privatized between 1993 and the beginning of the next century. Now it was deprivatized and renationalized by Putin. The lesson: "The Yukos affair saw the destruction of the nascent bourgeoisie's ability to pursue independent politics, and instead they became a subaltern class. Big business was subordinated politically to the state through ... deprivatisation."[36] The magnates who ran the big state corporations survived but on leashes held by

Putin who became, simultaneously, the facilitator and guardian angel of the new class. Ben Judah:

> Putin imposed a consensus on the oligarchs between when he turned on Berezovsky and destroyed Khodorkovsky. He … made himself indispensable to them. Putin became the arbiter, the deal-maker and the fixer. If you were on his right side, he was also the facilitator. This meant that these men actually came to want him. Most of them at first came to enjoy this stability. Despite making millions and billions the oligarchs had felt hunted throughout the 1990s. One whisper in Yeltsin's ear, or one sharp power play could cancel out fortunes. There was something comforting to know that [Putin] was always there. Some came to think, even in the 1990s, that they had always needed him. Knowing who was all-powerful, actually made them feel safe.[37]

When he was released from prison in 2013, Khodorkovsky fled to Switzerland. Breaking his promise to Putin to stay out of politics, in September he launched an online movement called "Open Russia." He was immediately joined by other exiled oligarchs. Their influence was minimal.

The renationalization of Yukos, known as the Yukos Affair, signalled Putin's triumph. Yukos was reorganized as the state-owned "Rosneft," which dominated petroleum exports to Europe. "[T]he Yukos Affair marked the Kremlin's growing commitment to the idea of a state-owned national oil champion."[38] It also indicated that the justice system was to be obedient to the state. It reminded many of the richest of the oligarchs that it was safer to remain abroad with their children and their money, many taking up British or even Israeli citizenship.

The reform of the Soviet economy didn't have to be like this, Stephen Cohen and Marshall Goldman had said, referring to the 1990s. Gustafson made a similar observation for the next decade: "Many observers, particularly Westerners, look back on the first half of the 2000s as a historic missed opportunity, Russia's road not taken, a battle for the country's soul in which the forces of change were defeated by the forces of reaction." No one of course predicted the escalator on which oil prices rode in the decade from 1999 to 2008, the crash of 2008, and the effect this would have on the Russian economy.[39]

By 2007, Putin's popularity rating was the highest in the world. Stephen Cohen:

> [In 2008], on the eve of the 2008 international financial crisis, Russia seemed to have recovered. Its economy had grown annually by 6 to 8 percent, doubling the GDP, and its gold and foreign-currency reserves were nearly $600 billion, the world's third largest ... Some of the new wealth had spread to the provinces and to the middle and lower classes, whose incomes were rising. But those advances ... were largely caused by unusually high prices for the country's oil and stood out mainly in comparison with the wasteland of 1998 ... More fundamental realities indicated that Russia was still in an unprecedented condition of peacetime demodernization and depopulation. Investment in basic infrastructures remained barely a third of the 1990 level. The government claimed that less than 20 per cent of its citizens lived in poverty, but the actual figure was probably closer to 50 percent and included 60 to 75 percent of families with two or more children, pensioners, and rural dwellers, as well a large segments of the educated and professional classes, among them teachers, doctors, and military officers. The gap between rich and poor ... had become "explosive."[40]

Putin, in power, had initially constituted a regime formed of the *siloviki*, a penumbra of former colleagues, lawyers, and security officials, the many of whom came from his home town, St Petersburg (thus called the "*Pitertsy*"). The system over which they presided has been called, with singular irony, a "managed democracy"; its economic policy, according to Richard Sakwa, has been characterized as "authoritarian modernization." Managed democracy was a mutant form of the German *ordoliberalism*.[41] Those oligarchs on the losing side scattered with their booty, while the *siloviki* wrapped their arms around the Russian state; the share of state-controlled production in the oil industry rose from 24 per cent in 2003 to 37 per cent in 2007.[42] The Yukos Affair of 2003 was a turning point.[43] "Capitalism with Stalin's face," commented the *Nezavisimaya gazeta* on the regime of Putin.[44]

In 2008, Putin stepped aside for Dmitri Medvedev. Hope rose among Russia's reformers. Putin stayed on as prime minister. "Modernization," an idea whose time had long since gone, was his slogan. In fact, Medvedev turned out to be a puppet with little more than a ceremonial role. He extended the presidential term from four to six years. By 2009, the western press had stopped referring to Russian as any kind of democracy. "Transparency International ranked Russia as more corrupt than 64 per cent of the world's countries ... In its 2010 report, the organization showed Russia as more corrupt than 86 per cent of the world."[45] In the Moscow city legislative elections of 11 October 2009, Vladimir Milov, a former government deputy minister and opposition candidate, ran as an independent. The electoral commission denied his registration. The leader of the Yavloko opposition party, Sergei Mitrokhin, was allowed to vote but when the votes were counted, Putin's party, United Russia, received 904 out of 1020 votes. Mitrokhin got none. Either the count was fraudulent or Mitrokhin voted for his rivals. In fact Russian elections have been called "election-like events" for the fact that they are elections in form only. In fact they were merely means to legitimize the ruling group's hold on power and their consolidation of authoritarianism.[46]

At the end of Medvedev's term as, "acting president," in March 2012, to the further dismay of liberals both within and outside the country, Putin became president again. After the interim period of Medvedev's presidency the political situation in Russia had become more feverish. The protest movement of the winter of 2011–12 demonstrated that discontent was vast and in the elections of December 2011, United Russia lost heavily.[47] In the presidential elections of March 2012, the screws were tightened, and protest against the regime was met with heavy repression. Critical intellectuals were arrested and even driven out of the country, and even members of the female punk group Pussy Riot were arrested and charged with "hooliganism." Religion, referred to as "neo-pietism," had rushed in as communism trickled out. Putin sometimes took the Orthodox patriarch, bearded and all in black like a jihadi, with him on trips abroad. By the autumn of 2013 the protest movement that had brought tens of thousands of people into the streets of Moscow and other cities had been suppressed.[48] Meanwhile many of the oligarchs had slipped out of harm's way.

Back in Russia, the prosecutor's office and the tax police launched attacks on the last remaining independent television station. Its owner Vladimir Gusinsky was arrested and upon release fled to Israel. Lebedev kept his hand in as coowner of *Novaya Gazeta*, which campaigned against corruption and authoritarian rule. Four of this newspapers' journalists had been assassinated. Of them, none was more heroic than Anna Politkovskaya who was gunned down for reporting the slaughter in Chechnya and the role of the *mafiya* in Russian politics. While a majority of Western writers have laid the blame for this on Putin, Richard Sakwa is more ambiguous, suggesting that the murderers were rogue members of one of the several factions that manoeuvered for power within the state administration.

## FRONTIERS: CHECHNYA AND UKRAINE

Chechnya is the small state of the Chechens, an autonomous, non-Russian people of the Caucasus who were conquered by the Russian czars in the nineteenth century. Their attempts to gain a degree of independence after the collapse of the Soviet Union have been thwarted by two major Russian invasions, the first in 1994–96 and the second in 1999–2000. There is general agreement that these wars, which have led to the deaths of as many as 160,000, were used by Putin to consolidate his power.[49]

There is a suggestive parallel between the Russian attack on Chechnya in September 1999 and the Soviet invasion of Hungary in October 1956. Both came at virtually the same moment as Western assaults on the European periphery: in 1956 as France, Britain, and Israel attacked Egypt, Soviet troops marched into Hungary; in 1999, NATO (that is, essentially, the US) launched its air assault on the Bosnian Serbs. "The Balkan interventions (Bosnia in 1995, Kosovo in 1999)" writes Layne, quoting Walter LaFeber, "aimed to 'strengthen Washington's control of NATO, the major institution for maintaining US influence in European affairs' and to 'project American power into the East Mediterranean region where it could link up with a growing U.S. military presence in the Middle East.'"[50] Perhaps it is too obvious to stress that the Chechens are Muslim. In fact Muslims form between 6 and 14 per cent of the population of Russia. At any rate, there the similarity ends; the Soviets did not pulverize Budapest in retaliation for revolt. The Russians wiped the capital of Chechnya, Grozny, off the map; as the Nazis had done to Moscow and Warsaw, and the Allies had Dresden. And whereas President Eisenhower intervened to force the British, French, and Israelis to back off from Egypt, President Clinton congratulated Putin on his atrocious destruction of the Chechen capital. The Russians claimed to the satisfaction of Brussels and Washington that the Chechens were terrorists. Clinton, who had unusually good relations with Putin, referred to him as the "liberator of Grozny." The German chancellor, Schroder, referred to him as a "flawless democrat."[51] Still, Russian-American amity was likely to go only so far; in March 2004 NATO expanded to encompass the Baltic states on Russia's doorstep. Reciprocally, ten years later Crimea and the eastern Ukraine were invaded by Russia. In the devastated Chechnya, a Russian puppet was installed.

The Ukraine was a second frontier of Russian expansionism. After Russia itself, Ukraine had been the most important part of the USSR. Kiev, the capital of Ukraine, was, even before Moscow, at the heart of historic Russia. From the late eighteenth to the early twentieth centuries Ukraine had been divided between the Russian and Hapsburg Empires, with Russia ruling the lion's share of the country. With the collapse of the Russian empire during World War One, the independence of Ukraine seemed likely. But, thanks to the diligent work of the Ukrainian communists, independence never happened, and in 1922 Ukraine became part of the USSR. Ukrainian "national communism" was permitted until 1930, but after that purges of mounting devastation ravaged the Ukrainian rural population, the middle class, and even the communist leadership, and all hopes for even limited autonomy were smashed.[52]

But Ukrainian nationalism was a sturdy and persistent plant, hardy and with deep roots. With the breakup of the Soviet Union in 1991, the movement for Ukrainian independence again sprouted. It was accomplished in December 1991 under the chairman of the parliament, Leonid Kravchuk (in power 1991–94), and, joining Belarus and Russia itself, came to form the Commonwealth of Independent States (CIS). In the 1994 Budapest Memorandum, signed by Russia, the UK, and the US, the Ukrainian state and territorial sovereignty were guaranteed in exchange for the removal of nuclear weapons from Ukrainian territory and the guarantee of accessibility for the Russian fleet to the Black Sea port of Sevastopol. As in Russia, the shock of capitalism was life-threatening. Ukraine was devastated by economic crises for the whole of the 1990s. Corruption triumphed.

With the greatest uncertainty, Ukraine lurched into the future. In 1996 a new constitution was adopted under the second president, the corrupt and thuggish Leonid Kuchma (1994–2005). Kuchma was replaced by Viktor Yushchenko (2005–10) who was elected by fraudulent means. Yushchenko was forced by massive demonstrations to yield power to a candidate of the West-backed Orange Revolution, Victor Yanukovych (2010–14). Yanukovych, who was advised by the

American diplomat Paul Manafort, was also driven from power, fleeing to Moscow with bags of money – an implausible $32 billion was mentioned, according to Andrew Wilson – as well as gold and other forms of moveable loot. His party evaporated.[53] Those who replaced him were determined to launch the Ukraine back into the arms of the West while Moscow searched or a way to maintain influence, if not actually dominate or dismember, its neighbour.

After Russian commandos seized the government in the Ukrainian province of Crimea on 27–28 February (2014), the peninsula, which had been attached to the Ukraine only since 1954, was formally re-annexed to the Russian Federation. This was not Afghanistan, a far away place about which most Russians knew nothing and cared less. Thus Putin proclaimed, "In people's hearts and minds, Crimea has always been an inseparable part of Russia." If Putin's claims were hot air, as some Western commentators claimed, so was chatter about "Russian imperialism." At any rate, with the annexation of Crimea, Putin's popularity skyrocketed. Hill and Gaddy of the Brookings Institute have suggested that the annexation was "the greatest blow to European security since the end of the Cold War," a predictable if hyperbolic suggestion.[54]

But Russian expansion did not stop there. After the seizure of Crimea there was a move to annex the Donbas, a degraded and polluted industrial region in eastern Ukraine. Russian infiltration had continued for months from April over the summer of 2014 and into 2015. The Donbas had a mixed population of Ukrainians, Russians, métis, and others. Ethnic Russians comprised 38.5 per cent (2001). Some 72 per cent of the population were Russian speakers.[55] It was infested with criminal gangs, some of them close to the Yanukovych family. By 2015 thousands had been killed in the anarchy that overtook the region. Thousands of Ukrainians were forced to emigrate from Donbas, not wanting to remain under Russian/Yanukovych misrule. There was a small separatist group in the Donbas who wanted the region to join Russia, as did Putin. His project appropriated the name *Novorossiya*. The idea enjoyed only a tepid popularity. Otherwise, people wanted peace under whatever rule.[56]

After an innocent overflying Malaysia Airlines passenger jet was shot down in July 2014 (using a missile supplied by the Russians to mercenaries), Putin was forced on the defensive. In Europe, there was more posturing and dithering than firm resolution. Even limited sanctions were opposed by Western banking and business interests who had previously touted for the money appropriated by Russian and Ukrainian oligarchs.[57] George Soros, the anti-Russian sugar daddy, railed against NATO inaction and the threat to Ukrainian independence. The *Moscow Times*, the Russian capital's English-language newspaper, declared "Russia Unfazed." A ceasefire was agreed upon between Kiev and the pro-Russian forces in September. By this time it was unclear which side the majority of the people in the Donbas region actually supported. There was speculation that an "Ulster-like" situation might last for years.[58]

With his Ukrainian policy triumphant, Putin's popularity continued to soar. From a low point of 44 per cent approval in 2013 his ratings climbed back over 80 per cent. He reached 86 per cent in May (2015). *Krym nash* (Crimea is ours) certain non-Russian Tajiks were quoted as exclaiming.[59] "What did Putin Want?" was a question that many in the West asked. One answer seemed to be the destabilization and even collapse of Ukraine and its reintegration into Russia as a buffer state.

And what did the Europeans want? To the extent that Western government actually cared, their politicians and ministries wanted an independent and stable Ukraine, more or less as the east of the West, and a Russian bear caged within its immediate post-Soviet frontiers. What Russia did in Sakhalin or Chechnya or even in Moscow seems not to have mattered much. Oligarchs, mafias, mercenaries, and models were, on the whole, okay.

And the Americans? Well, although elements in the media and think tanks may have hoped for a rerun of the Cold War, they had other problems – China, the Middle East, Mexico, Donald Trump. At any rate, rather than any serious sabre rattling, the Europeans and their American and Canadian allies satisfied themselves with limited sanctions.[60] The rest of the world – Asia, Africa, and Latin America – watched patiently but remained uncommitted. Since the price for Russian oil had fallen from around $100 to half of that, the Russian economy was suddenly plunged into crisis. The sanctions imposed by Washington and its allies, therefore, should have worked. Even though Russia had impressive currency reserves, it needed access to Western capital markets. But Russia had other friends, like China and Iran, so sanctions could not work the way they had in Saddam's Iraq.

Back in the Ukraine, according to Anatol Lieven, "[E]vents in the east and in Odessa make clear that a Ukrainian state that defines itself purely in pro-Western and anti-Russian terms is ... out of the question, because a great many Ukrainians will not tolerate this."[61] Andrew Wilson has written, "The Ukraine crisis in 2014 might bring an immediate end to the post-Cold War order. Or, like the original Crimean War in the 1850s, it might mark the beginning of a transition to something else." "I think the Cold War never finished in our region," Mamuka Kudava, a former Georgian ambassador to France, has commented. "Putin wants to make sure that no country in the region, like Ukraine, Georgia or Moldova, will ever be able to join any Western institutions like the EU or NATO."[62]

# 4

# East Asian Geese

The obliteration of Hiroshima and Nagasaki by atomic bombs in August 1945 flashed the dawning of a new age in Asia, an age more radically different than anything experienced either in Europe or the Americas. In the next chapter I will dealt with China, the Asian new age Goliath. In this chapter I will deal with Japan and South Korea – both of which were shattered by war only to become leaders of what the World Bank called, in its 1993 report, the "East Asian Miracle." With Japan as the leading economy and trailed by others, the pattern has been likened to that of a flyover of geese.

In a nutshell, in the decades between the early 1950s and the mid-1980s the economies of both major and minor East and Southeast Asian states[1] rose from desolation and subordination to triumph at a global level. So surprising was their resurrection that writers imagined that in an increasingly globalized world even the advanced countries of the West might be overtaken. The term "convergence" thus came into circulation. What the globalizers seldom foresaw was that the flood of goods from Asia, initially produced by cheap labour but later by increasingly sophisticated state-of-the-art technologies and digitization, would lead to the eastward flow of wealth and with wealth political and military puissance.

By the second decade of the twenty-first century the Asian developmental states, also known as newly industrialized countries (NICs), together with China, had come to account for about half the world's total manufacturing output. By 2030, it has been predicted, reversal and geopolitical reconfiguration would be a *fait accompli*. The flow of history thus would have been reversed with the East triumphant and the West descendant. Nothing would be left of the American Century and the American World Order but memories and recriminations.[2]

Or, perhaps, not. In the late 1980s the ascendancy of Japan "in America's place," was confidently predicted. In 1979 the Harvard historian, Ezra Vogel, later to write glowingly about Deng Xiaoping, published his *Japan as Number One: Lessons for America*. Alas, Japan never became Number One; declination rather than ascension seemed to be its fate from as early as the year after Vogel's book was published. By 2014, OECD projections referred to Japan's fiscal health as "the worst among major industrial economies" and predicted Japan's growth rate for 2014 at 1.2 per cent.[3] Would China's decline follow? Its GDP growth rate too declined from more than 12 per cent a year in the 1990s to less than 7 per cent by 2015. But no, again, for as Wang Hui argues, although "China's financial institutions have encountered grave difficulties ... the basic mode of development will not change. In short, China will continue to rise within the world capitalist system."[4] We will see.

## THE JAPANESE PHOENIX

Consciousness of the astonishing rise of Japanese capitalism and imperialism has been with the West since the second half of the nineteenth century. In the summary of John Dower: "Japan's emergence as a modern nation was stunning to behold; swifter, more audacious, more successful, and ultimately more crazed, murderous and self-destructive than anyone had imagined possible."[5] "Crazed," "murderous," "self-destructive," and these words from a sympathizer. Of course, Japan, like America, has always had its detractors, particularly those who have sought to minimize its achievements, point to its weaknesses, or even predict its imminent collapse. Here are the sharp, disparaging, words of Hilda Utley on the cusp of World War Two: "Japan is putting up a big bluff to the world ... Here is a country which claims to be the Britain of the East ... A country ... which believes it can take Britain's former place as the workshop of the world – or at least of Asia and Africa."[6] By 1936 when Utley's book was published, Japan had become Asia's most successful imperial power, having defeated the Russians in a great naval battle in the war of 1904–05, driven the British out of the region's rich markets, colonized Taiwan and Korea, and invaded China. Manchuria, the rich hinterland of both Korea and China, had become a Japanese protectorate with its own Japanese-commanded colonial army. With the preemptive, and to the Americans, "infamous," attack on Pearl Harbor in December 1941, Japan, which had already seen off the Russians and the British, replaced America as the greatest power in the East. The British colony of Hong Kong fell to the Japanese on 25 December 1941 and the garrison at Singapore crumpled and collapsed ignominiously on 15 February 1942. The Dutch threw up their hands in the East Indies in March 1942 and Americans surrendered the Philippines in May. The Asian age of capitalist transformation had begun with multiple bangs.

Japan's triumphant moment turned out to be premature. Overstretched, outgunned, and under-resourced, Japan succumbed to American naval and air power within a remarkably short span of time. At its peak in mid-1942, by August 1945 when the emperor surrendered, his empire had been shattered and home cities atomized. In common with her wartime ally Germany, Japan had been overrun by the army that had defeated her. The *shogun*, an upstart who had ruled Japan in the stead of the emperor up to the mid-nineteenth century, took the form of the American general, Douglas MacArthur (1880–1964), an "American Caesar."[7]

General MacArthur compared the Japanese to American twelve-year-olds. He stripped Japan of its military apparatus and purged the country of its militarists, hanging a few in the full glare of publicity for effect. The greatest of the war criminals, Emperor Hirohito (1901–1989), he preserved, on the argument that without him the Japanese would be difficult to manage. (This was at best a doubtful proposition; the Germans had, after all, adapted to living without their Führer almost overnight, while the Italians had actually shot and then strung up their own dictator without the help of anyone.)

General MacArthur, almost immediately upon his arrival promulgated "five great reforms" involving (1) "emancipation of the women of Japan through their enfranchisement"; (2) "encouragement of the unionization of labor"; (3) liberalization of the education system; (4) creation of a "system of justice designed to afford the people protection against despotic, arbitrary and unjust methods"; and (5) "democratization of Japanese economic institutions to ensure wide distribution of income and ownership." In the first postwar election in April 1946, thirty-nine women were elected to the lower house of the *Diet*, the Japanese parliament.

Japan's relationship with the United States was clearly established and would not change over the next half century; the principle of incorporation and subordination established during the occupation meant that Japan would remain a unique kind of valet state, ostensibly independent but unwaveringly faithful. Even as the credibility of US global hegemony came under pressure, Japan, dominated by the Liberal Democratic Party, remained in an obedient trance.

From before the war the Japanese economy had been dominated by a group of huge, vertically integrated monopolistic firms, the *zaibatsu.* These firms that were often managed by family or kinship groups had merged with other groups to form huge cartels. They had backed and profited from imperial expansion and had been especially active in Korea where they initiated that country's remarkable double-digit growth in the 1930s. By 1945 the ten largest *zaibatsu* controlled some 35 per cent of Japanese capital. Seen as essential to Japan's imperial policies, they were abolished by the American occupiers. However, they soon reformed, attired in the sheep's clothing of the banks that they controlled. These new conglomerates – banks and industrial firms – were now known as the *keiretsu*.

Yet beginning in the 1950s, and in large part because of the war in Korea for which Japan served as a forward base, everything turned around again. The war served as Japan's Marshall Plan. The United States spent close to $3 billion in Japan for war and war-related supplies between June 1950 and 1954: "a gift of the gods," according to one Japanese writer. Fearing depression in Japan with the cessation of hostilities, the Americans strategized the reestablishment of a neocolonial sphere with Japan as the metropolis and Korea, Taiwan, and Southeast Asia as dependent peripheries. There was little prospect of Japan exporting to the US, it was assumed, as "the Japanese don't make the things we [the United States] like." Communist China was to be left out of the loop.[8]

A decade later, Japan, like Germany, had become an economy on a tear. In fact on no economy was the term "miracle" ever lavished as relentlessly as on Japan over the decades to the late 1980s. We may ask why such enthusiasm for the success of what, quite recently, had been America's sworn enemy. John Dower has suggested that American modernization theorists in the 1950s were enchanted by Japan because it offered such an convincing example of anticommunist success, especially by comparison to China: a "non-Western capitalist counter-model to China," he has called it. This was one of the sustaining dogmas of the developmentalists in the World Bank and the IMF.

Even from the early 1960s Japan had began to export capital to its neighbours, searching for cheap labour and lower manufacturing costs and a base for declining and technologically obsolescent industries. First came Thailand and Malaysia, and after them other states in the region. It was by this means that Japan became the champion of Asian regional developments and that a high level of regional integration was effected, ultimately leading to all-Asian trade pacts, like the Association of East Asian Nations (ASEAN) formed in 1967 and AFTA (ASEAN Free Trade Area) signed in January 1992.[9] "Nearly half of the total capital outflow from Japan to developing countries by 1970 was in Korea (17.3 per cent), the Philippines (8.7 per cent), Indonesia (7.4 per cent), Taiwan (7.3 per cent), and Thailand (5.5 per cent)."[10] In the same decade came the war in Vietnam (1965–75), guaranteeing that Japan would become "the single largest beneficiary in absolute terms of the Vietnam War."[11]

When the historian Paul Kennedy launched his provocative study of the rise and fall of great powers in 1987[12] – with more than a nudge and wink at American vulnerability – he, or his editors, featured on the dust cover a cartoon which, in the convention of journalism in which states were portrayed as individuals, we see a caricatural Japanese businessman climbing up to the top of the globe and a resigned Uncle Sam sliding down its surface. (A British businessman with a bowler and a Union Flag is seen exiting the picture.) What was obvious from this was not merely that Japan had replaced Britain as the workshop of the world but that, fifty years later, it was going to push America aside – Toyota was going to accelerate past General Motors and Sony was about to outplay General Electric. China? Unsurprisingly, still not in the picture.

Although in 1979 "Japan as Number One" had become a stock phrase, within just three years after the publication of Kennedy's book, the Japanese economy went into free fall, its stock market and speculative land market having crashed. Whereas Japan's growth rate caught up with that of Britain and surpassed France by 1990, in the decades that followed while these two European states continued to plod along, Japan slowly decelerated. "Thus," writes Hamada, "it is no exaggeration to argue that the Japanese economy, *alone among developed economies*, has suffered from a long-lasting 'disease'" (my italics). Unlike the British economy, which stagnated in the 1970s and early 1980s and then expanded again, declined again, and revived again, the Japanese economy has remained consistently moribund for more than two decades. By 2015, demographic decline had replaced economic decline as the guarantee of Japan's slow collapse; not faltering exports but young people not having enough sex was the problem, suggested *The Guardian*.[13]

Japan's explosion as *the* iconic developmental state could not have happened without the patient godfathering of the US. Having uprooted the Japanese empire and incinerated its cities, the Americans then proceeded to rebuild Japan as its East Asian "Fort Apache," the base from which its cavalry could patrol dangerous territory against lurking communists. But to rehabilitate Japan as a sustainable base, Washington had to rebuild Japan's industry. This it did, with consummate effect, in a mere two decades, roughly 1950 to 1970. By the later date, Japan was more extensively and effectively industrialized than almost anywhere in Europe.

There is no argument here for *laissez faire*, the ancestor of neoliberalism, either; Japan attained its postwar development objectives through high levels of statist planning including a carefully monitored industrial policy and a prudent foreign exchange policy. Two ministries in particular guided the development state, MITI, the Ministry of International Trade and Industry, and the MF, the Ministry of Finance. At first rebuilding its heavy industries such as steel, shipbuilding, and petrochemicals, after 1975 Japan shifted its interest away from heavy towards more high-tech industries, leaving key heavy industries, excepting cars, to rival industrializing powers like South Korea. Not all initiatives were, of course, successful. In reaction to the oil shocks of 1973 and 1979, Japan had embarked on a policy of building mammoth oil supertankers and by 1970 had become the world's leading producer, but when the world demand for supertankers fell off, Japanese shipbuilding stagnated. Yet Japanese industry as a whole thrived and its recipe for success can be simply summarized:

> The essential function of government in Japan was to supply incentives to the market to foster long-term growth, principally, though not exclusively through industrial policy. It used quotas and high tariffs to protect sunrise industries in their infancy. The industries chosen for promotion did not conform to a single model of development. They spanned light industries and heavy industries; the selection driven essentially by considerations of economic, rather than political criteria, not least the potential for high value-added

> and spillover effects. Firms were encouraged to adapt foreign technology in order to spur increased production and returns to scale, thereby lowering production costs … The result [of the government's strategy] was a form of Japanese capitalism 'with few national political guarantees for organized labor, little emphasis towards the social welfare state, high degrees of mercantilism, limited penetration by foreign investment, and … exceptionally dependent on access to the US market.[14]

In spite of its dependence on the US market, after the US defeat in Vietnam in the mid-1970s, according to arguments such as those of John Dower and Paul Kennedy, the American development model began to be questioned. Other centers and other models had started to emerge. So while Japan remained bound in its clientage to the US at one level, it began to slip its ties at another. For their part, even before their defeat in Vietnam, the Americans began to review their relations with China, ultimately becoming convinced of the need for a better balance with the East even in spite of the fact that it was Red.[15]

## HEYDAY

Japan's unnerving economic success grew from the 1950s and peaked in the 1980s. And while they were largely distracted by unfolding events in Mikhail Gorbachev's Soviet Union, Westerners woke up to find the Japanese growth rate had exceeded that of the United States and that Japanese buyers were shopping around for major Western works of art and real estate; they shocked Western speculators when they bought up a version of Van Gogh's *Sunflowers* and the RCA Building in New York together with choice bits of California.[16] In Tokyo there was a property boom unprecedented anywhere in the world: it was said that the value of the land that the Imperial Palace stood on was greater than the entire value of real estate in Canada. More ominously, it was in the 1980s that the Japanese had become the principal holders of American government bonds and thus a key supporter of the dollar. No surprise, then, that alarm bells began to ring more insistently on Wall Street and in Washington. Remember, America had not yet got over military defeat in Vietnam, the Soviet empire was still intact, and in the think tanks the comforting term "unipolar" had not yet come into being.

All of the extravagance of the 1980s was possible because of the lending policies of Japanese financial institutions (banks and insurance companies, especially), which in retrospect seem reckless. In the beginning of the 1990s, when Japanese banking authorities reigned in their lending, to universal astonishment, collapse, and even a certain amount of chaos, ensued. The banks were suddenly forced to acknowledge that they held billions in bad debts. The value of real estate plummeted. Beginning in April 1991 inflation-adjusted GDP growth fell to the low level of 0.6 per cent per year. The political fallout was almost immediate; in 1993 the thirty-eight-year reign of the nepotistic and bourgeois Liberal Democratic Party (LDP) was brought to an end by a disenchanted electorate.[17] Two years later came what was unofficially dubbed *saryaku no toshi*, a term the British Queen had only a little earlier translated as *annus horibilus*. In November 1997, almost exactly a decade before the Western financial crisis of 2007–08, the same thing happened in the North Atlantic, several financial institutions disappeared beneath the waves. In 1997–98 Japan even experienced negative growth. Once more, the politicians of the ruling Liberal Democratic Party, ineptly, did too little, too late.

Yet in spite of this, as Gavan McCormack had warned, Japan was nowhere near basket-case status:

> Yet predictions of demise were greatly exaggerated … [for] Japan was fabulously wealthy, its GNP … more than 80 per cent of that of the United States, a nation nearly twice its size in per capita terms. Put another way, Japan's GNP was more than double the combined GNP *of all other* Asian nations, including those of the Indian sub-continent … With fewer than 120 million people, it was on track to become the largest economy in the world, perhaps even before the end of 1995, thus matching, and exceeding the highest ambitions, and the wildest dreams, of not only the preceding fifty years but of the century and a half since Japan began to pursue the path of Westernization and modernization. In 1995, unemployment was statistically insignificant. The biggest banks in the world … were all Japanese, as were the major trading companies and many of the major industrial corporations. Japanese investment funds flowed in waves that fed the growth of the region. It became the unquestioned "goose" behind which formed the ranks of the world's dynamic economies.[18]

Thus a paradox – dogged ambition, willing sacrifice, and heroic growth leading to the intoxication of prosperity, a blissful security, and comforting conformity, followed by crisis, a hangover of stagnation and inertia, debt, despair, recriminations. The hangover of economic stagnation began with the recession of 1990 and has continued to the present, with the economy recovering briefly and then falling back, apparently depleted. Malign nature played its part in the form of a devastating tsunami in March 2011, which struck the coast of the main island of Honshu killing nearly 16,000 people and costing more than $300 billion.

Between 1992 and 1999 average Japanese economic growth had come in at an unimpressive 0.73 per cent. Between 2003 and 2007, it rose to just below 2 per cent. Then came the global meltdown. In 2008, 2009, and 2011 growth was negative. By 2014 the *Japan Times* reported an OECD study that was nothing but more bad news: "Japan's fiscal health is the worst among major industrial economies, with public debt equivalent to more than 200 per cent of GDP. Central government debt topped 1,000 trillion yen last year for the first time ever." Growth in 2015 was 0.5 per cent.

Several problems affecting the Japanese economy have been identified although all of these emit a whiff of wisdom after the event; first of all, the apparent complacency of Japan's self-serving elite is stressed, notably the politicians of the LDP and their cronies in the state and in business. These failed to understand, among other lessons, that sustained development would require considerable investment in research and innovation and especially in tertiary education. Secondly, was Japan's swollen debt. The Japanese, who had always been gracious when requested by Washington to accept import restrictions or to bow down to the devaluation of the dollar in relation to the yen or to subsidize the American invasion of Iraq, owed more per capita than any other people in advanced countries and, as we see above, broke its own record in 2013.[19] Still, it has to be said that they owed most of it to themselves. Thirdly, was the problem of the increasing age of Japan's working population, to which no non-Japanese emigrants could be added. Even more than the most chauvinist of the Europeans, and certainly far more than Canadians or Americans, the Japanese think of themselves as a singular and superior people, possessed of qualities unattainable by other Asians who, in the view of the conservative elite associated with the ruling LDP, were inferior and certainly little worthy of accommodation. Throughout the Cold War they expressed this by simply turning their backs on Asia and in the case of the unforgettable victimization of Koreans and Chinese during World War Two, simply refused to acknowledge their war guilt.[20] As for Japanese relations with America, writers like Gavan McCormack seem embarrassed at the prostrations and policies of prime ministers like Junichiro Koizumi (2001–06) and Shinzo Abe (2006–07, 2012–present) but no more than the metaphysical outpourings of the likes of Prime Minister Mori Yoshiro (2000–01), credited with possessing "the heart of a flea and the brain of a shark," who encouraged such nonsense as the recognition of a Japan that was "a country of the gods centered on the emperor." McCormack:

> The Japan of Koizumi and Abe [cast] aside its inhibitions in the embrace of market fundamentalism and US hegemony just as the credibility of both was sinking to new depths around the world. Downsizing, deregulation and privatizing the state, they would simultaneously focus national coherence around patriotism, duty and a proud Japanese identity, while making every effort to give priority to serving the US.[21]

Abe Shinzo was elected prime minister at the head of the LDP for the second time in December 2012, the seventh occupant of the office in six years. He established himself among the most unshakeable of ultranationalists, unlike anything seen in the West except perhaps in the sunless recesses of the Republican Party. Like many Japanese politicians he followed his grandfather, a wartime cabinet minister of the imperial fascist stripe, and his father, into the *Diet*, being first elected in 2006 but lasting there, after a scandal-marked tenure, only until 2007. He distinguished himself by denying many of the most appalling crimes committed by Japan during World War Two – including the Nanjing massacre and the forcible recruitment and organization of Chinese and Korean women as "comfort women" to serve Japan's soldiers.[22] This refusal of "apology diplomacy" obviously rang the bells of certain chauvinist elements within the Japanese electorate – perhaps somewhat kindred to the neo-Nazis in Western Europe. Additional, if more subtle, chauvinism might be expected. A dismayed Gavan McCormack punned: "Abe Days are Here Again."

Abe days have featured "Abenomics," an attempt to solve Japan's slow growth problem by means of increasing the national debt through spending, especially on highways and railways but also on the Japanese military. A militarized Japan was seen as serving American ends in the region and, it was hoped, might feature as part of a complicated policy of confrontation and retreat with regard to both Koreas and China. When he was prime minister in 2007, Abe pursued the idea of a grand "Arc of Freedom and Prosperity," which sought to ally Japan with its neighbours (South Korea, Australia, Philippines, Indonesia) together with the US and India, to isolate China. When this confrontational policy was met with yawns in both the US and India, and with the Australians alarmed about antagonizing China, he resigned. In 2011, while he was enjoying the role of one of the more right-wing princelings of the LDP, his idea of encirclement and isolation of China was taken up by President Obama: in this scenario Japan was to become the "strategic pivot" of US hegemony in East Asia, "the Great Britain of the Far East." Or was this an American idea that Abe merely parroted? In any case, what was intended in Washington's strategy was less of a Japan as an economic powerhouse than as a faithful beat policeman or an unsinkable aircraft carrier, like Britain had been in Europe during the Cold War. In late 2011 it was disclosed that Washington was moving ahead with this provocative idea; plans included the establishing of port facilities and posting US Marines to sweltering Darwin, Australia. "The American military will be able to store equipment for an eventual conflict on Australian soil, much further from Chinese missiles than bases in Japan and South Korea," reported the *Financial Times*.[23]

In early 2013 Japan's aggressive policy towards the islands known as Diaoyu to the Chinese and Senkaku to the Japanese, raised the alarm in Washington where security guarantees had been made to Tokyo. Abe claimed, regarding the Senkaku islands, that Japan "simply cannot tolerate any challenge now, or in the future." Western media, like the *Financial Times*, relayed the opinion from Washington that the Chinese were training for a "short, sharp war." The Japanese economy remained, meanwhile, "mired in recession."[24]

## "THE KOREANS ARE COMING"[25]

Even more than Japan, Korea had remained sheltered from the assaults of Western capitalism and imperialism for much of the nineteenth century. With some justification Western writers caricatured the country as "the Hermit Kingdom," a title which goes a long way to explaining Korea's striking backwardness even by the standards of other Asian countries. With an almost completely preindustrial economy, and dependent entirely on human and animal transport, Korea even lacked a generalized money economy before the arrival of the Japanese replaced barter with the yen. Then, in the years that followed the Kanghwa Treaty of 1876 by which the Japanese forced the Koreans to open their doors to trade, capitalism began to trickle in. By the end of the nineteenth and into the early twentieth centuries, the Japanese had begun to eye Korea as a conveniently close hinterland for conquest and exploitation. In 1910, five years after defeating the Russian navy in the Sea of Japan, the Japanese invaded Korea outright. The peninsula, which had been a unified state since the seventh century and ruled by the same dynasty since 1392, now became a colony, a source, as usual, of markets, raw materials, and labour but also a corridor for entry into Manchuria and the rich wheatlands and resources of northern China. What distinguished the relationship between Korea and Japan, however, was that the Koreans and the Japanese, in language and culture, enjoyed a closeness that the French hardly shared with the Algerians (another colony just across the sea) much less the British with the Indians. Perhaps the closest colonial analogy would be the English and the Irish although over the centuries the English destroyed or at least subverted much of Irish culture and effectively retarded Irish economic development. While the Japanese, like the English, were chauvinist by most yardsticks, like the English, they did allow the Koreans to integrate at a high level in both the military and the colonial economy.

So the real difference between Japan's colonies, like Taiwan and Korea, and those of the French and British was that the Japanese industrialized them. As one historian points out: "What is striking about the colonial period [1910–45] to the student of Korean socioeconomic history is, first of all, the extent of industrial growth that did take place in spite of Korea's colonial status. Second ... is that colonialism did not preclude considerable numbers of Koreans taking an active part in such industrial growth." The "wafer-thin stratum of Korean capitalists ... was deliberately cultivated to further collaboration."[26]

For Japan, the takeover of Korea was a compelling proposition. Cultural factors aside, Korea had a strong central government, a peasantry disciplined by centuries of servitude, and a reasonably well-educated and competent bureaucracy. Among its resources were water power, iron, and coal in the north and agriculture in the south. In the early years of colonial rule, manufacturing represented less than 7 per cent of Korea's total output. By the end of the 1930s, by which time Korea had been transformed into a logistical base for the invasion of Manchuria, manufacturing had reached nearly 30 per cent. As well, a major shift in agriculture included a deepening commercialization. In 1910–12, when the Japanese took over, the market value of all crops stood at 318 million yen. By 1939–41, it had reached 1,875 million yen. Rice production increased from 67.4 million yen in 1910–12 to 142.8 million yen in 1939–41. It was this rare colonial transformation that marked the beginnings of Korea's industrial revolution.[27]

The cost of economic progress was high. While the Japanese had stimulated higher levels of agrarian production, turning Korea into a breadbasket, and laid the foundations for the modern development of manufacturing, transportation, and commerce, these advances were directed, unsurprisingly, more at annexing the Korean economy to Japan's than at fostering independent growth. Like modernization everywhere else in the world, not excluding the socialist economies, ruthless expropriation and exploitation of the peasantry was the price. Eui-Gak Hwang explains:

> According to statistics compiled in 1930 about 75 per cent of Korean farming families fell into serious debt. More than 70 per cent of those debts were payable to Japanese financial institutions, at interest rates of 15–35 per cent a year. The only way to avoid starvation was to abandon the farm; indeed, many went to Manchuria or Japan, only to find it no easier to settle there ... It is evident that [the] combination of land taxes, high rents, and the extension of Japanese ownership, in addition to curtailing domestic consumption, was the means employed to provide rice for export to Japan.[28]

Apart from migration and starvation, many Koreans who lost their lands became tenants, while others were absorbed by industry, mines, and railway work. In 1919 Korea had practically no working class; by 1941 it had nearly 1.3 million industrial workers. During World War Two, hundreds of thousands of these workers were shipped to Japan to toil, especially in the mines where around a quarter of a million laboured (and died) under the most appalling conditions.

During the war, as in other Japanese colonies, the screws were tightened down in Korea in the interests of the Greater East Asia Co-Prosperity Sphere, Tokyo's faux commonwealth. By 1942 the tax rate was three times higher than in 1936, and the Japanese were conscripting hundreds of thousands of Korean men and women for military, industrial, and other purposes. In an attempt to stifle the inevitable rising tide of nationalism, the Japanese interdicted the use of the Korean language, even compelling the Koreans to change their family names into Japanese. These repressive measures backfired, fanning rather than quenching the nationalist flames.

## LIBERATION AND DIVISION

With the collapse of the Japanese empire in August–September 1945, a power vacuum was created in Korea. Into the country from the north rushed the exiled Korean communists, thousands of whom had fought together with the Red armies in Manchuria and elsewhere in China. An East Asian communist revolution now became likely. On 6 September 1945, four days after the Declaration of Independence had been promulgated in Hanoi, the Korean communists, backed by Soviet forces that had crossed the border on 9 August, announced in Seoul the formation of the Korean Democratic People's Republic (KDPR). In the south the Korean People's Republic (KPR) was formed. Its antecedent was the Committee for the Preparation of Korean Independence (CPKI) many of whose members were also communists. But like the Vietnamese nationalists, they were Koreans first and communists second. The main planks in their program were the extirpation of Japanese influence in Korea, the support for popular mass politics and the social equality that this implied, and the reform of Korea's "feudal" legacy, feudalism being a code for gross inequalities in the allocation of resources, particularly land.[29]

Meanwhile, on the other side of the Pacific Ocean, different plans were being drawn up. At several stages during World War Two there had been loose talk about the liberation of colonial peoples generally. Some six months after the Atlantic Charter was signed in August

1941, President Roosevelt had implied that Korea was one of the countries from which the yoke of tyranny would be lifted. At the Cairo Conference in 1943, the Koreans had been referred to by the Americans as a people enslaved by Japanese imperialism. Then the tune changed, and the argument was made that Korea might be made into a trusteeship administered by the victors of World War Two; this trusteeship might last anywhere from five to twenty-five years. If this seems to have been a reprise of the mandates system that rose from the deathbed of the Ottoman Empire in the Middle East, it is because it was: minus oil, of course, which did make a difference.

When the Japanese surrendered, a revised version of the trusteeship plan was offered by Washington to Moscow; the Americans and the Soviets were to divide the peninsula between them, it was proposed. The 38th parallel was to be the dividing line. North Korea was to fall within the Soviet sphere, and South Korea was to become an American trusteeship. Both the Soviet Union and the United States wanted to deny as much territory as possible to their rivals and to create a glacis to protect their zones of domination. Talk of "security" was useful here. The term "responsibility," applying to the American role in South Korea, was also dusted off.

American troops arrived in South Korea on 8 September, two days after the announcement of the formation of the KDPR. They sustained the United States Army Military Government (USAMG) in the southern half of the country. This was in effect an occupation authority that was based on the implicit assumption that the Koreans in their zone were, like the Japanese, a defeated enemy. The USAMG involved 72,000 men and was originally designed for occupation duties in Japan. Although some of its officials spoke Japanese, almost none spoke Korean. It refused to recognize the Korean Peoples Republic (KPR). Under the USAMG, Syngman Rhee (1875–1965) was installed as de facto head of state. Rhee was supported by the Korean Democratic Party (KDP), the main organ of the Korean right containing, at the visible level, patriots, notables, and intellectuals, and, less visible, large landowners and wealthy capitalists, many of whom had profited by cooperation with the Japanese. Its founder was Kim Song-ju whose family in the period of the Japanese occupation had established the largest Korean-owned textile mill. The goals of the KDP, besides opposing reforms by the KPR, were vague – it could hardly admit to favouring landlordism, private ownership of industry, and the rehabilitation of opportunists and traitors. It stood reality on its head by claiming that the supporters of Korean independence were collaborationists and reactionaries. The party was to weld its fortunes to the interests of the Americans, who would be willing to support it rather than the more liberal and leftist groups.

Syngman Rhee had been a Protestant pastor and a longtime resident and lobbyist in Washington. He had much in common with other exiles over the next half century plus who had spent their lives abroad to return home to run their countries as reliable proconsuls lacking any local bases of power. Reactionary, manipulative, duplicitous, and, necessarily, ardently pro-American, Rhee and his American backers effectively declared war on the Korean left, attacking trade unions while stemming the tide of land reform. Although his victory was not easy, it was complete. By 1949, Rhee's supporters had effective control over the army of the Republic of Korea (ROK), the police, and the judiciary while the jails were full of nationalists and reformers of every stripe; political violence, carried out by the army and right-wing youth squads, had liquidated 100,000 of their opponents by 1950. A new model Asian state had been created with some remarkable similarities to the dictatorships that would come into being in Latin America in the 1970s; in its dependency on the United States, its repressive authoritarianism lasting until 1988, its embracing of the economic policies of import substitution industrialization (ISI) and in the 1970s, in its indebtedness, second only to Brazil. In the 1980s after both Rhee and his successor Park Chung-hee had passed on, Korea's policies, like those of Chile, were voiced by American-trained ventriloquists who directed the neoliberal phase of Korean development.

With the formation of the Republic of Korea in July 1948 the United States withdrew the bulk of its occupation forces. Its advisors were nonetheless active in the counterinsurgency campaign against the people of Cheju island and the mainland opposite, protest being stimulated by huge inequalities between the tiny elite and the masses of the poor. The campaign was marked by "nauseating atrocities ... Americans organized and equipped the southern counterinsurgent forces, gave them their best intelligence materials, planned their actions, and often commanded them directly."[30] Vietnam foreshadowed, then.

In North Korea the Soviets had been the occupation force. Upon receiving the Japanese surrender they had handed government over to Kim Il-sung, a communist guerrilla leader. Surrounding him were other guerrilla veterans of the war against the Japanese. Within a few months of liberation, a number of reforms had been enacted, including land redistribution, industrial nationalization, and formal equality for women. At the political level, a powerful mass party enrolling hundreds of thousands of Koreans and a rudimentary army had emerged. In 1948 the KDPR and the Korean People's Army (KPA) were formed. It was from among the leaders of these former guerrillas that the rulers of the DPRK for the second half of the twentieth century, like Kim Il-sung, were found.

## THE KOREAN WAR, 1950–53

The origins of the Korean War are still debated as if the war was a matter of one country invading another, like Japan's invasion of China or Germany's invasion of France or the Soviet Union. This is mistaken. The Korean War was a civil war; foreign intervention turned it into a theatre war between an alliance of communist Koreans and the People's Republic of China (PRC) on one side and an axis of capitalist states under the leadership of the US on the other. Wang Hui, presumably conforming to Chinese usage, has called it "the War to Resist US Aggression and Aid Korea."[31] It was the first and last major war of the Cold War fought on land by NATO armies under the camouflage of the United Nations. Under American command, these armies included fighting contingents from Australia, Belgium, Canada, Columbia, France, Greece, Luxemburg, Netherlands, New Zealand, the Philippines, Thailand, Turkey, and the United Kingdom, as well as the US and the Republic of Korea. The overall commander of the UN army was the imperious General Douglas MacArthur, seconded from his duties as American supremo in occupied Japan.

From 25 June 1950 the flow of events was as follows: the KPA, equipped with Soviet tanks, crossed the 38th parallel driving the Republic of Korea army southwards in disarray. Some 95 per cent of the national territory of Korea and 98 per cent of the Korean population fell under communist control. This sudden overturn of the status quo provoked an international crisis all the more so since Beijing, less than a year earlier having proclaimed itself a communist People's Republic, was so clearly allied to the Kim regime. The United States called an emergency meeting of the UN. A vote was taken, and it was decided to form a UN army under US command. The UN secretary general, the compliant Norwegian Trygve Lie, lobbied in support of an American resolution denouncing the North Korean attack. The Soviet Union might have defeated the resolution through its veto in the Security Council, but it was boycotting the UN for other reasons.

The US-led army only managed to block the North Korean advance at Pusan on the very southern extreme of Korea. Then, in a brilliant amphibious landing at Inchon on the west coast of the peninsula, near Seoul, the US army drove the KPA reeling back across the 38th parallel and then northwards right up the length of the peninsula to the Yalu River, the frontier of Korea and China. American fighter planes flew beyond the Yalu in pursuit of MiGs flown by Soviet pilots. While the UN armies were poised on the Chinese frontier, thousands of communists and their supporters to the south were slaughtered by the ROK army and police. Cumings refers to this as "The Atrocious Occupation."[32] Then, on 8 October 1950, the Chinese launched a surprise attack on the UN forces hurling them back across the 38th parallel and southwards.

The war now raked up and down the peninsula until an armistice, as opposed to a peace treaty, was agreed upon in July 1953. Korea, north and south, had meanwhile been devastated. Three million North Koreans and a million South Koreans had been killed, and half as many were missing. As well, between 500,000 and a million Chinese soldiers had died. In the process of the American carpet-bombing of the peninsula, more than 300,000 homes had been destroyed. According to the US air force general, Curtis Le May, "We burned down *every* [my italics] ... town in North Korea and South Korea."[33] The infrastructure of the industrialized north no longer existed – dams, factories, bridges, were all rubble. The large town of Sinuiju near the Chinese border, for instance, had been removed from the face of the earth. By 25 November, according to an official dispatch, a large part of the area between the Yalu River and the enemy lines to the south was "more or less burning." Soon the area would be a blackened and barren wilderness.[34] In fact, the scale of urban destruction exceeded that of Germany and Japan in World War Two.

The big winners in this devastating war were the Japanese economy and Syngman Rhee. Japan had become a forward military base and arsenal for operations in Korea, with American military spending and stockpiling meaning orders for machinery, steel, chemical products, and armaments. The surviving farmers of South Korea were inadvertent beneficiaries; during the occupation of the south, the KPA had carried out land reform. This was not undone. This reform had two main effects; first, it redirected capital away from the land towards industry, and second, it uprooted the conservative landlord class and created, over time, greater income equality. On the down side, Rhee's hold on power was consolidated.

## TROOPS, TRUNCHEONS, PROTECTIONISM, LIBERALISM

Rhee's regime thus became a dictatorship oiled by US military and Asian Development Bank aid and, hence, blessed by Washington. Under him developed an exceptional variety of the capitalist firm, the *chaebol*, a vertically integrated and notably sustaining heavy industry. *Chaebols* were modelled on the Japanese *zaibatsu* described above. They had barely existed before the 1950s, but afterwards they emerged under Rhee in their Goliath form, becoming the beneficiaries of the South Korea's import substitution (ISI) policy which was sustained by huge amounts of American and, to a lesser extent, Japanese aid. "No other country in the world received such large sums in per capita terms, with the exception of Israel and South Vietnam," writes Jung-en Woo. In her calculation, South Korea cost the US a billion dollars a year. And despite the views of the critics, aid worked its miracle supporting a Korean annual growth of 4.5 per cent a year between 1953 and 1962. Industry grew at 10.8 per cent a year.[35] This cost, and this success, eventuated not because of the simple miracles of aid and development but because Korea was, before and after the war that began in 1950, a "key containment country."

Yet, corruption became the undoing of Rhee himself. A student uprising forced him to resign in April 1960. He fled to Hawaii. His whole clan was thrown out of power and influence – like the South Vietnamese Diem clan in 1963 and the Marcos family in the Philippines in 1986. After a brief, faltering, attempt on the part of oppositional parties to form a government, in May 1961 a military dictatorship under General Park Chung-hee was installed. Park slipped into civilian clothes and held an election in 1963. His regime lasted until 1979. Dictatorship itself continued in South Korea until 1993, just three years longer than it lasted in Eastern Europe. But Eastern Europe could only gaze with admiration at the success of South Korea's capitalist development.

Park founded the Third Republic, the state that emerged from a war-ravaged ruin to become one of Asia's industrial giants. At first having doubts, the Americans, led by their ambassador in Seoul, soon came to view him ecstatically. (Of course, other dictators, in other countries, so long as they were no threat to American security and leadership were also viewed poured loans and grants into the country. In 1957 it provided Korea with $383 million. This dropped, rose again, and then dropped once more to a 1960s nadir of more than $252 million. Military aid in 1965 was $100 million and economic aid, $200 million. In addition, Korea signed a normalization treaty with Japan in 1965 by which the Japanese paid a total of $800 million, "no small sum for a country whose entire exports in 1964 amounted to $200 million," adds Woo.[36]

Military aid in fact was the payment for Korean bodies to fight in the American war in Vietnam. Initially, Korea sent 47,872 troops to Vietnam and a total of more than 300,000 by the time the war was over. "This was more men per capita than any nation in the world, including the United States ... The total cost to the United States of equipping and paying for these men was 'peanuts compared to what it would be for a comparable number of Americans' but those 'peanuts' went a long way to finance Korea's takeoff, and also to indulge Park Chung-hee into solidifying his dictatorial grip."[37]

"Vietnam marked the coming of age for some of Korea's largest conglomerates," notes Woo. "Vietnam absorbed a stunning 94.29 percent in the total Korean steel export, 51.75 percent of transportation equipments, 40.77 percent in nonelectric machinery and 40.87 percent in "other" chemical exports."[38] Steel production was of unequalled importance to Korea, as it was to other industrializing powers. As Park himself noted: *Ch'ŏl ŭn kunggyŏk*; "steel is national power."[39]

In some respects, in fact, Park's rule seems quite Jacobin; for he not only swept away the entirety of Rhee's corrupt establishment, threatening, dismissing, and even jailing thousands of those accused of incompetence and the "illicit accumulation of wealth" but also built a modern state and economy. To the question "Is democracy an essential aspect of development?" the South Korean answer is bound to be a confident "No." Perhaps a comparison of South Korea and East Germany is fruitful; both were war-ravaged dictatorships, one capitalist, the other communist, and both were half countries. In both, ordinary citizens were victimized by the secret police, repression was widespread, and, in both, quite apart from economic advance, health and education improved. But by 1990 when East Germany ceased to exist, its economy was still efficient only by Soviet Bloc standards while that of South Korea was advanced by Western standards and its society was much more free and prosperous. So three cheers for capitalist military dictatorships, on the Korean (if not the Pakistani) model.

In the 1960s, South Korea's per capita annual GDP matched that of Ghana; both stood at $230. By the early 1990s, South Korea was ten to twelve times more prosperous. Historical differences aside, the analogies with Latin America are also tempting because what stands out is how closely South America fits into the Cold War timetable, with nearly three decades of military dictatorship (1960–87) and then neoliberalism and a profound economic crisis (in 1997)[40] that followed. What is emphatically different is South Korea's singular success, which was in part due to the launching of the Third Republic right in the middle of the golden age of capitalism when international trade seemed to be on the verge of limitless ascent.

Thus stimulated by US military spending but now relatively independent of US economic control, South Korea, in the two decades of the Park dictatorship, enjoyed a period of unprecedented industrialization; so remarkable was it, in fact, that South Korea has since acquired iconic status as an instance of state-led development. Growth was thus a corollary of extensive military intervention: *dirigisme* ruled, backed up by an inflated military and a ubiquitous system of spies.

Vital to this militarized *dirigisme* was Park's nationalization of the banking system. The government, interventionist but hardly leftist, also implemented severe price controls, and it strictly monitored capital flight. Protectionism was everywhere. In the background was a draconian system of punishments for economic transgressors; according to Alice Amsden, "Legislation passed in the 1960s ... stipulated than any illegal overseas transfer of $1 million or more was punishable with a *minimum* sentence of ten years' imprisonment and a maximum sentence of death."[41] The shadow of the noose thus hung over the free movement of capital, although the threat did not apply equally to those at the top of the political pyramid. And a bristling protectionism was everywhere; it became so exalted that in the 1960s the smoking of foreign cigarettes was viewed as unpatriotic.

According to plan, exports took off. The pivotal years were 1964–65. In 1963 exports registered $86.8 million a year; by 1971 they had reached over a billion. Yet, far from the case of South Korea being an example of enlightened military rule, it was the civilian directors of the country's great, integrated, state-backed firms (including Hyundai, Daewoo, and Samsung), the *chaebols*, who remained firmly in the driver's seat – as they did as late as the time of president Lee Myung-bak (2008–13). If we wanted a name for South Korea under Park, we might, breathlessly, call it a "national capitalist developmental dictatorship"; "Korea Incorporated," in short. Yet the South Korean developmental dictatorship was not original as it had significant elements in common with late-nineteenth century Germany and Japan.

The state-*chaebol* alliance was critical to rapid growth, and the *chaebols* were to become some of the world's leading industrial conglomerates. This alliance was based on state-provided loans at low interest rates and the repression and extraordinary levels of exploitation of labour – indeed like China in the 1980s and '90s. Repressive labour policies kept workers' wages much lower than those of their counterparts in other countries and prohibited labour unions. By 1984 sales by the top ten *chaebols* accounted for 67 per cent of the Korean GDP. The growth rate in the period of the dictatorship stood at more than 12 per cent.

Why, asks Vivek Chibber, did the underdeveloped Korean bourgeoisie go along with the dictatorship? The reason seems plain; only the state had the economic means to subsidize the project of export-led industrialization. The native industrialists, often linked to Japanese firms, leaned on the state to provide the loans necessary to finance the production and export, and even the research, to make the break into the US market. Park got the money by nationalizing the banks. With the assistance of the developmental state "[t]he *chaebol* penetrated the US market at an extraordinary rate, initially filling the niches hitherto occupied by the Japanese, and then expanding into new, high-tech lines." Later, from about 1985, the *chaebols* acquired control over independent sources of finance. The developmental regime was cast aside in favour of neoliberalism under Roh Tae Woo and Kim Young Sam (together 1987–98).[42]

Thus by December 1987 when democratic elections were held for the first time since the Park coup in 1961, the recipe of export-led industrialization (ELI) directed especially at the US market seems to have succeeded in South Korea as in few other places. In common with other Asian economies, it was often claimed, South Korea had achieved the fastest reduction of poverty for the greatest number of people in history. As *The Economist* summarized:

> South Korea's expansion, like that of other Asian tigers, resembled the rapid development of communist states. In the 1950s some Eastern European economies achieved spectacular growth by squeezing more and more savings and labour out of their people. But this kind of authoritarian advance is neither pleasant or sustainable. South Korea's labour policies were especially unpleasant. The country was built by men who worked appalling hours, led by obsessive bosses ... Kim Woo Choong, who found the Daewoo industrial group in 1957, never took a day off until his son was killed in a car crash in 1990. His employees were expected to work 6 days a week, 12 hours a day, until the mid-1980s. Anyone who protested got fired, or jailed. Under Park Chung Hee as well as under South Korea's next soldier president, Chun Doo Hwan, labour disputes were normally resolved by troops, tear gas and truncheons.[43]

Even as late as 1986, South Korean manufacturing employees worked the longest hours in the world with wages that were lower than their counterparts in Brazil, Mexico, Hong Kong, and Singapore. As political commentator Perry Anderson asked, "Is it proper to speak about development if it creates as politically repulsive a society as South Korea?" The answer seems to be a qualified "Yes." In the mid-1990s on a visit to Seoul, Anderson noted, "What a Londoner notices first is the ways in which the city [Seoul] is more advanced than his own."[44]

Following disorders in Pusan and Masan in the summer of 1979, Park was assassinated in public view in October by the maddened head of the Korean CIA, whom he had offended. The murderer was hanged, and the show went on. But inflation had reached its highest point, the deficit had trebled and the GDP growth rate had slowed down to 6.5 per cent – from more than 10 per cent earlier. Riots spread everywhere. It wasn't until 1985, and after three IMF loans, that stabilization returned, and so, too, did remarkable growth. By 1988 it had reached 12 per cent and South Korea had become the envy of East Asia. By the early 1980s the great *chaebols* were up, running, and proliferating, and Korean capitalism no longer required the crutch of state support: "in purely quantitative terms, the average number of subsidiaries under each *chaebol* rose from 4.2 in 1970 to 14 in 1989."[45]

Park's successor, General Chun Doo Hwan, ruled South Korea as president from 1980 to 1987. His repression was even greater than Park's perhaps because under him the Korean economy was forced to open up to American imports and service industries: the protection of petrochemicals, heavy industry, and shipbuilding was removed, and in agriculture, American rice, grains, and even tobacco poured in. This was the Chilean road to neoliberalism, directed by the same team, mainly from Stanford, that had worked in the Southern Cone of Latin America. For the American banks in Seoul financial liberalization was a gold mine; in 1980 several of them recorded profits of as high as 359 per cent. "And profits kept going up."[46] The Russian road to neoliberalism lay just ahead.

Chun Doo Hwan's economic guru was Kim Chae-ik, a Stanford Ph.D. His fellow economic evangelists all had American doctorates. It was these economic reforms and the repression and protest that accompanied them that set the stage for the collapse of the military regime. "No other *economic* issue fueled such intense resentment and anti-Americanism in Korea as trade liberalization. For some, like farmers, it was a matter of livelihood ... but for others, like students, the trade issue was just another humiliating symbol of Korean lackeyism, of a state so ruthless at home but so feckless abroad."[47]

Chun Doo Hwan was succeeded by his hand-picked successor, another general, the dim and supine Roh Tae Woo, who held office until 1993. By this time there had been several quite breathtaking shifts in the geopolitical world – the Soviet Union had disappeared, India had embraced neoliberal reform, Japan was at the beginning of its quarter-century malaise, and China, in the last years of Deng Xiaoping's life, was pursuing its fate as a capitalist Goliath on hormones. Neoliberalism had crashed the party with Latin America being celebrated as its most successful testing ground. Despite the odd gloomy prediction, America was standing tall.

Despite the despotic decade plus of Chun and Roh (1980–93) and the violence, always viewed with toleration by the US whose soldiers were garrisoned in tens of thousands in South Korea, a democracy movement had continued to grow to the point of the June Uprising of 1987. This was South Korea's Tiananmen. It saw the mobilization of hundreds of thousands of students, workers, farmers, and even middle-class professionals who demanded Chun's resignation and the establishment of democracy. One commentator referred to this mobilization as "one of the most extensive, organized and courageous cultures of political protest in the world."[48] It was this movement, in fact, that brought the curtain down on South Korea's Cold War dictatorship and opened another curtain to the democracy that was manifest in the presidential election of December 1987 that Roh Tae-woo, South Korea's first democratically elected president, won. Roh's presidency (1988–93)[49] was the beginning of the end for military rule; he was the last general to occupy the presidential palace. On 30 September 1990, while he was in power, Moscow and Seoul established full diplomatic relations; two years later China and South Korea did the same. This was bad news for Pyongyang, which had played Moscow off against Beijing.

Roh's successor was Kim Young-sam who remained in power until 1998 to be succeeded by Kim Dae-jung (1998–2003). During the civilian presidency of Kim Young-sam, prosecutors brought charges of corruption and bribery against both Chun and Roh. At trial, it was disclosed that Chun had shaken down South Korean firms for $1.2 billion and Roh for $630 million. In 1996 a court found both generals guilty of sedition and sentenced Chun to death. Roh got twenty-two-and-a-half years in prison. Both were subsequently pardoned by Kim Dae-jung.

Left of centre, and a subtle critic of Washington, Kim Dae-jung was an open admirer of the neoliberal British prime minister, Tony Blair (1997–2007) and a leading advocate of the "Third Way," a hypothetical position between capitalism and socialism or, at least, reactionary capitalism and neoliberal socialism. His aim was to balance the demand for increased political and economic justice against the demands of the monopolist *chaebols*. This was made all the more difficult by the 1997–98 East Asian financial crisis, which was caused in large part by the over-borrowing and then bankruptcy of some of the largest *chaebols*. The financial crisis put South Korea in the pocket of the IMF from which it was forced to borrow $57 billion in the form of a rescue package.[50] The IMF, consistent in its support for neoliberalism, demanded not only fiscal deregulation and the removal of restraints on foreign financial services firms but also fiscal austerity. Behind the IMF was the US Treasury. "The US saw this as an opportunity, as they did in many countries, to crack open all these things that for years have bothered them."[51] Yet, despite the door being opened to market forces, the stranglehold of the *chaebols* was hardly reduced.

## SUNSHINE AND SUCCESS

As part of his role as a conciliator, from June 2000 Kim Dae-jung pursued a "sunshine policy" of reconciliation with the DPRK. For this he was awarded a Nobel Peace Prize and a high level of scepticism from the State Department of President George W. Bush, which insisted on seeing North Korea as part of an "axis of evil."

Kim was succeeded by his protégé, Roh Moo-hyun (2003–08), a lawyer who was also part of the 1980s human rights movement. Although Roh's ties were to the democracy movement, his policies led him to advance the neoliberal agenda. By late 2007, the Roh regime, like the military dictatorships that had preceded it, became haunted by the spectre of corruption. Roh, who had become unpopular for his willingness to throw himself at the feet of Washington – not only for the bilateral free-trade agreement that he signed but also for his volunteering troops for the invasion of Iraq – barely survived impeachment proceedings.[52] "A slew of bribery scandals, some of them involving Mr Roh's aides, had underlined the extent to which money still talks in Asia's third largest economy," reported the *Financial Times*. "Corruption remains endemic in Korean society," it added.[53]

In December 2007, Lee Myung-bak, "The Bulldozer," former head of Hyundai Engineering and Construction, a branch of one of the great *chaebols*, won a landslide election as president of South Korea. Amid the by now almost inevitable questions of corruption and protests against Lee's right-wing agenda and within a hundred days of his inauguration in February 2008, the new president's support collapsed. The streets of Seoul echoed to the cries of "*Dokje Tado!*" ("Down with dictatorship"). In June he threw himself on the mercy of the electorate: "I reproach myself for not serving the people properly," he apologized, cancelling his program for privatizing water, gas, and electricity and offering sops to small business and low-income families. He left office with as little popularity as his early role model, George W. Bush, but, also like Bush, having handed the leading capitalist firms (that is, the *chaebols*) even more influence and dividing the country even further (between Christians and Buddhists). Nor did he attempt to deal with questions of nepotism and corruption. Yet, in common with other of the smaller East Asian tigers, he managed to sidestep the 2007–08 economic crisis and kept unemployment (at below 4 per cent), debt, and inequality (according to the Gini coefficient lower than US, China, or Japan) at low levels.

Lee was succeeded in 2013 by Park Guen-hye, the daughter of Park Chung-hee, the military modernizer. She became the first female head of state in Korea's millennium-long history. In 2016 she was accused of corruption and cronyism in which she helped one of her friends fleece South Korean companies for tens of millions of dollars. In December 2016 half a million Koreans took to the streets of Seoul to celebrate her impeachment. Implicated in corruption was Jay V. Lee (Korean: Lee Jae-yong), heir to the founder of the Samsung Group, one of the leading *chaebols* and world leader in smartphones and memory chips. Lee got five years in prison. In July 2017 Samsung announced record earnings.

# 5

# Chinese Transformations

To understand the making of communist China we must go back several steps to the nineteenth century: while the states of the North Atlantic surged ahead becoming ever more industrialized and even more democratic, China, the "Celestial Empire," lapsed into a coma of despotism and backwardness. It hadn't always been this way, as Kenneth Pomerantz explained: "Core regions in China and Japan circa 1750 seemed to resemble the most advanced parts of Western Europe, combining sophisticated agriculture, commerce, and non-mechanized industry in similar, arguably more realized, ways."[1]

But backwardness was an invitation to disaster. At a time of dynastic weakness in China, the warships of Britain, riding a wave of unequalled dominance, arrived on the coast to further the interests of global mercantilism. Seeking to find an export that might be used in lieu of silver for the silk, tea, and porcelain that their consumers craved, British merchants hit upon opium that was grown in Bengal (which the British controlled) and trafficked eastwards by the East India Company, one of the world's first multinationals. When the Chinese officials attempted to block opium imports, the British declared war, battering China's obsolete navy and shattering her coastal defences. The Chinese surrendered and accepted British terms: the pushers had won the First Opium War (1839–42), the first drug war in modern history. China was then at the start of a long century of purgatory, punctuated by catastrophe, humiliation, and the threat of fragmentation. The Treaty of Nanjing ended the First Opium War and opened China to Western commerce; free-trade liberalism vanquished protectionism and autarky. In 1841 Hong Kong had been ceded to the British. Other European states claimed concessions along

China's coast and up her rivers. China, like Russia some 150 years later, went into a nosedive. The period from the Treaty of Nanjing to the establishment of the People's Republic of China in 1949 became known as the "century of national humiliation."

After the British, it was the turn of the Japanese. Like the British, their expanding empire needed raw materials and markets. Heeding the Chinese defeat to Britain in the Opium Wars, Japan had sought to protect itself through rapid industrialization and militarization. In 1894 during the Sino-Japanese war they conquered Taiwan, turning it into a Japanese colony and imposing on the island, in a way common for all empires, Japanese culture and Japanese economic requirements. Then, in 1910, they took over Korea. From Korea, in the autumn of 1931, they marched into China's northern territory, formerly called "Manchuria," and renamed it the Japanese "Manchukuo." Here they set up a puppet emperor. The conquest of Korea and Manchuria had more in common with the German conquest of Eastern Europe than with the British and French conquests of Africa in that it was (almost) a matter of terrestrial rather than maritime expansion and its victims were neighbouring people who shared elements of a common history and culture. At any rate, the Japanese lived up to Western standards of colonialism with their insistence on subordination and resource and labour exploitation: "China must in the first place be so reorganized as to become a producing country of crude materials needed for manufacturing" wrote one imperial advocate. But Japanese imperialism was different from European since the Japanese remained impressed by China's former cultural achievements in spite of their contempt for China's current predicament. Historically, the Japanese recognized, China had been the centre of Asian civilization, but by the 1920s the centre had shifted to Japan. One leading Japanese scholar wrote of his country's mission to spread "Japanese civilization and ways to every corner of the world." As he noted, with macabre satisfaction, "We no longer need to ask when China will collapse. It is already dead, only its corpse is still wiggling."[2]

Between 1932 and 1945 Japan expanded its hold on the East Asian mainland until it grasped large swaths of China, including Manchuria, and footholds in the coastal provinces. As the Japanese absorbed increasing space in northern and coastal China, the headquarters of the rump Chinese state moved to Chongqing in the southern, inland, province of Szechwan. This state was ruled by the Nationalist

Party, the Guomindang, the head of which was Jiang Jieshi (once familiar as Chiang Kai-shek), known by the Italianate title as "generalissimo." Jiang had inherited the mantle of nationalist leadership from Sun Yat-sen, "the Father of the Chinese Nation," whose family had strong connections to the West and who had sought rapprochement with the communists. When Sun died in 1925 he was succeed by Jiang, but by then the country had begun to break up with warlords seizing power in the regions. In the 1920s China had begun to look like continental Europe during the original Thirty Years' War (1618–48): mini-states, warlords, ravaging armies, intransigent ideologies, destruction, trauma, misery.

Conducting a guerrilla struggle, studying the actual situation of the peasants, and carrying out reform in the lands under its control was the Communist Party under Mao Zedong. Mao was one of the earliest members of the Chinese Communist Party (CCP) and justifiably recognized as a talented leader and strategist. The CCP had been established in Shanghai in July 1921. Even before it was founded, two Chinese students who had gone to study in France, Zhou Enlai and Deng Xiaoping, had joined the French Communist Party alongside the Vietnamese revolutionary, Ho Chi Minh. We can see here in the aftermath of the Bolshevik Revolution of 1917 the appeal communism and the Soviet Union had, especially for intellectuals, in the colonial East. It is no surprise that the Soviet model of dictatorship, known as "democratic centralism," came to impress the leaders of the Asian communist parties fighting against colonial oppression.

After forming an alliance with the Guomindang, which Jiang betrayed, the communists were forced to flee in 1934 to the poor and sparsely populated area of Yan'an, to the west of the Yellow River in Shaanxi province, far from the coast and the industrial and commercial centre of Shanghai. It was here that the most profound analysis of patterns of land ownership and the first experiments in Chinese communism, especially in land reform, were carried out. And it was here that the individual communists who led China over the second half of the twentieth century emerged. Mao Zedong became their leader. He was the first of the communist heads of China *not* to be selected by the Comintern in Moscow.[3] Like Ho Chi Minh, he had become a Marxist in the months of revolutionary ferment at the end of World War One. For two decades while China was consumed by civil wars, communism spread only slowly. Then came the

Anti-Japanese War, which broke out in 1937, and Mao's opportunity. By the end of the war, Mao's vision of Marxism, "Mao Zedong Thought" as it was later called, would shape the party for the next three decades. Other leaders who stood alongside him were Zhou Enlai, Liu Shaoqi, and Deng Xiaoping. These were among the "Eight Immortals," the apostles who were later revered as being virtually beyond criticism.

## MAO ZEDONG, 1945–76

During the Anti-Japanese War there had been a truce between the Nationalists and the Communists, but when the Japanese surrendered in August 1945, open civil war broke out, which lasted until 1949. By that time the Nationalists had been seriously demoralized by years of fighting and retreating, by the mass desertions of their press-ganged army, and the divisions and venality of their leaders who remained stubbornly hostile to the idea of land reform. Even those with urban property were dismayed by uncontrolled inflation. Unsurprisingly then, during the civil war it was the Communists who prevailed, defeating the Nationalists in battle after battle and driving them, clutching as much wealth as they could bundle up, to Taiwan. Despite Jiang's aversion to reform, his despotic and often ruthless style, and his support for landlordism, Washington remained on the side of the Nationalists providing credits and loans until the end of 1949. Yet US president Harry Truman had few illusions: "Chiang Kai-shek['s troops] will not fight it out. [The] Communists will fight it out – they are fanatical. It would be pouring sand into a rat hole [to give aid] under present conditions." Truman's secretary of state, George Marshall (of Marshall Plan fame) wrote, "He [Jiang] is losing about forty percent of his supplies to the enemy. If the percentage should reach fifty percent he will have to decide whether it is wise to supply his own troops."[4] President Truman's analysis was correct; rather than stand and fight, Jiang cut and ran.

Thus Taiwan became another Japan, an American Gibraltar on China's doorstep, a link in an archipelagic chain that ran from Japan, or even the Aleutians, to the Philippines. This arc of empire was known in US foreign policy circles as a "defense perimeter." Its function was containment. But the whole structure of international relations in Asia was in a state of flux; communism had arrived, imperialism was collapsing, and, most surprising of all, the Japanese model of liberal capitalism based on exports was still waiting behind the curtain for its cue.

In December 1949, just two months after the existence of the People's Republic of China (PRC) had been declared, Mao Zedong travelled to Moscow to meet Stalin. Stalin snubbed him, keeping him waiting for weeks. Perhaps more discouragingly for the leaders of the CCP, the Mongolian People's Republic, between China and the Soviet Union, was recognized by Moscow as independent and thus within the Soviet, not the Chinese, sphere of influence. But the Chinese realm continued to expand: in October 1950 the battle-hardened troops of the Peoples' Liberation Army (PLA) invaded Tibet. In an earlier epoch, the British in India may have reacted to this since Tibet, like Afghanistan, was the roof of their Asian empire, but by then the British had left India, and the Indian prime minister, Nehru, in the name of solidarity with China, was willing to turn a blind eye.

Over most of the decade that followed, Sino-Soviet relations seemed firm enough and Asian communism appeared to have a secure future. For sure, communist regimes ruled a third of the world and much of the massive and populous Eurasian continent. It is hardly surprising, thus, that there was panic in Washington where the term "the loss of China" became a familiar trope in foreign policy and journalistic circles. "To have Free China become Communist seemed a national disaster," wrote John King Fairbanks, the dean of American historians of China in his history of US–Chinese relations.[5] Stalin's visit to Beijing in December 1949 had confirmed the worst Cold War fears. Dean Rusk, long-serving US secretary of state (1961–69), was among those virtually blinded by outrage. The government of the People's Republic, he fumed in 1951, was "a colonial Russian government. It is not the Government of China. It does not pass the first test. It is not Chinese." Chester Bowles, an eminently liberal figure in the governments of President J.F. Kennedy and Lyndon B. Johnson (together 1961–69), warned in 1961, "We are going to have to fight the Chinese ... in two, three, five, or ten years."[6] Although the apprehension about war between China and America came and went over the next half century, Chester Bowles was, thankfully, wrong. Instead of a new Pacific war, after the Korean War, America and China settled down for two decades of mutual, fist-waving, antagonism with the United States and its allies effectively quarantining China by blockade. The isolation that ensued was thus hardly a matter of choice for the Chinese leadership, but it did have the effect of shrouding China in an impenetrable darkness.

With the defeat of the Japanese and the end of their occupation of the Chinese mainland and of Taiwan, Beijing, the new capital of the communist People's Republic, saw off the last of foreign occupiers on its mainland. With the Soviet promise to evacuate their enclaves in Lüshun and nearby Dailan by 1952, almost all of its territories had been redeemed except for Taiwan, the refuge of the Nationalists; Hong Kong, which the British were to hold on to until 1997; and Macau, a fragment of the Portuguese seaborne empire, which held out until 1999, the last European colony in Asia that had been turned into an East Asian Las Vegas.

The first priorities of China's new government were the elimination of assumed enemies and the extension of rural reform to the regions beyond Yan'an. In late 1950 into 1951 a reign of terror against "counterrevolutionaries" saw executions of as many as two million people in south China. Another two million were sent to the Chinese gulag for "reeducation." At the same time the Agrarian Reform Law of June 1950 toppled the landlord class and turned landless peasants into private landholders. By May 1951 land had been distributed to more than 13.5 million landless peasants and paupers.[7]

The next preoccupation was collectivization. Between 1954 and 1956 as many as 110 million peasant households, about 92 per cent of the total, were forced into production cooperatives. These featured the abolition of private property; the pooling of land, farm animals, and tools; and the setting of production quotas that were privileged above any needs the peasants themselves might have. The process of turning private lands into communes had been carried out in the Soviet Union where it had also been accompanied by terror on an apocalyptic scale.

After the evacuation by Chiang in 1949 there was a brief but short-lived period of peace. Then came the war in Korea. The war, considered in the last chapter, ended with a truce in July 1953. Four months earlier Joseph Stalin, ostensibly the role model for Soviet man, had died. This was regarded as a huge tragedy by the Chinese leadership. In the words of the Xinhua News Agency (10 March 1953), the mouthpiece of the People's Republic, "Joseph Vissarionovich Stalin, the greatest genius of the present age, the great teacher of the world

Communist movement ... has departed from the world ... Comrade Stalin's contribution to our era through his theoretical and practical work is beyond our estimation. Comrade Stalin is representative of the whole of this new era of ours."[8]

At Stalin's funeral, Premier Zhou Enlai, the number two figure in the whole of the Maoist era, occupied a privileged spot in the midst of Stalin's successors (and not alongside other foreign mourners). Solidarity was repaid with material generosity; the Chinese Five-Year Plan, also introduced in 1953, was carried out with the help of thousands of Soviet experts and Soviet materials. Mixed Sino–Soviet companies were formed for mining and aviation. The plan achieved a dramatic increase across a broad range of enterprises from coal mined to bicycles assembled. What doubt could there be in the Western world that the solid Red ice sheet that was already grinding down peoples from the Baltic to Tibet was on the move?

In industrial terms, then, the first Five-Year Plan was a roaring success. Although the commanding heights of the economy (banking, trade, railways, heavy industry) were nationalized, initially certain firms had been left in private hands. Thus the British and other Europeans who had established themselves in Shanghai, many from the nineteenth century, were allowed to return to their businesses, at least until the mid-1950s. More important to the resurrection of the Chinese economy was the role of Soviet experts who for a decade after 1949 supervised several areas of Chinese industrial development.

In agricultural terms development was less remarkable, although in certain respects substantial gains were made. Not the least of these was the dissolution of the backward regions and their linking to the expanded national market. The object of providing cheap agricultural products to feed the urban population was thus met. It was to accomplish this that the peasants had been shunted into co-operative units. Little was invested in their health and welfare. But even simple measures of public health had their benefits; according to the 1953 census, the first taken using modern methods, China's population totalled 582.6 million; by 1957, the number had reached 646.5 million.

Throughout the 1950s China's international prestige grew, especially in the Third World. China's relations with its neighbours – India, North Korea, and the Mongolian People's Republic – were good and getting better. Internationally, premier Zhou Enlai increased China's visibility by attending the Geneva conference in April 1954 – a meeting convened to discuss détente in Asia and which continued on to fix the future of Indochina. The Chinese made an even greater splash with their participation at the 1955 Bandung conference. The presence of Zhou in Indonesia, a populous and potentially rich Asian country with a large and well-organized Communist Party, did not pass unnoticed in the West. Chinese solidarity with the Third World continued until 1978, a date of monumental significance for the political orientation of China, as we shall see.

In the meantime international communist solidarity went into free fall. In the Soviet Union, especially after the denunciation of Stalin by his successor, Nikita Khrushchev, in 1956, the idea of the continuing revolutionary agitation of society, as opposed to a plodding stability, appeared to be passé: in China this counterrevolution waited for another couple of decades. In fact although Stalin had treated Mao condescendingly, the Chinese leader viewed his Soviet counterpart with admiration. The Chinese view of Khrushchev was different; he was regarded as reckless and buffoonish, and, worst of all, lacking Stalin's steely conviction.

The differences between the two countries erupted in the spring of 1957. In the months before, Mao himself had encouraged China's intellectuals to speak out against political abuses. "Let a hundred flowers bloom, let a hundred schools of thought contend," he had said, and criticism of the party followed. Would there be a softening of communism, as in the Soviet Union, or liberalization, as was attempted in Hungary? Neither. Suddenly and viciously the party leaders, including Liu Shaoqi, Mao's heir apparent, and Deng Xiaoping, turned on the intellectuals, accusing them of being anti-revolutionaries. "Revisionist" was the word they used, meaning deviant, a vice leading to the "capitalist road," the highway to hell. Abandoned by the party leadership, including Mao, the intellectuals found themselves exposed and defenceless, and a political massacre unprecedented in the postwar years followed. Jonathan Spence comments,

> By the end of the year [1957], 300,000 intellectuals had been branded 'rightists,' a label that effectively ruined their careers in China. Many were sent to labour camps or to jail, others to the countryside not just to experience life on the land for a year, but into what was essentially a punitive exile that might last for life …

> a whole generation of bright young party activists were similarly penalized, among them some of China's finest social scientists, scientists and economists.[9]

Although Spence mentions a figure of 300,000 victims, other sources suggest 400,000 to 700,000. Their punishments presaged those that would be inflicted later on the intellectuals accused of "rightism" during the Cultural Revolution (1966–76). Deng Xiaoping, later to become the celebrated godfather of a renewal of capitalism in China, was at the centre of the "Anti-Rightist Movement." Like Nikita Khrushchev who willingly participated in Stalin's Great Terror in the Soviet Union and then became a reformer, Deng didn't scruple at supporting Mao Zedong but then, when the tide turned, shifting to leading China to a version of capitalism.

## GREAT LEAP FORWARD AND THE GREAT PROLETARIAN CULTURAL REVOLUTION, 1958–70

The "Great Leap Forward" was an aspirational phase connected to the Second Five-Year Plan (1958–62). Its main objects were to increase industrial output and modernize China's backward agricultural sector. Chinese planners had talked about catching up to the West in fifteen years. By 1959 it was claimed that "England" would be left behind in steel production.

The planners had become disenchanted with the Soviet Union, which they regarded as having become retrograde. So Mao decided that lest the Chinese suffer from a slackening of the revolutionary spirit, they should have a new slogan and a set of new projects; the slogan was "More, faster, better, cheaper." In the agricultural sector the new project took the form of the introduction of communes; no more cooperatives, no more private plots. The 740,000 cooperatives were merged into 26,000 communes. These accounted for 99 per cent of the peasant population. In them everything from dinners to tractors was shared.

At first, the plan went swimmingly. The harvest of 1958, when the Great Leap Forward reached it apogee, was remarkable. Deng Xiaoping spoke of a future when "all citizens would have sixty-six pounds of pork annually, and five pounds of grain and a half pound of apples daily; and all women would walk around in high-heeled shoes and use lipstick. We can have as much as we want!" he exclaimed. An excited Mao Zedong gave a speech attributing the successful increase in production to "the all-round, continuous leap forward in China's agricultural production and the ever-rising political consciousness of the 500 million peasants." Few in China's governing circles even dared to disabuse him.[10]

Stark reality punctured the dream of a Great Leap Forward. The record harvest of 1958 was exposed as a bureaucratic fraud; the reported 375 million tons of grain had not been harvested; rather, perhaps as little as 215 million were brought in. Worse, the enforced introduction of communes and forced procurements led to a devastating famine that swept China from 1958 to the early 1960s. Tens of millions of peasants starved to death in the worst manmade famine in history; one estimate is of 45 million deaths. If this is the case then the Great Leap Forward caused far more deaths than the Anti-Japanese War.[11] The blame for this has to be laid at the feet of China's rulers and especially Mao Zedong although he escaped almost entirely from criticism.[12] Yet because the famine rose from political, not natural, causes, recovery, for those who survived it, was rapid. By 1964 output levels in agriculture were back to pre-Great Leap levels. Nevertheless, as one argument puts it, the Great Famine turned China's peasants against collectivization and sowed the seeds of reform.[13]

By the early 1960s the coherence of global communism was at an end although in the West this was barely understood. The disenchantment of the Chinese leadership with the Soviet Union had become complete; the Sino-Soviet relationship, overtly fraternal, occasionally warm, although generally cautious and sometimes strained, was now at an end. In 1960 the Soviet aid experts in China were recalled in their hundreds, and the next year Beijing attacked Khrushchev for revisionism. From this point began a new and final epoch in the distinctive history of communist China, one in which the Soviet Union, while it lasted, played a generally antagonistic part. This epoch was marked by the final, wrenching, spasm of actual communism, the Cultural Revolution. For many this proved conclusively that socialism in its communist form could not be the answer. Underlining this was, as we shall see, the deaths of several of the giants who had dominated Chinese history since the 1920s.

The Cultural Revolution (1966–70) was a radical political intervention that sought to revivify – like blood-letting had been in premodern medicine. Mao Zedong had become convinced that the Chinese revolution was losing its conviction and was surrendering its impetus to a swollen bureaucracy. He and his comrades proclaimed a comprehensive attack on the "four olds" within society: old customs, old habits, old culture, and old thinking. On the losing side of the radical program were the "revisionists" also known as "capitalist roaders." These were, like Stalin's successors in the Soviet Union, leaders who wanted to creep gradually and carefully on a track parallel to, but separate from, the capitalist road.

Exceptional factors also partly explain this autumnal revolution; the "Great Helmsman" himself was seventy-three and realized that his days at the tiller were numbered. What if the party bureaucrats were to take control and push him to one side? Other matters must have preoccupied him: What did he think, for instance, about the overthrow of Sukarno and the butchery of hundreds of thousands of communists in Indonesia in 1965, of the twenty years war in Indochina (1954–74), of the painfully slow growth of the economies of the Warsaw Pact, or the remarkable advances of managed capitalism in Japan, South Korea, and Taiwan?[14] Or the decline of fervour in China that both preceded and succeeded the Cultural Revolution?

The radical ultracommunists who fomented the Cultural Revolution had their base in Shanghai, the former centre of capitalism in China. Mao himself was their leader. Their enemies, the capitalist roaders, were headquartered in Beijing. Liu Shaoqui, the vice chairman of the party and Deng Xiaoping, the general secretary, were the leading lights of the capitalist roaders. In 1967 Deng had said, "As long as we increase production, we can even revert to individual enterprise; it hardly matters whether a good cat is black or white – as long as it catches mice, it is a cat." This homely metaphor, coined as a pragmatist's attempt to put economic planning ahead of political rectitude in the shadow of the Great Leap disaster, was to plague him for the next four decades.

On Mao's side was his third wife, Jiang Qing, an actor who had become convinced that China needed a cultural cleansing. She was soon to become a leading figure in the Cultural Revolution Authority, the inquisitional bureaucracy of the revolution. She claimed that China was "under the dictatorship of a sinister anti-Party and anti-Socialist line which is diametrically opposed to Chairman Mao's thought. This sinister line is a combination of bourgeois ideas on literature and art

[and] modern revisionist ideas." Later, Jiang Qing was to be a part of the Gang of Four, conspirators who sought power in the immediate aftermath of Mao's death. Beside her was Lin Biao, one of the Maoist immortals who had been at his side since the darkest days and who propagated the basic canon of Cultural Revolution Maoism as contained in a small booklet with a plastic cover called *Quotations of Chairman Mao* – known as the little red book. By the early 1970s this book was known virtually everywhere in the world, except within the Soviet bloc.

In the spring and summer of 1966 the revolution spread throughout China. All pleas for caution were cast aside as central governmental institutions and leading officials were attacked, purged, and sometimes even destroyed. Chaos reigned for three years as squads of high school and university students, calling themselves Red Guards and waving their little red catechisms, roamed the country in a destructive frenzy. Lin Biao led the cheering. His description of Mao as "our great teacher, great leader, great supreme commander and great helmsman" became the standard description of the Chairman. At a mass rally on 19 August 1966 Lin declared that "Chairman Mao is the most outstanding leader of contemporary times. The greatest talent of contemporary times." "Long live Chairman Mao! Long live!, Long, long live!" he raved.[15] The Cultural Revolution peaked at the beginning of 1967. By that time schools and universities had all been closed and monuments connected with the past – temples, old buildings, and art objects – had been demolished while teachers, administrators, party leaders, and even parents had been publicly criticized and humiliated. By late 1967, in the eyes of China's ruler, the revolution had reached an intolerable level. Within two more years, having consumed thousands of victims, many of whom had committed suicide, and with many institutions shattered by investigations and purges, revolutionary ardour had cooled. Mao decided that the Cultural Revolution had gone far enough. The People's Liberation Army (PLA), which was under the authority of the communist party rather than the Chinese state, now turned to restoring order. The teenage Red Guards were sent back to school, and the terror abated. Many of the victims of the terror languished in the countryside for years to come. Deng Xiaoping's son, Deng Pufang, had been so badly beaten by the Red Guards during the Cultural Revolution that he was disabled for life. Xi Jinping, China's present strongman and son of Vice Premier Xi Zhongxun, was banished to the countryside for six years. His older half sister committed suicide after enduring brutal treatment.[16]

In the early 1970s China entered a period of relative calm. Then, suddenly, in February 1972, and to the astonishment of the whole world, the US president, Richard Nixon (1969–74), hitherto the most ardent of anticommunists, embarked upon a visit to Beijing. He was accompanied and guided by the ruthless but brilliant realist, Henry Kissinger. What this sudden détente foretold was at the time entirely opaque; like the sudden fall of the Berlin Wall, it was a chapter in the Cold War that was beyond immediate interpretation.

Nixon was to boast that his visit "changed the world," a verdict that seems to be roughly accurate although it takes no account of the swing back from the Cultural Revolution, led by Chairman Mao himself, that had already taken place.[17] One of its most palpable symptoms of this swing was the quite surprising vilification of Lin Biao.

The tragedy of Lin has all the elements of high melodrama and, in its official version, is not entirely believable. Having taken over the PLA, he abolished all ranks and insignia. When, under Mao's guidance, the PLA moved to keep the military safe from the depredations of the Cultural Revolution, Lin was isolated. By 1970, with revolutionary zeal and ideological purity no longer in demand, his position worsened. According to the official view, driven to desperation with the collapse of his stratagems, he then planned the assassination of Mao. When this aborted, he seized a passenger jet and, together with his family, attempted to fly to the Soviet Union. On 13 September 1971, the plane ran out of fuel over Mongolia and crashed, killing its entire crew and all of its passengers. In 1972 Premier Zhou Enlai announced that Lin had been a "renegade and traitor."

By now, the mass of the population of China had already showed signs of having become disenchanted with the exaggerated purgings and blood-lettings of official ideology. Jonathan Spence:

> The most violent strains in Chinese society had been given free rein and the basic organizational structures stretched to the breaking point. The Great Leap Forward had at least had a meaningful economic and social vision at its heart, the Great Proletarian Cul-

tural Revolution showed that neither Mao nor the CCP seemed to know how or where the nation should be heading.[18]

Mao's health continued to deteriorate between the time of the visit of the US president and September 1976, when he died. His last public appearance was in 1973 at the Tenth Party Congress. His passing was preceded by that of Zhou Enlai who died in January 1976. Just a year earlier, Mao's old antithesis, Jiang Jieshi, founder of the Chinese republic in Taiwan, had also passed away. The founder of the PLA, General Zhu De, had died in July. With the demise of Jiang, Zhou, Zhu, and Mao, and before them, Liu Shaoqui and Lin Biao,[19] a generation that had risen in the wake of the great political turmoil that followed World War One, and that had steered Chinese history for over half a century, were no longer.

## AUDIT

The Chinese revolution was second only to the Bolshevik Revolution as the greatest political upheaval since the French Revolution. It owes pride of place to its Bolshevik predecessors since it was they who inspired, mentored, and served as a role model for the Chinese communists from the 1920s to the 1950s. But unlike the communists who in the end liquidated the Soviet Union, the Reds who ruled China never surrendered their claim to being the inheritors of revolutionism. Thus the present ruling oligarchy of China, billionaires and all, still manages to maintain the pretence of being communist. Hence the claim that what exists today is a "socialist market economy," although "capitalism with Chinese characteristics" or even a "statist market economy" would be closer to the mark. Yielding nothing to the critics of monumental and widespread corruption and waste and the rise of a Chinese "new class," the title of the final speech of President Hu Jintao at the Eighteenth Party Congress in November 2012 was "Firmly March on the Path of Socialism with Chinese Characteristics and Strive to Complete the Building of a Moderate Prosperous Society in all Respects."[20]

Eric Hobsbawm, whose verdict reflected a lifelong commitment to European socialism but evinced little feeling for the world east of the Mediterranean, has showed scant sympathy for the distinctiveness of Chinese communism. He noted begrudgingly, however:

> However much we may be shocked by the record of the twenty Maoist years, a record combining mass inhumanity and obscurantism with the surrealist absurdities of the claims made on behalf of the divine leader's thoughts, we should not allow ourselves to forget that, by the standards of the poverty-stricken Third World, the Chinese people were doing well. At the end of the Mao period the average Chinese food consumption (in calories) ranked just above the median of all countries, above fourteen in the Americas, thirty-eight in Africa, and just about the middle of the Asian ones ... The average expectation of life at birth rose from thirty-five years in 1949 to sixty-eight in 1982, mainly owing to a dramatic and – except for the famine years – continuous fall in mortality rate.[21]

In 1979, thirty years after the PRC had come into existence and just three years after Mao's death, even the World Bank looked on China with barely concealed admiration. Despite a 2 per cent growth in population, "rapid expansion of industrial output has caused national income per person to grow fairly fast. With adjustments for international comparability, per capita GNP appears to have grown at an annual rate of 2.0–2.5% in 1957–77 and, because of a spurt in the last two years, 2.5–3% in 1947–79. Even the former rate is significantly above the average for other low-income developing countries (1.5% in 1960–78)."[22]

What the Bank was observing was that as a consequence of a second spasm of agrarian reform, the household responsibility system propelled peasant production forward, causing agricultural output to leap up by a third and peasant incomes to rise from 30 to 44 per cent of national income.

## CAPITALISM WITH CHINESE CHARACTERISTICS

In the years after the death of Mao Zedong in September 1976, the "reform" period was launched and a new China was born. Justin Lifu Lin: "The change in China's fate started in December 1978 when the Third Plenary Session of the 11th Central Committee of the Communist Party of China ushered in the reform and opening strategy – to reform the economic structure and open the economy to more foreign trade." "Mao's dream of a self-sufficient China," explains Stephen Roach, "was replaced by Deng's gamble of externally led development."[23]

This revolution is associated with Deng Xiaoping (1980–92), a leader caricatured as a rightist and feudalist during the Cultural Revolution, purged and vilified in 1966 and 1976, attacked by his rivals after the death of Mao Zedong, but exonerated in November 1979 by which time he had become China's supreme leader. In that year he had reassured his comrades of the Four Basic Principles that would guide China's future: "First, we must adhere to the socialist faith; second, we must adhere to a dictatorship of the proletariat; third, we must adhere to the leadership of the Chinese Communist Party; fourth, we must adhere to Marxism–Leninism and Mao Zedong Thought." That said, the door was closed on socialism and opened to capitalist globalism. At the Fifth Plenum of the Eleventh Central Committee (23–29 February 1980) Premier Zhao Ziyang explained further:

> In economic work, we must abandon once and for all the idea of self-sufficiency, which is characteristic of the national economy. All idea and actions based on keeping our door closed to the outside world and sticking to conventions are wrong ... By linking our country with the world market, expanding foreign trade, importing advanced technology, utilizing foreign capital, and entering into different forms of international economic and technological cooperation, we can use our strong points to make up for our weak points.[24]

Thus China adopted the same globalist and liberal economic model as Japan and the Asian geese. Many in Taipei, the capital of Taiwan, must have rubbed their hands. Soon they would put them in their pockets to draw out the capital that would be needed to stimulate mainland industry. Between 1970 and 2007, China's exports went from 5 per cent of GDP to 36 per cent; the bulk of these being produced by subsidiaries of companies often owned by "overseas" Chinese.[25]

Over the decade 1979–89, after he had routed his left-wing enemies and put himself securely in power, Deng introduced capitalist relations to selected parts of the Chinese economy while dissolving certain communist arrangements such as communes. State-owned enterprises (SOEs), however, not only continued to exist but expanded while the banking sector remained state-controlled. Key elements in the commanding heights of the economy were given over to management by Mao's closest comrades and later, their children, the

"Princelings." The Princelings in fact fulfilled the same nepotistic function in postcommunist China as the oligarchs did in Russia – they ate the lunch that in communist theory, at least, had been prepared for the masses.

Besides Deng, other Mao cronies were up there in the scramble for former public properties. Unlike the case of the *nomenklatura*-into-oligarchs in Russia, these were not a "new class" so much as an old ruling class with unleashed bourgeois instincts. Still, unlike the case in Russia where leading elements in the economy like oil and banks were privatized and benefited some hundred families, in China much was kept in the hands of the state. Peter Nolan lauds the Chinese model of elite engrossment:

> The essence of China's enterprise reform policy was crystallized in the slogan "grasp the large, let go of the small." By the late 1990s most of the small and medium enterprise sector had been removed from state ownership, and a wide array of institutional structures emerged from the process. Although this was broadly referred to as "privatization," the latter term does not fully capture the complexity of the process or its outcome. The non-state sector, which consists of mainly small and medium-sized enterprises, has made a vital contribution to China's growth. Removing the constraints over this sector unleashed the force of the country's vibrant tradition of entrepreneurship, which had been smothered since the mid-1950s under the administratively directed economy … Alongside the rapid growth of the non-state sector, *the commanding heights of the economy remained under state ownership* [my italics].[26]

Central to this strategy was the plan to put mammoth state-owned conglomerates at the centre of the manufacturing economy – that is, to create the Chinese equivalent of General Electric and General Motors to be run by the government. The models for this had already been established in Japan and Korea. In Japan they were called the *zaibatsu* at first, and later the *keiretsu*, and in Korea, *chaebols*. In China they were called *yangqi* and there were around 110 of them.[27] In 1998 Vice Premier Wu Bangguo explained: "Japan relies on its six large enterprise groups and Korea relies on ten large commercial groupings. In the same way now and in the next century our nation's position in the international economic order will be to a large extent determined by the position of our nation's large enterprises and groups."[28] These "large enterprises and groups" have become familiar enough by now: telecoms, oil and chemicals, automobiles, power equipment, metals and mining, heavy engineering, and so on, not to mention the banking sector where Chinese banks stand out as the largest in the world. In the *Financial Times* list of the world's 500 largest corporations, the FT500, there were nine Chinese banks. In the Fortune 500 list of top companies, as of 2003, a dozen were Chinese. Canadians will be especially aware of the great, vertically integrated oil and gas firms, CNPC, Sinopec, and CNOOC that bought into Canada's oil patch.[29] PetroChina, a subsidiary of CNPC, became the world's largest listed oil company, surpassing even ExxonMobil.

To summarize: after the Chinese revolution itself, "reform and opening" was the second major transformation of the twentieth century.

As a consequence of reform and the township and village enterprises (TVEs), hundreds of millions in the rural areas and even more in the cities walked away from poverty. In 1978, 30 per cent of rural residents, about 250 million, lived below the poverty line. By 2009 this figure had dropped to 36 million. President Richard Nixon's much-celebrated visit to China in 1972 is seen as foreshadowing this remarkable change although, as we have noted, this "Sinamerica" interpretation of Chinese history exaggerates the American role.[30] Underplayed in this view is the fact that since the 1930s as the Communist Party had slowly extended its influence over the whole of the country the most massive land reform in history had taken place. This reform was completed in the first decade of communist state power in 1949. Following this land reform, which was revised again, industry was made a priority. So, while peasants were mercilessly exploited in order to create a surplus to be invested in factories, the country was industrialized. By the reform period, that is, from around 1980, China could already boast many features of a middle-range developed country. Both peasants and workers had been guaranteed employment, food, and a modest degree of education. It was this widespread primary education in China that meant that when the moment of reform arrived, there existed a massive population of potential workers who understood the rudiments of collective (i.e. classroom) discipline and who could read. Compared to India, the only other BRIC state with a huge population and massive poverty for most of the twentieth century, China has remained outstanding. By the second decade of the twenty-first century, in certain key areas a much greater concern for the health of the Chinese majority is evinced than in the case of India – for instance India spent 1.2 per cent of GDP on health while China spent 2.7 per cent. In India in 2011 half of all Indian households did not have access to toilets; the figure for China is one per cent. And of course there never was in China a strata of society comparable in perennial oppression and poverty to the Dalits in India who comprise some 300 million people, a quarter of India's population.

## TIANANMEN

There had been in the aftermath of the death of Mao Zedong a guardedly open debate about democracy and human rights in China as well as a movement to limit the privileges of the party leaders, functionaries in the government, and officers in the military. The corruption involved the privileged children of the party leaders, (called *zilaihong* meaning "born red"). By the late 1980s the tension within the party over several questions had increased. The reformers especially wanted more economic freedom and further opening of the economy to the West.[31] The conservatives wanted to tighten party control. During the 1970s and '80s the social and political climate had become more hopeful and free.[32]

Debate reached crisis point in the spring of 1989. In January of that year, Hu Yaobang, a liberal reformer who had been defeated by Deng in 1987 and who warned about the corruption of the party, died. On 16 April 1989 a huge mobilization involving thousands of students, workers, civil servants, teachers, and even entrepreneurs marched into Beijing's Tiananmen Square. It was there in the great central plaza that the birth of the People's Republic had been announced in October 1949, forty years earlier. The mobilization in the spring of 1989 was to demand more democracy, more political freedom, and less corruption. Banners were carried with the slogans "Long Live Democracy," "Long Live Freedom," "Down with Corruption," and "Down with Bureaucratism." Similar demonstrations took place in more than a hundred cities throughout China, like Chengdu in the southwest.[33] The "Democracy Movement" had been born. The state-controlled organs of mass media, like the *People's Daily* and the Xinhua News Agency, suddenly enjoyed "something approaching 'a period of press freedom.'"[34]

Crisis loomed at the highest levels. China's leadership, divided on how to handle the mass movement, decided that its existence was threatened. Deng, who was chairman of the Military Affairs Commission and thus in charge of the PLA, made threats in the press. One claim from the leadership noted that the protests were organized by "an extremely small number of people with ulterior motives" who were opposed to "the leadership of the Communist Party and the socialist system." This had little resonance. By the end of April the crowds in the streets continued to increase. In mid-May when Mikhail Gorbachev visited Beijing, the students crowded into Tiananmen in even larger numbers. On 17 May, a million people marched through Beijing in support of the students' demands.

Led by Premier Li Peng and Deng Xiaoping, the party leaders decided to meet the protests with repression by declaring martial law. In the first days of June, tanks and armoured vehicles were sent against the demonstrators. On the evening of 3 June troops unleashed an attack. "Down with Deng Xiaoping!" the protesters cried as they fled. In his testament to their persistence and valour, Tim Brook has written:

> The night was over. So too was the Democracy Movement and everything the students and their supporters hoped to achieve. By taking the Square, the People's Liberation Army had crushed opposition to the Party. It had also shattered the minds of an entire city and an entire generation. The students trudged ... to their campuses like people in a nightmare, some hysterical, most in tears, all dazed and exhausted. The dream was over. From now on it would be the old story: intimidation, settling of scores, silence.

Thereafter it was illegal to use the term "June 3" or to comment on Tiananmen on the internet. The word *jiquanzhuyi*, "totalitarianism," was also banned.[35] Often the party used the word "democracy" or "democratic centralism" but with a special meaning; that is, it meant "dictatorship" or "party dictatorship." Any threat to the dictatorship of the party, it was claimed, would lead to instability and chaos. For this reason all forms of dissent, on whatever grounds, had to be crushed.

Of those killed in early June, most were workers and clerks, fewer were students. Estimates range from 2,600 to 3,000 dead, 20,000 wounded, and up to 7,000 arrested in Beijing alone. Goldman makes the point that "although the student and intellectual leaders were interrogated, subjected to arrest, deprived of their jobs, and put under surveillance, they were not executed as were scores of workers who had participated in the demonstration." Brook adds, "It was the workers who were the fodder for PLA guns, not the students."[36]

Even those at the apex of power were sidelined. Zhao Ziyang, general secretary of the Communist Party, who had urged compromise was accused of trying to "split the party" and was dismissed. He was to spend the final sixteen years of his life under house arrest. China's democracy movement was now declared dead, but what was to follow remained unclear. After the Tiananmen massacre and the ensuing purges, the program of economic liberalization paused to gather its breath and then plunged on. A dozen years earlier, at the end of December 1978, agreement had been reached to sell Coca-Cola inside China. Soon a bottling plant would be opened in Shanghai. In December 1990, a dozen years later, the Shanghai Stock Exchange opened, and, by the end of next year, it had as many as 100,000 investors. A new class structure bloomed. Among the other delegates to the National People's Congress, there were thirty-one with at least a billion dollars in personal assets. Another fifty-two billionaires were delegates to the Chinese People's Political Consultative Confluence.[37] After Tiananmen some twenty to thirty million closed-circuit video (CCTV) cameras were installed across the country and a Bureau of Public Opinion was created to measure the pulse of the public.[38]

## THE MIDDLE CLASS ON THE CAPITALIST ROAD

For Deng, as he announced in 1992, "Development is the only hard truth." He allowed that some people would get rich before others. Then, in 2002, Jiang Zemin, a Deng protégé, declared that the party would dedicate itself to the success of the "new middle-income stratum," that is, the middle class. One author described the rising Chinese middle class as "the moral force behind civilized manners. It is the force necessary to eliminate privilege and curb poverty. It is everything."[39]

The size of the middle class depends on how it is measured. He Qinglian has explained that the Chinese elite comprises about seven million people, or about 1 per cent of the employed population, the middle class a further 110 million (16 per cent), the working class around 170 million (25 per cent), and the unemployed and pauperized rural population, 100 million (14 per cent).[40] When Hu Jintao spoke at the Seventeenth National Congress in 2008, he spoke of a "socialist harmonious society."

By then the top 10 per cent of urban Chinese were earning 9.2 times as much as the bottom tenth. It was on his epochal Southern Tour in early 1992 that Deng had assured his listeners that the only way forward for China was as an export economy. China should become the fifth of the geese behind Japan following the lead of Hong Kong, Taiwan, South Korea, and Singapore. Visiting Shenzhen, the site of a Special Economic Zone, he made it clear that "In reform and opening it is necessary to be bolder and to open on a larger scale … whoever is opposed to reform must leave office." He was commended for this by Chinese interest groups, reformist intellectuals, and foreign pundits. A month later, the *People's Daily*, the main mouthpiece of the regime, announced that "active and prosperous financial markets will bring the country innumerable benefits" and "a joint-stock economy can serve our socialist construction."[41] In the same year, the Fourteenth Party Congress approved further economic deregulation. This was further entrenched at the next party congress in 1997. At the Fourteenth Congress, Party Secretary Jiang Zemin, praised his mentor as "the general architect of reform and opening up and of the modernization drive in relation to socialism in China."

China's capitalist revolution was bound to be contested. During 1993, despite the repression that had followed Tiananmen, "peasant uprisings occurred in 20 of China's 29 provinces; in the same year industrial workers ... staged more than 6,000 illegal strikes and joined more than 200 riots." Sixty per cent of these were over "land grabs" in which unscrupulous local officials had illegally sold off to developers private plots owned by farmers.[42] Millions of workers and peasants had been dislocated by the reforms and were bitter at the corruption and inequality that arose from it.

While the reform program was being advanced, Deng had purged and liquidated those within the leadership of the CCP who threatened his grasp on power. His smashing of protest marked the last gasp of socialism and the beginning of the new order – of what? Already there had been talk of "a socialist market economic system." And recall that the Germans had patented what was called a "social market economy."

The differences were huge: in China, for instance, the state ran the SOEs and the banks, and a Red aristocracy ran the state. In 1992 Schell and Lappin put their finger on China's "strangely eclectic economy," but perhaps this misses the point that all capitalist economies are mixed with the state, in spite of the rash of privatizations in the 1990s, variously running railways, guaranteeing mortgages, organizing banking, and providing health care and education.[43]

China's capitalist counterrevolution recalls the destruction of the Soviet bloc at the beginning of the 1990s; we might note that the Tiananmen demonstrations and the breaching of the Berlin Wall, which preceded the breakup of the Soviet Empire, both happened in the same year, 1989. Wang Hui: "1989 was for me significant in many ways: it was a farewell to the old era."[44]

In 2001 China's recognition as a capitalist power had been acknowledged by its welcome into the World Trade Organization. Writers in the liberal American journal, *Foreign Affairs*, celebrated the fact that Beijing "has begun to embrace regional and global institutions it once shunned and take on the responsibilities that come with the great-power status." What did "responsibility" mean here? It meant acceptance of Western norms and, of course, the rules of the prevailing form of world capitalism. It was noted, with a certain complacency, that China was too dependent on US investment and technology to become a challenge to American economic dominance; in fact foreigners owned 50.4 per cent of the firms that produced China's exports and another 26.3 per cent were joint ventures with Chinese partners. The Chinese state owned a mere 10.3 per cent. Obviously, then, "the vast bulk of Chinese exports are produced by fully foreign owned multinationals."[45] Although in 2013 China owned around $1.3 trillion of US debt and this was by any accounting an alarming amount, it was less than the cost of the invasion of Iraq.[46] It wasn't a problem that China's sovereign wealth fund, the China Investment Corporation (CIC), had $575 billion under management.[47]

In 1990 China was warned about currency manipulation and in 1992–94 it was named as a manipulator. Currency manipulation is the practice of keeping the national currency artificially low as a means of increasing exports. Although China was accused of unfair trading practices and the subject of regular complaints of cheating, no sanctions were put into place against it. But currency manipulation together with "predatory pricing," dumping, the abuse of intellectual property rights, and cyberhacking were all considered part of the "China gripe," that is the complaints that have regularly been issued against China's trading practices.

Even in spite of the griping, enthusiasm for the dynamic, reformed, and stable China peaked in 2008 when the summer Olympics were held in Beijing. By this time while it was apparent that the world capitalist economy had not yet fully recovered, the Chinese economy appeared unshakable. In a massive investment boom in 2009–10, the Chinese spent four trillion renminbi on projects like high-speed railways, highways, and airports.[48] Three cheers for China, it was thought, whose busy industries and fantastic savings accounts would put the global capitalist economy back on its feet.

But the problem of China's rise seemed reluctant to stay dead. The grievances paraded in journals like *The Economist* and by the writers who took up the same cry were followed by further upsetting reminders: Arvind Subramanian's *Eclipse: Living in the Shadow of China's Economic Dominance* (2011) had a cover photo of President Obama apparently bowing to China's Hu Jintao. Subramanian, boasting of being a fellow at the Peterson Institute for International Economics[49] and formerly of the IMF and GATT and of Harvard and Johns Hopkins, wrote: "[T]he economic dominance of China relative to the United States is more imminent (it may already have begun), will be more broad-based (covering wealth, trade, external finance, and currency), and could be as large in magnitude in the next 20 years as that of ... the United States in the aftermath of World War II."[50] Subramanian's fictionalized "Introduction," flashed forward to February 2021 when a newly installed American president made his way to the Chinese head of the IMF to request $3 trillion in emergency financing. Of course the application of crippling "conditionalities" might have to be applied to America as they had been to Ghana or Sri Lanka.[51]

Cassandras seemed to be everywhere. The three most important words in the past decade, according to Gerard Lyons, chief accountant of Britain's Standard Chartered Bank, were not "war on terror," but "made in China."[52] Barry Eichengreen, eminent economic historian and author of the biography of the hegemonic dollar, warned in the *Financial Times*: "The dollar's days as a reserve currency are numbered";[53] the renminbi was on its way to the top. To this Ho-Fung Hung, an American but hardly an America Firster, added a further account to the story of the transformations of contemporary global capitalism with a chilling anecdote about the vulnerability of the dollar:

> In November 2007, a midlevel central government official in China made a remark in an international financial forum. He said that the Chinese government should consider reducing the portion of its assets denominated in US dollars and diversify the current mix of its gigantic foreign exchange reserve, which exceeded 1.5 trillion in US dollars and has been the biggest in the world since 2006. Within a few hours, the value of the dollar in the international currency market plunged.[54]

Then there was the shopping problem. With its apparently limitless wealth, China could buy almost anything including American (and Canadian) businesses and resources. It could elbow its Western rivals away from their former African, Middle Eastern, and Latin American clients, at unfairly low prices. The Chinese state-owned China Ocean Shipping Company (COSCO) even bought control of the Greek port of Piraeus, famous in the annals of Western civilization for the long walls that joined it to Athens. The Western media had a great deal to say about this, even more than Chinese investments in and migration to Africa and Latin America, as we will see more of in the last section of this chapter and in chapters 8 and 9. So China could be blamed for anything, even the 2008 meltdown. The economic catastrophe of our times was to a significant degree the fault of China, at least according to the Dutch economist, Helen Mees who spelled it out in a forthright article, entitled "How China's Boom Caused the Financial Crisis,"[55] published in a leading American journal.

Something, obviously, had to be done and that something was a rebalancing of the trade between China and its major partners, especially the EU and the US. Both Michael Pettis and Stephen Roach, outstanding western commentators on the Chinese economy, addressed this problem although not without a certain alarmism. "Balancing" became the new "convergence" in the lexicon of development economist. *The Great Rebalancing. Trade, Conflict and the Perilous Road Ahead for the World Economy* (2013) sums up the concerns of Pettis, professor of finance and economics at Beijing University; *Unbalanced: The Codependency of America and China* (2014) is Roach's title. Roach had worked as the chief economist of Morgan, Stanley in Asia and taught at Yale. In common with Paul Krugman, he was a public intellectual, well enough known to nonspecialist readers who were bound to be concerned not just with

America's shrinking hegemony but with the state of the global economy. Both were cautious about accepted truths. Pettis stressed that Chinese growth figures were hugely exaggerated ("over optimistic") and that the Chinese economy was unbalanced. He predicted that while some Chinese economists expressed the likelihood that the Chinese economy could expand by 6 to 7 per cent in the next few years, in fact it might grow at only half that level.[56] Roach wrote about the "mutual pathology" of Sino-American codependence and the impossibility of nations like the United States "to get out of their own skin and assess the ever-changing developments in China."[57] Both Pettis and Roach speculated that another global crisis might happen soon – that is, in the next few years. Yet they were both optimists, perhaps like most economists they ignored "externalities" such as geopolitics and environmental changes.[58]

This vilifying of China was not surprising given that from the time of President Ronald Reagan and the "Evil Empire" there had been a steady stream of hostile rhetoric against those states that failed to do America's bidding and were accused of a democratic deficit and a failure to guarantee human rights. The Chinese were doubtless aware of this growing hostility. Human rights abuses in China had long since been criticized, though ineffectually: They had improved only slightly.

The criticism of the Chinese role in global capitalism was, however, quite unacceptable. In spite of demands, the renminbi was not devalued – or, at least, not until August 2015. Instead of deflating and introducing austerity, Beijing went on a spending spree, pumping public money into roads, railways, ports, and property to the tune of four trillion renminbi. In the city of Wuhan, government officials "planned to build 140 miles of new subway lines in the seven years that New York City set aside to build 2 miles of the Second Avenue subway."[59] Chinese cities took on the look of Singapore; North American cities looked increasingly like Detroit. In all of China's major centres property boomed, as it had in Japan at the end of the 1980s, before the collapse. In the West, struggling with the aftermath of 9/11, 2008 and a global economy suffering from the slowest economic growth rate in twenty-five years, there was resentment. Nothing was more gratifying than the stories of the corruption of China's ruling group, which were splashed on the western media at regular intervals. Even *Maclean's* ("Canada's National

Magazine"), in early 2012 carried the banner headlines "The China Crisis. Massive corruption. Political unrest. Factories at a standstill. How serious trouble in the world's most important economy is going to hit us all."[60]

By the end of 2013, the air was crackling with news about General Secretary Xi Jinping's anticorruption drive as dozens of businessmen and women, and especially officials who were members of the Communist Party, were manacled and marched to the courts to be sentenced to long terms in prison. Evan Osnos quotes Xi Jinping warning that corruption would "inevitably lead the Party and the nation to perish." Economic crimes, in fact, seem to have spiralled into the stratosphere from 9,000 in 1980 to 77,0000 by the end of the decade. By 2000 the regime was indicting more than 2,500 senior officials a year. Bribe size had exploded from 4000 renminbi in 1984 to 272,000 renminbi in 2005.[61]

Is corruption going to sink the Chinese boat? Wen Jiabao seemed worried. Speaking at the National People's Congress on March 2012, he warned that:

> Now reforms in China have come to a critical stage, without a successful political reform, it is impossible for China to fully institute economic reform and the gains we have made in these areas may be lost, and new problems that popped up in Chinese society will not be fundamentally resolved, and such historical tragedies as the Cultural Revolution may happen again in China.[62]

Recall that the Cultural Revolution had been launched as an attempt to deflect China from the "capitalist road," and one of the demands of the students and workers protesting in Tiananmen Square had been the ending of corruption. Is corruption, influence peddling or "rent seeking" really a problem? Stephen Roach is unworried. "China's corruption is deep-rooted and systemic. It is a serious problem. But the question at hand is whether corruption has the potential to bring the economy down or have a material bearing on the codependency between the US and Chinese economies. The answer is, no." China is more corrupt than Brazil but less than India and Russia, all BRIC economies – yet Brazilian corruption has led to a huge crisis and Russian corruption seems out of control, with the economic growth of both countries continuing to deteriorate.[63]

Will President Trump be able to put China back in its place? No, says Kenneth Rogoff, Harvard economist and former chief economist of the IMF. "If the Trump administration tries such crude tactics with China [as it has done with Mexico], it will be in for a rude surprise. China has financial weapons, including trillions of dollars of US debt … The US cannot 'win' a trade war with China."[64]

# 6

# South Asian Avatars: India and Pakistan

The Mughal Empire, between the empires of Ottomans, the Safavids, and the Manchus was one of the great terrestrial states of Asia. Its rule spread by conquest over most of India and Pakistan from 1526 for more than two centuries before its domains were slowly subdued by the army of a British private company. The chartered East India Company gradually expanded its control of the subcontinent from a base in Calcutta, defeating both local rulers and rival Europeans. Then in the middle of the nineteenth century it was superseded by what was essentially a British colonial administration. This lasted until 1947. For a century, then, the Raj, as colonial India was called, became the greatest of Britain's overseas domains, the source of wealth, employment, soldiery, and palpable self-satisfaction.

The Raj was both the first and the greatest of the European colonies to become free after World War Two; the word "freedom" rather than "independence" marks the perception that the British had taken away autonomy, if not actually freedom in the Western sense, and then, in 1947, the Indians claimed it back. In what is incontestably the most stirring speech given by the head of a newly independent state, as freedom approached on the evening of 14 August 1947 Prime Minister-elect Jawaharlal Nehru affirmed that, "[L]ong years ago we made a tryst with destiny, and now the time comes when we shall redeem our pledge, not wholly or in full measure, but very substantially. At the stroke of the midnight hour, when the world sleeps, India will awake to life and freedom." Freedom thus came at midnight on 15 August 1947, just more than two years after the war in Europe had ended and less than two years after the Pacific War ceased. This freedom, coming at virtually the same moment as the Cold War began, is thus one of the most decisive markers of the postwar period. That this had not been achieved "in full measure" reflects the fact that immediately prior to independence, the British had excised from its Indian domain the state of Pakistan.

In the pages that follow I will reduce the question of India's recent past to a number of simple concerns: first, politics, the struggle between the different classes, castes, and political constituencies for a share of the bounty of development; second, development itself, that is the development of capitalism and the relative merits of dirigisme and neoliberalism; and finally, I will mention the partition of Pakistan itself, the emergence of Bangladesh, and the question of Pakistan's tortured relationship with America on the one hand and jihadism on the other. But first, the backstory.

## THE MUGHALS AND THE RAJ

The Mughals, a conquering dynasty and a ruling class, were a mixture of Persians, Afghanis, Turks, and native Indian converts to Islam who ruled India from 1526 to 1857. Their capital was Delhi. Unlike the Muslim dynasties that became the rulers of the Maghreb, Egypt, the Arab Middle East, or the Ottoman Empire, all of which converted most of their subject populations to Islam, the Mughals did not convert the majority of Indians. Some of the leading officials of the Mughal Empire were, in fact, Hindus; others had Hindu mothers. Although Buddhism was founded in India, Hinduism remained *the* unique religion of India; its origins and development were exclusively Indian and it remained, by far, the most widely practiced religious ideology both in India and among the worldwide Indian diaspora. Islam became India's second religion, and even after the 1947 partition of India into India and Pakistan and the migration of Muslims to the new country, the population of Muslim Indians remained at around 15 per cent.[1]

The British rule that had begun in 1757 when the East India Company defeated the Mughal army took over what was a rich and populous province. No export crop was as profitable as the opium from Bengal that was exported by British firms to China and led to the Opium Wars (1839–42 and 1850–60) and the fatal weakening of the Chinese state. Calcutta in Bengal, the headquarters of the British East India Company, remained the capital of British India until 1912 when New Delhi, on the other side of the country, was built by the British alongside the former Mughal capital of Delhi.

For a century, while British control and influence spread throughout the subcontinent from Calcutta, the Mughals continued in power. Then, in 1857 in the aftermath of a revolt of Indian soldiers against East India Company rule, the Sepoy Mutiny,[2] the British Crown took over, extirpating the Mughals but leaving more than 500 princely states of various sizes to rule over much of the country under British tutelage. Britain thereafter pulled the strings, manipulating local princes until 1947 when, simultaneously, India became independent and partition took place, separating India from the newly created Pakistan, a state ostensibly for India's Muslims but one divided into two parts, West Pakistan and East Pakistan, the two separated by a thousand miles. This politically bifurcated Pakistan lasted until 1971 when East Pakistan became independent as Bangladesh.

## POLITICS

Perhaps the greatest of the colonial world's nationalist parties was the Indian National Congress, founded in 1885 and dominating Indian politics until the elections of 2014. The Congress can claim to be not only one of the first but also the longest surviving nationalist political party. It was, as well, the model for other colonial parties like the African National Congress (ANC) of South Africa. It was tolerated by the men who ruled the Raj because its first leaders and members were literate and, for decades, biddable. Broadly secular, with few extremists whether Hindu, Muslim, or communist among its leaders, the Congress did not embrace violence in the style of the Russian revolutionaries or the Balkan or Irish nationalists in the years around the Great War. The last spasm of armed protonationalism, the Sepoy Mutiny had ended nearly thirty years before the Congress was founded. After that, for decades, in the minds of the rulers of the Raj, at least, there was complacent acceptance of foreign domination. The British, who might still on occasion gun down their Indian subjects (as in Amritsar, Punjab, in 1919) or starve them (as in Bengal in 1943) or lead them into slaughter in its global wars,[3] did not thus indulge in mass repression of the native literati. Besides, they needed them to manage India's government and economy. Although the British allowed remarkably few Indians into the upper reaches of the elite Indian Civil Service (ICS) – by 1880 there were a mere sixteen Indians among the 900 British members of the service

– they expected a small minority Indians to become, more or less, Englishmen and for this reason established several Indian universities in the middle of the nineteenth century. By the early twentieth century some members of this tiny minority had travelled to Britain to study either at private schools or even to universities. Mohandas K. Gandhi (b. 1869), the father of Indian independence, went to Alfred High School in India and law school in England. He became what was essentially an English barrister, a trade that he practiced in South Africa before returning to India. His successor as head of the independence movement was Jawaharlal Nehru (b. 1889). Nehru was a Kashmiri Brahmin whose antecedents had served the Mughals. He had an education at the poshest of private schools (Harrow) and the most illustrious of universities (Cambridge). If he hadn't been an Indian he might have been qualified to join the English ruling class as a Brahmin version of Benjamin Disraeli (a Jew who converted to Christianity and prime minister of Britain, 1868, 1874–80). Although Gandhi was a Gujerati of a merchant caste, most of Nehru's cabinet colleagues were of the superior Brahmin caste; this, his resolute nonalignment, his British manners, and his moral posturing explain why Nehru was so strongly disliked by the Americans, especially their redneck politicians.

The Congress monopolized all discussions about independence for more than half a century. It went from being a respectful spectator of British rule, to a noisy nationalist party in opposition, to a majority shareholder in independent India. From January 1930, at a meeting in Lahore where Nehru was chosen president of the party, the Congress began to advocate *purna swaraj*, "complete independence." Gaining power at independence, it ruled India almost continuously until May 2014, when it lost to the right wing and chauvinist Bharatiya Janata Party (BJP).[4] For the better part of this century, the Congress has been dominated by the Nehrus. Nowhere in any democracy in modern times can any family match this record.

Factions within the Congress Party existed from the beginning, but these were often quite unstable. Nehru himself declared in the 1940s for socialism. Like many British socialists, he remained a toff despite his adherence to left-wing ideals. In the 1950s he wobbled more towards liberalism. His leading colleagues, like Morarji Desai and Vallabhbhai Patel, led the conservative wing of the party.

In the other corner of the political ring were the two main communist parties, strong in Kerala and West Bengal where they enjoyed consistent electoral success and were a regular challenge to the Congress. In Kerala they launched a successful land reform program and devoted relatively large expenditures to education and health care. Although among the poorest states in India, Kerala was thus the most egalitarian and had the best-educated and healthiest population in the country. So although the Congress made promises about reducing poverty and increasing equality, it was unable to keep them as well as the communists. In West Bengal, India's fourth largest province, a common front led by the Communist Party of India (Marxist), ruled for thirty-four years, from 1977 to 2011. By the time of the elections of 2014, however, it was but a shadow of its former self, winning only sixteen seats. "For the first time since Independence," commented Aijaz Ahmad, "the communist left has no significant presence in the Indian parliament."[5]

By adopting socialism Nehru was on common ground with other leaders of countries that were fighting their way to a postcolonial world. These often sought a "third way" between capitalism and communism, accepting a limited kind of national welfarism with the commanding heights of the economy, including banks and railways, controlled by the state but the rest of the economy in the hands of either local capitalists or multinationals. India was also resolutely "third worldist" being one of the most active participants in the Bandung Conference of April 1955 where twenty-nine Asian and African leaders got together and proclaimed a third way in pursuit of progress. Of equal status to Nehru among nonaligned leaders was Zhou Enlai of China whom many of the Congress elite felt was a natural ally. Most of the countries at Bandung, after all, were sympathetic to the Soviet Union and many, like India and Indonesia, had substantial communist parties. Yet even tolerating communism, the governing aspiration of the Bandung participants was nonalignment, an ideology detested especially by the titans who ruled the world from Washington.

Nehru was especially optimistic that an India–China entente could be established: *Hindi-Chini bhai-bhai.* Together, he hoped, they might establish a left-leaning but neutralist Third World power bloc that would be able to face the capitalist West and communist East on equal terms. Both would naturally oppose any form of colonialism or neocolonialism. But the fly in the ointment was Tibet. Tibet and China had been antagonistic for centuries; Tibet invading China when it was strong, China invading Tibet when it was weak. In 1949 China invaded Xinjiang, and in October 1950, just after the Korean War broke out, it invaded and annexed Tibet. In both places it proceeded with the settlement of Han Chinese. In the view of Beijing, Tibet and Xinjiang were now as much Chinese territories as Alaska was American. In March 1959 the Tibetan leader, the Dalai Lama, together with a large number of Tibetans, fled to India. These Tibetan fugitives tended the flames of the "Free Tibet" movement just as fugitives from communist Cuba kept the dream of their Caribbean homeland alive in Florida.

In the early 1950s Nehru was guardedly optimistic that the matter of Tibet and the question of the virtually unmapped frontier between Tibet and India could be settled amicably. Then, in April 1954, India officially recognized Tibet as part of China. Still, the Chinese did not recognize the McMahon Line, the frontier between Assam in India and Tibet, drawn up by the British, nor did they accept that the principality of Ladakh, neighbouring Kashmir, owed allegiance to India. Although the Indians expanded their influence to the east beyond Assam and the Chinese built a road near Ladakh that joined the Chinese province of Xinjiang to its neighbour Tibet, since both were pledged to eternal amity, no problems were anticipated.

This honeymoon between the two Asian colossi lasted until 1962 when the Chinese clashed with Indian troops in the Himalayas to the west and east. There was panic, first in tea-rich Assam to the east as the frontier war escalated and then in New Delhi as unprepared Indian troops, commanded by dithering generals at the head of which stood an incompetent chief of staff, were driven out of the contested areas. In the end, after the Indian defence had virtually disintegrated, the Chinese called a halt to their advance. The Indians lost 1,383 soldiers killed and another 3,908 as prisoners of war; no figures are available from the Chinese side. Nehru, who had been forced to appeal to President Kennedy for arms, had been humiliated, and his dream of Third World solidarity and nonalignment turned to dust.

After having a stroke in January 1964, Nehru remained prime minister until May when he died in office, psychologically depleted by India's defeat in the Himalayas. After a brief interval, he was succeeded by his daughter, Indira Gandhi, who ruled from 1964 – with a short interval between 1977 and 1980. While in office Indira Gandhi commanded her fellow Indians with the authoritarianism of a Russian czarina, relying heavily on her son, Sanjay. In August 1971 New Delhi signed a treaty of Peace, Friendship and Cooperation with the Soviet Union and between 1972 and 1975 her government carried out a series of nationalizations, at the same time tightening her grip on the Indian political process. The two acts – one apparently economic and the other political – were connected; the nationalization of commercial banks placed increased opportunities for patronage in the hands of the government. Import quotas and industrial licences were used for the same purpose. Corruption and the abuse of power thus increased significantly. Unlike her father, Indira Gandhi had little taste for compromise, or for Coca-Cola. In the late 1970s in a decided snub of Washington, Coke and IBM were expelled.[6]

By 1975 with sinking popularity and having been found guilty of electoral malpractice by the largely independent judiciary, Indira Gandhi declared a state of emergency. The business community applauded this and supported the government's firm hand; Ramachandra Guha quotes a hotel owner in Delhi admitting to one journalist that with the emergency, the situation was "just wonderful. We used to have terrible problems with the unions. Now when they give us any troubles, the government just puts them in jail." J.D.R. Tata, the Mumbai industrialist and plutocrat, admitted, "The parliamentary system is not suited to our needs."[7]

The Brazilian solution seems to have arrived. The Indian Constitution was neutralized and more than 100,000 people were imprisoned without trial. Between 1975 and 1977, with 400 million living on the knife-edge of starvation *and* its democracy annulled, Indian seemed bound to become a Third World dictatorship, in the mould of the Latin American republics, or, given India's warmness to the Soviet Union, a new pro-Moscow satellite in Asia. It even boasted a secret police, the Research and Analysis Wing, which Indira Gandhi unleashed against her opponents.

Surprisingly, perhaps, with the jails full to overflowing, in early 1977 Indira Gandhi called an election. The Congress was thrown out; both she and Sanjay, her cosseted son, in fact lost their seats. Romish Thakur echoes a common view: "In voting Mrs Gandhi out in 1977, Indians showed that while they can put up with much economic injustice, they would not tolerate tyranny. In accepting defeat gracefully, Mrs Gandhi confirmed that the norms of democratic transition of power had been internalized at the highest levels of India's political elite."[8]

Her party, defeated by the a coalition known as the Janata (People's) Party, Indira Gandhi was succeeded by Morarji Desai, Nehru's long-term rival by now an eccentric octogenarian, who remained in power for just two years until Gandhi's return to power in January 1980. Among those elected were two leading lights of the Hindu chauvinist Rashtriya Swayamsevak Sangh (RSS), Atal Bihari Vajpayee and L.K. Advani. They were members of the Bharatiya Janata Party (BJP), the political front of the RSS.

Indira Gandhi's autumnal years were hardly peaceful. In June 1980, Sanjay accidentally killed himself stunt flying. Elsewhere, inflamed by her sending the Indian army to occupy their Golden Temple in Amritsar, a sect of radical Sikhs plotted her assassination. She was Sten gunned down by her Sikh bodyguard in August 1984. In response, the Congress politicians close to her organized a pogrom against the Sikhs; at least 3,000 died and another 25,000 were left homeless.[9]

Vivek Chibber provides an epitaph for the high noon of the Nehru era, the Indira–Sanjay decade:

> A ... strategy Indira and Sanjay Gandhi used was to intervene in the normal practices of promotion and circulation of top-level bureaucrats, so that the plum posts and perquisites went to those most loyal to them personally ... This was a change of momentous consequences for Indian political development. Internal conspiracy, Byzantine intrigues, shifting alliances – all this had always been a staple of Congress internal politics, even in the time of Nehru ... But the politicization of the bureaucracy was an innovation for which Indira and Sanjay could take all the credit. The natural consequence of such interference was a drastic demoralization of top level bureaucrats, under this dispensation, the criterion on which decisions were assessed was no longer their conformity to rules but their fidelity to the ruling family.[10]

After Indira's assassination in August 1984, she was succeeded by her second son, Rajiv (1984–91) who was swept to power on a huge wave of sympathy for his mother. Rajiv's time in power was, in retrospect, the last hurrah for the Nehrus and their dynastic political vision. This was the vision of an upper class privilege as exercised by an

Anglicized secular Brahmin autocracy that was relatively progressive, nonaligned, and more than just a little venal. This vision was bound to be only of limited success in breaking with the oppressive caste system and thus liberating those below them from poverty and despair. On the whole, India's substantial Muslim population continued to supported the Congress party, while Dalits and tribals moved their votes elsewhere.

Rajiv's reign also hastened the end of the idea of a "development state" boasting of the modest but hardly inconsequential "Hindu rate of growth," a growth sustained by an import substitution industrialization (ISI) that built India's factories and benefitted selected captains of industry like the Tatas of Bombay who backed it.[11] As the ISI-based economy was gradually superseded by neoliberalism, the signs seemed propitious; the economy of India actually lurched forward and poverty declined for the first time in decades. But the price of growth was increased foreign debt as well as swelling fiscal and trade deficits. Crisis returned in 1990–01 when a debt forced India to accept the IMF's "structural adjustment" program. The effect of this was to open up India to foreign competition and to further dismantle the welfare provisions of the ISI state. But, as we shall see, the reforms of the 1990s led to the "take-off" to a period of high growth rates.

Rajiv's government received praise from unsurprising quarters. The *Wall Street Journal*, the American probusiness Bible and neoliberal advocate, blessed the Indian prime minister with the moniker "Rajiv Reagan."[12] However, opposition to economic reformism both from the advocates of the poor, like the parties of the left, and from Indian business, which had profited from the exclusion of foreign firms from the Indian market, soon mounted, and Rajiv was forced to limit his advances.

But in May 1991 Rajiv was assassinated, not gunned down like his mother had been by Sikh fundamentalists from the north but by a Tamil woman from Sri Lanka to the south who used a suicide bomb to protest the Indian army's involvement in the civil war in her homeland. The grand old party of Indian nationalism would never again rule alone; when it returned, it would need more than a little help from its friends who represented a rainbow of regions, castes, classes, and ambitions.

With the assassination of Rajiv Gandhi, P.V. Narasimha Rao (1991–96) became prime minister. A quiet man, disliked by journalists for his aloofness and much disparaged by the leaders of the Congress Party, Rao has been called "the father of economic reform." His most significant act may have been to appoint another quiet man, Manmohan Singh, as finance minister. Singh, an Anglophile Punjabi, had written an Oxford thesis in the 1960s advocating trade liberalization. Back in India, he went to work as a civil servant, becoming governor of the Reserve Bank. With his appointment by "PV" Rao came Singh's chance to put theory into practice – he implemented the IMF's structural adjustment program by devaluing the rupee, removing quotas for imports, reducing tariffs, encouraging exports, and welcoming foreign direct investment. What has been described as a "great economic transformation," otherwise called an "economic miracle" and "the Manmohan Singh reforms," followed. " A new India bounded into existence," claims the journalist Rajdeep Sardesai breathlessly, "restless, aspirational, with access to the information superhighway, the silicon economies, multinationals and global opportunities. The explosion of purchasing power, the shopping mall culture, the booming service industry, new industries in leisure and tourism ... all contributed to a society where the consumer marched one step ahead of the citizen. This new India wanted efficiency, good services and the ability to get rich fast."[13]

If the future of the RSS and its political front, the BJP, was now brighter, this was not immediately apparent. The party would have to wait until the elections of 1998 before it gained real recognition and legitimacy within the Indian political system.[14] Meanwhile it increased its elected members of parliament while its RSS cadres went about the country organizing, in their hundreds of thousands, the take-over of both political and cultural organizations. "The RSS," writes Aijaz Ahmad, was to succeed in commanding "quite literally, thousands of fronts across the country, for every conceivable social category in Indian society, whether defined by caste or profession or language or religion or whatever." Its objective, he writes, was "not merely to win elections and form governments but to transform Indian society in all domains of culture, religion and civilization. Acquisition of political power is seen as a means towards that end."[15]

Not for the first time, nor the last, in the 1990s India seemed to be entering a period of accelerating crisis with fluctuating coalitions but no stable government. The phrase "India's growing crisis of governability" began to be taken up. London's liberal *Financial Times* alarmingly declared: "The Raj is now nearing collapse" and concluded that Nehru's dynasty and his economic program had been at fault. Neoliberalism was on a roll. The conventionally conservative *Economist* made the point that, "The government must dismantle an unbelievably complicated system of restraints and rewards that, over the past four decades, has securely enclosed every area of life ... India must be opened up."[16] But at the political level another development was becoming manifest: the Congress, under Sonia Gandhi, was losing altitude and the BJP was gaining. Then, in 2009, came a reprieve with the Congress forming a government at the head of a salad of smaller parties.

In the national elections of the late 1990s no party seemed able to win a clear majority although the Congress did survive. Smaller regional parties, of which there were more than forty that won one or more seats, rose and fell in popularity with their leaders attracted to the possibility of lucrative alliances. In 1999 the BJP, under Atal Bihari Vajpayee, won the election at the head of a coalition of more than twenty of these. It was he with whom the slogan "India Shining" was to become associated. But not immediately as the Congress Party had one last throw of the electoral dice: Vajpayee was succeeded in 2004 by Manmohan Singh, P.V. Rao's finance minister. Behind Singh, or perhaps at his elbow, hovered "Sonia," another Mrs. Gandhi, Italian-born and raised, widow of the martyred Rajiv and mother of Rahul. Winning the elections again in 2009, it looked like the Congress party was back in the business of ruling India, at least until the shocking corruption scandals of 2011–12 became apparent.

## GENERAL ELECTION: 2014

In the general election of April–May 2014 Indians had two main choices to replace Prime Minister Manmohan Singh who had opted for retirement. The first choice was Rahul Gandhi, Brahmin, millionaire, princeling (*shezada*) of the ruling Congress dynasty, "the family raj," whose mother, Sonia, was head of the Congress party. The second was Narendra Modi, the one-time low caste tea seller and preacher who had become chief minister of Gujarat, one of India's most dynamic states. Modi had become the darling of the RSS and the BJP. A spiffy dresser and quite telegenic, he had done wonders for the economy of Gujarat, his native state, as was broadly acknowledged especially by the local captains of industry. His popularity among Indians generally, and especially the aspiring urban middle class, had also risen prior to the election while that of Rahul Gandhi had stalled. *The Economist*, in a scathing comment on Rahul after the Lok Sabha (lower house) election results came in, noted: "Rahul, who had been long groomed for leadership, is a dud; earnest, but lacking in energy, ideas, strategy, and, crucially, the ability to connect with party workers and voters."[17] While hope still breathed in the breasts of the Congress party faithful that Rahul's sister might ditch her dodgy husband and take up the family patrimony, it did look like the Gandhis, in common with other Third World dynasties that came to power with the end of colonialism, had reached the end of the line.

Modi carried quite different baggage. The BJP, unlike Congress, which was ostensibly secular (if run by and for the two top castes), was devotional. The party ideology was centred on "Hindutva," Hindu supremacy (in a country which, it was predicted, was soon to have the largest Muslim population in the world). But more alarming: in Gujarat, while he was chief minister, he had turned a blind eye to a February 2002 pogrom in which at least 1,000 Muslims were slaughtered by frenzied Hindu militants. Modi may even have approved of this pogrom. In any case, Edward Luce, at the time a South Asian correspondent for the *Financial Times*, wrote, "For three days and nights, mobs of fanatics went from house to house armed with electoral rolls (to identify the religion of each household), dragged women and children out of their homes, poured kerosene down their throats and ignited them to crows of cheering onlookers. The police in Ahmedabad and other Gujerati cities did not intervene [for 72 hours]." Six months later Modi was reelected as chief minister of the state in a landslide. He was banned from visiting the US and Britain.

Jawaharlal Nehru had labelled the RSS a "fascist element."[18] In power, it had undertaken a program to "saffronize" the Indian curriculum in schools and even in universities (saffron being the colour sacred to Hinduism). The attempt to wipe out rival interpretations of history, in this case Indian history, has been called by Wendy Doniger, the leading American historian of Hinduism, appropriately, "fascist bigotry." Yet while others commented on the fascist aspects of the BJP ideology, writers in the business press praised Modi's emphasis on economic reform, Gideon Rachman of the *Financial Times* among them, who wrote, "Mr Modi emphasizes economic policies that are focused on encouraging growth, helping business and reducing the size of government. This kind of liberal agenda is no longer so fashionable in the west. But it has been crowned with economic and political success in Gujarat."[19]

The election of 2014 was held amid a slowing economy, a record high current account deficit, and a falling rupee. In the election results announced on 16 May, the National Democratic Alliance, a coalition led by the BJP, won 336 out of 543 seats. The party itself scored 282 seats, 53 per cent of the total and quite enough to govern without partners. "It's a Tsunami!" trilled Rajdeep Sardesai in his study of the 2014 election.[20] The United Progressive Alliance led by the Congress was crushed with a mere fifty-eight seats and the tiny, reforming, Aam Aadmi party, regarding which there had been much speculation and journalistic chatter in the weeks before the election, won a mere four seats, all in Punjab. Regional parties also scored victories; the regional party of Tamil Nadu in south India, led by the colourful Jayalithaa, an ex-actress and long-time pork-barreler, for instance, won thirty-seven seats.[21] She was not to be, alas for her followers, much longer in this world.

By June it was obvious that the BJP-led government strongly supported the removal of measures that, according to neoliberal economists and representatives of business, were "holding back job creation in the country." The object of this labour legislation was meant to conform to the government policy of increasing the share of manufacturing from the present 15–16 per cent to 25 per cent by 2020 and, thereby, create 100 million new jobs. India, thus, would step into the shoes of China whose preeminent position as "workshop of the world" would be undermined by the increase in worker's wages. In the "flying geese" metaphor, India would become the leading goose as China, like Japan, fell behind the flock.

The left-leaning *Economic & Political Weekly* was unsurprised by Modi's program (as opposed to his populist promises). In an article with the title "Saffron Neo-liberalism," Anand Teitumbde, leading commentator on the condition of the Dalits, noted:

> Modi has been setting the ground for the creation and opportunities for trade and investment for the benefit of big business, which invested heavily in him. While the reforms have always been sold

> in the name of the people and justified with the dubious "trickle-down" theory, they are actually meant to promote the interests of capital through the laissez-faire economy and are therefore anti-labour. Privatisation of public sector units, commercialisation of public services, handing over of natural resources to the private sector, reliance on the market mechanism for pricing, fiscal measures to incapacitate the state to undertake any economic activity and thereby promote private interests, are the typical contents of neo-liberal policies.[22]

But the honeymoon of Narendra Modi was sooner or later bound to end. This came in early February with a municipal election in the city-state of New Delhi. In that election the AAP won a stunning 67 out of 70 seats, with the BJP winning only three, and the Congress gaining not a single seat. Commentators, excluding those who were aligned with the Congress, used the words "spectacular" and "turning point" to describe the outcome. "Is the Congress finished?" asked Rajdeep Sardesai of the once-commanding party of the freedom movement.[23] Perhaps. But if so it was perhaps not alone in its fate. In the legislative assembly elections held in October–November 2015 in Bihar, the poorest Indian state, the BJP campaign came unstuck and the opposition coalition, grouping six parties, cleaned up. *The Times of India* pronounced that, "Modi's honeymoon is over."[24]

## THE ROAD TO NEOLIBERALISM

By 1950 an estimated 360 million people lived in India with 85 per cent of them living in villages and deriving their livelihoods from agriculture. But agriculture was in dire straits as food production had increased only marginally since the beginning of the century and was not keeping up with population increases. Although there was no excess of land in India, the country's main problem was inefficient and undercapitalized farming. Compared to other countries, India's rice and wheat yields per acre were low – indeed India's average crop yields were among the lowest in the world. Food had to be imported and paid for by exports. Even with imports, Indians suffered from malnutrition and the diseases associated with it such as tuberculosis.

Even before independence, however, several major projects had either been planned or put underway that sought to increase food production and make it more efficient. In 1951 India launched its first Five-Year Plan, a pioneer in Asia and from a page of the Soviet manual of rapid industrialization by privileging heavy industry over the production of consumer goods. India's markets, like those of other economies that had adopted the dirigiste model, thus became limited by high duties or even closed to all but the most necessary imports, with the result that a huge range of Indian consumer goods, from cars to ceramics, continued to be Indian made.

We might back up a bit by reminiscing about economic growth in general. First, remember that our yardstick is called "growth rate of per capita GDP," that is, the annual rise in economic increase of each person in a country, or the national GDP growth divided by the population. (If growth occurred from year to year without any population increase then it would be much higher on a per capita basis; ie. the same number of people would be producing more stuff.) Second, recall that in the last half century of colonial rule, India's national income grew at a rate of 0.7 per cent per year.[25] It seems fair to say that this has been seen as the most telling criticism of colonialism – that is, that it retarded economic development and thus guaranteed widespread poverty.

To jump ahead, the Indian GDP growth rate attained 5.9 per cent in the 1990s and 7.6 per cent from 2000–11 reaching, in 2006–07, a vertiginous, and probably hallucinogenic, 10.8 per cent. This was seen as the justification for neoliberalism and proof that the BJP motto "India Shining" might be actually realized. The improved growth rate seemed to fit in nicely with the 1950s theory that economic development, that is industrialization, would globally "lift all boats," that it would benefit rich and poor alike, although obviously not in equal measure. As we shall see, although this passed for common knowledge, or even economic theory, right into the 1980s and '90s, it was mistaken. By 2016 the richest 1 per cent of the world's population controlled half of global wealth.[26]

Back to India: while Nehru explicitly claimed that he, and by extension, India, were socialist, both were quite distinct from the communist leaders and parties of Europe who called themselves socialist but were more accurately described as communists and their states, dictatorships. Rather than the socialist states of Eastern Europe, the economy of India up to the 1980s resembled several postwar economies in Latin America in that it was dirigiste, and its key development policy was "import substitution industrialization" (ISI), as we have mentioned above. This policy called for heavy state intervention in the market to assure that sovereign, national, industries would have a chance against the more well-developed and advanced exporters from the West. So in India, like Argentina, foreign-made cars carried such a heavy import tariff that locally produced cars were bound to be cheaper. What was more, with ISI Indians would gain experience in manufacturing; peasants would become proletarians. In India a car manufacturing industry circumvented the expensive experimental stage by copying the design of British Austins, Italian Fiats, and Japanese Suzukis. As a consequence, these were practically the only cars on Indian roads until the 1980s. But the real importance of ISI was that it led to the development of export markets of manufactures of all kinds. Alice Amsden calls ISI "the mother of exports," arguing that, in spite of its name, ISI was a necessary first step in any strategy of export growth.[27]

There were several consequences of Indian development policy. On the positive side, industry did expand, and the Indian economy did diversify away from agriculture, which British colonial policy had seen as the natural function of subordinate economies. Too, both the class of national capitalists and the working class expanded. This guaranteed the existence of left-wing politics, the Indian form of which was communist rather than socialist parties. But these communist parties, like those of France and Italy, worked within and not against the liberal democratic state. On the negative side, preference for local manufactures and local capitalists stifled innovation while an overweight and often indolent bureaucracy, which supervised the entire manufacturing economy, choked initiative. Too, small Indian entrepreneurs obviously could not compete against the state-supported giants. Agriculture was stifled. The export in agricultural commodities was governed by restrictions in the form of trade quotas or licences; growers of cotton, for instance, had to wait upon bureaucrats who set prices and quotas. Private investors were hampered in their response to signals from the market. It was this multiplicity of permits and procedures needed for permission to carry on capitalist economic activity of most kinds that led India to be known derisively as the "Permit Raj."

Now the Permit Raj had slowly unfolded under a handful of what Nehru had called the "kings of industry," rulers of the manufacturing branch of the national bourgeoisie. In the view of these kings, a strong state role in the economy was consistent with assuring their own monopolies within the national economy. The state would provide a trellis of economic regulations up which certain Indian industries might climb. "From the very earliest discussions of Indian industrial planning, the domestic capitalist class was given every assurance that the new state would be singularly committed to using public monies as a means of accelerating the development of private industry."[28] But industry was only part of the story, for in common with other Third World economies where agriculture provided between 30 and 50 per cent of national income, India's agriculture accounted for half of India's export earnings.

Recall that in the first decade of independence the Indian economy was expanding at a faster rate than ever before although this was during the *Trente Glorieuses*, the Camelot years of global capitalism. In the last half century of colonial rule, as we have mentioned, national income grew around 0.7 per cent per year; from 1948 to 1969 it grew at 3.3 per cent per year. In recent decades it has grown at between 5.2 and 7.6 per cent per year. In 2014–15 it grew at 7.3 per cent.[29]

So up through the 1950s and into the 1980s we see a dirigiste India becoming increasingly, and even remarkably, industrialized under the aegis of ISI. Then in the 1980s, after several decades of criticism of the corruptions and restrictions of free enterprise by the regulations of the "Permit Raj" by big business and, increasingly, its international partners, there were two changes.[30] First, Prime Minister Rajiv Gandhi initiated the liberalization of the Indian economy under pressure from General Agreement on Trade and Tariffs (GATT), the global organization dominated by the G7 economies, especially the United States. His first reforms came in early 1985. Between 1986 and 1994 GATT, supported by the World Bank, organized the Uruguay Round of free trade agreements. Right across the board tariffs in developing countries dropped sharply – in Argentina average tariffs fell from 38.2 per cent to 30.0 per cent, in Brazil from 40.7 per cent to 27 per cent, and in India from a whopping 71.4 per cent to 32.4 per cent.

## CHEERS AND FADING LUSTRE

Still, in the early 1990s, despondency reigned both over the state of the Indian economy and particularly over its management by the ruling party. But, surprisingly, as the next decade rolled on, the economy of India, by now under the spell of neoliberalism, picked up. In 2002 – when the acronym BRIC was coined – India, together with Brazil, Russia, and China, looked like they might drive global economic growth for the next decade. Two years later with the Congress-led United Progressive Alliance (UPA) in power, Manmohan Singh, the Oxford-trained, neoliberal finance minister, became prime minister. Suddenly, India was able to boast of an investment boom and a quite remarkable level of growth. Praises were duly hymned by a range of liberal writers while conservative economists, their predictions apparently fulfilled, approached ecstasy. In 2009 the UPA under Singh triumphed once more. But the dark side of India's economic miracle remained studiously ignored. "Under the current incumbent, Manmohan Singh," Anderson pointed out at the time:

> [corruption] has reached an all time high, with the defalcation from the public purse of some $40 billion in crooked telecom contracts alone, while the Prime Minister – everywhere lauded as the image of probity – looked the other way. As the costs of securing a seat in parliament have risen vertically, so it has increasingly become a club of the super-rich; one out of five MPs is a dollar millionaire, and the total assets of its 543 members can be reckoned at $2 billion, in a society where over half the population lives on less than $2 dollars a day.[31]

After the BJP government fell in 2003 India's GDP growth had continued to rise – from 5.9 per cent in 1999 to a stellar 8.3 per cent in 2003 and a wondrous 10.4 per cent in 2010 before dropping to just over 7 per cent in 2014. This led to lavish predictions and confident assumptions that neoliberal prescriptions had worked. Deepak Lal spoke of an "economic miracle": "[T]he acceleration of industrial growth from 6.4 percent to 8.4, and to 10.8 percent in 2006–07, suggests that the economic effects of the ending of the Permit Raj in 1991 and India's growing integration with the world economy are now at last bearing fruit ... India's recent trends augur well for the future growth of the industrial sector." Fareed Zakaria, the most successful Indian-born journalist in America swooned.[32] Under his hand, in April 2004, *Newsweek* announced that India was no longer a backward Third World country; "it was now 'a good place to do business,' indeed, 'an investment-worthy partner.'"

Thomas Friedman, *The New York Times*'s irrepressible champion of globalization, explained hyperbolically in 2005 that twenty years earlier India "was known as a country of snake charmers, poor people, and Mother Teresa. Today its image has been recalibrated. Now it is also seen as a country of brainy people and computer wizards." Jeffrey Sachs in *The End of Poverty* cheered "India's historic escape from poverty." He proclaimed that "the return of China and India to global economic prominence" would "reshape global politics and society" in the twenty-first century. In a 2011 book, still praising globalization and confident in the economies of China, India, and Brazil, although apparently alarmed by the loss of jobs in the US and the huge levels of pollution consequent to Chinese industrialization, Sachs reassured his readers that "the modern market economy is an amazing human contrivance." The term "New India" became current.[33]

Statistics, of course, did capture the giddy reality of India, even though Zakaria, together with others of the globalization drill team, ignored them in favour of anecdotal evidence. As a consequence, the actual transformation of the Indian economy remained obscured with its cheerleaders failing to acknowledge that it was services, especially information technology (IT), not industry and manufacturing that had been the main growth agent since the 1980s. The development economist Dani Rodrik, an often sceptical Keynesian, warned about this:

> As India's example demonstrates, it may be possible sometimes to generate growth on the back of tradable services, such as software and information technologies (IT). But as India also shows, there are limits to the extent of structural change such a model can accomplish. The trouble is that IT industries rely on education and skills that only a small part of the country's huge workforce possesses. Manufacturing industries have much greater potential to absorb the surplus labour presently employed in traditional agriculture or informal activities. As India has not been able to demonstrate comparable success in manufactures, its economy generates far too high-productivity jobs for the unskilled workforce with which it will remain abundantly endowed for some time.[34]

The point that well over two-thirds of the population lived on less than two dollars a day, the poverty line accepted by the UN and most aid agencies, was absent among the cheers of the enthusiasts. *The Times of India* reported on 12 July 2010 that eight Indian states had more poor than twenty-six of the poorest African nations. Four years later (7 July 2014) the same newspaper reported that by one yardstick 29.5 per cent of the population lived below the poverty line and by another the figure, 21.9 per cent. Wikipedia noted that India had 17.5 per cent of the world's population and 20.6 per cent of the world's poorest in 2011. So by 2012, the average per capita monthly income of Indians was still less than half of that of Chinese (€240 compared to €520).[35]

In 2011, in common with the economies of the other BRIC states, not to mention much of the EU, India's economy stalled. Prometheus, it seems, had flown too close to the IT sun; writers like Jayati Ghosh had warned in the first years of the century that while India's Silicon Valley computer and call centres had provided a remarkable 1.3 million jobs, this was out of a workforce of 400 million. Rural employment had in fact declined and so had industrial employment.[36] By 2012 GDP growth was down to 5 per cent; better than the "Hindu rate," to be sure, but only half the 2010 rate. There was talk of the miracle "emerging economies" like India, declining. In the last quarter of 2013, GDP growth sank to 4.7 per cent where it remained for fiscal 2013–14. Manufacturing had fallen by 1.9 per cent compared with the previous year. With more than half of India's 1.2 billion people under twenty-five years, the growth rate would have to remain at about 8 per cent to generate enough jobs for the 13 million people entering the workforce each year.

In 2008, Amit Bhaduri wrote of "predatory growth," that is the enrichment of the top decile of the population at the expense of the lowest. Thus, according to *Forbes* magazine, in 2007 India claimed the distinction of having forty billionaires, Japan had a mere twenty-four, China seventeen, and France, fourteen. "The combined wealth of Indian billionaires increased from $106 to $170 billion in a single year," he complained. At the same time 303 million lived in "utter misery." "Nearly half of Indian children under six years suffer from underweight and malnutrition, nearly 80 per cent from anaemia, while some 40 per cent of Indian adults suffer from chronic energy deficit ... [M]ore than three in four Indians do not have a daily income of $2."[37] By 2012, the average per capita monthly income of Indians was less than half that of Chinese (€240 compared to €520). Two writers in the *Financial Times* commented on the precarious position of the middle strata as the growth of emerging economies began to slow down. Indians themselves seemed to recognize the inability of their government to manage the economy.

In 2014 the list of Indian billionaires had expanded to one hundred, again according to *Forbes.*[38] And according to the UN by 2020, India will be the most populous nation in the world.[39] By then, unless the present downward trend in growth is again reversed, there could be two hundred billionaires and two billion paupers.

Several questions have been prompted by India's roller coaster ride and its comparison to China, two of which were asked of the Indian economist, Jayati Ghosh, in the website of the German newsmagazine *Der Spiegel* in August 2013.

> *DER SPIEGEL*: China is suffering from a banking crisis, and in India ... economic growth has almost halved, and panicking investors are abandoning the rupee. Is the Asian Era over before it has even begun?
> GHOSH: Our two countries have big problems, but the situation is completely different. China is fundamentally strong; it has a huge trade surplus. India, however, suffers from a huge current account deficit, which we are trying to partly fill with hot money, or speculative investment, from abroad. China first and foremost has to control its illegal shadow banks, but that is not at all comparable to the mess that we are now facing in India.
> *DER SPIEGEL*: India in particular is falling behind in the race to catch up to industrialization. Why is it so much more difficult for your country than for China to escape poverty?"
> GHOSH: We can't manage the simplest things, because our starting point was completely different. When China began its reform process at the end of the 1970s, almost everybody there already had enough to eat. There were roads in almost every village, and there was medical care. In China, society was by and large equal. In contrast, a third of Indians still don't have electricity. We fight against the legacy of a caste system, which condones inequality and discrimination. India's elites put up with conditions which are extremely damaging.[40]

Not mentioned here are the questions of global warming and pollution. With air pollution twenty times higher than the safe limit,

Delhi was moving up there to pass Beijing and certain Polish cities in the championship league of metropolises with unbreathable air.

## PAKISTAN

Pakistan was invented by the British and has continued to exist thanks to the life support of the Americans. It is therefore like Israel, a neocolonial protectorate that has survived thanks in large part to the postwar patronage that derived from the Cold War. Both, Pakistan, born at midnight on 15 August 1947 and Israel, born on 14 May 1948, were the result of partitions: one of India, the other of Palestine. The partition of India, hasty and arbitrary in conception and catastrophic in fulfilment, is known to history simply as "the Partition."[41]

After British power crumbled in South Asia and the Middle East, both Pakistan and Israel were sustained by America. And both have claimed to be, in the words of General Ayub Khan (1958–69), America's "most allied ally." But their fates have been radically divergent. Whereas Israel has continued to expand, Pakistan, impractically conceived in two unequal parts separated by a thousand miles, in 1971 broke into two. When the army from West Pakistan launched an invasion to prevent the separation of East Pakistan it was defeated by the Indian army, not for the first time. Israel's defence force has, by contrast, won wars against all comers.

With the breakup of the original Pakistan, West Pakistan became simply "Pakistan." Quite conceivably this Pakistan should have included Kashmir, which at the time of Partition in 1947 was predominately Muslim although ruled by a Hindu prince. But the Indian army intervened and occupied the province that has remained in a state of siege ever since with Muslim insurgents, supported by the Pakistani army and guided by the ISI, the intelligence branch of the armed forces, regularly attacking the Indian forces of law and order.

The newly separated Pakistan was dominated by Punjabis but with large and powerful populations of Sindis, Pushtuns, and *muhajirs* and occupied the historic lands of the Indus or Harappan civilization.[42] Its influences were from the Arab Middle East, Iran, and Turkic Central Asia, and it shared frontiers with the states of Central Asia, especially Afghanistan, as well as India. East Pakistan became

"Bangladesh." Its population was more homogenous being mainly Bengali; its people therefore were close in culture to the Hindus of West Bengal state in India. Both East and West Pakistanis were predominately Sunni Muslims.

From its birth, the population of Pakistan skyrocketed. In 1950 the population of the undivided Pakistan was just over 40 million; by 2014 the population of Pakistan proper was 182.5 million and that of Bangladesh 157 million, together some 20 million more than the population of the US.

## PRAETORIANS

It was popular from the late 1950s to refer to any number of bumbling despots in uniform as "praetorians."[43] Pakistan has regularly, even normally, been ruled by such praetorians since the time of Ayub Khan (1958–69), a Punjabi general from one of the families with the largest landholding in the country. Although he was educated in colonial times at Sandhurst, Britain's hatchery for martinets, Khan saw the writing on the cheques and quite efficiently grabbed on to America's coattails, turning himself into Washington's faithful ally by enrolling Pakistan in Asia's main anti-Soviet military alliances, CENTO (Central Treaty Organization) and SEATO (Southeast Asia Treaty Organization), both Asian imitations of NATO.[44] India was a member of neither.

Ayub Khan made himself the chief of the general staff, prime minister, and president and ruled over Pakistan during its golden years, such as they were. In 1962, after India was defeated by China, he sent several thousand soldiers in mufti to stir up rebellion in Kashmir. This was a failure and led to the second war between India and Pakistan, the first having taken place at the time of Partition (1947).[45] It was under Khan that Pakistan's military intelligence organization, the Inter-Services Intelligence (ISI), began to meddle in the affairs of Afghanistan. The strategy was to create a counter-weight against the loss of Kashmir and the threat of India. The dominant population of Afghanistan was Pushtun, whose numbers were in fact greater on the Pakistanis side of the border. (The division of the Pushtuns on both sides of the artificial Durand Line was another disastrous partition organized by the rulers of the British Empire to shore up the defence of Central and South Asia.)

Now, the Pakistani military, dominated by the ISI, absorbed somewhere between 25 and 70 per cent of the Pakistani federal budget. It was in fact a state within a state, "an army with a country," with its own hierarchy and its own sources of finance, sustained by its own industries, which included heroin production.[46] Still, it was strongly supported by Washington as a regional ally against Soviet expansion. The American secretary of state for most of the 1950s, John Foster Dulles, had praised the Pakistani military for having the "moral courage to do its part in resisting communism." It was Dulles who explained that "the United States of America does not have friends, it has interests."[47]

The moment of opportunity for the ISI came with the Soviet invasion of late 1979 and the rise of the Taliban, the irregular force of Muslim fighters. Many of the leading Pakistani generals were to become supporters of the Taliban; more than merely advisers, they organized logistical support and training especially from Peshawar, the major Pakistani *entrepôt* on the road to Kabul. While funding for the *mujahideen* came from Saudi Arabia and the Gulf states, military *materiél* continued to be routinely shipped from the US through the port of Karachi, the US supplying 27 per cent of Pakistan's arms supplies.[48]

The role of the ISI in both Afghanistan and Kashmir was hardly a secret. General Musharraf who seized power in Pakistan in 1999 had warned Washington, "Remember my words; if the ISI is not with you and Pakistan is not with you ... you will lose Afghanistan." In November 2008 a team of Pakistani suicide gunman associated with the al-Qaeda-linked, Kashmir-based jihad organization Lashkar-e-Taiba, landed from the sea to attack targets in Mumbai, India's commercial capital, killing more than 180 people. The only survivor of the attack admitted to having been trained by the ISI.[49]

Ayub Khan was succeeded by Zulfikar Ali Bhutto of the Pakistan Peoples' Party. Bhutto, a brilliant populist and more than a little in the mould of Juan Perón, was certainly the most outstanding figure in Pakistan's short history. His threats to the military and to the civilian bourgeoisie menaced the status quo and he was overthrown by his own army chief-of-staff, Muhammad Zia-ul-Haq (1977–86), a fate similar to that which was to befall radical populists from Argentina to Haiti, to Ghana, and to Indonesia. Although there was global protest against the victimization of Bhutto, the Pakistani judiciary stood at the side of the military, and Bhutto was hanged.

It was Zia who turned Pakistan towards the Gulf and to the jihadist dogmas of Wahhabi Islam, which were implicitly anti-American. We will see more of this in the next chapter. But Zia's grip on Islamic radicalism soon evaded his, and his successors' control. In 1979, the year of the Iranian revolution and the hostage crisis in Tehran, radicals burned American cultural institutions in Pakistan and besieged the American embassy. Zia apologized, but from then on relations with Washington were always uncertain. He seemed, nonetheless, to have made powerful enemies within the ruling groups of the country, perhaps even the ISI. He was assassinated in August 1988 aboard a redesigned luxury Hercules C-130, together with the US ambassador and a number of key military advisers. The FBI investigated, but the assassins remained undiscovered or at least unacknowledged.[50]

With the immolation of Zia-ul-Haq power returned to the class of civilian plutocrats and oligarchs. For most of the 1990s it was shared between Benazir Bhutto (b. 1953), daughter of Zulfakir Ali Bhutto, and Mian Nawaz Sharif (b. 1949), one of Pakistan's richest men. After the execution of her father, Benazir had fled to London with her husband, Asif Zardari, in his early years known as "Mr 10 per cent" and later upgraded to "Mr 20 per cent." Both Benazir and Sharif sought to repair the damage done by Zia to Pakistani–American relations. One columnist in the English-language newspaper, *The News*, referred to Sharif and his brothers as "the greatest lackeys of the Americans that we have ever had."[51]

## DARKNESS

Pakistan stands out from the richer states of the region like India or Iran for the fact of its apparently irreducible poverty. This has been guaranteed by its unreformed, feudal, landholding system and the commanding role that the army, which forms a privileged enclave and consumes an overwhelming proportion of national finances, plays in its politics and economy.[52] As far as feudalism is concerned, 2,000 families own around 70 per cent of the cultivable land. Four out of five seats in Pakistan's national assembly have normally been held by this oligarchy or their nominees. Beneath this elite, the countryside sustains a thin layer of middle and rich peasants and below them a mass of landless, impoverished, indebted, and immiserated farm labourers that some sources refer to as serfs. Nearly two-thirds of Pakistanis (60.3 per cent) live below the UN's statistical poverty line, about the same figure as in the poorest Indian state, Bihar (61.3 per cent).[53] This figure should also be compared to India's 22–29 per cent. There are, in fact, proportionately fewer paupers in most African states than there are in

Pakistan. Here is Ahmed Rashid, author of the indispensible trilogy that examines the question of "Pakistan on the Brink":

> The UN estimates that Pakistan's 185 million population will grow to 275 million by 2050. Despite its primarily agricultural economy, Pakistan can barely support its existing population, and it is difficult to see how water, food, land and services will be available for 90 million more people. One-third of Pakistanis today lack drinking water, another 77 million have unreliable food sources, and half the school-age children do not go to school. The literacy rate is 57 per cent, the lowest in South Asia and not much better than the 52 per cent that prevailed at the creation of Pakistan ... The country needs at least 9 percent annual growth rate to employ its under-twenties who make up 60 percent of the population.[54]

In the elections of December 1988 Benazir Bhutto was elected as prime minister. At the age of thirty-five she became the first woman to head a government in a contemporary Muslim state. In February 1997 Sharif succeed her and remained in power until October 1999 when there was another military coup that installed General Pervez Musharraf in power. It was Musharraf who ruled on 9/11 in the aftermath of which President Bush insisted that Pakistan should be 100 per cent for or 100 per cent against America in the War on Terror. Bush's deputy secretary of state made it clear that if Pakistan opted for the Taliban it "should be prepared to be bombed into the Stone Age." The general prudently opted to support the Americans.

Musharraf remained president of Pakistan from 2001 to the end of 2007 while the invasions of both Afghanistan and Iraq became more horrendous. In this period, while Musharrif's government officially conformed to the demands of Washington, the jihad, in the form of the TTP (Tareek-e-Taliban Pakistan), spread to the borderlands between Pakistan and Afghanistan. In 2008, Musharraf ran for office again. Misjudging his popularity, his party was crushed and he was forced to step down in the face of impeachment proceedings.

The ISI clearly considered the TTP an asset. The TTP announced their presence by carrying out attacks and suicide bombings against security forces, Shi'as, Christian churches, and civilian groups. On 16 December 2014 it was responsible for the killing of 132 school children in an assault on a military-run school in Peshawar. In retaliation, American drones killed TTP militants together with hundreds of innocents that the drone operators had mistakenly identified as enemies.[55]

In his first major speech after the coup that brought him to power, General Musharraf had stared into the abyss of what seemed to be Pakistan's future: "Fifty-two years ago we started with a beacon of hope and today that beacon is no more and we stand in darkness. There is despondency and hopelessness surrounding us with no light visible anywhere around. The slide down has been gradual but has rapidly accelerated in the last many years." Between 2003 and 2013, there were more than 40,000 terror-related casualties in Pakistan including sixty suicide bombings in 2007 alone.[56]

In December 2007 Benazir Bhutto returned to Pakistan and on the 27th she was assassinated. A month earlier, London journalist Tariq Ali had written gloomily: "In Pakistan ... the long night continues." In September 2008, Asif Ali Zardari, Benazir's much-vilified husband, was elected president, just in time to see Pakistani–Indian relations reach their lowest point with the attack on Mumbai of the Lashkar-e-Taiba.

In early 2011, while Zadari was president, the "holy warrior sheikh," Osama bin Laden, was "martyred" by American Special Forces in his house in Abbottabad, near the Pakistani military academy. Officially, at least, the Pakistanis claimed ignorance of the assassination, Zardari congratulating President Obama when he learned of it. The distinguished American journalist, Seymour Hersh, however, claimed that the assassination was a setup and that both the Pakistanis and the Americans had long planned it. At the end of the same year the cover of the *Atlantic Monthly* referred to Pakistan as "The Ally from Hell."[57]

With the regular slaughter of Pakistani civilians by American drones, the assassination brought US–Pakistani relations to a new low. What was to be done? Although military aid alone cost Washington $2–3 million a year, the country remained dominated by praetorians some, at least, who backed the Taliban in Afghanistan and *Lashkar* in Pakistan. The praetorians for their part were unnerved by the agreement between president Obama and Prime Minister Modi, which aimed to strengthen US–Indian ties.[58] The Americans were anxious lest if they cut and ran, as they had in Iraq and Afghanistan, the *mujahideen* might seize a state with nuclear weapons. Bin Laden had called on Pakistan to "prepare for the jihad" that should "include a nuclear force."

# 7

# Middle East Islamisms

In the late 1980s two Muslim men, both Sunnis, one an Egyptian and the other a Saudi, established a secret militant network that was called in Arabic, *al-Qaeda,* a word meaning, simply, "the base." The Egyptian was the physician, Ayman al-Zawahiri, who became the network's leading ideologue and the Saudi, Osama bin Laden, son of a fabulously wealthy contractor who was, himself, a Yemeni but who operated in Saudi Arabia. In December 2001, three months after 9/11, al-Zawahiri posted online a text called *Knights under the Prophet's Banner* in which he rationalized the attacks on New York and Washington. He called the US, "the faraway enemy" (to distinguish Americans from "the nearby enemy," the corrupt apostates who ruled the Middle East and the Maghreb). He signed the text, and extracts were published in a London-based Saudi newspaper. In it he proclaimed that the struggle between Islam and the West was universal and that the former was bound to prevail.[1] This struggle was considered a jihad and those who undertook it, *mujahideen*. They also came to be known as Salafists, jihadists, jihadis, and, in French, *intégrists.*[2] Their essential doctrine was a puritanical form of Islam known as Wahhabism, which had been established in Saudi Arabia in the eighteenth century and came to be the governing ideology there.[3]

The time was ripe. With the defeat of the Soviets in Afghanistan in early 1989, the polyglot army of foreign jihadis that had aligned themselves with the Afghani Taliban and made Peshawar in Pakistan their headquarters, began to disperse to new homes and new struggles in Bosnia, Algeria, Egypt, Tajikistan, and Chechnya. The jihad intensified in 1992. In February 1993, the first attempt to blow up the World Trade Centre (WTC) in New York was made. Thereafter jihadi activity was marked in Egypt, Bosnia, Algeria, West Africa, and in Western Europe.[4]

The war of the jihadis was guided by the writings of a succession of Muslim thinkers including the Egyptian Sayyid Qutb whose prominence had threatened the secular nationalist Colonel Abdul Gamal Nasser (1951–70). These writings were but an element in a long line of struggles against Western powers that went back to the nineteenth century. In the postwar period – before the invasion and occupation of Iraq in 2002 – the most violent of these was the *guerre sale* of the Algerians who sought independence from France. Smoldering at the end of the war in Europe, the Algerian war had burst into open flame in 1954 and lasted until 1962 when Algeria became independent. Fought in France as well as Algeria, this war was essentially secular. It installed a dictatorship that was broadly progressive and "Third Worldist" but by the 1980s had come to have much in common with the secular dictatorships elsewhere in the Arab world – for instance in Egypt, Tunisia, and Iraq. Those dictatorships, avowedly anticommunist, were normally backed by the West.

From independence, Algeria had been ruled by the Front de la Libération Nationale (FLN), which led the struggle against French colonialism. Although Islam had always been present in the politics of colonial Algeria, Islamists, in the contemporary sense, had been a permanent feature of national political life only since the 1980s. Their main political party, the Front Islamique du Salut (FIS), founded in early 1989 after a political upsurge in October 1988, made an impressive start in the elections of June 1990, taking control of the majority of provincial (*wilayat*) governments and those in all major cities. But the ruling FLN, increasingly aligned with France, had other plans. Those included securing the dominance of its own oligarchs. Although the chiefs of the FLN may have expressed a rhetorical concern for the well being of the country's impoverished urban youth (growing in numbers) and their yearning for less poverty and inequality, its ties to the West and particularly France demonstrated its neocolonial moorings.

As in Iran in the 1970s, in the 1980s Algerian youths fell in behind FIS leaders to fight the FLN oligarchs for power. A second savage war was the outcome. This took place between 1992 and 1997. It peaked in 1994–95 and was arguably, like the revolution in Iran, no less of a religious than a class struggle; if this is indeed the case then the question might be less about "the war for Muslim minds," the title of Gilles

Kepel's study, and more about the war for Algerian bodies and control over Algerian oil. At any rate, in the end, unlike Iran where the shah was driven into exile and his entourage liquidated, in Algeria, as later in Egypt, the *ancien régime* prevailed, and after huge bloodshed the Islamist movement was crushed. And like Iran, and indeed almost all of the former Third World, Algeria's FLN rulers emerged from the crucible of social struggle more than ever devoted to neoliberalism and neocolonialism.[5]

In 1992 bin Laden and al-Zawahiri set up a sanctuary in the Sudan by oiling the pariah regime of Hassan al-Turabi with hundreds of millions of dollars. From there for several years (1992–96) they would direct operations against their enemies on all sides – especially the Muslim regimes including, obviously, all Shi'a regimes, like Iran. They also set themselves against all regimes, like those in America, France, and Israel, which actively sought to dominate the Middle East and oppress Muslims. Even the Saudi monarchy that had embraced the dogmas of Wahhabism and bankrolled the Salafis, as well as anti-Shi'a forces like Saddam Hussein's, was denounced as being heretical.

It was Khartoum that was to become, like Moscow in the 1930s, the headquarters of an international conspiracy to change the world. Al-Qaeda would be the new Comintern.[6] Other centres, including London (called "Londonstan"), would be branch headquarters from which propaganda work, often via the Internet, and finance would be organized. While in the West after the fall of the Soviet Union there was a period of comfortable economic expansion and a certain political euphoria, in the Muslim world these were years of tension marked by the consolidation of neoliberalism, the dictatorship of the mullahs in Iran, and of increasing Wahhabi and Salafi radicalism sustained by money and propaganda provided by Saudi Arabia and the Gulf monarchies. The American invasions of Iraq in 1990–91 and then again in 2003, of Afghanistan in 2001, and of Somalia in late 1992, the struggles of the Bosnian Muslims against the Serbs in the mid-1990s, and the war in Syria from 2011 all provided the justification for and stimulated the recruitment of volunteers to fight against the Americans and their allies. These recruits, originally from the Middle East, the Caucasus, and Central Asia, were joined by a motley stream of volunteers from Europe and North America. By 2015, there were as many as 35,000 of these who had sworn oaths to the ISIS would-be caliph.[7]

In June of 1995, an attempt was made on the life of the Egyptian dictator, Hosni Mubarak, during his visit to Ethiopia. Mubarak responded by cracking down on the Egyptian Salafists. Zawahiri reacted, in turn, by blowing up the Egyptian embassy in Islamabad in November. Then, an even more spectacular assault: on 7 August 1998 his followers destroyed the US embassies in Kenya and Tanzania, killing hundreds of innocents. In May 1996, bin Laden flew to Kandahar, the second largest city in Afghanistan and the capital of a makeshift emirate ruled by the Taliban. From Afghanistan bin Laden issued a "declaration of jihad against the Americans occupying the land of the two holy sites"; the sites being Mecca and Medina. This was, in other words, a war against the Americans in Saudi Arabia. With the agreement of the Saudi king, the Americans had established bases on the peninsula from which they had attacked Iraq in the operation known as Desert Shield. There were more than twice as many Americans in Saudi Arabia as had worked for defence contractors in Iran on the eve of the revolution there.

The jihadi assault took the form of two major attacks against American installations in Saudi Arabia. At Khobar, in the oil-rich eastern province, in June (1996) an American air force barracks was blown up, killing twenty. On 12 October 2000, a dinghy packed with explosives blew a huge hole in the side of a guided missile destroyer, the USS *Cole*, which was refuelling in the harbour at Aden. Seventeen sailors died. In June 2001 Osama bin Laden boasted of the feat in an al-Qaeda recruitment video. Videos, like cell phones, were ubiquitous aspects of the proliferation of social media that had spread with globalization. By this time a complex war had unfolded that involved Afghanistan, Pakistan, and Central Asia. This battlefield was called by Washington "Afpak." But while havoc reigned from Kabul to Kenya to Kabilya, Egypt, the intellectual heart of the Muslim world, for the time being remained tranquil.

## NASSERISM AND THE EGYPTIAN REVOLUTION

With the end of European colonialism in the immediate postwar years, from Algeria to Iran a cohort of secular republicans took over the reins of newly sovereign states. Where they found kings, these were often liquidated – packed off to exile if they were lucky, like king Faruq of Egypt in 1952 and Idris of Libya in 1969 – killed if they were not, like the king of Iraq, Faisal II, in 1958. The shah of Iran nearly shared their fate but was saved by the Anglo-American coup of 1953, at least until he was finally ousted in the revolution of 1979. A few kings did survive, not just in Saudi Arabia but also in the tiny desert states such as Jordan and those like Kuwait and Dubai in the Gulf. Most of those used oil money to buy American protection.

With the revolution of 1952, Egypt, which served as a hinge between the Middle East and Maghreb, had, after World War Two, retained its role as both the most influential and coherent state in the whole region. The 1960s were the heyday of the influence of Egyptian secular nationalism. "By the 1970s," Roger Owen has written, "it seems safe to say, apart from the states in the Persian Gulf, the direct influence of Arabism and the colonial legacy had been transformed into autonomous indigenous political structures, each with its own logic, its own dynamic and its own modes of operation."[8]

The colossus of postwar Arab nationalists was Colonel Abdul Gamal Nasser of Egypt. After taking power following the coup in 1952, he cast his spell over the whole region until his premature death in 1970. In 1957 the head of intelligence in Lebanon wrote of him, "Political propaganda in Nasser's favour is what mostly occupies the spirit of the Muslim masses who consider him the only leader of the Arabs. They care for no other leader but him thanks to the influence of Egyptian and Syrian radio stations and his achievements in Egypt."[9]

"Nasserism" was a uniquely regional form of republican secular nationalism. The domestic enemies of the Nasserites included communists, radical Islamists (like members of the Muslim Brotherhood) and even Western-style liberals. Israel was the main foreign enemy. The Israelis had not only dispossessed the Palestinians but also defeated the Egyptians and their allies, first in 1948 and then in the 1957 Six Day War. Outrage at Israel was complicated by America being Israel's protector. The Soviet Union became the Nasserites new best friend in the later 1950s and '60s but then was stiffed as Anwar Sadat (1970–08) Nasser's successor, cozied up to Washington.

When Nasser died in September 1970. Egyptians in their tens of thousands wept inconsolably, but in the chancelleries of the West, in Israel, and even in some mosques there were nods of satisfaction. There was no Abdul Gamal Nasser *bis*, no son, to inherit the deceased colonel's mantle. So Nasser was succeeded as president by one of his fellow revolutionary officers, Anwar Sadat, who came to resemble the shah or, further away, the most egregious sort of Latin

American *caudillo* – corrupt, unpopular, gaudily uniformed, and ignominiously pro-American. His jihadi enemies referred to him as "pharaoh."

Reckoning on being among the world's selected band of "presidents for life," Sadat's duration was surprisingly truncated. It was he together with the business elite of his National Democratic Party (NDP) who brought neoliberalism (Arabic: *infitah* = "opening") to Egypt, officially in 1974. "[T]he *infitah* helped to create a new wealthy comprador class, serving as the local agents for import/export companies and as representatives and junior partners of foreign capital."[10] They were dubbed "the *infitah* bourgeoisie."

Muhammed Hassanein Heikal, the Egyptian journalist and author best known in the West (and a tireless admirer of Nasser) summed up Sadat's regime: "Indeed," he wrote, "Egypt was not being transformed from a planned to a market economy, but rather to a supermarket economy … Egyptian society was now divided between the 'fat cats' and their hangers-on, perhaps 150,000 people at most, on one side, and the rest of the population on the other." World Bank statistics confirm the double escalator effect; the rich rode up ever higher, while the poor descended ever lower. By the late 1970s, Egypt's total exports amounted to $26 million, its imports $609 million, "most of which was spent on luxury products."[11] The Egyptian economy floated on a puddle of profit from the export of oil – the price for which shot up due to the October (1973) Yom Kippur War between Egypt and Israel and the Iranian Revolution (1979) – rents paid by users of the Suez Canal, and on foreign remittances, notably from Egyptians working in the rich states of the Gulf. After Egypt's third, 1973, defeat and Sadat's 1979 peace treaty with Israel, Washington's subsidies to the Egyptian military, like its donations to Pakistani's praetorians, replaced those of the Soviets and kept the colonels and generals sweet. Vali Nasr notes that after the peace deal with Israel, America poured more than $30 billion into Egypt, most of which went to the army. As in Pakistan (and Turkey) the military controlled a huge part of the Egyptian economy.[12]

Sadat was assassinated spectacularly at a military parade on 6 October 1981. His assassins were soldiers who were normally represented in the media as jihadis, although, as Heikal points out, there was more to the assassination than met the eyes of Western commentators:

> At the time, a good many people in the West saw the assassination of Sadat as just another of those apparently senseless acts of

> violence which have destroyed ... so many prominent public figures ... Nothing could be further from the truth ... The forces that conspired against Sadat were just as much part of the mainstream in Egyptian society as were the forces which overthrew the Shah from the mainstream in Iran ... This was tragically and graphically illustrated at his funeral, when he was taken to his grave by a most imposing galaxy of foreign statesmen, including three former Presidents of the United States and the Prime Minister of Israel, but with only a handful of his own fellow-countrymen as mourners.[13]

The unlamented Sadat was succeeded by Hosni Mubarak who reigned for more than thirty years (1980–2011). Mubarak possessed most of Sadat's vices although to different degrees. Above all, he took the degradation of the Egyptian economy and the elevation and enrichment of the elite a step further than his predecessor. He depoliticized and hand-fed the generals, removing them at will and keeping them at a safe distance from power. In an era of inflated military budgets, even while Egypt's GDP increased (from around $17.8 to $188 billion between 1980 and 2010), he ran the army into the ground. In the place of the army, Egypt under him became a security state crawling with spies. But more than that, it was a state in which the security apparatus was subservient to Washington in the way that the Stasi in East Germany was subservient to Moscow: "I am very comfortable about dealing with the United States, and I will continue to do so and to enhance our relationship," Sadat fawned.[14]

Mubarak sought to insinuate his son, Gamal, as his successor. Gamal was trained as a banker in the West and brought in his entourage a cohort of wheeler-dealers who depended on corruption and connections to the West to enrich themselves. Gamal and his peers, from "Baby Doc" Duvalier in Haiti to the princelings of China, formed a cadet branch of the global "developing markets" plutocracy that became evident in the 1980s. Some were, of course, more plutocratic than others, although none could match the Saudis and their Gulf neighbours or, for sheer weight of numbers, the Chinese. Still, they tried. (According to the writer Marwan Bishara, the son-in-law of Ben Ali, the ruler of Tunisia, owned "among other things, a shipping cruise line, concessions for Audi, Volkswagen, Porsche and Renault, a pharmaceutical manufacturing firm, and real estate companies."[15] Not the three billion accumulated by Wen Jiabao, but a not insignificant sum for a small and poor country.)

By 2011 Mubarak's Egypt was on the verge of a double transition. First, not surprisingly given the threat of Islamism across the Muslim world, his regime wanted to ensure that the growing political influence of the Muslim Brothers was stifled. Although Mubarak's NDP retained a comfortable control of parliament, the Brotherhood, "the closest thing to a real political party in Egyptian politics under Mubarak,"[16] was becoming increasingly popular and effective. Mubarak needed a degree of assurance before handing the Egyptian state over to Gamal.

Politics in Egypt was a matter of elections in which, despite their manifest fraudulence, every party normally participated. In the elections of December 2010, concluded just a month before the Egyptian revolution that began on 25 January 2011, the candidates of the ruling NDP won a comfortable majority of 93.3 per cent of the seats of the national assembly. All opposition parties together won 3 per cent and the undeniably popular Muslim Brothers elected but one member. As one member of the Brotherhood noted, "These were not elections with rigging; it was rigging with a hint of elections."[17] Then came the Arab Spring.

## MOSSADEGHISM AND AYATOLLAHISM

Eric Hobsbawm has called the Iranian revolution "one of the major social revolutions of the twentieth century." More than that, it was also a classic instance of long-term "blowback," a useful word for the unintended, usually calamitous, outcome of a political initiative.[18] Although the long-term origins of the revolution are to be found in the prewar Western interventions in the Middle East, its precipitating causes are in the American and British overthrow of the progressive, secular, nationalist, Mohammad Mossadegh in 1953. Mossadegh must count as one of the most dedicated reformers in the postwar history of the Middle East, and, unlike the officers who ruled Egypt, Algeria, Turkey, and, briefly, Iraq, he was a civilian. According to Steven Kinzer:

> Many Iranians ... were ... drawn to him because of his commitment to social reform. Mossadegh had freed peasants from

> forced labor on their landlords' estates, ordered factory owners to pay benefits to sick and injured workers, established a system of unemployment compensation, and taken 20 percent of the money landlords received in rent and placed it in a fund to pay for development projects ... He supported women's rights, defended religious freedom, and allowed courts and universities to function freely.[19]

With Mossadegh's overthrow, Shah Muhammed Reza (1941–79) got his throne back. He had acceded to it when his father, the military strongman and dictator, Reza Shah, who had established the ruling dynasty in 1926, was forced to abdicate by British and Soviet troops in 1941. By sidelining the shah and becoming elected as president of the *majles* (parliament) in 1951, Mossadegh assured the nationalization of the Anglo-Iranian Oil Company. This firm, a major jewel in the British oil crown, which paid the Iranian state a scandalously low level of royalties and housed its workers in "pigstyes," had been resolutely insistent on its rights to exploitation. So when Anglo-Iranian was nationalized, the British were unforgiving. Under a recently elected Conservative government they embargoed exports from their former refinery at Abadan, at the head of the Gulf, in order to put the screws to Iran. In 1953 agents of Britain's MI6, in cahoots with the CIA, organized the overthrow of Mossadegh, much to the delight of the royalists, the reactionary heads of the army and even many of the mullahs, including one Ruhollah Khomeini. When he was brought to trial, Mossadegh defended himself vigorously: "My only crime," he argued, "is that I nationalized the Iranian oil industry and removed from this land the network of colonialism and the political and economic influence of the greatest empire on earth."[20] Too popular to hang, he was kept under house arrest for the remainder of his life.

Although the British were outraged that the Iranians under Mossadegh would nationalize oil, Britain's most valuable overseas asset, they, themselves, had nationalized their own coal industry only a few years earlier. The Americans, more than any of their European allies, were concerned with the fact that Mossadegh might become a neutralist like many Third World leaders in the 1950s. Neutralists, like Nehru and Nasser, tended not to be subservient to Western capital and strategic interests. It was always thought to be a good idea to overthrow them.[21]

After the overthrow of Mossadegh, the role of the US in Iran, if not its effects, came to resemble Washington's role in Latin America in the 1970s. Juan Cole:

> The United States ... helped train [the shah's] secret police, and enabled one of the more repressive capitalist dictatorships in modern history. The shah became more and more megalomaniacal, favoring gaudy costumes that would have put a Las Vegas lounge lizard to shame. He built up a coterie of billionaire cronies, while millions of villagers, unable to get government loans for their small farms, were forced to migrate as day laborers to squalid urban slums. A massive apparatus of domestic spying and surveillance filled the shah's jails with prisoners of conscience. The shah began assaulting, in the name of secular nationalism and the monarchy, key symbols of Islam.[22]

In recompense for the Anglo-American assistance in restoring him to the throne, the shah partially denationalized Iranian oil, keeping revenues from 50 per cent of production and dividing the remainder between British Petroleum (BP), the successor to Anglo-Iranian Oil Company (which we shall meet below), and other Western oil firms, American, British, French, and Dutch. The Iranian share allowed the shah to invest in the selective modernization of the country, sustaining the building of dams, hydroelectric schemes, and the modernization of Tehran. The population of Iran shot up from 19 to 30 million. His own royalties kept the shah and the swelling cohort of hangers-on and middlemen in clover. His income ballooned from $34 million in 1954–55 to $181 million just two years later, and that was before renationalization in January 1973. He became the country's biggest landowner and his Pahlevi Foundation, a tax shelter, was the means by which the shah transferred as much as two billion dollars to foreign bank accounts. To top this off, in October 1971 the shah sponsored a bacchanal that vindicated his own rule by ostentatiously celebrating 2500 years of Iranian monarchy. As many as 22,000 imported bottles of wine were drunk in a city with no serviceable sewer system.

But there were other beneficiaries, as well, for Iran was not the kind of wretched dictatorship that had emerged in poor backwaters like Gabon or Haiti. One area of expansion was education, although, as it would be at the time of the Arab Spring, this became a problem for the status quo. As one writer has commented, "Politically conscious Iranians had condemned [the shah] as an American puppet ever since the CIA returned him to his throne in 1953. And the expansion of education in the sixties and seventies greatly increased the number of such politically conscious people."[23] And in the absence of the repressed Iranian Communist Party, the *Tudeh*, many of the swelling population of students joined local revolutionary parties like the Marxist, anticlerical Fedayan-i-Khalq and the Islamic but leftist Mojahedin-e Khalq. The Fedayan, founded by university students, carried out its first armed raid, against a police post, in February 1971.

By the 1970s Iran possessed the world's fifth largest military, and, alongside Israel, Saudi Arabia, and Pakistan, had become one of the ramparts of the American preoccupation for regional hegemony in the Middle East and Central Asia. American arms manufacturers and salesmen and, on the buying side, members of the royal family and senior military staff, all rubbed their hands contentedly. Ervand Abrahamian: "Arms dealers began to jest that the *shah* read their manuals in much the same way as other men read *Playboy*. Western defense contractors were as conspicuous as they were ubiquitous. By 1977 there were 60,000 of them working in the country. Many Iranians resented their high salaries and ostentatious lifestyles."[24]

By the late 1970s the Iranian class structure looked like a pyramid: at the summit was a bourgeoisie composed of the ruling family, top officials, civil and military and court-connected entrepreneurs, comprising 0.1 per cent of the total population. Below them, a middle class of 23 per cent of the total, divided into two sections, a modern element (10 per cent) including professionals, bureaucrats, and students, and a traditional section, comprising bazaaris, clerics, and farm, workshop and factory owners. Some of the clerics had huge wealth. Finally there were the bottom classes, the "masses," totalling 77 per cent, also bifurcated into a modern, urban sector (32 per cent) that included mainly workers and soldiers, and a traditional rural sector that mainly comprised peasants, both landless and smallholders.[25]

The small shopkeepers of the bazaar, the bazaaris, had tight relations with the mullahs, supporting them and their institutions. The bazaaris were affected by the competition of foreign firms and by price controls, and were excluded from Iran's most profitable businesses, arms imports, and oil.

Under the shah, who was dismissive of religion, many of the mullahs, too, were aggrieved. The shah's land reforms had weakened the grip of the clergy on the countryside. (The same reforms under the communists in Afghanistan who seized power in 1978 had the same effect on the clergy and led to the same explosive results, namely a loss of hegemony by the secular state.) Unusually for Shi'ism, historically marked by the quietism of its leaders, there were dissident mullahs even at the highest levels. One of the most vociferous of the leaders of these mullahs was Ayatollah Khomeini, a populist firebrand who had preached against decadence and corruption since the 1940s but had also opposed Mossadeq *and* America. Even before he was exiled in 1964, Khomeini had picked on the United States as Iran's principal foreign adversary: "Let the American President know that in the eyes of the Iranian people he is the most repellent member of the human race," he proclaimed.[26] Rather than dispose of him by more bloody means, the shah drove Khomeini first to Turkey, then to the Shi'a shrine city, Najaf, in Iraq (1964–78), and finally to Paris (1978–79). The bazaaris bankrolled Khomeini to the tune of millions. Having left Iran in the mid-1960s, he did not return again until February 1979 by which time the shah had fled.

Meanwhile, in Khomeini's absence, SAVAK, the shah's secret police "imprisoned and tortured Islamic clerics and other dissidents by the thousands, using methods and equipment provided by the CIA."[27] Still, Washington and London backed the status quo in Iran. President Jimmy Carter (1977–81) explained, "Iran, because of the great leadership of the Shah, is an island of stability in one of the more troubled areas of the world."[28] At the same time he saw the need to exert pressure on the shah to liberalize Iran's civil society by protecting the human rights of the shah's critics. The message seems to have gone over the shah's bejewelled head.

By the first half of 1978, Iran's remarkable rate of annual economic growth that had ranged from 11.3 per cent in the 1960s to 7.4 per cent in the 1970s, plummeted, in part because of the decline in oil prices. The opposition, encouraged by the mullahs and a wide variety of other groups including the two major guerrilla organizations mentioned above. These became increasingly bold. Between February 1971 and October 1977, 341 student guerrillas were killed, with 177 of those deaths coming in gun battles, ninety-one by execution, and a further fifty murdered in jail cells. Most of those killed were under thirty-five years of age, and thirty-nine of them were women.[29]

By the end of the decade the regime was mowing down the protesters in unprecedented numbers – seventy theology students in Qom in January 1978, 300 in Tabriz in February, one hundred in Yazd, forty in Mashhad, one hundred in Isfahan, 4,000 on 8 September in Tehran on one of the holy days of *Eid al-Fitr*, 700 more in Tehran, and 135 in Bazvin on the holy days of *Muharram* beginning on 2 December (1978). The wealthy, called in Iranian *taghuts* or "devils," who lived in a world of exaggerated affluence even by the exalted standards of Middle East oil producers, panicked. In September (1978) employees of the Central Bank of Iran released a statement showing that 177 members of the Iranian elite had recently sent $2 billion abroad; thirteen top military officers had alone exported $253 million. Ordinary soldiers were paid $1 a day. By the end of December French intelligence was reporting that the shah could not survive politically.

After a couple of years of rising tumult and thousands of deaths, on 16 January (1979) the shah got the message and fled, ultimately to Cairo. Crownless, throneless, and powerless, but hardly penniless, the dying king followed the setting sun to New York for medical treatment and, afterwards, to obloquy in Egypt where he died of cancer. His family settled near Washington. In his absence, what was left of his regime was overthrown. In the place of the monarchy came the mullahs, but not just any mullahs for Khomeini made sure that the new government was staffed with his disciples. On 1 February (1979), Khomeini flew back to Tehran from his exile in Paris. There was confusion in Washington: the American ambassador in Tehran was confident that the ayatollah was a "Gandhi-like" figure and not a communist. The CIA was sure that a revolutionary situation did not exist in Iran.

With the shah in full flight and the ayatollah at the head of the government, for the first time in the twentieth century, an essentially religious revolution had taken place. Whereas in Egypt the regimes that took power after the July (1952) revolution were headed by secular soldiers and sustained by soldiers and policemen, in Iran the new regime was headed by ayatollahs, the princes of Shi'ism, and sustained by armed theology students, the *pasdarans*. It was they who, like the *sans culottes* at the time of the French Revolution, drove the terror after the revolution; almost immediately after attaining power, Khomeini had some hundred generals, including the head of SAVAK, executed. One school headmaster commented: "Thank God! Those bastards have shed blood in every family in the land."[30]

Between February 1979 and June 1981, the new regime liquidated nearly 500 victims. It also executed religious nonconformists, especially Bahais, one of the sects that had split off from orthodox Shi'ism in the nineteenth century. Between June 1981 and June 1985, in a second spasm of repression, revolutionary courts passed a further spate of death sentences this time lynching 8,000 leftists. Finally, in 1988, as Khomeini lay dying, the clerics hanged a further 2,800, mainly leftists. Their crime was "apostacy."

A decade earlier, with the destruction of the shah's regime, the flames of anti-Americanism that had risen to new heights in the 1970s leaped even higher, fanned by a pumped-up clerical hysteria: "Death to America" and "Down with the Great Satan" became the chants of the foot soldiers, who were, like the Red Guards in China, often students. In November 1979, the US embassy in Tehran was occupied by the ayatollah's supporters. American officials were turned into hostages and most were held for 444 days. The shock felt right across the United States was palpable; bewildered self-righteousness, underpinned by innocence, and massaged by the media, peaked. Worse was to come in the next decade.

Iran's rivals did not remain impassive. On 22 September 1980 Saddam Hussein, seizing the moment and assuming, more or less correctly, that the Iranian army was utterly disorganized, invaded Iran. For most of the decade that followed, the Americans continued to throw their weight and their technologies behind the secular Saddam as a counterweight to the clerics who ruled Iran. The conservative monarchies of the Gulf did their part; Kuwait gave Saddam $50 billion worth of assistance and Saudi Arabia $60 billion. Israel sold US arms and spare parts to Tehran. "Ostensible allies, Israel and the United States thus found themselves supporting opposite sides in a war in which *both* warring parties were stridently anti-Israel *and* anti-American."[31]

Over eight years of war some 262,000 Iranians and 105,000 Iraqis died. In northern Iraq the Kurds had enjoyed the support of the shah against Baghdad. With the shah removed, Saddam turned against them using poisoned gas to drive rural people into the arms of the waiting Iraqi army. Between eighty and a hundred thousand people were killed in this way. Later, in the war against the revolutionary regime in Iran, Saddam used gas attacks against the Iranians.[32]

By the time of the Iranian Second Republic, founded the year of the ayatollah's death in 1989, the country was in the hands not only of conservative clerics but, simultaneously, an elite for whom zealotry was as much aimed at profit as piety. "It is perhaps ironic that since Ayatollah Khomeini's death Iran's new leaders have sought to re-establish as far as possible the economic (as well as some of the politico–military) ties that existed between Iran and the West during the shah's regime."[33] The same elite had no misgivings about engrossing its collective self; after the briefest of intermissions, venality was back and the chasm between rich and poor began again to widen. In the late 1980s the top 10 per cent of households received nearly 42 per cent of the national income and the bottom 20 per cent only about 4 per cent; by the early 1990s, the share appropriated by the top stratum had increased. "After parliamentary elections in 1992, under the leadership of the … Supreme Guide, Sayyid Ali Khamenei [Khomeini's successor] … the government reversed the nationalizations, which had reached their high-water mark in 1982, and sold off state-owned industries in the industrial and service sector. This was consistent with the development plan for 1994 that stressed privatization and marketization of the economy, including the liberalization of foreign trade."[34] The government adopted macroeconomic policies favoured by the IMF and encouraged by the World Bank. By early 1995 Coke and Pepsi, formerly demonized, had returned. So in spite of the rantings of the mullahs against the West, Iran had now joined the world of neoliberalism: New York had thus become, like Najaf, a Holy Place and Wall Street, a Holy Way. "Ayatollah-ism" had mutated to become neoliberalism in a black turban, the world's only neoliberal theocracy. No new society had emerged. According to Fred Halliday, "By the early 1990s the story was circulating in Tehran that there was now only one authoritative Ayatollah left in the country: his name was "Ayatollah Dollar."[35]

By the mid-1990s Iranian messianism had thus run out of prayers. Controlling 80 per cent of the economy, the clerics had shown themselves to be not merely reactionary but often idle, incompetent, and extravagantly corrupt. Agriculture had stagnated and small-scale industry was stalled. Effective social reform, in the form of better housing, education, and public health had only mixed successes. The condition of women was appalling; the protection of their rights as guaranteed by the family protection laws of 1967 and 1975 had been repealed; polygamy was back, and unilateral divorce was again legally sanctioned. Under President Akbar Hashemi Rafsanjani (1989–97), probably the richest man in the country and the leader of Iran's business class, the "free-market" economy expanded.[36] Abbas Amanat confirms the "corruption and racketeering of the Islamic Republic's elite, the failure of economic policies and industrial projects, massive institutional and individual kleptocracy, the striking levels of drug addiction, prostitution and other social ills [and] political suppression."[37] Then, for a moment, at the end of the century, there seemed to have been hope. Christopher de Bellaigue refers to the election of President Mohammad Khatami 1997–2005) as a "springtime."[38] Bellaigue accepts, however, that Khatami's regime was more beneficial to Iran's considerable middle class than to the masses of the poor.

So winter returned with Khatami's defeat and the election of Mahmoud Ahmadinejad (elected 2005, reelected 2009, defeated 2013). Yet Ahmadinejad was widely unpopular with both young people and many liberals and had to resort to repression, on top of the usual doses of religious obscurantism, to keep a population, disappointed over domestic decline and international isolation and aching for change, under control. Isolation deepened when Iran was declared a part of the "axis of evil" and made subject to crippling sanctions (which were removed in early 2016). In the elections of June 2013, Hassan Rouhani, another moderate like Khatami, was elected. After "eight acrimonious years," wrote *The Guardian*, an "extraordinary political transformation" had taken place. Rouhani was a protegé of Akhbar Hashemi Rafsanjani, alongside Ali Hosseini Khamenei, one of Khomeini's two main disciples. He was not only a graduate of Glasgow's Caledonian University but was a nuclear negotiator. To almost universal relief, except on the part of Israel and its allies on the American right, the first stages in the removal of all sanctions was implemented. In return, Iran gave up almost its entire nuclear stockpile. According to different estimates the removal of sanctions would provide Iran with a windfall of between $50 and $100 billion.[39] On 14 July 2015, Bastille Day, after two years of talks and attempts by Republicans and a major pro-Israel lobby group in Washington to prevent agreement, an accord was signed between the five members of the UN Security Council, together with Germany (the P5+1), and Iran.

In spite of a change in leaders and in economic policy, the clerical dictatorship represented in the Iranian regime's Guardian Council remained in place. In the words of Ayatollah Ali Khamenei, Iran's supreme leader since 1989, "If the agents of penetration [ie. the secular politicians] somehow manage to enter [the] foundations of the Islamic Republic, they will weaken the bases of the system and will eat them from the inside like termites."[40] By the end of 2016, the battle to replace Khamenei was under way with the reformists and the hardliners each fielding candidates.[41]

## THE LIQUIDATION OF SADDAM HUSSEIN

For several years after World War Two it may have seemed that Iraq's destiny was to become a an oil-rich British protectorate, the home, as well, like Egypt, of air bases that served as the guardians of Western interests in the Middle East. The British-owned Iraq Petroleum Company had been given a seventy-five-year lease by the compliant Hashemite dynasty that had been put in power by the mandate government at the end of World War One. But the throne of the Hashemites was never secure, in large part, at least in the conventional explanation, because its incumbents were Sunnis from Arabia and the majority of its people were Shi'as.[42] In 1933, the year after Iraq became officially independent according to the provisions of mandate rule, the Iraqi king, Faisal I (1921–33) complained, "In Iraq there is still ... no Iraqi people, but unimaginable masses of human beings, devoid of any patriotic ideal, imbued with religious traditions and absurdities, connected by no common tie, giving ear to evil, prone to anarchy, and perpetually ready to rise against any government whatsoever."[43]

In 1958, following the example of the Young Officers of Egypt in 1952, nationalist officers overthrew the monarchy. The king and the followers of the powerful Anglophile prime minister, Nuri al-Sa'id, were murdered. The leader of the officers, their Nasser, was Abd al-Karim Qasim (1914–63). Qasim proclaimed Iraq a republic and announced that land reform would take place. Membership of the American-dominated CENTO (also known as the Baghdad Pact) would end; Iraq would become neutralist. Alarm bells rang.

Qasim's military dictatorship lasted until 1963 when it was overthrown by a rival army clique led by Colonel Abd al-Salam Arif of the Arab Socialist Ba'ath Party. (Coincidentally, in the same year Hafiz al-Assad, another Ba'athist, carried out a coup in Syria that secured the position of the Alawite ruling class.) Arif was backed by the CIA: "We came to power on a CIA train," admitted the incoming interior minister.[44] Washington was relieved to see the end of Qasim and rejoiced in the repression of the local communist party that followed his ouster Arif himself was overthrown in 1968 in what became known as the "17 July Revolution." Saddam then stepped into power, first under Hasan al-Bakr, his kinsman, who was both president and prime minister until 1979, and then as a dictator on his own. He executed as many as 500 members of his own Ba'athist party before turning to Iraq's Islamicists, more than 200 of whom he also slaughtered. Among them was Muhammad Baqir al-Sadr, one of Shi'ism's most highly regarded theologians.

Iraqi petroleum production peaked at nearly 6 per cent of the world total.[45] As his influence increased, Saddam appointed his cronies and kinsmen to key offices in the army and intelligence bureau and continued to purge his rivals. Public hangings became a hallmark of his regime but so was land reform. In 1972 the Iraq Petroleum Company had been nationalized. Its assets became part of the Iraq National Oil Company (INOC). Between 1970 and 1982, according to Cleveland, 264,000 farmers received land.

> Because of its oil wealth, Iraq could afford to pursue the creation of a social welfare state. The government was able to reduce taxes, subsidize basic foodstuffs, establish free health care, and abolish university tuition fees. These measures, when combined with plentiful employment that accompanied the extensive development schemes, led to an improvement in the living conditions and income levels for the population at large. Thus, although the ... regime of al-Bakr and Husayn [sic] may not have been loved, the prosperity that accompanied its consolidation of power in the 1970s at least led to its acceptance.

Widespread reforms to the status of women and especially their education were an aspect of Saddam's reforms. By 1982 over 30 per cent of university students were women.[46]

Then came the 1979 revolution in Iran. Washington saw this as a huge threat to its dominance in the Middle East. Recall, too, that the

Soviets had invaded Afghanistan in December 1979. In August of the same year, Carter signed a presidential decree authorizing military aid to the *mujahideen* who had risen up against the pro-Soviet government in Kabul, thus launching a civil war that was to last up to the present.

Saddam, too, had every reason to fear the ayatollah. Again, to stress the conventional explanation, although he and his cronies were Sunnis, the majority of the population of Iraq were Shi'as. The great shrine cities of the Shi'a, Karbala, and Najaf, were actually in Iraq. The ayatollah had charged Saddam with "attacking Islam and the Quran" and characterized his government as being dominated by "the infidel Ba'ath Party." In Iraq's north, the Kurds, although Sunnis, were seeking their independence from Baghdad. The ayatollah had abrogated the agreement made between the shah and Baghdad that had guaranteed no support for the Kurds from Tehran.

The Iraqi invasion of Iran in 1980 was a cataclysm without a resolution. Over the decade of the 1980s more than a quarter of a million Iranians and even more Iraqis were killed. The United States, Kuwait, and Saudi Arabia all provided Saddam with huge military aid while the regime in Syria backed Iran. Far from dislodging the Iranian revolutionary regime, when Iraq announced a cease-fire on 11 March 1988 – followed by Tehran on 20 April 20 – the regime of the ayatollah was even more secure. Meanwhile, arms dealers made spectacular profits.

The war with Iran had been over for two years when, in August 1990, Saddam invaded oil-rich Kuwait and claimed it as an Iraqi province. His justification was that this enclave really belonged to Iraq. This time, Washington took sides against Baghdad. When Saddam refused to withdraw, on 17 January 1991 the Americans launched "Operation Desert Storm" and pushed the Iraqis out of Kuwait. This involved launching air strikes against Iraq itself, destroying the invading Iraqi forces and lacerating the Iraqi infrastructure. A cease-fire was announced on 24 February after a mere hundred hours of combat.

It was on 27 February (1991) that President George H.W. Bush announced that Kuwait had been liberated. "By God," swore the American president, a few days later, "we've kicked the Vietnam syndrome once and for all." For the Americans, "the best decade ever" followed. This was the time of economic growth at around 4 per cent a year, of the "Great Moderation," unipolarity, and of President Bill Clinton

(1993–2001) who unseated Bush.[47] It ended with the cataclysm of 11 September 2001 at the hands of dissident Saudis.

Between 1990 and 2003 the United Nations undertook to prevent the rehabilitation of Iraq through the imposition of draconian sanctions. Justifying these on the basis of weakening Saddam, the sanctions amounted to carrying on war in violation of its own principles against a defenceless civilian population. Patrick Cockburn:

> [Under the sanctions regime] Iraqis saw their social and economic standards fall from the same level as Greece to those of Mali. The World Health Organization said that in 1996 'the vast majority of the country's population has been on semi-starvation diet for years.' The UN estimated that between six and seven thousand Iraqi children were dying every month as a result of sanctions. Millions of Iraqis who had once held good jobs and lived in comfort were reduced to poverty and often to crime. The country's once high-grade education and health services collapsed ... There were shortages of electricity and drinking water because power and water treatment plants were targeted in the bombing campaign of 1991 and only partially rebuilt. The US-led invasion destroyed the Iraqi state and army, but sanctions had already shattered the country's society and economy.[48]

With the war against Iran (1980–88), the defeat in Kuwait, and the American attack on the Iraqi homeland, the long night of what had been one of the Middle East's most prosperous and developed societies had begun. It was resumed in March 2003, when, under the banners of the War on Terror, "Operation Iraqi Freedom" was launched. It lasted from 19 March to 1 May (2003) and involved a mere twenty-one days of major combat operations. The pretext for this invasion was the false claim that Saddam had formed a compact with the jihadis under Osama bin Laden and was in possession of chemical and bacteriological weapons of mass destruction (WMDs). The British, under the Labour Party leader, Tony Blair, confirmed this and broke with Germany and France to send troops. On 1 May 2003, on the deck of an aircraft carrier off the coast of California the US president declared the end of "major combat operations." Over the flight deck of the carrier a sign had been hoisted: "Mission Accomplished," it read.

In Iraq, as his army was destroyed and his regime crumbled, Saddam fled. The state that he had run was soon replaced by mere anarchy. Initially, from March 2003 until June 2004, an American administrator ran the country on behalf of the Coalition Provisional Authority. The administrator, appointed by President Bush, was the famously incompetent L. Paul Bremer III. Bremer sought to privatize as much of Iraq's infrastructure and oil resources as possible. His most disastrous blunder was to disband the Iraqi army – the effect of this was to turn a large number of the 400,000 unemployed soldiers into anti-America militiamen. Under him, too, nearly $9 billion of Iraqi money earmarked for reconstruction disappeared.

Bremer was succeeded by an interim and provisional government and then from the spring 2006 by a permanent government under Nouri al-Maliki. In 2008 negotiations with major Western oil companies began. Al-Maliki was succeeded in 2010 by Ayad Allawi. It was during Allawi's rule that Iraqi oil, under national control for forty years, was actually auctioned off to foreign oil companies, advancing beneath the national banners of "energy security." It is widely accepted that that the ultimate object of the coalition, that is, the American and British invasion, was the securing of Iraq's oil under conditions and at a price attractive to the great oil companies like the giant BP and other of the oleagenous "sisters," Shell, Exxon Mobil, and Total. "Oil lies at the heart of Iraqi politics" explained Greg Muttitt in a closely argued account of the attempts of mainly Western oil companies to get control of Iraqi's abundant oil reserves.[49]

In the vacuum that the Americans and their allies had created, sectarian violence broke out between Sunni and Shi'a militias. It was there that Abu Musab al-Zarqawi, head of Jama'at al-Tawhid wal-Jihad, first became conspicuous. Later, in October 2004, this organization mutated to become "al-Qaeda in Iraq." We will see more of him below. In the decade that followed, violence ebbed and flowed while as many as a quarter million Iraqis were killed, two million displaced, and a further 2.2 million made refugees in other countries. According to the "Iraq Body Count" that documents "civilian deaths from violence," up to 24 February 2015 between 135,322 and 152,799 Iraqis were killed. Others trekked as far as Scandinavia in search of refuge.

By 2015 the desolation of Iraq has been ongoing for thirty-five years, and Iraq, created by the machinations of the British and

French during the Great War, has ceased to exist as a coherent state. No country since the end of World War Two, not even Vietnam, has suffered so intensely for so long nor has any major state been so utterly erased.

Saddam had fled from the American invasion but was captured and later hanged (on 30 December 2006). Douglas Feith, chief strategist to US defense secretary Donald Rumsfeld and one of the leading advocates of the invasion of Iraq, had said that America's aim was to transform not just the Middle East but the "broader world of Islam generally."[50] According to General Wesley Clark, sometime NATO commander, the invasion of Iraq was to be followed by attacks on a number of other Middle East states over a period of five years. Here was *mission civilisatrice* risen from the dead. There is little proof that the American public was behind Rumsfeld here and some evidence that the invasion of Iraq led to a growing isolationism.[51]

Violence in Iraq has diminished significantly since 2008, and the occupation of Iraq officially ended in December 2011. While the cost to Iraq in lives and the very fabric of civilization was incalculable, the cost to America was at least three billion dollars and 4,486 lives; more Americans were thus killed in the invasion of Iraq than in 9/11. Of those who benefitted from the destruction of Iraq, none was more unintended than Iran, which, to the chagrin of its regional rivals, gradually returned as regional hegemon. And yet, the Americans had not entirely evacuated the country. Although most had left in 2014, as late as October 2016 there were still 5,000 in Iraq (as compared to more than 8,000 in Afghanistan).

With the destruction of Saddam Hussein, yet another secular ruler of the Middle East, one with no ties to any form of Salafism, had been removed, the prospect of increased democracy had withered. The Western domination of the oil of the Middle East had become even more assured.

## THE ARAB SPRING AND THE SYRIAN CIVIL WAR

Consider the conclusion from one of the State Department's most active agents in the Middle East in the Obama era: "We are now fairly certain that in the new Middle East, the fruit of the Arab Spring will not be a rising liberal Arab order, but an ascendant Islamist one that, if it is able to assert itself, will be ... an enemy to the United States and Israel."[52]

The Arab Spring marked an attempt right across the Middle East at replacing oligarchs with democrats and substituting the neoliberal economic regimes the oligarchs had imposed with unspecified systems that would solve the basic problems of economic stagnation and overpopulation. The Spring may be said to have lasted from December 2010 until the overthrow of the democratically elected but increasingly unpopular Muslim Brotherhood of 2014 by the Egyptian military (with the blessing of Washington).[53] It stimulated popular revolts in Libya, Yemen, and Syria, none of which were successful in installing regimes that were in any normal sense democratic. Like the failed European revolutions of 1848, their effect was to throw the whole of the region into turmoil. This had a profound impact right across the Mediterranean on the states of the European Union to which refugees fled in numbers unprecedented since World War Two. Ultimately, its reverberations affected politics across the Atlantic even to Canada.

The genesis of the Arab Spring was in Tunisia in mid-December 2010. There, in an unplanned revolt, the unpopular dictator Ben Ali, a favourite of Paris and Washington, was overthrown. Other uprisings followed in 2011 in Yemen and Libya. In Libya the West intervened and in an air war, copied from the campaign against the Serbs in Yugoslavia and referred to as "the Balkan Solution" (aka "Hillary's War") the state was destroyed. Civil war followed. As in Iraq, where there had been dictatorship there was now anarchy. Thousands fled, joining those fleeing the wars from Syria to Afghanistan flooding into Europe. In Egypt, in a spontaneous popular uprising centred in Cairo, Hosni Mubarak was overthrown to be ultimately replaced by a dictatorship under Field Marshal al-Sisi. Mubarak is said to have taken much of his family's $70 billion fortune with him. Once again the prisons filled up and the economy declined.

## CIVIL WAR IN SYRIA

Iraq was a majority Shi'a state dominated by Saddam's Sunni regime; Syria was a majority Sunni state dominated by the Alawite Shi'a regime. Besides Sunnis and Shi'as, Syria had a minority population of Christians, Kurds, and Druzes.[54] The government of Hafiz al-Assad that had gained power after a coup in 1963 and then increased incrementally in the years that followed was sustained by a largely Alawite officer corps. But Assad's power was not simply based on Alawites,

Druzes, and Christians. It was also supported by the Sunni bourgeoisie and at least one large Sunni clan. What is more, according to Charles Glass, not only have "a considerable proportion of Syrian Sunnis ... not taken up arms against the regime," not all Alawites have supported the regime.[55]

In common with the regime of Saddam of Iraq, the Assad regime had been dominated by the Ba'ath party, a nationalist and resolutely secular formation that rose in the postwar years to accelerate the demise of Western domination in the Middle East. It embraced the idea of "Arab socialism," which prescribed high levels of state control of the economy. Like both Nasser and Saddam, Hafiz al-Assad aspired to turn Syria into the leading Arab state; for a period Syria and Egypt merged to form the United Arab Republic (1958–61), but this proved disastrous, and the marriage was soon dissolved. But, more like Saddam than Nasser, Assad never achieved universal popularity among the majority Sunni population, for the obvious reason that he was an outsider and to some, a heretic. In 1982, antiregime forces led by the Muslim Brotherhood who had seized control of the city of Hama called for a jihad against the ruling regime. In one of the greatest bloodbaths in the modern history of the region, Assad's forces crushed the revolt with tanks leaving as many as 20,000 dead and large sections of the city utterly destroyed. The Muslim Brotherhood in Syria was thus annihilated. The regime's destruction of Sunni Hama was echoed by its unflinching support for Iran against Sunni Iraq during the Iraq–Iranian war that followed the Iranian Revolution of 1980.

When Hafiz al-Assad was succeeded by his son, Bashir, in 2000 the family grip on power was tightened: Bashir's brother, Maher, became the country's second most powerful man. He commanded the Republican Guard, a sort of dedicated elite, as well as an armoured division. Assef Shawkat, Bashir's brother-in-law, was made head of military intelligence – until he was assassinated in July 2012, possibly by Sunni rebels. Other members of the family became leading bankers and intelligence operatives; the family thus ran the Syrian equivalent of both CIA and FBI. Like the family of Mubarak in Egypt, their rule was a festival of self-enrichment.

Although the economy of Syria became increasingly dilapidated from the mid-1990s, the wealth of the country became even more unevenly distributed under Bashir's neoliberal policies than in the time of his father. By 2007, according to Goldsmith, "a third of the population lived in poverty on less than $50 US per month, while 12.3 per cent of Syrians lived in extreme poverty with a maximum monthly income of $32." Even the traditional support base of the Ba'ath party, the rural peasants, the workers, and the petty bureaucrats, among whom Alawites were heavily represented, grew disenchanted with the government. One commentator has noted that there were only two classes in Syria, the 500 people who controlled most of the wealth and who included the top families that surrounded Bashir al-Assad, and the rest.[56]

Bashir, a student of ophthalmology in London when his father died, at first seemed inclined to a degree of reform at home. For reasons of security, given that his neighbours were not of the same ideological inclinations – being either Sunnis (Turkey, Jordan, Saudi Arabia, and the Gulf states), Israelis, Kurds, or Christians (Lebanon) – and had powerful Western backers (especially Washington), he remained close to revolutionary Tehran and at no great distance from Russia. There he found financing for his gargantuan appetite for arms, inherited from his father. He seemed indifferent to popularity with the Arab world. As his father had gained notoriety by the massacre at Hama (not to mention his supporting the Druzes against the Palestinians in Lebanon), Bashir made himself unpopular by blowing up the Lebanese prime minister, Rafik Harari, the popular "Mr Lebanon," in February 2005. Quite suddenly, he became caricatured as one of the of the region's violence-prone fiends – a lesser Saddam Hussein. But not much less. International opinion forced the Syrians to withdraw from Lebanon in April 2005 after a twenty-nine year stay. In late 2012, Hizbollah, the guerrilla and "terrorist" organization operated from Tehran, entered the picture on the side of Assad.[57]

The launch date for the Syrian Civil War came at the very end of winter, 2011. On 26 January (2011), by which time Egypt's "eighteen days of revolution" had begun, it was noted that there was not a "peep of protest" in Damascus. On 31 January, Assad acknowledged that although the rebellions in Tunisia and Egypt were ushering in a new era in the Arab world, Syria was immune. On Friday, 2 February, *The Guardian* correspondent in Damascus reported that "over 15 Facebook groups have emerged this week rallying people to take to the streets for a 'day of rage' today and tomorrow, calling for solidarity with Egypt and an end to emergency law in the country." Nothing apparently happened.

The beginning of the antiregime Syrian uprising was not until 15 March 2011. In the months that followed, the support of the regime hung in the balance and although individual Alawites joined the resistance, the majority remained either passive or faithful to Assad. The rise and conquests of Sunni ISIS in Iraq and Syria assured their fidelity.

In most Western states there was confusion as to whether Assad should be toppled, like Saddam and Muammar Gaddafi, or allowed to stay. The Russians supported the status quo as Assad promised them bases in the eastern Mediterranean. The Americans and their allies were indecisive. Secretary of State Hilary Clinton said, "President Assad is not indispensable and we have absolutely nothing invested in him remaining in power."[58] By the end of 2012 it was believed throughout the American intelligence community that the anti-Assad rebels were losing the war.[59]

By mid-January 2012 the UN estimated that 5,000 had been killed by the Assad regime; by May the UN estimate was 9,000–12,000 killed and 30,000 refugees. By early 2014, the *Financial Times* claimed 140,000 dead and nine million displaced "in what the UN describes as the worst humanitarian catastrophe since the second world war." Jonathan Littell, quoting the Syrian Network for Human Rights, estimated that "as of September 2014, the [Assad] regime had killed 124,752 Syrian civilians, including 17,139 children, as opposed to 831 civilians (of which 137 were children) killed by Da'esh [i.e. ISIS]." Andrew Cockburn supposed "upwards of 200,000 people."[60] There was, thus, no Arab Spring in Syria – instead, a prolonged, devastating, civil war that began in 2011 and continued into 2017 with a chaos echoing that in Iraq, Libya, and, further away, Afghanistan.

## A NEW CALIPHATE?

Abu Musab al-Zarqawi was a Bedouin from Jordan.[61] He had fought against the Soviets in Afghanistan in 1989. He then left the country in 2000 when he had a disagreement with bin Laden. After the fall of the Taliban in late 2001, he moved to Iraq where he declared himself, first, head of "al-Qaeda in Iraq" and then Jama'at al-Tawhid wal-Jihad, "the Party of Monotheism and Jihad." Andrew Bacevich has explained that Zarqawi had not been able to gain a foothold in Iraq until the American invasion destroyed Saddam and his authority.[62]

A branch of this party was established in May 2007 in Syria. Ghosh has made the point that although al-Zarqawi's rhetoric was similar to bin Laden's, his objects were different. "Zarqawi directed his malevolence at fellow Muslims, especially Iraq's majority Shiite population." He organized the bombing of the Imam Ali shrine in Najaf, Shi'ism's holiest place in Iraq. This gave him star status among the jihadis although that didn't last long. In June 2006 his rise to fame was terminated when the US air force bombed his headquarters north of Baghdad. The American thinking was that by destroying leading jihadis the situation could be rectified. But this was erroneous; the graveyards of the Middle East were full of leaders, but as they filled up the situation got worse, not better.

Zarqawi was succeeded by Ibrahim al-Samarri, a mediocre student of Islamic religion, whose *nom de guerre* was Abu Bakr al-Baghdadi. Samarri/Baghdadi, like Zarqawi, had earned his notoriety as a bloodthirsty commander who had claimed the title of caliph, head of the Muslim community. His organization was known in English as ISIS, "the Islamic State of Iraq and Syria." In Arabic it is called Da'esh from its acronym.

Jabhat al-Nusra had been founded in early 2011 by two of Baghdadi's lieutenants but remained dormant for a year, building up support among Syria's impoverished Sunnis. In one explanation:

> Of all the armed factions in Syria, al-Nusra subsequently received the most fighters, hundreds of poor Sunnis who lacked the means to feed their families and whose grievances allowed them to become politically disposed to the groups' sectarian narrative, if not their whole ideology. These poor Sunnis were paid $400 a month, more if they were married and had children. Al-Nusra raised money from selling oil from the Syrian fields that it had captured. In many respects al-Nusra was like the Taliban – one had oil and the other opium.[63]

So the war in Syria and Iraq, and the borderlands in between, involved two rival jihadi forces, the Assad regime, the Free Syrian Army, the Iraqi army, and their various Western and non-Western supporters – the French, British and Americans mainly in the air (except for their Special Forces), the Russians in the air and at sea, the Turks in the air, the Saudis and other Gulf Arabs at home writing cheques, and the Canadians who withdrew their air force but left their Special Forces.[64] In 2015, as we have seen, the Americans became more cordial in their relations with Tehran. Tehran sustained Hizbollah. The Americans also supported Israel, which Hizbollah attacked. As well, Washington supported Saudi Arabia where the cheque-writers remained unmolested.

By September 2015, there were 4 million displaced persons living in UN-registered camps in Lebanon and Jordan, and 1.7 million living in Turkey. Russia, which had a base for its Black Sea fleet at Tartous and built an airbase outside of Latakia, pledged to support the regime of Bashir al-Assad while Western air forces pounded ISIS. Several writers suggested that air policing was ineffective and destructive of civilian populations.[65]

# 8

# African Dark Days

Between the beginning of World War Two (c. 1940) and the independence of Ghana in 1957, there passed uncertain decades during which projections for the future of Africa were urged, formulated, revised, argued, interpreted, and discarded, then renewed. The British drew up the first of these plans in London at the very beginning of the war and the Free French at Brazzaville on the Congo River in early 1944.[1] The Belgians, ravaged by German invasion, at the end of the war hardly had a coherent plan for the postwar period, and the Portuguese simply assumed more paternalism and exploitation. At the nascent United Nations the word "colonial" was seldom mentioned; the "sacred trust" of "self-government" and "the progressive development of ... free political institutions" was mentioned in Article 73 of the UN Charter that was drafted in San Francisco in 1945. Then, as now, there was waffle to conceal uncertainty and a longing for a blameless return, as far as possible, to the status quo. Invariably these plans were formulated in the West and redacted in the colonial capitals. Emerging from these plans were distinct scenarios that I have addressed under several headings.

## CAPITALISM

In the imperial capitals of Europe, there was an overriding assumption that Africa was to continue to be a continent obedient to the rules of capitalism as certified at the many conferences from Berlin in 1885 to Versailles in 1920 to Bretton Woods in 1944. All accepted Western hegemony if not outright colonialism. After World War Two "Washington's main concerns were the Cold War ... and the economic organization of the core areas of the capitalist world in ways that would firmly tie the underdeveloped world of their needs."[2] Africa was small yams compared to Asia.

It was accepted that the colonial frontiers and zones of economic influence would be sacrosanct. Still, the French did not trust their rivals, the "Anglo-Americans." We will see this even as late as the Rwanda crisis in the 1990s.[3] In the view of the leading Euro-American powers, adjustments, even if they were aimed at creating homogenous tribal states, would not be tolerated; there could be no ethnically cleansed African Turkeys, no independent Biafras for the Igbo peoples, or Congo homelands just for the Congolese. Economies, too, would remain the same; Senegal would adopt the CFA franc and Nigeria, sterling; French experts would supervise the ministries of finance in Francophone Africa, British economists would guide Anglophone Africa. Shipping lines like Elder Dempster and Messagerie Maritime would connect the ex-colonies to their former metropolises. Myths of eternal amity between the colonies and metropolises would be cultivated; the title of one Nigerian governor's memoirs was *But Always as Friends*.[4] Any measures, however retrograde, could be used on the excuse that communism had to be kept out of Africa. The Belgians shot Patrice Lumumba, the British ousted (he claimed) Kwame Nkrumah, the French let the Moroccan Mehdi Ben Barka be kidnapped on the streets of Paris by French policemen and taken to the suburbs to be tortured to death.[5] In the 1970s the British Conservative government justified arms sales to the apartheid regime in South Africa – used mainly for internal repression – ostensibly on the basis of Cold War considerations.[6]

## CLASSES

Independence would see the birth of a new Western-oriented wannabe ruling class and petty bourgeoisie, replacing the colonial governors and functionaries. The new leaders of Africa were obviously going to be sustained in power by clientism in its several forms, including tribalism. (In international terms, this African elite was part of the global comprador class, later better known, more than a little dismissively, as "gatekeepers.")[7] The French thought highly of elite assimilation, that is, of *évolués*, who would be reliably French in taste and above all in loyalty. In no African country was there any kind of dominant caste like India's Brahmins that could be collectively transformed into modern rulers of entire states, although in the colonial period there had been regional rulers, like those of India's princely states, in parts of Uganda, Nigeria, and elsewhere. These rulers, variously regarded as chiefs or kings or emirs, were generally semiliterate and conformist and were encouraged to distinguish themselves by gaudy ceremonials and dress. Their sons were often educated in special schools, sometimes in Africa and occasionally in Europe.

Everywhere, in the postwar era, there was turbulent social change. This had been stimulated by the demands on colonial Africa of wartime Europe and of the return to Africa of soldiers who had fought in colonial armies in Africa and Asia. Senegalese and Moroccan soldiers even fought (and surrendered) alongside the French and *Legionnaires* at Dien Bien Phu in 1954, the battle that ended French dreams in Southeast Asia.

In the centres of European influence like the colonial capitals and the mining towns, postwar change was especially rapid, in the outback, less so. This meant that tribes inevitably were in a state – of what? – "mutation and decay," said some, "development and progress," said others. Education, it was apparent, was a solvent of the precolonial status quo. In colonial Africa it ranged from the laudable, as was the work of missionaries in southern Gold Coast, to the lamentable, as were the parsimonious efforts in the Muslim areas of colonial governments in northern Gold Coast and Nigeria. In the Belgian Congo and Portuguese Africa it was virtually nonexistent. The education of women was not contemplated.

## *A New Class*

Few of the Africans who inherited the state from the British, French, Belgians, or Portuguese from the late 1940s into the 1970s had paper qualifications beyond primary school certificates and almost none had administrative experience beyond typing and filing. The ancestral figure of the clerical class was "Mr Johnson," the fictional creation of Joyce Cary, a British District Officer in the first decades of colonial rule in Nigeria, who later became a novelist with a taste for the picaresque.[8]

Throughout the continent, the Western-educated tended to come from some tribes and not others, and their education depended on the influence on those tribes of European missionaries. Muslim areas, where missionaries were often discouraged by colonial administrations, tended to be, in terms of Western-educated strata, cripplingly backward. Ignorance was preferable to dissidence. Nor was Arabic used for purposes other than religion; where there was scholarship such as there had been around Timbuktu for nearly a thousand years, it was more of a pious than an enquiring nature. When we exclaim that Europe underdeveloped Africa we must acknowledge that pre-colonial Africa below the Sahara was a backwater compared to most of Asia and much of Latin America. A few Africans, often associated with coastal trade and with missionaries, had become literate in European languages by the nineteenth century, but it was not until the beginning of the twentieth that education produced a new class of literate subjects, many of whom found work in colonial regimes throughout the continent. George Orwell was largely correct when he wrote in 1946 that, "backward people are more easily governed than civilized ones."[9]

Then, after 1945, the first elections took place. Since social classes in colonial Africa were barely more than vestigial, electorates tended to be mobilized on the basis of tribal affiliations. In certain colonies, or regions within colonies, however, the colonial rulers justified the promotion of some tribes above others: the Buganda in Uganda, the Tutsi in Rwanda and the "Hausa-Fulani" in northern Nigeria benefitted from this. This policy proved to be disastrous when Africa became independent.

## DEVELOPMENT

Especially from about 1940 came the idea of development, the antecedents of which go back to the nineteenth century. Development, that is the theory and practice of turning the ex-colonies into subordinate economies and that was simultaneously utopian and myopic, ruled the council chambers and secretariats of Africa from about 1940 to about 1980, or even slightly longer in some places. Its effects were stagnation, corruption, and continued subordination. On the whole while both capitalist and communist Europe were transforming themselves in the aftermath of World War Two, the plan for Africa was evolutionary gradualism in the direction not of independence but of some sort of clubby, dependent, associationism. This was where the Commonwealth came in, at least before it found itself irreconcilably divided on the issue of apartheid.

Development "aid" fell off at the end of the Cold War.[10] By then it had withered away to be replaced by a torrent of neoliberal measures insisted on by such institutions as the World Bank and the IMF. From the 1980s these institutions had begun to propound the idea of "structural adjustment," a euphemism for austerity. By the second decade of the twenty-first century Western institutions of development had been largely superseded by a combination of handwringing charities sometimes publicized by global celebrities and by increased military intervention. "R2P" (responsibility to protect) became the code for the right to invade. Picture French *paras* and American drones flying about with Jeffrey Sachs and Bono hymning in the background about poverty. Accompanying the death throes of developmentalism, from around 1980 came actual economic decline, accentuated by rampant corruption, spiralling debt, and infrastructural deterioration. Dark days, indeed.

Immediately after World War Two, colonialism, while still cherished by the European governments that possessed colonies, was deplored by the Americans who railed against it – although when it came to the matter of "security" against the spread of communism, they made exceptions for certain colonialist regimes. Almost no one noticed that independent Liberia was hardly different from the colonial Belgian Congo to the extent that it was run by a single firm, Firestone, for the exploitation of a single tropical commodity, rubber, which was essential to the economy of a single Western state, the US.[11]

In Britain and France there was, before the 1950s, certain discussion but little real debate over the political and economic form the management of the African colonies would take, although it was generally agreed that the slow spread of education would permit the expansion of a class of Europeanized African subordinates who would sustain the colonial economies on behalf of Manchester and Lyon. In 1954 there were nearly 12,000 of these cultural métis in the Congo alone. In Monrovia, Freetown, and to a limited extent in Lagos, the elite were often the descendants of repatriated slaves from North America. The French were actually quite tolerant about letting a miniscule number of Africans join them in ruling Africa.

## NEOCOLONIALISM

So Africa became independent. Or did it? The term "neocolonialism" was quite widely used in the 1960s; Jean-Paul Sartre used it in the introduction to Frantz Fanon's *The Wretched of the Earth* in 1961. Sartre referred to it as "that idle dream of mother countries ... [that was] ... a lot of hot air." But at independence, he thought, many countries only achieved "a simulacrum of phony independence."[12] Otherwise it was seldom defined, perhaps because, like other terms such as "populism," it remains perpetually feral.[13] Yet it was an idea whose time had come even as the hour of colonialism was passing. Kwame Nkrumah, the pioneering African nationalist leader, warned of it after he had been removed as president of Ghana in early 1966. Nkrumah thought that his removal was the work of foreign powers, principally, one assumes, the British. The journalist, Jack Woddis, took up the idea, popularized, and expanded it.[14] Marxists like Woddis claimed that capitalist colonialism and neocolonialism created poverty and inequality and that so-called "development aid" was the cosmetic means of covering up the scars and disfigurements that colonialism left behind. Thus no matter what form aid took, it had its critics. Development aid, it was argued, was neocolonial to the extent that it served to maintain control over the future of African economies by foreign interests.

The patently neocolonial term "Françafrique" was invented by Félix Houphouët-Boigny (in power 1960–93), the first and long-time president of independent Côte d'Ivoire. Like almost all of former French Africa, the Ivory Coast remained within a bloc of ostensibly independent states that continued to use the franc, in the form of the "CFA franc," which was tied to the French franc. Other ties were cultural. Wrote *Time Magazine*, with swooning approval: "The Ivory Coast's First Lady is coiffed by one of the most exclusive Paris hairdressers ... and dressed by Dior whose salon is strategically located across the street from the Houphouët-Boigny's apartment ... The affluent Houphouët-Boignys also have a villa in the stylish Swiss resort of Gstaad (their six-year-old adopted daughter Hélène is attending school in Switzerland)."[15]

A more telling symptom of Houphouët-Boigny's willingness to prostrate himself to gods of the Quai d'Orsay was his apparent, but somewhat shrouded, complicity in the overthrow of both Kwame Nkrumah and the later, and equally radical, Thomas Sankara of Burkina Faso, "Africa's Ché Guevara" (in power 1984–87), one of Africa's few reforming leaders. Other forms of subservience were apparent with the voting within the UN of the former French colonies almost invariably following the lead of France itself.

Frantz Fanon (1925–1961), the West Indian psychiatrist who served on the side of the Algerian nationalists, wrote angrily about the corruption of the neocolonial elites. Besides *The Wretched of the Earth*, another of his books was called, pointedly, *Black Skins, White Masks*. He likened the heads of the new one-party states in Africa to "chairmen of the board of a [company] of impatient profiteers." He flayed them for their corruption: "Scandals are numerous, ministers grow rich, their wives doll themselves up, the members of parliament feather their nests and there is not a soul down to the simple policeman or customs officer who does not join the great procession of corruption."[16] J.-F. Bayart, reflecting on exposés of official corruption by the Policy Planning Unit of the Ministry of Foreign Affairs in Paris has noted that,

> Deaf to the paeans of the aid donors who saluted the advent of market-based democracies south of the Sahara, [French officials] celebrated the merits of good governance, praised the virtues of decentralized co-operation and gave an inaugural blessing to an emerging African "civil society" ... [Although] one researcher [within the Policy Planning Unit] ... was more inclined to postulate that tenets in Africa more closely resembled 'a return to "the heart of darkness."'[17]

## DARK DAYS IN GHANA

Ghana was the first country in sub-Saharan Africa to gain independence, and Kwame Nkrumah (1910–72) was independent, postcolonial Africa's first head of state. Young, articulate, university educated, and a civilian, J.F. Kennedy-ish, in fact, Nkrumah embodied a number of the most attractive characteristics of Africa's new postcolonial leaders. Although a sympathizer of the Non-Aligned Movement, and the very embodiment of Pan-Africanism, unlike Nehru, Nasser, or Sukarno, Nkrumah had little apparent interest in socialism either in the Fabian, social democratic, Soviet, Chinese, or any other doctrinaire form. Nor was he, like Patrice Lumumba (July to September 1960), the first prime minister of the Congo, at all apparently anti-Western before his overthrow.

Conscious of the value of the peaceful protests that had brought independence to India in 1947, Nkrumah, at the head of the Convention Peoples' Party (CPP), audaciously exploited British uncertainty about the costs of repression and the future value of one of their most advanced African colonies. He guessed correctly that neither the British Labour Party in power (1945–51) nor the postwar British public, had the stomach for a colonial war over cocoa, the Gold Coast's main export. Cocoa was produced by African smallholders, not European settlers like the tea planters of India or the rubber growers of Vietnam. In fact in Ghana there was no settler community, as there was in Kenya where it had gone from 23,000 in 1939 to around 60,000 by the late 1950s, able to rally support from politicians in the British capital. In fact Westerners of all sorts cheered on Nkrumah – leftists, churchgoers, liberal idealists, anthropologists, black nationalists. They saw in the Gold Coast the dawning of the new, free, postwar, world that they had longed and many had fought for. As for America, where Nkrumah had gone to university, it was clear that here was an ally in the struggle against European colonialism and the pursuit of liberty. And in the nascent Third World there was a widespread attempt of overthrow the assumptions of colonialism.

But Nkrumah didn't have much of an idea of how to create an independent state where none had existed before – and especially a state where literacy was rare and industry nonexistent. Even though Ghana had a Westernized elite, educated in schools in the south of the country by missionaries since the nineteenth century, this was by any measure quite small. All that left him was the rhetoric of effort. He explained:

> The dependent territories are backward in education, in agriculture, and in industry. The economic independence that should follow and maintain political independence demands every effort from the people, a total mobilization of brain and manpower resources. What other countries have taken three hundred years or more to achieve, a once independent territory must try to accomplish in a generation if it is to survive. Unless it is, as it were, "jet-propelled," it will lag behind and thus risk everything for which it has fought.[18]

The problem for Nkrumah and for Ghana as a whole was that the newly independent country had to be inserted into a system of mature capitalism desperate to rebuild itself after World War Two. For Ghana's Western trading partners, the main object was metropolitan profit not "development." The means of obtaining that profit had led to the sharpening of techniques over the entire period of colonial rule. How could Ghana envisage wandering into the counting houses of Europe with its bags of cocoa and its bars of gold and expect an outburst of fair trade?

Gold Coast did have just enough going for it to allow optimism to survive in the short term. There was the fact of sterling reserves, for instance, the deposits that the Gold Coast had been forced to leave with the Bank of England during World War Two. These could be withdrawn and invested. Then there was the matter of an increased demand for cocoa; this seems quite exaggerated in retrospect – even the huge British taste for sweets had its limits. What else? Perhaps if Ghana industrialized quickly it could satisfy some of the demands of its neighbours in countries like Côte d'Ivoire and Nigeria. The problem of course was that these countries also had peasant economies and peasants had very limited spending power. On top of this was the fact that both Nigeria to the east and the French African colonies to the west and north were tied up by British and French firms.

In retrospect, it is clear that the Ghana of Kwame Nkrumah couldn't possibly work without a lot of help. It barely lasted a decade and in that decade mass nationalist parties spread across the continent – to Nigeria, Ghana's next-door neighbour that became independent in 1960, and to most of French Africa, to the west and north of Ghana that was freed later in the decade. Only Portugal's African territories (Guiné, Angola, Mozambique, Cape Verde Islands), as well as Namibia, Southern Rhodesia (Zimbabwe), and South Africa remained under colonial or white-minority rule after the 1960s. As I have stressed, Portugal itself was one of the most retarded of West European states; its Brazilian colony was far more advanced than the mother country and would in the distant future, as we shall see, become a global power as Portugal itself shrivelled within the EU.

Ghana in the late 1950s struggled forward. With £200 million in sterling reserves and the world price for cocoa on an apparently endless escalator, there seemed to be every reason to design ambitious programs of national economic development. Of course, the whole world in the 1950s, communist as well as capitalist, was tantalized by the dream of sweet, even chocolaty, tomorrows. In Ghana, an extensive harbour and industrial park were built at Tema, along the coast east of Accra, and the massive Akosombo Dam was raised on the Volta River to provide hydroelectric power for the country and its infant industries. Ghana was, development optimists predicted, moving out of the agricultural and into the industrial stage of development. Still the future was not without clouds; in spite of wishful thinking to the contrary, Ghana's economy remained resolutely peasant-based. The modern elements of the economy, like the banks and the trading and mining firms, were few in number, miniscule in size, and almost entirely British-owned. Even petty merchants in the markets were often foreigners – Lebanese in some cases, Indian, Pakistani, or even Greek-Cypriot in others. In fact it was the continued hold of Britain over Ghana that led Nkrumah to argue, after he had been deposed, that his country had gone from colony to neocolony without actually becoming independent.

Other obstacles in the way of Ghanaian development seem not to have been foreseen either by the Ghanaians or their British advisors. Even in the expansive postwar years there was the commodity roller coaster. Cocoa prices had climbed from £190 to £352 per tonne between 1948 and 1958, and then, in the early 1960s, swooped sickeningly downward. Rising export prices had allowed an increase in imports that had stimulated a "feel good" atmosphere in the run-up to independence. Falling cocoa prices and diminishing sterling reserves had just the opposite effect. As his critics both inside and outside the country moved against him, Nkrumah, fatally convinced of his own messianism, became more isolated and dictatorial. By 1961, Ghana's considerable foreign currency reserves had been almost entirely depleted. In 1964 Nkrumah turned Ghana into a one-party state. This only decreased his popularity, running at low levels among the cocoa farmers who were suffering from low prices and the workers who were made to endure low wages and high living costs.

While he was in China on his way to Hanoi in February 1966, Nkrumah was deposed in a military coup. There was dancing in the streets. In London, the day after the coup, *The Times* wrote unctuously that if the militarists behind the coup "generate confidence, and want help, Ghana would be worth salvaging again." The newspapers' editors didn't have to say in whose interest the country would be "worth salvaging," but its readers knew. On the same day Nkrumah sent a telegram from Beijing to his secretary: "Don't forget that world imperialism and neo-colonialism hate my guts and all I stand for. They know I am in the way."[19]

After the fall of Kwame Nkrumah, the senior officers who overthrew him failed to generate confidence. They were, instead, as one African leader suggested, "musical comedy generals" who knew nothing of how to manage an independent economy under the difficult conditions that affected Ghana – especially the dependence on only a few resources and with low levels of investment and agricultural productivity. Yet, the generals marched on, wheeling about in a generally right-ish direction, one group succeeding another, each changing the colours under which it misruled: a "National Liberation Council" gave way to a "Presidential Commission" that was succeeded by a "National Redemption Council" until the last awkward squad was marched off the parade square and its beribboned officers confined to their barracks. In 1970 the Ghanaian economy went into free fall.

The generals' nemesis was a young air force officer, Jerry Rawlings (b.1947), who, having turned them out in a coup, returned power to a civilian regime before deciding that it, too, was incompetent and so seized power himself once more. Over the long duration of his rule, from December 1981 to 2001, Rawlings was, like Nkrumah, at first, remarkably popular and then unmistakably unpopular. His appeal diminished sharply from 1983 when the "Economic Recovery Program" (read: "austerity program") insisted on by the World Bank and the IMF led to the dismantling of much of Ghana's public health and welfare schemes and destroyed any prospect of even modest import substitution industrialization. Paul Nugent:

> [T]he retraction of the state from the economic sphere ... had ... damaging consequences. In the 1980s, most of the support for peasant agriculture was withdrawn on the basis that subsidies bred price distortions. This had a detrimental impact on peasant agriculture, and contributed to a mounting food import bill. In the 1990s, pressure was placed upon government to privatize state enterprises, wholly or partially, as part of the package of conditionalities. This meant that the Nkrumah-ist vision of the state as an engine of development was effectively disabled. The Bretton Woods institutions [ie. the IMF and World Bank] predicted that inward foreign investment and reinvigorated local entrepreneurship would take up the slack, but this happened in an uneven

manner. Manufacturing and food production never recovered, whereas gold mining and the cocoa economy flourished. However, government revenues covered only 56 per cent of spending in 2000, which meant that the state remained heavily dependent on external aid.[20]

Yet, overall, less due to the programs of structural adjustment ("conditionalities") than to lashings of aid and borrowed money, living standards in Ghana improved. According to Nugent, [I]n 1998, Ghanaian life expectancy stood at 50 years, which was above the African average and an improvement on the average of 45 years in 1960. Moreover, over the ten-year period from 1978 to 1988 infant mortality is estimated to have plunged from 77 to 60 per thousand while the percentage of immunized children is estimated to have risen from 31 to 56 per cent over the five years after 1988." In the period from 1988 to 2008 the infant mortality rate (of live births) dropped a further 77 to 50 per 1,000.[21]

Rawlings remained in power until the new century when he withdrew in favour of John Kofi Agyekum Kuofor in January 2001. Having served two terms, Kufuor was succeeded by John Atta Mills (2009–12) and John Mahama (2012–17). Ghana remained relatively democratic, with a free press, and was considered one of the more prosperous and stable of African states having escaped, unlike its neighbours, Sierra Leone and Liberia, civil war and crude dictatorship. Considered a middle-income state, its annual per capita GDP ($1,850) was higher than its neighbours like Mali ($696) and Senegal ($1,023) but lower than oil-rich Nigeria ($3,006). Accompanying the development duo of Jeffrey Sachs and Bono on a trip to northern Ghana in 2012, John Mulholland of *The Observer* made the point that, "By any measure Ghana is a success story." It was, he noted, "one of the most stable and economically successful countries in Africa." A small but significant part of its well-being continues to derive from foreign aid. Although increases to Canada's foreign aid had stalled and in many cases fallen, aid to Ghana increased by 4 per cent, making it one of the Canada's major aid recipients.[22] By 2014, however, Ghana was again struggling, with exports and currency reserves down and debt and inflation up. The president, "Mr Power Cut," John Mahama said that support from the IMF would be sought. In January 2017 he resigned.

## THE CONGO CAKE

After suffering what was probably the worst colonial administration in the whole of Africa, independence came suddenly to the Belgian Congo on 30 June 1960. At its eve, dozens of parties materialized, apparently out of nowhere. One leader stood out, Patrice Lumumba. Patrice Lumumba was more radical, more secular, more cosmopolitan, and less tribalist than his rivals – more than a little like Kwame Nkrumah of Ghana. Lumumba had visited Ghana in December 1958 and been swayed by Nkrumah's speech at the All-African Peoples' Conference. Infatuated with the idea of independence and excited by Nkrumah's rhetoric, he was determined to lead a united Congo into the future. His vehicle was to be the mass-based Mouvement National Congolais (MNC), a southern cousin of the Gold Coast's Convention Peoples' Party. A month after he returned from the Gold Coast, there was rioting in the Congolese capital and the Belgians, now trapped in the headlights of a global anticolonialism, panicked. They advanced the timetable for local elections, which were to be in the run-up to independence. More anticolonial violence followed. Again the Belgians pushed the deadline for independence. They consoled themselves that the Congolese, deficient in skilled personnel of any kind, would need them. They would remain in control of the economy, especially the mining monopoly. This was the essence of neocolonialism. In any event, here was one of the largest and richest countries in Africa where the total number of educated people, including priests, was in the hundreds. In the year of independence there were only 136 children in secondary schools, barely more than in any one of several secondary schools in Ghana or Nigeria.

Just before independence, elections were held. The party of Lumumba, the MNC, won the largest number of seats, and he was therefore in a position to become the first prime minister of the independent Congo. In July an army mutiny swept the country while Lumumba became caricatured by the Belgians, and more importantly by the Americans, as a maddened stooge of Moscow. (*Lè yo vie touye chen yo di'il fou* – "When the people want to kill a dog, they say it's rabid" – is the appropriate Haitian aphorism.)[23]

In December (1960) Lumumba was arrested and in January, with agreement between Brussels and Washington, not to mention the United Nations, and to the satisfaction of his political rivals, he was tortured and then shot by a firing squad commanded by Belgian officers. When the news got out there were demonstrations right across the Third World. Africa had now got its own martyr to stand beside other victims of the Cold War.[24] In Moscow, a university was named after him: "Patrice Lumumba University of Peoples' Friendship." In the Congo itself, decades of repression, civil war, invasion, and plunder would follow. The West had reproduced a Haiti in Africa – a neocolony celebrated for the profits of its proprietors and the horror of its regimes. Its Papa Doc Duvalier was Joseph-Désiré Mobutu, also known as Mobutu Sese Seko (in power 1965–97).[25]

If Mobutu was ushered into power by the Belgians, he was approved of by the Americans. In 1971 he changed the name of the Congo to Zaire. Adam Hochschild recalls Mobutu's allies:

> US military aid helped Mobutu repel several attempts to overthrow him. Some of his political enemies he ordered tortured and killed; some he co-opted into his ruling circles; others he forced into exile. The United States gave him well over a billion dollars in civilian and military aid during the three decades of his rule; European powers – especially France – contributed more. For its heavy investment, the United States and its allies got a regime that was reliably anti-Communist and a secure staging area for CIA and French military operations, but Mobutu brought his country little except a change of name.[26]

Of the benefits Mobutu showered on himself, Jean-François Bayart comments:

> He was said to control between 17 and 22 per cent of the national budget for his personal use ... Mobutu ... seems to have amassed most of his fortune from exporting ... copper, ivory and, above all, diamonds ... In 1982 his foreign assets were estimated at $4 billion. His wealth within the country was immense. The Head of State was one of the first beneficiaries of Zairianisation, and he grouped his acquisitions into a conglomerate ... which, in 1977, employed 25,000 people (including 140 European managers).[27]

Since Mobutu's corruption was beyond parody, we are bound to ask further how he was able to endure – that is, by what means other than with the support of the United States, France, and Belgium. His secrets to success were several. Leaving aside terror, Mobutu was able to mobilize the support of local allies by giving them crumbs from the cake of national wealth. Assets worth as much as a billion dollars were distributed to those whom he favoured. As Bayart notes, in 1973 he "Zairianised" agricultural estates and small businesses, removing them from their foreign owners and handing them over to the "sons of the country." Thus, ownership by expatriates – Belgians, Greeks, Portuguese, and even Pakistanis – was terminated and the new class of Zairois property owners was expanded. He also took over a golden goose in the form of the Union Minière de Haut Katanga – the sprawling Belgian monopoly that was to become the mainstay of the economy. Union Minière was, among other of its claims, one of the world's greatest copper producers.[28] Of course, many of the beneficiaries of the distribution of spoils were simply greedy incompetents, transforming their boons into consumer goods rather than investing them. From 1974, due to corruption and mismanagement, while the economy of Zaire regressed, its civil service payroll grew.

Besides local allies, Mobutu had built up a network of foreign partners, most of whom licked their chops over the prospects of Zaire's mineral and petroleum wealth and what remained of its domestic markets. Thus, mining speculators, oil explorers, and manufacturers all crowded into the president's palace anxious to conclude deals. General Motors, British Leyland, and French Renault all assembled cars while Goodyear made tires. Krupp refined palm oil and made soap, and, in 1975, Gulf began to produce oil from offshore deposits. The mineral producers and the oil wells, of course, were largely in foreign hands although they generated a certain amount of wealth for the state and its rulers, the gatekeepers. The goods the various assemblers and manufacturers produced were more expensive than imports. No one had yet thought of land grabbing although that would come later.

The 1973 nationalizations may be seen as the beginning of the end of Zaire as a viable national economy. Of the approximately $800 million the nationalized copper mines produced annually, officials stole as much as $270 million. The situation worsened in the 1980s and '90s as corruption deepened, copper profits dipped, export costs increased, and the countryside could no longer feed the swelling urban population. Even by 1960, 36 per cent of the population was urban and by the end of the century this had risen to nearly a half. Despite talks about rehabilitating the agrarian economy, virtually nothing was done as roads from the countryside became impassable and transport vehicles collapsed. Nor was there any attempt at agrarian rehabilitation through the normal means of rural credit or investment in improved practices and seeds. As certain sectors of the agricultural economy went into decline – such as cotton and palm oil exports that had thrived under the colonial state – imports took their place. By 1980, then, there was simultaneously economic stagnation and population growth.

And to shift the country down a gear from bad to worse, there was structural adjustment, first laid on the country by the IMF in 1977 and then brought down again a decade later. More retrenchment, further sales of public assets, removal of exchange controls, and a massive loss of jobs as the civil service was slashed and industries closed down. By the early 1990s the national economy was in complete ruins and Mobutu's former supporters in the West turned their backs on him while the IMF expelled Zaire as a voting member. These were indeed bad times for despots; Jean-Bedel Bokassa (1966–79), the demonstrably maniacal dictator of the Central African Republic, who had been overthrown by French paratroopers in September 1979, found refuge in France, at least before returning to Africa to be tried and convicted for mass murder. Idi Amin, "the Butcher of Uganda," fled in the same year, settling among the pious in Saudi Arabia. Across the Atlantic, Papa Doc's son and successor, Jean-Claude "Baby Doc," had abandoned Haiti, also for France, in February 1986. The rule of the military dictators of Argentina, Brazil, and Chile came to an end in the same decade. Suharto in Indonesia (1965–98), another friend of the West, on the other hand, lasted ten more years.[29]

## CONGO REDUX

In May 1997 Laurent-Desiré Kabila, a Luba from Katanga in the mineral-rich south of Zaire, a gun runner, gold smuggler, and, fitfully, anti-Mobutu rebel, marched his ragtag army right across Zaire into Kinshasa. He was backed, perhaps secretly, perhaps not, by Washington and, later, by the tyrant Mugabe of Zimbabwe.[30] Mobutu fled; he was now part of the motley procession of fugitive postcolonial rulers – King Faruq, Kwame Nkrumah, Odumegwu Ojukwu, Baby Doc, the Shah, and perhaps we should include Sihanouk and certainly Idi Amin. London and Paris have always been favourite boltholes for fleeing tyrants, but Mobutu was spoiled for choice since he owned property in France, Switzerland, Portugal, Spain, and Morocco. He chose the Riviera. His estate at Cap Martin, "Villa Del Mar," had, appropriately, formerly belonged to King Leopold. Its estimated worth was £3.2 million (about $5 million). This sealed the fate for his palace in Gbadolite, his hometown 1,000 km north of Kinshasa, that had cost in excess of $10 million to build. It was looted and fell into ruins. The dictator's actual end came in Rabat, Morocco, in September 1997 where, like the Shah of Iran, he died of cancer. Meanwhile, his successor, Kabila, even before he reached Kinshasa, had cut deals with the international mining companies.[31] One Western diplomat was quoted as observing, "It's the best thing for Zaire and offers the best chance of a peaceful transition."[32]

With the demise of Mobutu began another chapter in what Gérard Prunier has called "Africa's World War" and Adam Hochschild has referred to as "a bewilderingly complex civil war in which millions have died."[33] The first stage of this war, which lasted from October 1996 to May 1997, is known as the "First Congo War." It was followed from August 1998, by the "Second Congo War," which lasted five years until June 2003 when a peace deal was signed in Pretoria. This war, which was both civil and international, involved nine African countries and thirty militias. Even after the war had officially ended, bands of armed men of no particular fixed allegiance roamed the country. As late as 2007, as many as 45,000 casualties were reported. Van Reybrouck:

> The Second Congo War disappeared from the international media reports because it was considered incomprehensible and obscure. And indeed, there were no clearly delineated camps: even more, there was no clear division of roles into villain and underdog. After the Cold War, Western journalists increasingly came to apply a moral frame of reference reporting on armed conflicts; in Yugoslavia, the Serbs were the major culprits; in Rwanda, the Tutsis were the innocent victims. In both cases that led to disastrous misrepresentations and policy measures. In Congo it was not particularly easy to find a "good" side. Anyone viewing the conflict from close up knew that all those involved had their own skeletons in the closet ... The Second Congo War became a conflict in which everyone found everyone else just a shade more culpable, so that hitting back was allowable and an endless spiral of violence could ensue. The Western media turned and left.[34]

In the meantime, Kabila had renamed his country the "Democratic Republic of Congo." He ruled it in customarily autocratic and incompetent fashion at least until January 2001 when he was assassinated by one of his bodyguards. He was succeeded by his son, Joseph.

In April 1994, in Rwanda, a genocide in which hundreds of thousands were slaughtered took place. This came to be regarded as the most horrendous of the postwar world. Its victims were mainly Tutsis, a large minority living among the majority Hutus. While there has been some debate how this genocide started, it does seem clear that the *genocidaires* enjoyed the full support and even military assistance of the French government. It is surmised that Paris, feeling threatened that a vital part of Françafrique might be appropriated by its Anglo-American rivals, felt compelled to support the *genocidaires.*

In the Congo in 2006 Joseph Kabila was elected. Yet again, disaster ensued. In the east of the country a breakaway party was formed under General Laurent Nkunda and in January 2008 another civil war. The death toll seems an almost unimaginable five million plus people, making it, according to the International Rescue Committee, the deadliest conflict since World War Two. *Foreign Policy* magazine referred to Joseph Kabila as "Congo's New Mobutu," stressing the ruthlessness of his reign of terror ("one of the world's worst human rights records"), the wretchedness of the lives Congo's citizens, and the unflagging support he continued to claim from the leaders of the West.[35] No longer invisible, behind the scenes lurked those who were greedy for the Congo's rich minerals, including the Western multinationals. The minerals produced in the war zones of the Congo were known as "conflict minerals." The most valuable of them are the "3 Ts" – tin, tantalum, and tungsten – together with gold. According to the Enough Project, "Locals in mining communities are often forced to take part in the illicit mining economy. Money earned from the sale of conflict minerals is used for personal profit and to further violent causes."[36]

But "kleptocracy" doesn't tell us as much as we need to know: "coltan," a compound of columbium and tantalum, one of the "3 Ts," tells us more. Coltan is an ore available in huge quantities in the Congo. It is essential to the manufacture of cellphone components. While a little comes from Australia, the Congo is the main source. In 2000–01 its price rose from $30 to $300 dollars a pound and its export value to Rwanda from which it was shipped, around $240 million.

> In an increasingly globalized economy, governments were only intermediaries in a mass of complex, international, and rapidly mutating trading networks. Kagame and Museveni [the ruler of Ugan-

> da] were not at the end of any supply line; it was the multinational mining companies, shady fly-by-nights, notorious but highly evasive arms dealers, and crooked businessmen in Switzerland, Russia, Kazakhstan, Belgium, the Netherlands, and Germany who made a killing by selling Congo's stolen raw materials. They all operated in an extremely free marketplace. In political terms Congo was a disaster area, but in economic terms it was a paradise – at least for some. Failed nation-states are the success stories of runaway, global neoliberalism.[37]

According to the UN's Human Development Index, in 2013 the Democratic Republic of the Congo (DRC), certainly one of the most richly endowed countries of the world, stood 186th out of 187 and 49th out of 50 in Africa. A new source of wealth had opened up for foreign investors: land. As one Congolese explained to the journalist Stefano Liberti in 2010, "In Congo, the government signs agreements with large foreign companies without consulting us. The most fertile land is handed over to agribusiness firms, who convert it into monocultures of jatropha and palm oil for export to Europe."[38]

Joseph Kabila, reelected in 2011, had promised to honour the constitution and not seek election for a third term. But the poll, due in November 2016, was postponed. In fact what had happened was nothing short of a coup. An editorial in *The Observer* commented:

> [T]hat the leadership of another African country appears ready to ride roughshod over democracy and laws is clear. The DRC has never had a peaceful transition of power since independence in 1960 ... Last year the presidents of Burundi, Rwanda and Congo-Brazzaville overrode constitutional requirements that they step aside. In Burundi's case, violence and displacement resulted. In Uganda, Yoweri Museveni looks determined to go on forever. Robert Mugabe's Zimbabwean "presidency for life" and José Eduardo dos Santo's Angolan ascendency provide further examples of endemic disregard for democratic principles.[39]

## SOUTH AFRICA'S APARTHEID

South Africa remains the richest, most economically advanced country in Africa and the last to be ruled by non-Africans.[40] Between 1652 when the first Dutch settlers stepped off ships headed for the East Indies and 1994 when the last white prime minister stepped down, South Africa became Africa's preeminent colony of white settlement on which, until they were abandoned by Britain, both Kenya and Southern Rhodesia (Zimbabwe) were modelled. But unlike these, or Algeria, home of French settlers for merely a century, the roots of European and Asian settlement in South Africa extend over three centuries. No settler colonialism in Africa or Asia could compare to this.

The whites in South Africa were to become Africans if only because they were nothing else. Of them, the preeminent group was that of Dutch origin – these became the Afrikaners and their language, Afrikaans. By 1793 there were about 15,000 Afrikaners at and around the Cape of Good Hope. Thriving in a Mediterranean climate, they had farms but not plantations and owned about 15,000 African slaves. The Bantu-speaking Zulus who emigrated from the northeast and drove other Africans before them had yet to enter the country. (The centre of the Zulu settlement was to become the modern province of Kwa-Zulu Natal to the east of the Cape.)

From the nineteenth century other Europeans and Asians of diverse origins immigrated to South Africa to work in and manage the mines, to labour in the sugar plantations, and to develop export crops and even wine. The Europeans included people from Britain, French Huguenots who had settled even earlier, and Jews from Lithuania; the Asians were mainly from India from where they had been brought in the nineteenth century as indentured labourers, a modernized form of serfdom. Besides the Europeans and the Indians there were the descendants of the Malay-speaking people who had been brought as slaves in the eighteenth century (called "Malays") and métis, that is people of mixed race, called "coloureds." So blacks, whites, Asians, and coloureds, all with different assigned roles in a repressive and deeply unequal world, coexisted. Always, the white Europeans ruled over the rest; the African majority suffered every kind of exploitation and humiliation and was kept under control by a well-oiled apparatus of repression and violence.

In the postwar period, under a Nationalist Party government, South Africa adopted an import substitution industrialization (ISI) model of economic development, with several features in common with countries in Latin America, India, and elsewhere. Previously, between the time of the Anglo-Boer War (1899–1902) and World War Two (1939–45), under the banners of *Volkskapital* ("peoples' capitalism"), the white settlers established a modern economy of which they took control of key elements. This included its agriculture, its manufacturers and, above all, its mines.

The central political doctrine of the state in the postwar period was one of racial supremacy, known as apartheid ("apartness"). This racist, populist, pseudo-philosophy, rooted in nineteenth-century British colonial mining ordinances and sustained by the teachings of the local Calvinist Church, was a latecomer, not emerging in full bloom until the 1930s.[41] Its central object was to condone and enforce extreme inequality on the basis of racist criteria.

The crowning of the South African apartheid system was constitutionally enacted by the Nationalist Party in 1948, the year after much of South Asia became independent. Thus, the year, in which Congress secured political power in India, its opposite, the white-racist Nationalist Party, won a surprising election in South Africa. Support for the Nationalists was principally by the Afrikaners. Opposition to the Nationalists among the Europeans came from within the English and Lithuanian-Jewish populations many of whose members were attached to the African National Congress and the Communist Party. Communism was a natural home for dissident whites in the postwar era as it had been for dissident Europeans in Europe in the 1930s. But for most emigrants from poor and grim postwar Europe, there was no reason to complain as apartheid South Africa was a gift that kept on giving. In their thousands they emigrated – between 1962 and 1970 some 30,000–40,000 of them with around 40 per cent being British.[42] Most of these voted for the Nationalist Party.

The Calvinist Dutch Reformed Church had certain points of similarity with the Southern Baptist Church of Texas and the US South. Both had fought wars to guarantee their way of life and both sought to keep people of African origin in a subordinate position, just a notch above outright slavery. Education was a sore point; the less of it for Africans, the better. Assimilation, thus, was hardly a goal. "[B]lack education should be aimed at developing a higher Bantu culture and not at producing black Europeans."[43]

## HEAVEN

From 1948 to 1972, and especially from 1964 to 1973, the South African economy boomed with the country experiencing one of the highest growth rates in the capitalist world, in some years exceeding 5 per cent.[44] Foreign investment flooding into the country permitted South African defence expenditures to increase from $63 million to $1 billion between 1960 and 1975, "defence" in this context referring to the role of the state in both sustaining apartheid against the majority of the population and destabilizing neighbouring Angola and Mozambique which, after Portuguese colonialism collapsed at the time of the Carnation Revolution in 1974, came to be ruled by regimes that were anticolonial and nominally Marxist. (Portugal itself joined the EEC in 1986.)[45]

To those, white settlers and foreign investors alike, despairing of the crises afflicting the rest of the continent, South Africa was a haven where investments could be assured of peaceful increase and labour remained cheap and in infinite supply. This remained the case at least until the 1980s when the implacable tide of African protest, a debt crisis, a slowing growth rate, and international pressure, especially from the United States, caused the more liberal members of the white ruling class to reexamine the premises of white rule, cross their fingers, and accept democratic elections.

Slowly, partly due to external pressure but mainly a result of the high price demanded to maintain the repressive apparatus, the apartheid state weakened. In some ways its decline resembled that of the postwar European dictatorships (Spain, Portugal, Greece), in other ways it seemed like that of the dismal military regimes of Latin America in the 1980s. The economy, which had grown lustily in 1979–81, fell back after 1983. Then there was internal pressure, particularly in the form of the Black Consciousness movement led by the remarkable Steve Biko (1946–77), a medical student. Biko was arrested and assassinated by the government ("died in police custody"), but the equipoise that the apartheid state had previously enjoyed was lost. From the mid-1980s, control of the townships, the massive urban slums to which Africans had been legally consigned, was lost. Other factors pushed it further; sanctions in the West, loss of military credibility in Angola at the hands of the Cubans, and, finally, the fall of Communism in 1989.[46]

In February 1990 Nelson Mandela, the leader of the African National Congress (ANC), a common front of Africans and whites, nationalists, liberals, and communists, was freed from the prison in which he had been held for twenty-seven years. The ANC itself, previously banned, was unbanned, that is, its members were allowed full political rights. Even the Communist Party was permitted to emerge from the shadows. For many, this was a gobsmacking turn of events. Nelson Mandela who became the first president of a nonracist South Africa was almost immediately, and universally, feted as a hero in a pantheon that included other leaders, like Gandhi and Martin Luther King, who had led the struggle against racism and for equality. Although few African or Asian leaders have ever been held in such remarkable esteem, even liberal parties in the West had trouble recognizing that Mandela was a genuine democrat and that his cause was one that many Westerners could take as their own. In Canada, while there was widespread popular support for African liberation, the ruling Liberal Party showed itself wishy-washy. Its leaders, like those in the Conservative Party in Britain, were conspicuously more concerned with investment than human rights in South Africa. Certain noisy political figures on the right even sought to undermine the credibility of the ANC and Mandela altogether. The views of the Canadian backwoods Conservative MP, William Vankoughnet, for instance, are only a slight exaggeration of this tendency. "No-one wants to accept that the whites have done a lot of good things for blacks," he explained. "Communists are trying to destroy what white people have built. If the black people come to power, that will be destroyed."[47]

## LIBERATION

In South Africa's first democratic elections, held 27–29 April 1994, the ANC won power with a whopping 62 per cent of the vote. "Rwanda is our nightmare, South Africa is our dream," wrote Wole Soyinka, Nigeria's Nobel Prize–winning novelist and playwright.[48]

The supporters of the Nationalist Party, mainly whites together with some sectors of the coloured population, won 20 per cent. The party soon disappeared altogether. Nelson Mandela became head of state. He was seventy-six. A negotiated transition, with remarkably little strife, took place bringing to an end nearly three and a half centuries of white advance and black retreat. Now, nowhere in Africa were Africans ruled except by other Africans.

Even before the end, the writing was on the wall. In an article in January 1989, professor J.L. Boshoff, himself an Afrikaner, had confessed:

> What an appalling human tragedy apartheid has been. The Afrikaners' Frankenstein; their own creation has degenerated into a monster which now threatens to destroy them ... How reasonable

> and intelligent people could have voted for this laughable conception and endorsed it with ever increasing majorities, is one of the great mysteries of democracy. I am guilty myself. I voted for it.[49]

Others had anticipated the end even before Boshoff; from 1984 secret negotiations had been taking place between proxies of the Nationalists and the ANC. Mandela himself, like the leaders of the Indian National Congress in the prelude to Indian independence, had been in talks while still in prison. Not before time, the leaders of some of the grandest of the capitalist firms in South Africa realized that the apartheid state had reached the end of its tether. Profits would have to be assured according more conventional liberal–democratic arrangements. Capitalism and Afrikaner privilege, they prayed, would survive.

The 1994 election was a moment of great euphoria, not only in South Africa but right across the democratic world. The British, the Americans, the Canadians, and the Indians, among others, had all watched and waited for democracy to banish racism in South Africa. There was talk of pages being turned and new chapters being opened in African history. The lost decade of the 1980s when a mere seven out of the forty-five states of sub-Saharan Africa could boast of democracy, was temporarily forgotten. Perhaps the crazed dictators like Idi Amin of Uganda and Jean-Bedel Bokassa of the Central African Republic had, after all, fled in 1979. Julius Nyerere, turned into an icon by Western students and developmentalists, had kept hope alive, at least until he retired in 1985. Mobutu still held on but against increasing pressure. Elsewhere, well, perhaps a great deal of wishful thinking.

## AFRICAN NATIONAL CONGRESS IN POWER

In the beginning, the new ANC government introduced an ambitious Reconstruction and Development Program aimed at redressing social inequalities; all South Africans were now to enjoy the fruits of emancipation. The program abolished all of the ten homelands and extinguished the legal residues of apartheid. And above all of this stood Nelson Mandela. If the miracle of South Africa's transformation was contrived, Mandela's saintliness seemed genuine. "Mandela spoke from the heart about the need for reconciliation and for everyone to pull together for the sake of the country. Coming from a man who had spent over a third of his life in jail and who had refused all compromise in order to be free, this was magical stuff. Moreover, the man had grace, a sense of humour and a complete lack of grandeur ... The country and the world embraced him for all that."[50]

In 1999 Thabo Mbeki (b. 1942) replaced Mandela as president. Mbeki, who had become the effective head of the ANC after independence, had spent his whole live in the party. Indeed, he was a consummate *apparatchik*: doctrinaire, manipulative, vindictive, secretive. Brushing aside Mandela's pleas for reconciliation between all of the races, Mbeki brought back racial politics by stressing the existence of two separate nations, black and white. And, he claimed, it was the turn of the black nation, or at least the black members of the ruling party and the small black middle class, to prosper. "An aspirant class of black capitalists" championed by Mbeki, was thus in the making.[51]

But while there was prosperity for the few, for the mass of Africans, especially the poor in the rural areas, times were as bad as ever they had been under apartheid. By early 2003, on one measure, unemployment stood at 42.1 per cent and was rising. Among African women it was more than 50 per cent. This was a partial explanation for the rise of prostitution and spread of HIV/AIDS. In spite of all the brave talk about transferring wealth from whites to blacks, then, what was really happening was a transference of some wealth from a mainly white to a mixed black and white minority. One of the world's most unequal societies, usually mentioned in the same breath as Brazil, was becoming even more unequal.

As for the whites, many migrated. The English speakers (usually of English and Jewish backgrounds), comprising about a third of the white population, tended to go to English-speaking countries, like Canada. Although the Afrikaners stayed put, the white population of South Africa plummeted from 16 per cent in 1980 to 9 per cent in 2011. Most members of the coloured population, which roughly equalled that of the whites, remained in South Africa. The Asian population, comprising 1.2 million or about 2 per cent of the total, also stayed. The Chinese population that had shrunk under apartheid, shot up again in the postapartheid era reaching as many as half a million, the largest in Africa.[52] Postapartheid Chinese emigrants soon outnumbered native Chinese. A ruling passed by the High Court in 2008 established that for purposes of the Black Economic Empowerment Act, the native Chinese were officially "black." Filipinos were also black although other Southeast Asians, most of who had come from the Dutch East Indies (ie. Indonesia) and were called Malays, were classified as "coloured."

The most egregious failure of the Mbeki regime (1999–2008) had not been its inability to improve the living standards of black South Africans but was its refusal to deal with the catastrophe of the HIV/AIDS epidemic that has devastated the country. "Every senior UN official, engaged directly or indirectly in the struggle against AIDS, to whom I have spoke about South Africa, is completely bewildered by the policies of President Mbeki," Stephen Lewis, the UN Special Envoy for HIV/AIDS, has written.[53]

The HIV/AIDS epidemic has, in fact, had a short, if lethal, history. The first significant group of sufferers was reported among Malawian workers in South Africa's mines. Thereafter, the sexually transmitted disease spread rapidly. Mandela's government promised to give the AIDS campaign high priority but, in fact, did little about it. Mbeki and his colleagues at first even denied its existence. One of his ministers actually claimed to a parliamentary caucus that it was a plot by the CIA in alliance with the drug companies. As R.W. Johnson, who has called Mbeki a "clever, paranoid and unbalanced man," noted at the time:

> By mid 2003 the AIDS pandemic had secured its millionth victim and the death rate ... was rising fast. Another 5.3 million South Africans were HIV positive ... Despite this the government was still trying by every means to delay and postpone the delivery of anti AIDS drugs. The sheer callousness of the new ANC elite towards the black unemployed and those suffering from AIDS was difficult to describe, surpassing the cruelties of ... the old [Nationalist] elite.[54]

"Something has gone wrong with the post-Mandela government," commented Stephen Lewis.[55]

In September 2008 Thabo Mbeki was defeated as head of South Africa's ruling party. His successor was Jacob Zuma, a member of the Zulu tribe (the largest in the country). The Zulus immediately took control of the key "security" ministries – the police, intelligence, and justice –and maneuvered their province, KwaZulu-Natal, into the leading position within the ANC.

Zuma was a Zulu all the way. He had six wives, more than twenty children and a royal compound that cost the state in excess of £27 million: "[A]ll his marriages are conducted in traditional Zulu style, with Zuma dressed in leopard skins and holding a spear."[56] Of course, South Africa was not the Congo so any resemblance between Zuma and Mobutu was bound to be coincidental.

In the 2009 elections the ANC won heavily in Zuma's home province and lost ground almost everywhere else, but as it was in control it managed to steamroller over opposition from rival groups and seize control of the media that had been, for a time at least, relatively independent. Economically the downhill slide continued with increasing debt and decreasing credibility among investors. "The country has become utterly corrupt under ANC rule," R.W. Johnson wrote in London's *Evening Standard* at the end of 2013. "Government ministers enrich themselves more or less openly. Civil servants, teachers and the police are all massively corrupt. Community riots against poor service delivery occur once every two days."

South Africa remains the most industrialized economy in Africa, although its manufacturing sector declined from 19 per cent in 1993 to 17 per cent in 2012. In common with other industrialized economies right across the globe, while industry had declined as a proportion of the economy overall, the services sector, with the acronym FIRE (finance, insurance and real estate), has increased in importance. South Africa's per capita GDP growth rate has dropped from 4.6 in 2004 to 2.8 in 2014 although gross government debt as a percentage of GDP is a modest 42. (We may compare this to Greece at 158.5, Portugal at 123, and Iceland at 100 if we require a little good news.) Unemployment, however, is the rain on the parade: youth unemployment has been around 50 per cent and unemployment in general half of that, never having been below 20 per cent since the end of apartheid. Inequality actually rose since the end of apartheid. As Simon Kuper reported in the South African business newspaper *Business Day*, it was 0.59 in 1995 but 0.63 in 2013. "Inequality is the new apartheid. The ruling classes pass on their status by sending their children to exclusive schools, much like in apartheid Johannesburg." Gerry Caplan, a longtime Canadian campaigner against apartheid, has stressed the connection between the rise of neoliberalism and the fall of apartheid, adding that it was South Africa's misfortune to have Nelson Mandela followed by "two singularly unworthy successors; Thabo Mbeki, the twisted AIDS denier, and the ethically challenged Jacob Zuma, who has come to symbolize the victory of the venal present over the honourable past." In a final flourish, he asked, "Will political power in South Africa remain in the hands of what one union leader impolitely called 'a powerful corrupt and demagogic elite of political hyenas'? Or will a new generation emerge to steer the country towards the glass half full?" In common with other liberation movements that attained power in Africa, Roger Southall has written, the ANC has "not merely failed to live up to expectations, but [has] become an increasing threat to democracy."[57] As late as mid-2017, attempts were being made to impeach Zuma.

# 9

# Latin America: Populism, Dictatorship, and the Super-cycle

In the early decades of the nineteenth century, as it moved to independence, Latin America was on its way to becoming the richest part of the non-Western world.[1] In economic terms, we might think of this first age of independent Latin America – say from about 1820 until the period beginning with Vargas' "New State" (1938–45) – as the classic moment of mercantilism. Here was a world of plantations, mines, and ranches, of coffee, copper, and corned beef, with industry still waiting for a program that would advance its importance, expand a working class, and sustain a class of national capitalists who would be able to overthrow the agrarian export elites who ruled over the cattle ranches, the coffee *fincas*, and the sugar mills and who supported the conservative parties.

By the twentieth century, following a surge in the growth of world trade that had begun in the middle of the nineteenth, many of the larger states of Latin America enjoyed ever-brightening prospects. The most populous Spanish-speaking state in South America, Argentina, had the highest GDP growth rate in Latin America; in 1913, its per capita income was higher than both France and Germany. Its agricultural labour force had shrunk to 34.2 per cent of the total. Canada's, comparable in several respects, was 37. And like Canada, the limitless agricultural frontier could only make farming more profitable. But Canada could boast nothing to compare to the capital of Argentina: "Buenos Aires was comparable only with New York in vitality and modernity in the New World, a thriving cosmopolitan centre unique in Latin America."[2] By 1919 it had a population of more than two million. Other cities in the major states of Latin America were also growing fast: in 1920, Rio de Janeiro had a population of 1,150,000 and São

Paulo of 570,000. Mexico City had a population of 693,000. In 1921 Montreal, Canada's largest city and its commercial heart, had a population of 619,000.[3] Unsurprisingly, most people in Argentina, Uruguay, and Chile, at least in the cities, saw themselves as living in an extension of Europe rather than in the Third World.[4] All the more since the majority actually came from Spain and Italy. The indigenous population counted for little.

Brazil, the largest state in Latin America, was already more populous and prosperous than Portugal by 1800. The fact that Argentina, Uruguay, and Chile also looked welcoming to prospective European emigrants was in part due to their swelling urban centres and their substantial agricultural and mineral exports. Brazil's population, by contrast to the more Europeanized Latin American states, was remarkably mixed because of its former slave population, yet, like Argentina in the 1880s, it attracted 200,000 free, overwhelmingly European, emigrants a year. By the middle of the twentieth century, these states were still booming: between 1939 and 1945 Chile's rate of GDP growth was an impressive 4 per cent and Mexico's a sizzling 6.2 per cent. But Brazil's economic growth was even steeper – between 1930 and 1980 it was a stunning 6.5 per cent, before the rise of China probably the fastest in the world.

In Latin America, Chile had an exemplary tradition of democratic elections, while Mexico avoided the fate of dictatorship altogether after 1910. The Latin American role model, Europe, by comparison, in the first decades of the twentieth century, was lashed by hurricanes of political turbulence and economic uncertainty; rising nations, teetering states, collapsing empires, seething racial and religious enmities, civil wars, fugitive populations, financial crises. It is hardly surprising that Europeans as well as Levantines fled in their millions to Latin America.[5]

Argentina and Brazil, which we will consider below, remain the largest and most populous countries in South America, covering between them 63.3 per cent of the continental area, 60.2 per cent of the population, and almost 70 per cent of the GDP. Both experienced dire periods of military rule and dirty wars, beginning in 1964 in Brazil and 1976 in Argentina; democracy was regained in 1983 in Argentina and in 1984 in Brazil and consolidated with difficulty in the following years. Economically, over the twentieth century both countries moved in parallel from heavy reliance on agro-exports through a phase of import substitution and toward an opening along neoliberal lines. Both have seen privatization of public utilities, trade and financial deregulation, equal treatment of local and foreign capital, deregulation of domestic markets, tax, and labour market reforms. Both were charter members of the neoliberal vanguard, Chile, first of all, and then Argentina and Brazil.[6] But neoliberalism was just one more moment in the region's Sisyphian struggle for development; by 2015 the miracle of Latin American growth had reversed itself, and the heavy weight of inequality and underdevelopment was rolling back over the struggling economies.

## ARGENTINA: IMPERISHABLE POPULISM

Until the Depression of the 1930s Argentina had been ruled by an oligarchy with a rural economic base. Known as the *burguesía pampeana* (the pampas bourgeoisie), its main economic preoccupation was the production of wheat and beef for the export market. Its main social concern was in guaranteeing its own reproduction and hegemony in relation to other Argentines. This oligarchy was connected to the officer class of the military. To most senior officers, rapid, unguided change, meant chaos or even anarchy and communism. From the 1930s through World War Two, many of them openly expressed an admiration for European fascism – that is, the political solutions of Mussolini, Franco, and Salazar. The appeal of fascism was not surprising; at a time of social and economic turbulence it offered the solution of order and the promise of racial patriotism. Yet, in general, Argentine fascism had a different face and different manners than the fascism of Europe. Racial purity, for instance, was not a serious concern although the emigration of Jews from Europe was a question that disturbed a minority of Argentines.

By the end of World War II, Argentine politics had changed radically. The Depression, over which people in Latin America had little control, had weakened the economic and therefore the political power of the *burguesía pampeana.* Then, during the war, overseas demand for processed and manufactured goods from Argentina had increased and the industrial workforce had taken off; between the mid-1930s and the late 1940s the number of workers in industry increased from around half a million to about two million. A massive migration from the countryside to the cities, and to Buenos Aires in particular, became a flood. Alongside the working class was a growing middle class, including small entrepreneurs. Sensing the decline of the bourgeoisie and a change in the established social order, Argentina's officer class panicked and on 4 June 1943 carried out a coup that put its own generals in office.

One officer among the rest – Colonel Juan Domingo Perón (b. 1895) – held particular ideas about political management. In the new military government of 1943 Perón became undersecretary in the War Department and labour secretary, two offices that allowed him to simultaneously build up his own following in the army and cultivate the growing and increasingly muscular working class. He succeeded in the latter by encouraging a series of reforms that included health benefits, job security, and pensions. By drawing the trade unions to himself, he detached them from their previous allegiances (particularly to socialism and anarcho-syndicalism). The workers were now given instructions not by the political leaders or trade unionists but by the managers of the Peronist state.

Perón's popularity soared. Amid the shouting, "Peronism" was born. The army realized what was happening only too late. In another coup in October (1943), his superior officers forced Perón to resign. Organized by Perón's followers in the labour movement, crowds flooded into the streets of Buenos Aires. The army vacillated and then backed down. By the time Perón ran for the presidency in 1946, he had become the most popular man in the country. Postwar economic buoyancy confirmed his hold on the masses; here was the Argentine *age d'or*, in part financed by the $1.5 billion sterling and dollar balances that Argentina had accumulated by selling supplies to the Allies during World War II. The country could spend lavishly without having to borrow.[7]

The postwar populism associated with Perón stressed cooperation between the state, capital, and the unionized working class while denouncing the inequalities that had pervaded Argentina since colonial times: "Argentina was a country of fat bulls and undernourished peons," Perón claimed in 1946. To fatten the peons he allowed generous wage hikes for the nascent working class – 12.6 per cent in 1947 and 5.3 per cent in 1948. At the same time he stabilized farm prices. Naturally, the *burguesía pampeana* detested him, never more than when a Peronista crowd pillaged the Jockey Club, their cherished haven, or Perón abandoned his compact with the church, legalized divorce, and put parochial schools under state control. Here was Quebec's Quiet Revolution two decades before it happened in Canada, Argentina's northern twin. But there was one major difference – the seigneurial elite, which had long since disappeared in Canada and been marginal at the best of times, retained its hold over the export economy of Argentina for much of the twentieth century.

Perón was no less detested by foreign investors for he nationalized the run-down British-owned railway system, as well as the American-owned telephone company, and the French-owned dock facilities. In 1947 he paid off the whole of Argentina's foreign debt. All of these nationalist and popular moves were, as we shall see, later reversed, and Argentina became, once again, foreign-owned and profoundly indebted.

Perón succeeded, in the short term, in guiding the Argentine state along a developmental path that saw the country continue as an economic leader in Latin America. He did this during the first decades of the Cold War when local conservatives, largely within the upper and middle class and especially within the army and the church, were preoccupied with preventing the radicalization of the working class and especially its shift in the direction of secularism and socialism. The undoing of Peronism came when he and his third wife, Isabel, who succeeded him, were overthrown in a military coup in March 1976, a dozen years after that in Brazil. If James K. Galbraith is correct, this was the end of road for Argentina "as one of Latin America's most advanced and successful economies." Here was "economic failure" made worse by "ineffective or misguided market reforms in the 1990s."[8]

But Peronism was more than mere developmentalism plus antichurch (and anti-American) populism, and this is why certain liberal economists, as well as nationalists, disparaged it. While Latin America's most eminent economic planner, Raúl Prebisch, supported ISI he looked askance at Perón's actual program that involved printing money, widespread subsidies, a bloated public sector, unrestrained military spending, and the support for uncompetitive small industries throughout the country.[9] It was, he was right to think, a sure recipe for inflation, debt, and, ultimately, economic crisis.

## POST PERÓN

Isabel Perón (1974–76) was replaced by the army chief of staff, General Jorge Videla, who turned out to be one of the most implacable monsters in the political history of Latin America. The years between

1976 and 1983 were the most agonizing in Argentine history, for this was the sunless age of military rule, dungeons, mass terror, and murder. Of Videla, the American columnist Jack Anderson claimed he was "one of the most flagrant violators of human rights since the mad dictator of Uganda, Idi Amin." In these few years of the "Dirty War," roughly the same span of time in which the Nazis dominated Germany (1934–45), as many as 30,000 Argentines were murdered by state-supported death squads while hundreds were tortured. For those whom they destroyed, a new term was coined, *los desaparecidos* ("the disappeared").[10] In the view of Edgar Dosman, Argentina's descent into barbarism under Videla and his henchmen was worse than other regional nightmares such as those suffered by the Chileans.[11]

The military hierarchy of Argentina and the death squads they commanded were linked to their opposite numbers in Chile, Uruguay, Brazil, and Paraguay through Condor, a Washington-supported state terrorist organization that served as a continent-wide secret police in the Southern Cone of Latin America. Through the Condor organization, these five states became involved in "committing human rights violations on a massive scale never before seen in Latin America."[12] Washington may have been on the whole uneasy about dictatorship and especially about Videla's Dirty War waged by the Condor organization but for the most part accepted both as a Cold War necessity.[13] This changed with the assassination by car bomb in September 1976, in broad daylight in Washington DC, of the exiled former Chilean foreign minister, Orlando Letelier. The bomb was placed by an agent of the Chilean secret police, DINA, who was connected to the Condor organization.

Beneath the politics of repression lay the economics of crisis. Already by the mid-1950s, Argentina had entered a period of increased uncertainty with per capita income barely growing at the low rate of 1.3 per cent, less than half of India's "Hindu Rate." By the 1960s, inflation had reached 30 to 40 per cent. As incomes and purchasing power dropped, the spectre of stagnation loomed and political confrontation increased. A civil war, reminiscent of that in Cuba in the 1950s between leftist guerrillas and the military, was fought out in both the countryside and the cities. Captured guerrillas and suspected supporters, including women whose babies were adopted by the military, were murdered in captivity.

The generals who stepped in could not solve the problem of stagnation even though they resorted to the nostrums of neoliberalism, free trade and deregulation. Unsurprisingly, the sovereign debt of Argentina increased, as did inequality, as working-class wages stagnated and the gap between the city and the country widened. Thus the generals' capacity for problem solving was shown to be as deficient as that of the regime that they replaced. Videla himself resigned while the army was still in command and was succeeded by another general, Viola, in early 1981. Viola was pushed aside by the hapless General Galtieri in December 1981. Galtieri lasted less than a year before going one transgression too far by engaging Britain in a war over the ownership of the Falkland Islands (in Spanish, *las Malvinas*) in 1982. The chant "Las Malvinas son Argentinas" was, however, bound to fall short against the British military, one of NATOs best armed and anxious to strap on its rusting armour in order to prove its fitness. The finest hour of British prime minister Margaret Thatcher (1979–90) had arrived. There followed the most bizarre of the wars fought during the Cold War period, with two US allies fighting one another using weapons from the NATO arsenal over territory of neither strategic nor economic significance.

With declining popularity at home, Thatcher dispatched an armada including a nuclear submarine and a destroyer flotilla to the South Atlantic. The submarine sunk the Argentine cruiser *General Belgrano* with the loss of more than 300 lives while British paratroopers and guardsmen forced surrender on the dismayed invaders. But the war was not entirely one-sided: several British ships, including the destroyer HMS *Sheffield*, were sunk by missiles launched from French fighter-bombers bought by the Argentines from a state-owned French defence contractor. Of course, France was Britain's NATO partner. The war was short and conclusive, lasting from 2 April to 14 June 1982 with the Argentines suffering 649 killed (mainly due to the sinking of the *Belgrano*). On the British side 257 died, little compared to the slaughter during the wars in the Middle East that were to come in a couple of decades.[14]

Having surrendered in the Falklands, the junta trooped off the stage in disgrace and fell from power in the face of massive civilian protests. Several of its leaders were accused of human rights abuses. Some of his colleagues wanted Galtieri executed by firing squad, but he got ten years instead. In the opinion of *The Economist*, "He might have been forgiven by at best some of his fellow Argentines for his ruthlessness, but not for his stupidity."[15] Decades later, in December 2010, a judge at Videla's trial referred to Videla as having manifested "state terrorism," a term underemployed in the trials of dictators in the postwar era. In 2012 he got life. He died in prison, ostensibly from concussion caused by a fall in the shower. The civilians, waiting in the wings, returned to a country still in the grips of an economy in crisis. In 1965 Argentina had been the tenth most wealth country in the world, but ten years later real per capita income had fallen 20 per cent.

## POST JUNTA

The first civilian politician to emerge from the anguish of military rule and become president was Raúl Alfonsin of the Radical Party who took office in December 1983. Alfonsin's main tasks were reconciliation and dealing with a debt exceeding $45 billion and consuming more than 50 per cent of export earnings. On his left were the Peronistas who controlled organized labour, which was against any kind of austerity. On his right the military glowered. To his credit Alfonsin created CONADEP,[16] the commission that investigated the atrocities of the military regime and oversaw the trial of the first of the culpable military leaders. At the same time, bending under the pressure from the IMF, he initiated a package of fiscal reforms, at the centre of which was the creation of a new currency called the "astral." It was the "Astral Plan" under which certain state industries were privatized. Although it was successful in the short term, the plan created a deep recession, the first of several in the postdictatorship era. This, together with the hostility of the army, which took the form of several small coups, led to a break in the consensus that had been stitched together with the moderate wing of the Peronistas and the Radicals during the elections of May 1989. The election of the colourful and crooked Peronista, Carlos Menem (1989–99) followed. Neoliberalism had meanwhile reached its high-water mark. Privatization in Argentina was carried out with remarkable speed. "Between 1989 and 1993, the state airline, telephone monopoly, highway toll concessions, oil and electricity companies were sold." Slowing down in the mid-1990s privatization picked up speed again in 1997–98 when the selling off of the post office and thirty-three state-owned airports took place. Correspondingly, in December 2001 inequality had also climbed to the highest level in the history of the country.[17]

Menem was a conservative infatuated, perversely for an Argentine, with the ideas of Margaret Thatcher, champion in the struggle for *las Malvinas* and one of the twin pillars of 1980s neoliberalism. Following her prescriptions and those of her American homologue, Ronald Reagan, the closed doors of the Argentine economy were thrust open to foreign investment and ownership and the assets of the state auctioned off at bargain prices – when Menem came to power, thirty-six of the country's most important firms were owned by foreigners; in 1998 when he exited, foreigners owned sixty-seven. "By 1994, 90 per cent of all state enterprises had been sold to private companies, including Citibank, Bank Boston, France's Suez and Vivendi, Spain's Repsol and Telefonica. Before making the sales Menem ... had generously performed a valuable service for the new owners; [he] had fired roughly 70,000 of their workers."[18] The opening up of the Argentine economy after the years of Peronism and military rule was a hit with the country's consumers who enjoyed a flash flood of foreign goods. The middle class rejoiced, the national debt, underpinned by more IMF loans, skyrocketed and corruption increased. Job losses, like the national debt, went through the roof.

Menem went down to defeat in 1999 and was followed by a succession of governments that could do no more than worsen Argentina's economic problems. Riots and looting ensued while debt and capital flight drained wealth from the country. The incomes of both the middle and the working classes declined and 24 per cent of bank deposits actually fled the country. According to the daily *La Nación*, 56 per cent of the population lived in poverty while 17 per cent found it difficult to afford a single meal daily. "Consumption even of basic foodstuffs has been declining in Argentina, which is both a reflection of the continuing recession and one of the elements that is keeping it going; declining consumption has led to a string of failures of businesses producing consumer goods. The IMF meanwhile stepped in to bail the country's economy – later admitting that it was a mistake. Argentina, once the wealthiest land in Latin America, was now a showcase of economic and political bankruptcy."[19] The chapter on Argentina in Edwin Williamson's *Penguin History of Latin America* is called "Argentina: The Long Decline." The penultimate paragraph begins, "In the course of the twentieth century Argentina proved unable to modernize itself either by revolution or by reform."[20]

In 2002 Argentina defaulted on its debt. In the years that followed there were debates and negotiations with the mainly American holders of that debt. Most of the bondholders agreed to take a "haircut," that is a reduction in payments. But few, owning only 7 per cent of the debt, held out. In 2014 they took Argentina to court.[21]

## KIRCHNERS

"Comes the moment, comes the man" or, at least, "comes the fiscal crisis, comes the man." In 2003 Néstor Kirchner (2003–07), a minor Peronista state governor, was elected president. He severed the linkages with organized labour and reconstructed the Peronist PJ (Partido Justicialista) as "a patronage-oriented machine party."[22] What made him especially popular were his public attacks on neoliberalism. In spite of this, the Kirchner administration did not carry out a major expansion of state ownership in the area of production. It did however renationalize Aguas Argentinas, the national water company that the French company Suez had bought, as well as one of the two main firms in electricity distribution, the national post office, and the main national airline, Aerolíneas Argentinas.[23]

Even after renegotiating its debt, Argentina did not return to its privileged place among rich nations. By 2004 Argentina's per capita GDP was $10,880, just below that of Poland ($11,000) and a long way below that of Greece ($19,000). Kirchner shifted the country's foreign policy in a nationalist and radical direction by conspicuously embracing Fidel Castro and Hugo Chávez. He could do this, of course, since communism was hardly the threat to the hemisphere that it had seemed to be, to Washington at least, during the Cold War. The attack on America on 9/11 seems also to have drawn the attention of that country's leaders away from the Americas and towards the Middle East. In 2006, Argentina's GDP growth continued its return to a healthy 7.9 per cent. In the general elections of October 2007, Néstor Kirchner was succeeded by his wife Cristina Fernández de Kirchner. This was not a good time to take hold of the reins of power anywhere.

In October 2010, Néstor Kirchner died of a heart attack: "Argentine Ex-Leader Dies; Political Impact Is Murky," headlined *The New York Times.* But the fog soon dissipated and a new Eva Perón, no longer shadowed by a husband, appeared. Cristina Fernández de Kirchner was reelected in a landslide in October 2011. Her policies were of the order of populist–nationalist, lubricated, naturally, by cronyism. By 2013 there was regular speculation about how much she and her followers and the oligarchs around her had misappropriated while championing the cause of the downtrodden: "a small fortune" speculated the *Wall Street Journal.*[24] Ominously, 2013 is the year that the commodities super-cycle ended.

In the summer of 2014, an American judge ruled that all American debtors, those who had accepted the haircut as well as the "vultures" who had refused, would have to be paid in full. The judge's decision was sidestepped, and the Argentine Congress passed legislation effectively accepting a second default, called by Standard & Poor's a "selective default." Kirchner announced that the legislation was an "historic event." She announced "Argentina wants to pay, can pay and is going to pay all its debts to all its bondholders." The debt deadline of $200 million was not met. The bond agencies downgraded the country's status. "Internationally, it is nothing new for Argentina to be labeled an economic disaster, and there was no stark market rout in Buenos Aires. The Buenos Aires index has been stable in response to Kirchner's hard line, and the world keeps turning as she said it would ..."[25]

Yet Perón's earlier dream of greater equality was still far short of realization. According to a 2007 survey, "of every $100 generated by the process of economic growth [since 2003], $62.5 went to the wealthiest 30 per cent, leaving $37.5 to be shared out between the remaining 70 per cent of the population, the poorest 70 per cent of the population gain[ing] only $12.8."[26] Poverty remained, in 2008, at 34 per cent, higher than it had been in the 1990s. And as far as the role of the United States in the world, a Chicago Council on Global Affairs Multinational Survey of 2007 disclosed that 84 per cent of Argentines rejected the idea that the United States "should continue to play the role of pre-eminent world leader." Stephan Phelan of *The Guardian* commented:

> Many in Argentina viewed the borrowing to buy US dollar Treasury bonds by the military juntas of the 1970s as the root of the country's economic problems. This view is relatively common in Argentina, where the outstanding national debt is contaminated by still-painful memories of the unelected dictatorship that first ran it up, and the later neoliberal governments whose failure to control it led to the domestic deficit crisis of 2001 and the biggest default in history.[27]

During the incumbency of the Kirchners, Argentina's annual growth rate had bounced up and down erratically; from 2003 to 2007 it had been around 8 per cent, in 2009 it was nearly 0, in 2010–11 it was back around 8 per cent, and in 2013 it was 3 per cent. By 2013 it seemed likely that the growth figures had been regularly massaged by the government and that real per capita GDP growth between 2005–13 had been around 5.6 per cent, a full percentage point less than had been officially stated. Later, as Fernández de Kirchner was preparing her handover to a successor, that same GDP growth was assumed to have been only 4 per cent in the decade prior to 2015. "Our [recent] history is divided into two halves," said Dante Caputo, a foreign minister during the 1980s, who has claimed that, "Argentina was the country with the fastest rise between 1880 and 1930, and then the country with the most notorious fall." He added that he doubted whether the next government would significantly alter the current downward trajectory. "Sadly," added Sonia Benedetti, a housewife quoted by Mander, "I don't think the next president will change this country. We don't just need a new president, we need a whole new political class. Out with the lot of them!"[28]

Cristina Fernández de Kirchner was constitutionally barred from running again in the elections held in two stages in October and November 2015. Heading a coalition of more than a dozen parties representing the Argentine left was Daniel Scioli of the "Front for Victory" alliance. In opposition was Mauricio Macri heading the centre right coalition, "Cambiemos" ("Let's Change"). Although the outcome was close, Macri became the new president.

*The Economist* saw the outcome with gloating satisfaction. Under the heading "The ebbing of the pink tide," it made the point that Cristina Fernández de Kirchner

> has ruthlessly subordinated Argentina's economy and some of its institutions to a single aim: preserving her own popularity ... She ran down the Central Bank's reserves to next to nothing to maintain an overvalued official exchange rate. She ran up a fiscal deficit of 6% of GDP and spurned an inevitable deal with holdout creditors, raising the eventual cost.

Little favourable could be said about Daniel Scioli, added the British weekly: "an essentially moderate man" and an adherent of "Ms Fernández's autarkic brand of populism." For his part, Scioli had claimed that Mauricio Macri "was the puppet of evil global forces such as the IMF, foreign multinationals, 'neoliberal adjustment' and so on." *The Economist* continued with the prediction that Macri's victory had "broken Peronism's seemingly iron grip on political power ... [A]fter 15 years of domination by various shades of the left, his victory may herald a shift back to the centre for South American politics." "The markets love that his cabinet is full of former CEOs of multinationals," commented Mabel Thwaites Rey, a professor of political sociology at the University of Buenos Aires. Perhaps surprisingly, *Forbes* magazine, a rival of the *Economist* and also from the right, headed its coverage of the Argentine election with support for the Peronists: "Why Macri's Win is Bad News for Argentina." Mark Weisbrod, the article's author, praised the reign of the Kirchners in no uncertain terms: "In the past 13 years, Argentina made enormous economic and social progress ... poverty fell by about 70%, and extreme poverty fell by 80% ... Unemployment fell from more than 17.2% to 6.9%, according to the International Monetary Fund." *Forbes* continued, hinting at the consequences of *The Economist's* prediction that the "pink tide" had turned:

> [M]acri has demonstrated his overwhelming loyalty to the United States government, which had been previously made clear in confidential US embassy cables published by WikiLeaks. One of his very first statements after being elected was to denounce Venezuela and threaten to have the country suspended from the Mercosur trading bloc ... The issue wasn't of pressing concern to Argentine voters, so it may very well be related to a US-led international campaign to delegitimize Venezuela's government and the elections to the run-up to its Dec. 6 elections.[29]

## BRAZIL: DEVELOPMENT AND DISORDER

The motto on the Brazilian flag, *Ordem e Progresso*, was coined by the French positivist philosopher Auguste Compte (1798–1857). Compte also invented the term "sociology" for the study of society, although he never actually crossed the Atlantic to apply it to Brazil; if he had he might have thought of a more catchy and appropriate motto, something like *Desenvovimento y Desordem*.

Brazil is the India of the Americas – massive, populous, fractious, hot, unequal, intellectually radiant and ecologically disastrous, and, above all, divided and unpredictable. One Brazilian writer has referred to it as "Belindia," a small rich Belgium within a larger, poorer, India or, as Drèze and Sen have said of India, it was like "islands of California in a sea of sub-Saharan Africa."[30] The differences between

Brazil and India are of course huge and historic, and none more significant, in the modern period, than Brazil's becoming independent more than a century before India.[31] Then there is the matter of travesties: in the 1990s, it was assumed that inequality and ecological devastation were Brazil's most scandalous transgressions, but in recent times, as we have seen elsewhere, India may have jumped ahead at least on the scale of unrepentant inequality. In both Brazil and India poor people tend to be darker than rich people; this is due to Brazil's history of slavery and colonialism in the modern period, while inequality in India was prescribed by the Vedas some three millennia ago. Since the beginning of the present centuries both countries have been considered members of the BRIC group and described as "emerging economies," at least when it was felt that assured economic growth was in their futures. While the economy of independent India uncoiled slowly at the "Hindu Rate" of around 3 per cent over the half century from 1930 to 1980, even through the period of military rule the Brazilian economy grew at an average rate of 6.5 per cent. Between 1968 and 1972 it expanded at a rate of 10.7 per cent. "It was similar to those registered by several Asian economies in more recent years," writes Michael Reid, "So Brazil had its 'China phase.'"[32]

Dramatic social change began to accelerate in Brazil, as in the other large economies of South America, in the 1930s. The Second World War was a watershed. Under President Getúlio Vargas (1930–45, 1951–54), "the Father of Modern Brazil," ISI was seen as the guiding prescription for the future. So the role of the state swelled, population increased, the urban working class and the cities expanded, and prosperity seemed assured.[33] In fact in the golden years of the postwar boom, emerging economies right around the Third World made ISI-based development look like a plausible economic strategy.

Varga's successor, Juscelino Kubitschek (1954–60) also benefited from the postwar boom. He was an economic modernizer with an erector complex who continued Vargas' development strategy, promising fifty years progress in five. It was he who built the new capital of Brasilia, a modernist architectural marvel, deep in the country's hinterland. In a 1964 report for the Economic Council for Latin America (ECLA) the achievements of the Brazilian state were highlighted with enthusiasm; it owned and operated most inland rail and waterway transport, as well as the state's petroleum production, steel making capacity, electrical energy, and iron and steel production. Again, the parallels with Indian statism are tempting.

The end of Kubitschek's tenure overlapped with the Cuban revolution in 1958–59 and the corollary panicky shift of Washington's attitude towards Latin American politics. This was all the more critical in light of Brazil's growing mood of anti-Americanism. Janos Quadros (1960–61) did nothing to quell American anxieties when he legislated a tax on profits exported to the United States and cold-shouldered the American-inspired Alliance for Progress that was meant to be an antidote to the example of the Cuban Revolution.[34] Quadros's award of a notable state honour to Che Guevara and his improved relations with the USSR and China did little to assuage the fears of the anti-Communists. Unsurprisingly, given the times, Quadros's tenure as a president lasted a mere six months and ended with his resignation as he watched the intensification of CIA activities in Brazil. To the extent that he was unpopular, it was due not to his foreign policy but to the economic problems, especially inflation, left him by Kubitschek.

Quadros was succeeded by his vice-president, another populist, João "Jango" Goulart who saw himself as Vargas's spiritual successor in the struggle to liberate Brazil from US domination. Goulart who was hardly a radical leftist, much less a communist, was overthrown in a military coup on 1 April 1964. "On the evening of the coup, tons of paper was thrown from the windows of apartment houses and office buildings – obviously by people of the middle class. White candles of victory were lighted in middle-class apartment windows in Rio de Janeiro. And a march of ... victory [took place] a day or so later. Evidently the middle class was pleased; it was relieved to have the military in charge." Writing this in 1968, the historian, Charles Wagley, commented, "It looks as if the Brazilian government will be dominated by the military for many years to come. If this should happen, then the middle class will have made a bad bargain. As a result of its basic economic, social, and political dilemma, the Brazilian middle class opted for stability over change."[35] In fact, the military was to remain in power for nearly two more decades, until 1985. President Goulart fled to Uruguay where, it was alleged, he was poisoned.

Goulart was replaced by General Humberto de Castelo Branco, a close friend of the CIA chieftain General Vernon Walters. The Kennedy administration in Washington, having failed to stifle the revolutionary regime in Cuba, backed the general. From 1962, the CIA had funnelled money to the opposition. Although the left and the trade union federation opposed the coup, as we have mentioned it was widely backed by the middle class that was fed up with strikes and with inflation that had gone from 55 per cent in 1962 to 81 per cent in 1963. The large Catholic population of Brazil was responsive to the claims that communism, along the lines of Cuba, was a real danger. As Goulart had moved to the left in order to support his reforms, the centre had moved to the right. In a telegram to the US Secretary of State, the American ambassador in Brasilia claimed that the fall of Goulart was a "great victory for the free world." Although it was a victory for the Brazilian right and a relief for Washington, despite claims of the Brazilian left ever since, the coup was domestically engineered and not "made in America" as, for instance, the coups in Iran in 1953 and Guatemala in 1954 had been.

## *OS ANOS DO CHUMBO* ("THE LEADEN YEARS")

Dictatorship in Brazil lasted for two decades, from 1964 to 1985, and has been recalled as the most dismal period in the history of the nation. Thousands were arrested, many of who were tortured and murdered.[36] Congress was suspended, the independent judiciary disappeared, and 133 university professors and researchers were deprived of their rights. Economic nationalism, in the form of the program of ISI, however, was maintained while simultaneously it was felt necessary to keep the country open to foreign capital and especially multinational firms. In sum, the formula worked. Michael Reid:

> Brazilian dirigisme had succeeded in creating by 1980 what was the largest and most sophisticated industrial base in the developing world. Some of the seeds planted by the military governments ... would germinate later; Petrobras and offshore oil; a petrochemical industry: Embraer (the aircraft manufacturer), huge hydroelectric dams; ... Land under crops expanded from 19.1 million hectares in 1950 to 49.2 million in 1980 ... Brazil ceased to be dependent on coffee, as a host of non-traditional exports including cars, aircraft, arms and soyabeans came into being.[37]

Although Maria Helena Alves has testified that, "[d]uring the 1969–1974 period it was difficult to meet a Brazilian who had not come into direct contact with a tortured victim or been involved in a search and arrest operation" a comparatively modest 379 people were killed or "disappeared," compared to some 30,000 in Argentina and more than 3,000 in Chile.[38] Among those tortured was Dilma Roussef (b. 1947) who was a member of a small guerrilla group. She was "repeatedly subjected to electric shocks on various parts of her body as well as to the *pau de arara* ("parrot's perch"), which involved being suspended upside down and naked from a stick, with wrists and ankles bound. She was jailed for three years."[39] Later, in 2011, she succeeded Lula as president of Brazil.

Economic growth in the minds of many in Brazil vindicated the sacrifice of democracy; people at the time spoke of the "Brazilian miracle" and the need for stability with a firm hand at the tiller. Although income per person grew to the point that it was close to that of Argentina by 1980, the major beneficiaries of the miracle were, unsurprisingly, the top 10 or 20 per cent of the population, in earlier times known as the "bourgeoisie." The top 10 per cent of the population actually absorbed a full 75 per cent of the total increase in Brazilian income by the 1975, midway in the two decades of military rule. This decile benefitted even further when the military government opened up Brazil's interior to foreign investment and suspended laws that had restricted the flight of profits out of the country. Otherwise, it conformed to the wishes of Washington when it broke off relations with Cuba and sent Brazilian troops to join in the US invasion of the Dominican Republic in April 1965. The army itself got to spend more on arms, often expensively purchased abroad, and on itself – guaranteeing its officers high salaries, security, and prestige, together with a system of welfare otherwise available only in advanced social democracies or in military dictatorships like Turkey, Egypt, and Pakistan. To justify their privileges, the officers wrapped themselves in the cloak of national security, asserting that secrecy was necessary if Christian civilization was to be defended against communism.

Of course shopaholicism whether military or otherwise was expensive. Between 1974 and 1977 Brazil's debt increased from $12 billion to $50 billion. The IMF loaned more money to Brazil than to any other single country in Latin America. By 1980 Brazil's debt payments represented 259 per cent of its total earnings. Insecure because of their declining popularity, the colonels began to release their grip on society. Protests increased; even the middle class joined in, having presumably felt a kind of collaborator's remorse for having underwritten the death certificate for Brazil's democracy. The army became divided between the hardline anticommunist conservatives and the nationalists. The debt burden became staggering. Regime collapse was inevitable; slowly the generals retreated from power. When military rule finally ended in 1985, it was followed by the period of the "New Republic."

By 1983 a government study was able to show that 70 per cent of the population had a daily caloric intake "lower than necessary for human development."[40] One study in the 1970s revealed that the number of abandoned and needy children was as high as fifteen million. Another, focusing on the north of the country, reported that nearly 45 per cent of children had been abandoned by their families.[41] This was like China at the edge of collapse in the late nineteenth century; India in the era of the Nehrus had no equally embarrassing claim.

## OUT OF THE DARK

When military rule ended, José Sarney (1985–90), an oligarch of the classic mould who had been president of the government party during the dictatorship, which he supported loyally, and Fernando Collor de Mello (1990–92), who had also emerged during the period of military rule, came to power. Neither could find his way out of the Brazilian labyrinth of debt and disorder. And while they were in the ascent, so was the inflation rate, which reached 230 per cent per annum in 1986. As Brazil emerged from the darkness of military rule, a different depression fell over the country – the burden of debt repayment had become too high to sustain Brazil's social responsibilities. To compensate for the cost of debt repayments, Brazil had to borrow. Borrowing led to inflation. Inflation ate away at the incomes of the poor.

Although food subsidies were kept in place, there were food riots throughout the country. The authority of the Sarney administration, already diminished, was further eroded. Outside of the cities was an additional source of conflict; there was open warfare between the big ranchers and the 10 million landless peasants. When the Amazon region was opened up by the government to relieve the problem of landlessness, the burning of the rain forests caused severe environmental problems that have continued to the present. This also increased human rights issues as the native peoples who lived in the Amazonian area were marginalized and even murdered.[42]

The return to democratic politics ("redemocratization") in the 1980s and '90s coincided not just with economic crisis at the national level but with the heyday of neoliberalism when the idea of selling off state assets was thought to be a brilliant solution to the financial problems of states everywhere. The political reaction to the economic crisis slowly emerged from 1982 in the form of a new political party; in fact this was one of the few new political organizations to surface globally in the late twentieth century, virtually flowing against the tide of neoliberalism. The Worker's Party (*Partido dos Trabalhadores* or PT) was led by Luis Inácio da Silva ("Lula"), a man from the very bottom levels of the proletariat who was born in the northeast. It expanded in popularity attracting at first autoworkers and, increasingly, the votes of the big cities, and even, for a time, the support of the perfidious middle class. Yet, the merely poor and the utterly destitute initially remained afraid that radical change would decrease their security and gave their votes to Collor, who won the national elections of 1989, defeating Lula again.

When Fernando Collor de Mello took office in March 1990, Brazil was in the midst of another deep crisis. Inflation had reached 2,000 per cent per year, and the toll of murders in Rio stood at 7,720 a year. A privatizer and modernizer who offered more state-owned industries for sale to the private sector, Collor promised a renewal of Brazilian capitalism by means of neoliberal reforms. Although he pledged to settle 500,000 families on agrarian-reform projects, instead he abolished the Ministry of Agrarian Reform altogether. As Paul Cammack predicted in late 1991, "Collor's perfection lay more in his ability to reflect the needs of the Brazilian bourgeoisie than to meet them; his record in office suggests that the crisis which produced him will also devour him."[43]

Gradually there was a political shift. The urban middle class, which had supported the PT, slipped away from it while the much more numerous poor, especially in the northeast, rallied to it. Then came the fulfillment of Cammack's prediction: Collor's impeachment for corruption in 1992. In fact the impeachment, much more than a mere story of corruption as we see in Russia or China, was the stuff of soap operas. Collor's campaign manager Paolo César Farias had shaken down some $160 million from the Brazilian bourgeoisie to sustain Collor's campaign. Keeping a few millions aside allowed Collor to invest in an apartment in Paris as well as a mansion in Brasilia. When the story blew up, Farias fled to Thailand with his twenty-something mistress. Safely out of harm's way, he assumed, he explained to her that their affair was at an end. She shot them both. Collor, however, had no such a dramatic last act. In 1994 he was exonerated by the

Supreme Court and later became elected to the Senate and an ally to both Lula and Dilma Rousseff.[44]

In his short stay as president, Collor had in fact managed one or two accomplishments – above all he had ensured that universal suffrage be extended even to the nation's huge population of illiterates. The voting age became sixteen years. This meant that there was a huge vote bank, especially in the poor northeast, ready to cast their ballots for such simple amenities as food and water as well as health, education, and universal pensions. Collor also took steps to reform the economy by putting an end to import bans and licences and selling off state companies. Here, the resemblance to the policies of Rajiv Gandhi of India, soon to be one of Brazil's BRIC partners, was evident.

Still, no joy for Lula. Despite the downfall of Collor, in the elections of 1994 a surprising candidate won. Henrique Cardoso, is a Marxist academic widely celebrated for his critique of developmentalism, the son of a general, and the descendant of a line of notables; a toff with a social conscience, thus a type familiar everywhere. His party was called the Party of Brazilian Social Democracy (PSDB). A little oddly, it simultaneously extended neoliberalism by selling off state assets and expanded the level of state interventionism, in, perhaps, a tropical variation of the German *ordoliberalism*. Kurt Weyland:

> [Cardoso] completed Collor's trade liberalization, lifted stifling state monopolies in the economy, and privatized important public enterprises (but not the state oil company, Petrobras). Yet since neoliberalism never attained strong support in Brazil, these market reforms did not seek to establish a free market economy ... In fact, at the same time that Cardoso reduced state interventionism in some areas, Brazil's total tax burden grew from an already high 26% of GDP in the early 1990s to a striking 35.9% in 2004 ... which is unusually heavy for a Latin American country. Thus, during the advance of market reform, the state actually captured an increasing share of national wealth![45]

Cardoso appeared to fit comfortably among the neoliberals *and* the tax reformers of his times. In the decade between 1991 and 2002, in fact, Brazil sold off partial or complete control of 119 companies, some, to the profit of their buyers, vastly undervalued. It is true that some of these performed better in private hands than under state control – this was the case of Petrobras, which lost its monopoly, and the national telecoms company where both became more efficient. But the three big federal banks were also left in public hands and electricity remained in the domain of state governments. And, thanks to an impulse for protectionism that was the antithesis of neoliberalism, imports remained low – just 13 per cent of Brazil's GDP in 2012. In spite of the tornado of poverty, debt, inflation, dictatorship, and corruption, Brazil had managed a remarkable level of industrialization.

By the mid-1990s, during Brazil's worst stagnation of the century, Cardoso presided over what was still one of the most polarized countries anywhere and certainly one of the most wretched large states in the Americas. In the mid-1990s Susanna Hecht described Brazil:

> With one of the higher levels of GNP per capita in the developing countries, Brazil has also the worst income distribution in the world. The minimum wage now fluctuates at less than fifty dollars a month with its purchasing power at almost the lowest level in the postwar period. In São Paulo, the rich centre of the richest state, more than a million people live in *favelas* – shanty towns – while another three million live in what are called *cortiços*. These are collective dwellings, basically old houses, which are divided up into small cubicles. Thirty families might thus share a bathroom, kitchen, and washing facilities. In this context, it is valuable to repeat yet another statistic: 54 per cent of Brazil's children live in families earning less than $35 a month. Of these, more than 25 million deprived children, some eight million, now live on the streets, occasionally returning home. Children have now replaced subversives as the main targets of death squads and policemen who routinely beat up, torture and kill children in order to hamper mugging and petty theft. Last summer [1993] child assassination by death squads hit international consciousness as eight kids were gunned down while they slept. [The Institute for Social and Economic Analysis, run by the Catholic Church] calculated from very sparse accounts that close to a hundred children a month are assassinated in Brazil's major cities. Indeed, in the 15–17 age group, 65 per cent of deaths are violent.[46]

In apparent contradiction to this horrifying story, an odd statistic emerges, "after 1998 Cardoso's presidency was marked by steadily declining inequality in Brazil," an inequality that was undermined by the fact that the extreme poverty that Susanna Hecht mentioned had fallen from 12.4 to just 5.9 per cent of the population. James Galbraith, whose main concern has been the economics of inequality, has put this down to three changes: the reduction of the relative income of the financial sector, an improvement of incomes of the primary sector, and an increase in the relative size and income of the public sector.[47] Bankers thus got less, civil servants and teachers got more, the poor survived, and the sales of orange juice and soybeans rocketed.

## THE PT: TROPICAL KEYNESIANISM AND THE COMMODITIES SUPER-CYCLE

On his third try, Lula, surfing on a remarkable social movement known as "Lulismo," won the presidential election of 2002. And in spite of early corruption scandals, he won two more elections with astonishing results and thus remained in power until the end of 2011. The PT had become Latin America's biggest and most successful social democratic party, this at the same moment that communism was disappearing in eastern Europe and in the West social democracy was mutating towards the Blairite form of neoliberalism. The secret to the success of the PT lay in the fact that Lula and many of his comrades were not Marxists in the old Latin American, Salvador Allende, sense; they were left-wing pragmatists who had abandoned the idea of state socialism – hence no renationalizations. Lula presented himself, or was presented, thus not as a latter-day Fidel Castro but as a New Age guru with a taste for "change"; *Lulinha, Paz e Amor*, "Lula, Peace and Love" was his song. Certainly he was not like India's Narendra Modi (elected prime minister in 2014), also, as we have seen in chapter 6, a man who had come from humble beginnings but who became a prophet of profits. Lula was, perhaps, the most effective social reformer of his day, and, under him, in the view of James Galbraith, "Brazil was one of the success stories of the early twenty-first century."[48] Of course, in retrospect, not everyone has remained enthusiastic. Wendy Hunter:

> [T]he central policies of the two Lula governments were a far cry from what the PT had promised in its opposition role. Whereas structural reforms to develop the economy and redistribute Brazil's substantial wealth characterized the party's program well into the 1990s, conforming to market dynamics were the order of the day in recent years. Macroeconomic policy displayed marked continuity

> with the model of market reform set in motion in the early 1990s. In social policy there were few innovations or significant extensions, notwithstanding the popular income transfer program Bolsa Familia [family allowance] … Expedience ultimately won out in the methods the president chose to gather legislative approval.[49]

To Lula's good fortune, at the global level the early years of the twenty-first century were marked by two overlapping features; first, the US was preoccupied in the Middle East and complacent with regard to the politics of the larger states in Latin America. Castroism was hardly likely to spread. Overlapping this, from the end of the 1980s to 2008, the US experienced a period of unusual economic calm that led to what one economic thinker called a period of "great moderation"; that is, a period, like the golden years, in which, it was confidently claimed, there would be no more economic anguish. Neoliberalism, of course, was to be credited for this, especially the removal of any controls on speculation. This period of doubtless American leadership was characterized by an insatiable commodity boom, the commodities super-cycle, stimulated by devaluation of the Brazilian currency in January 1999 and with Chinese demand for Brazil's primary exports – soya and iron ore – seeming limitless.

The emergence of the Chinese market in fact drove Brazil out of the economic doldrums and ended, for the time being, its dependency on markets in the North Atlantic. It came at a time of radical change in Latin America although to what extent it guaranteed or even stimulated it is not clear. Essential to the change that transformed poverty in Brazil was Cardoso's earlier economic reforms and especially Lula's *Bolsa Família*, a children's allowance sent to 14 million households of the lowest income, given on the proviso that to receive it children had their health checked and were sent to school.

When Lula finally stepped down he had become one of the most popular democratic politicians in the emerging world – a Nelson Mandela on the other South Atlantic shore. The status of Brazil had been transformed; it was now considered one of the BRIC countries. His successor in the presidential elections of 2011 was Dilma Rousseff, handpicked by Lula but not actually elected. By the time of her anointment, the Workers' Party had come to enjoy thumping majorities in both the Brazilian Congress and Senate especially thanks to support from the poor, desiccated, northeast. Alas, by 2014, the beginning of Rousseff's second term in office, the northeast was enduring its third straight year of drought. Since Rousseff took office she had distributed 670,000 water tanks across the country in the "Water for All" program. The campaign to get water to the dry region was part of the "Brazil Without Poverty" (*Brasil Sim Miséria*) campaign that proved to be not just popular but effective. In September 2014, the UN Food and Agriculture Organization removed Brazil from its World Hunger Map. In the previous year social spending as a proportion of GDP had reached a level higher than in any other Latin American country outside of Cuba.

What has been called Brazil's "new middle class" had now come to include about 100 million of Brazil's more than 200 million people. *The Economist*, no admirer of reformist governments but a devoted observer of the growth of the world's middle classes, noted that "[t]he number of comfortably off by developed-world standards has ... grown from 14 m. in 2003 to 30 m. Between 2003 and 2013 median income rose by 87% in real terms, that of the poorest tenth more than doubled. Inequality fell, partly because of handouts but more because of paid work. Just 5% of Brazilian's were jobless."[50] More than just moving up the development scale, the whole of Latin America seemed to be moving out of the underdeveloped into the middleweight category of powers, with Brazil, in one conjecture at least, replacing the United States itself as the regional leader in a period in which the continent was transformed by a long-term growth cycle. "Washington must ... understand that Brazil, not the United States, is the model the region is following."[51]

By 2014, however, as the commodities super-cycle continued to peter out, the euphoria connected with the era of Lula also became disappointingly deflated. Writing in 2011, after the first decade of "Lulismo," Nicholas Lemann in *The New Yorker*, waxed enthusiastic about the transformations that had been wrought by the reforms of the PS and the competence of the country's managers. One is reminded again of the hype that was heaped on India just a few years earlier:

> Until recently, Brazil has been one of the most uneducated, economically imbalanced countries in the world. Now its economy is growing much more rapidly than that of the United States, and it was not hit hard by the Great Recession. The gap between the rich and the poor in the U.S. is widening alarmingly, but in Brazil it is beginning to narrow. Twenty-eight million Brazilians have moved out of severe poverty in the past decade, while poverty in the U.S. is at its highest rate in years. Brazil is at peace. It has forsworn nuclear weapons. It

> has a balanced budget, low national debt, nearly full employment, and low inflation. It is, chaotically, democratic. It has a free press ... Brazilians usually rank at the very top in international measures of how optimistic the citizens of a nation are about its future.[52]

But, Lemann warned, in 2005, a year before Lula had been reelected, Brazilian newspapers had broken the story that the PT had been bribing its fickle allies to keep them sweet. Two of Lula's top aides had been forced to resign. It was their resignations that opened the space for the rise of Dilma Rousseff. By the end of her first term in office (2011–14) growth averaged only 2.2 per cent a year. By 2014, it hardly grew at all. Since the government refused to cut spending, however, it kept unemployment at the remarkably low level of 4.8 per cent.[53]

## DOUBTING DILMA

After Rousseff's reelection in October 2014, she ran into further problems when the former director of Petrobras alleged that members of her staff – but not, apparently, Rousseff herself – had received commissions on oil contracts. Bribes, in short. In the elections of 2014, she had stood against the probusiness Aécio Neves, a former state governor and grandson of the former would-be Brazilian president and perennial schemer, Tancredo Neves. From the beginning, against a background of growing economic problems, the electorate had become increasingly polarized between the rich south and southeast that supported Neves and the impoverished northeast together with Rio de Janiero, which voted for Rousseff. "Dilma Rousseff's policies are pitting the country's rich against poor and rural areas against the cities in a class war," tut-tutted the *Financial Times* during the election. The newspaper pointed out that the Brazilian economy had grown by an average of only 1.6 per cent per annum – *The Economist*, as we have seen, claimed 2.2 per cent – since Rousseff's presidential election but that under Lula it had grown at an average of 4.1 per cent a year.[54] Nonetheless, Rousseff won the election.

Calls for her impeachment, voiced by the members of rival parties, rose.[55] Her enemies, led by Eduardo Cunha, the president of the chamber of deputies, who had himself been investigated for a large-scale money-laundering scheme also involving Petrobras, were unrelenting. Balanced against the side favouring impeachment was her unreliable ally, the president of the Senate, Renan Calheiros, "a shady figure who some years ago had to resign to avoid being removed from office on corruption charges." Calheiros was one of a number of politicians, like Eduardo Cunha, who was accused of having stolen billions. In August (2015), it was the turn of José Dirceu, one of the founders of the PT and Lula's former chief of staff, to be arrested. In March the PT treasurer, João Vaccari Neto, was charged with corruption and money laundering. According to the police, Lula himself may have benefited from kickbacks from Petrobras. In early September (2015) Standard & Poor stripped Brazil of its investment-grade credit rating and downgraded it to junk status while Petrobras was declared unworthy of investment. In the cities, thousands of middle class Brazilians now took to the streets to express their frustration with the rule of President Rousseff.[56] Once again, class struggle was on the agenda.

"To believe that the major issue facing Brazil today is the impeachment of Dilma Rousseff or her struggle to hold on to power would be naive," Eliane Brum has written in *The Guardian*. "What is at stake is also the inexhaustible capacity on the part of the country's elites to feign indignation in order to create more space to re-establish their interests and keep their privileges intact." In common with Argentina and Venezuela, both beneficiaries of a decade-long commodity boom, Brazil's economic future seems to have curdled.[57]

Brazil had tied its future significantly to the global, and especially China's, demand for commodities – so much so that the connection between the two countries, the equivalent of "Chinamerica," was known as "Chinzila." This had underpinned the long boom under Lula but had ended in 2012 when, as one commentator has noted, "China's growth model was running out of road."[58] As the Chinese market for commodities shrunk, so did the exports not only of emerging markets like Brazil but also of developed countries like Canada and Australia, not to mention Germany. In common with its Latin American neighbours, Brazil appeared to be at a loss as to how to adjust both domestically and externally. In fact, the fortunes of the whole of the region seem to have turned. Boasting of a GDP growth of 6 per cent in 2010, Latin America's GDP growth continued to drop from 4.8 per cent in 2011 to 3.1 per cent in 2012, 2.9 per cent in 2013 (the year the super-cycle is said to have ended), 1.3 per cent in 2014, and minus 2 per cent in 2015. By 2015 Brazil's GDP per capita ($16, 000) was still below that of the other large states of Latin America – Mexico ($16,300), Argentina ($22,500), and Chile ($24,170).

AFTERWORD

# Reversal of Fortunes

Over the seventy years of the story that I have tried to tell here, there have been a number of wrenching convulsions, some awesome reversals, and a shocking number of unanticipated realignments. These have encompassed the entire globe, nowhere with greater impact than the broad, populous, landmass of Eurasia. To take but a couple of examples, Russia, the largest single state in the landmass and the roof of the entire continent, has gone from being a ravaged but undefeated giant, the possessor of what appeared to be the newest empire of the twentieth century, to being a sore and resentful second class, twenty-first century, petropower: irredentist, aggressive, and economically less successful than any of the reborn former communist states of eastern Europe or East Asia. The ideology that Russia once fostered and that found adherents from Beijing to Buenos Aires, has become barely visible in the dustbin of history. Another example: in 1945 when I entered primary school there was a British Empire. Over the front blackboard of my class was a framed poster featuring the Union flag and, in copperplate, "One Flag, One Fleet, One Throne." The message of invincible British greatness was inescapable. Some decades later only crumbs of empire remain and these often as laundromats for ill-gotten gains. The Commonwealth is as much a phantom as the Comintern. Having abandoned the Commonwealth for the EU, the British have now abandoned the EU. *Albion perfide?*

The fates of the states of East and Southeast Asia – Japan, South Korea, China, Taiwan, Vietnam, Singapore, Malaysia, Indonesia – had, by the end of the twentieth century, become starkly different from the Soviet giant to the north. This was, it has been frequently repeated, thanks to globalization, widely believed, at least during its golden years – the years of the "Great Moderation," which I shall mention below – to be a virtual panacea. In East Asia, where nearly a third of the world's population lived, between 1975 and 2001 GDP per head reportedly rose at nearly 6 per cent per year. China, which existed in a fog of Western incomprehension until the death of Mao Zedong in 1976, became the new workshop of the world. In the first decade of the twenty-first century its GDP reached 10 per cent; that of the most potent western economies sputtered in its shadow at around 2–3 per cent. In 1978, 30 per cent of China's rural population, about 250 million, lived below the poverty line. By 2009 this figure had dropped to 36 million.

Right from the get-go the new century has been witness to a sequence of remarkable shocks. One economist, blogging at the beginning of 2017 about "the magnitude of the post-WTO China shock to manufacturing [in the West]" put China's continuing economic success within "the China market" (i.e., the market for Chinese goods) down to "import-substituting industrial policies," that is, ISI.[1] In other words, success, the Chinese leader, Xi Jinping's, "Chinese Dream," was brought about due to a policy that has been the antithesis of the neoliberal doctrine. Was neoliberalism merely a supplement to the achievements of ISI? Were the policies of the Washington Consensus, the Ten Commandments of neoliberalism, essential, or were they irrelevant? And what is the connection between neoliberal reform, as in Russia and China, and kleptomania?

Globalization has been inseparable from America; an American president, the brilliant if vulgar Richard Nixon (1969–74), opened the US market to China, which had long been autarkic, that is, virtually self-sufficient. By the 1990s Chinese goods began to swamp the US market. The reaction to this was ultimately the election of Donald Trump. The process of cheap imports replacing domestically produced goods and leading to the Trumpist reaction might come under a heading called "Sweet and Sour." So Nixon's brilliant manoeuvre led to what most people would see as a catastrophe – the rise of Trump. Nixon kicked the ball, but China scored and America lost. No trade in modern times came so suddenly as that which led to the blossoming of "Chinamerica." One unanticipated upshot was huge job losses in the West, most notably in industrial America, and another was the reversal of status between West and East. As Branko Milanovic has explained it, China, which was poorer than the countries in the Balkans in the nineteenth century, will see its mean income catch up with the EU average by around 2050. "This would be," Milanovic stresses, "a remarkable reversal of fortunes." All the more intolerable, some might think, with world economic power shifting towards Asia as "convergence" gains speed. In fact, two years before Nixon visited China a watershed had already been reached in the United States. From 1970 onwards, American growth began to decline. Whereas real GDP per person had reached 2.41 per cent between 1920 and 1970, it dropped to 1.77 between 1970 and 2012.[2]

But ironically neither in much of Asia nor in large areas within the rest of the world has there been the peace that was supposed to be guaranteed by prosperity. Virtually from the end of World War Two America and its allies have pummelled and subverted regimes that threatened their hegemony, overthrowing or attempting to extirpate governments that were merely reformist and secular – like Iran in 1953 or Egypt in 1956 or Indochina in 1965 or Iraq or Libya in the early twenty-first century. Few states in the greater Middle East were safe from the interventions, usually high-sounding, of America and, in some cases, its local hoplites. This chaos ultimately spread, virtually unimpeded, from Algeria to Afghanistan to Nigeria, despite talk and frugal action by the penny-pinching powers of NATO on the need to stem it. (Thus we see, among other macabre ironies, the dispatch of Canadian Special Forces, trained for Arctic warfare, instructing one group of Syrians to shoot another while a Canadian warship patrolled the shores of the Black Sea.) The price of freedom, sometimes called "security," has become, therefore, not constant vigilance but endless war. During the administration of President Obama (2009–17) not a day passed without America being at war somewhere – "a record unmatched in American history."[3]

Thus while America, through its insistence on globalization, has brought prosperity to billions, it has also godfathered a million orphans. The "peace dividend" of the Cold War, then, has been havoc. "The first point is to understand that military interventions should not create more disorder than already exists," lectured the former French foreign minister Dominique de Villepin to an American audience.[4] The second point, however, is that "in the United States today, wars are fought by the poor (including many who are not even US citizens), are financed by the middle class, and benefit the rich."[5]

For Central and South America, once the midnight of American interventionism had passed the hemisphere entered a sunny period of prosperity and optimism – at least as long as the commodities super-cycle prevailed and the Chinese moved in on the oil, copper, and soy that the South Americans produced. When the commodities super-cycle sputtered and died in 2013, however, the prosperity of the continent faded and its celebrated political leaders like Chávez and Lula fell into disrepute. Although papered over by circuses like the Olympic Games, the states of Latin America had once again entered the cycle of class struggle and repression with "convergence" between classes and nations a forgotten daydream. In Brazil, for instance, the champion of unequal societies, inequality increased until around 1950 and remained stable at a high level until the governments of Fernando Henrique Cardoso and Lula (together, 1991–2011) pushed it down. "The decrease has by now lasted sufficiently long, more than a decade, that we can see it as a real and important development. This does not mean that this development cannot be overturned."[6]

What can we say about Africa that is not simply discouraging? Promoted by the cheerleaders of development in the 1960s and '70s, its heroes – Nkrumah, Nyerere, Rawlings, Mandela – fell one after another with the continent slipping backwards from the 1980s. This was of course in part due to the ministrations of the IMF and the Western aid agencies that opted for the Washington Consensus as a tonic to flaccid economies. Then there came, from the same Western source of righteousness, the evangelical doctrine of R2P, the "right to protect" – the upgrade of the nineteenth century imperial doctrine of *mission civiliatrice*. By the end of our period, parts of Africa were in a worse condition than they had been at the beginning of our period, that is, in the last days of colonialism. The end of the commodities super-cycle didn't help, either.[7]

Whither America now, we are bound to ask? If we look at America at around election time 2015, we see a confused and convulsed polity full of doubt about its global role, the campaign slogan of one of its presidential candidates being "Make America Great Again." This seems to be a long way from the America as the terminus of world progress expressed in the "End of History" thesis. A reading of German opinion in *Der Spiegel*, for instance, would suggest a great deal of nervosity.[8]

What has happened to America (and its economic dependencies, like Canada) in nearly any telling seems to be if not quite a chorus of lamentations then some persistent worries. Two disorders stand out. One is the matter of economic growth that we have mentioned. The second is inequality, a subject that suddenly manifest itself on the curriculum of Western politicians and planners somewhere around the end of the twentieth century. From being the Cinderella of a small circle of Keynesians besieged by whooping tribes of neoliberals pouring out of business schools and economics departments chanting "the market is always right," inequality was catapulted into princess status even before the crisis of 2008. By 2014 when the French economist Thomas Piketty wrote his blockbuster, *Capital in the Twenty First Century*, a book received with the same levels of adulation (but by a different readership) as *The End of History* had a quarter of a century earlier, the question of inequality was everywhere. And of course, so was the reality.

Neoliberal economists had argued that globalization would make people better off. They did not explain that the removal of the regulations governing postwar capitalism, the leading tenet of neoliberalism, would make some much better off than others. Certainly the claim of the globalizers applies to the tens of millions in China who have flocked to the cities to see their lives improve, although, as Joseph E. Stiglitz has pointed out, "Large segments of the population in advanced countries have not been doing well; in the US, the bottom 90% has endured income stagnation for a third of a century. Median income for full-time male workers is actually *lower* in real (inflation-adjusted) terms than it was 42 years ago. At the bottom, real wages are comparable to their level 60 years ago ... [health statistics] indicate "that life expectancy among segments of white America is declining. Things are a little better in Europe – but only a little better."

Not just the poorer deciles but even the middle class has suffered, in America shrinking from one-third of the population in 1979 to 27 per cent in 2010.[9] The decline of the American middle class, and its echo in parts of Europe, has had immense political repercussions and led to the penning of a thousand commentaries and ten thousand anxious conversations. Upsetting as it may seem, there is a larger threat than global inequality and that is global warming. I had intended to deal with that in the present essay but was persuaded to put it aside.[10]

In the final section of his *Age of Extremes* Eric Hobsbawm commented, "What I have written cannot tell us whether or how humanity can solve problems it faces at the end of the millennium."[11] The same can be said for my attempt at a follow-up to Hobsbawm, composed in the second decade of the new millennium.

APPENDIX

# Statistical Data

The following statistical data is intended to clarify some of my arguments, by providing comparative data on specific aspects of national economic growth, inequality, and quality of life between individual countries. Readers need to be aware that all overarching data (aggregated data) from which these indices are derived have inbuilt biases and omissions in part because of how and by whom the data was collected.

I have included three sets of information for selected countries to highlight many of the differences between them. In most cases the statistics provided relate to the countries discussed in the text itself. The three sets of data are as follows (see following 5 tables).

## AVAILABILITY OF DATA

It is possible for the reader of this book to check additional statistics produced in particular in the World Development Indicators data set or the UN Human Development Index, on the web. These data sets are in fact open source documents available to any enquirer.

Table 1.1

GDP in 5-year increments from 1990–2005 (in current billions of US$)

| | 1980 | 1985 | 1990 | 1995 | 2000 | 2005 |
|---|---|---|---|---|---|---|
| Argentina | 77.0 | 88.4 | 141.3 | 258.0 | 284.2 | 198.7 |
| Brazil | 235.0 | 223.0 | 462.0 | 785.6 | 655.4 | 891.6 |
| Canada | 274.0 | 364.7 | 594.0 | 604.0 | 742.3 | 1,169.3 |
| China | 191.1 | 309.5 | 361,0 | 734.5 | 1,211.3 | 2,286.0 |
| France | 703.5 | 555.2 | 1,275.3 | 1,610.0 | 1,364.8 | 2,283.6 |
| Germany | 946.7 | 730.0 | 1,765.0 | 2,591.6 | 1,950.0 | 2,861.4 |
| Ghana | 4.4 | 4.5 | 5.9 | 6.4 | 5.0 | 10.7 |
| India | 189.6 | 236.6 | 326.6 | 366.6 | 476.6 | 835.2 |
| Iran | 94.4 | 180.2 | 125.0 | 96.4 | 109.6 | 220.0 |
| Italy | 475.7 | 450.7 | 1,177.3 | 1,170.8 | 1,142.0 | 1,852.6 |
| Japan | 1,087.0 | 1,384.5 | 3,103.7 | 5,449.3 | 4,887.5 | 4,755.4 |
| S. Korea | 67.8 | 103.7 | 284.5 | 559.3 | 561.6 | 898.1 |
| Norway | 64.4 | 65.5 | 120.0 | 152.0 | 171.3 | 308.7 |
| Pakistan | 23.7 | 31.1 | 40.0 | 60.6 | 74.0 | 109.5 |
| Russia | .. | .. | 516.8 | 395.5 | 260.0 | 764.0 |
| S. Africa | 80.5 | 67.0 | 122.0 | 155.4 | 136.3 | 257.7 |
| UK | 565.0 | 489.3 | 1,092.3 | 1,320.2 | 1,635.4 | 2,508.0 |
| USA | 2,862.5 | 4,347.0 | 5,979.6 | 7,664.0 | 10,286.0 | 13,093.7 |

The gross domestic product (GDP) is one of the primary indicators used to gauge the health of a country's economy. It represents the total dollar value of all goods and services produced over a specific time period (a year); you can think of it as the size of the economy (www.investopia.com, 2017). Source: World Development Indicators prepared by the World Bank.

Table 1.2

Annual GDP from 2007 to 2015 (in billions of current us$)

| | 2007 | 2008 | 2009 | 2010 | 2015 |
|---|---|---|---|---|---|
| Argentina | 287.5 | 361.5 | 333.0 | 423.6 | 584.7 |
| Brazil | 1,397.0 | 1,696.0 | 1,667.0 | 2,209.0 | 1,803.6 |
| Canada | 1,465.0 | 1,549.0 | 1,371.0 | 1,613.4 | 1,553.0 |
| China | 3,552.2 | 4,598.0 | 5,110.0 | 6,100.6 | 11,064.6 |
| France | 2,663.0 | 2,923.5 | 2,694.0 | 2,647.0 | 2,419.0 |
| Germany | 3,440.0 | 3,752.4 | 3,418.0 | 3,417.3 | 3,364.4 |
| Ghana | 24.7 | 48.0 | 26.0 | 32.2 | 37.5 |
| India | 1,201.0 | 1,187.0 | 1,324.0 | 1,656.5 | 2,089.0 |
| Iran | 337.5 | 397.2 | 399.0 | 467.8 | .. |
| Italy | 2,203.0 | 2,391.0 | 2,185.0 | 2,125.2 | 1,821.5 |
| Japan | 4,515.2 | 5,038.0 | 5,231.4 | 5,700.1 | 4,384.0 |
| Korea, Rep. | 1,122.7 | 1,002.2 | 902.0 | 1,094.5 | 1,378.0 |
| Norway | 400.9 | 462.0 | 386.4 | 428.5 | 386.5 |
| Pakistan | 152.4 | 170.1 | 168.2 | 177.4 | 271.0 |
| Russia | 1,300.0 | 1,661.0 | 1,223.0 | 1,525.0 | 1,365.8 |
| S. Africa | 299.4 | 286.8 | 296.0 | 375.4 | 314.5 |
| UK | 3,063.0 | 2,875.5 | 2,367.0 | 2,430.0 | 2,861.0 |
| USA | 14,477.6 | 14,718.6 | 14,419.0 | 14,964.3 | 18,036.6 |

The gross domestic product (GDP) is one of the primary indicators used to gauge the health of a country's economy. It represents the total dollar value of all goods and services produced over a specific time period (a year); you can think of it as the size of the economy (www.investopia.com, 2017). Source: World Development Indicators prepared by the World Bank.

Table 2
GDP % Growth, 2000–2015

| | 2000 | 2005 | 2006 | 2007 | 2008 | 2009 | 2010 | 2011 | 2012 | 2013 | 2014 | 2015 |
|---|---|---|---|---|---|---|---|---|---|---|---|---|
| Argentina | -0.8 | 8.9 | 8.0 | 9.0 | 4.1 | -5.9 | 10.1 | 6.0 | -1.0 | 2.4 | -2.5 | 2.6 |
| Brazil | 4.1 | 3.2 | 4.0 | 6.1 | 5.1 | -0.1 | 7.5 | 4.0 | 1.9 | 3.0 | 0.5 | -3.8 |
| Canada | 5.2 | 3.2 | 2.6 | 2.1 | 1.0 | -2.9 | 3.1 | 3.1 | 1.7 | 2.5 | 2.6 | 0.9 |
| China | 8.5 | 11.4 | 12.7 | 14.2 | 9.7 | 9.4 | 10.6 | 9.5 | 7.9 | 7.8 | 7.3 | 6.9 |
| France | 3.9 | 1.6 | 2.4 | 2.4 | 0.2 | -2.9 | 2.0 | 2.1 | 0.2 | 0.6 | 0.6 | 1.3 |
| Germany | 3.0 | 0.7 | 3.7 | 3.3 | 1.1 | -5.6 | 4.1 | 3.7 | 0.5 | 0.5 | 1.6 | 1.7 |
| Ghana | 3.7 | 5.9 | 6.4 | 4.3 | 9.1 | 4.8 | 7.9 | 14.0 | 9.3 | 7.3 | 4.0 | 3.9 |
| India | 3.8 | 9.3 | 9.3 | 8.6 | 3.9 | 8.5 | 10.3 | 6.6 | 5.5 | 6.5 | 7.2 | 7.9 |
| Iran | 5.8 | 4.2 | 5.7 | 9.1 | 0.9 | 2.3 | 6.6 | 3.7 | -6.6 | -1.9 | 4.3 | .. |
| Italy | 3.7 | 0.9 | 2.0 | 1.5 | -1.1 | -5.5 | 1.7 | 0.6 | -2.8 | -1.7 | 0.1 | 0.7 |
| Japan | 2.8 | 1.7 | 1.4 | 1.7 | -1.1 | -5.4 | 4.2 | -0.1 | 1.5 | 2.0 | 0.3 | 1.2 |
| S. Korea | 8.8 | 3.9 | 5.2 | 5.5 | 2.8 | 0.7 | 6.5 | 3.7 | 2.3 | 2.9 | 3.3 | 2.6 |
| Norway | 3.2 | 2.6 | 2.4 | 2.9 | 0.4 | -1.6 | 0.6 | 1.0 | 2.7 | 1.0 | 1.9 | 1.6 |
| Pakistan | 4.3 | 7.7 | 6.2 | 4.8 | 1.7 | 2.8 | 1.6 | 2.7 | 3.5 | 4.4 | 4.7 | 4.7 |
| Russia | 10.0 | 6.4 | 8.2 | 8.5 | 5.2 | -7.8 | 4.5 | 4.3 | 3.5 | 1.3 | 0.7 | -2.8 |
| S. Africa | 4.2 | 5.3 | 5.6 | 5.4 | 3.2 | -1.5 | 3.0 | 3.3 | 2.2 | 2.3 | 1.6 | 1.3 |
| UK | 3.7 | 3.0 | 2.5 | 2.6 | -0.6 | -4.3 | 1.9 | 1.5 | 1.3 | 1.9 | 3.1 | 2.2 |
| USA | 4.1 | 3.3 | 2.7 | 1.8 | -0.3 | -2.8 | 2.5 | 1.6 | 2.2 | 1.7 | 2.4 | 2.6 |

This is expressed as a percentage difference in GDP from one year to the next. Source: World Development Indicators prepared by the World Bank.

Table 3
Per Capita GDP since 1990 in 5-year increments (current US$)

| | *1990* | *1995* | *2000* | *2005* | *2010* | *2015* |
|---|---|---|---|---|---|---|
| Argentina | 6,990.60 | 10,129.80 | 11,810.10 | 13,817.70 | 18,334.00 | 20,338.20 |
| Brazil | 6,639.80 | 8,050.20 | 8,987.20 | 10,860.50 | 14,114.60 | 15,473.70 |
| Canada | 20,107.80 | 23,354.30 | 29,185.40 | 36,134.60 | 40,027.20 | 44,261.80 |
| China | 986.6 | 1,869.50 | 2,933.30 | 5,092.60 | 9,333.10 | 14,450.70 |
| Egypt | 3,887.20 | 4,681.10 | 5,989.70 | 7,297.30 | 9,897.70 | 10,913.40 |
| France | 17,640.70 | 20,845.80 | 26,192.70 | 30,603.50 | 36,027.00 | 41,016.70 |
| Germany | 19,421.80 | 23,565.70 | 27,277.10 | 31,968.50 | 39,263.20 | 48,041.70 |
| Ghana | 1,240.70 | 1,506.40 | 1,801.40 | 2,277.10 | 3,021.50 | 4,210.50 |
| India | 1,146.00 | 1,500.70 | 1,998.50 | 2,860.90 | 4,315.40 | 6,104.60 |
| Iran | 6,575.60 | 7,976.60 | 9,436.00 | 13,011.70 | 17,163.10 | – |
| Italy | 18,546.20 | 22,271.60 | 27,006.40 | 30,051.80 | 35,075.80 | 37,217.40 |
| Japan | 19,229.70 | 23,416.60 | 26,795.20 | 31,663.50 | 34,996.30 | 40,763.40 |
| Korea, Rep. | 8,436.20 | 13,372.00 | 18,083.10 | 24,219.80 | 30,465.20 | 34,647.10 |
| Norway | 18,431.30 | 24,306.60 | 36,928.00 | 47,772.40 | 57,995.90 | 62,083.90 |
| Pakistan | 1,975.80 | 2,452.70 | 2,775.60 | 3,586.40 | 4,209.70 | 5,010.80 |
| Russian Federation | 8,012.80 | 5,611.70 | 6,825.40 | 11,822.40 | 20,497.90 | 25,186.20 |
| S. Africa | 6,401.20 | 6,691.40 | 7,702.50 | 9,847.80 | 11,785.60 | 13,195.50 |
| UK | 16,739.10 | 20,182.80 | 26,030.70 | 32,274.80 | 35,740.70 | 41,801.00 |
| USA | 23,954.50 | 28,782.20 | 36,449.90 | 44,307.90 | 48,374.10 | 56,115.70 |

This is a measure of the total output of a country that takes gross domestic product (GDP) and divides it by the number of people in the country. The per capita GDP is especially useful when comparing one country to another because it shows the relative performance of the countries (www.investopia.com, 2017). This approach includes changes in population size in the calculation. Source: World Development Indicators prepared by the World Bank.

Table 4
Inequality-adjusted Human Development Index

| HDI *Rank (2015)* | *Country* | *2010* | *2011* | *2012* | *2013* | *2014* | *2015* |
|---|---|---|---|---|---|---|---|
| 45 | Argentina | 0.655 | 0.661 | 0.662 | 0.694 | 0.702 | 0.698 |
| 79 | Brazil | 0.527 | 0.527 | 0.534 | 0.545 | 0.556 | 0.561 |
| 10 | Canada | 0.825 | 0.828 | 0.83 | 0.842 | 0.838 | 0.839 |
| 90 | China | 0.539 | 0.546 | 0.554 | | | |
| 111 | Egypt | 0.486 | 0.511 | 0.516 | 0.521 | 0.523 | 0.491 |
| 21 | France | 0.801 | 0.804 | 0.807 | 0.81 | 0.816 | 0.813 |
| 4 | Germany | 0.839 | 0.853 | 0.855 | 0.855 | 0.86 | 0.859 |
| 139 | Ghana | 0.414 | 0.382 | 0.386 | 0.396 | 0.385 | 0.391 |
| 131 | India | 0.408 | 0.423 | 0.424 | 0.433 | 0.439 | 0.454 |
| 26 | Italy | 0.767 | 0.782 | 0.772 | 0.773 | 0.78 | 0.784 |
| 17 | Japan | | | | 0.787 | 0.79 | 0.791 |
| 18 | Korea (Republic of) | 0.737 | 0.742 | 0.744 | 0.74 | 0.751 | 0.754 |
| 1 | Norway | 0.877 | 0.888 | 0.882 | 0.892 | 0.897 | 0.898 |
| 147 | Pakistan | 0.36 | 0.363 | 0.372 | 0.379 | 0.384 | 0.38 |
| 49 | Russian Federation | 0.694 | 0.703 | | 0.706 | 0.72 | 0.725 |
| 119 | S. Africa | 0.439 | | | | 0.428 | 0.435 |
| 16 | UK | 0.814 | 0.823 | 0.824 | 0.823 | 0.83 | 0.836 |
| 10 | USA | 0.807 | 0.774 | 0.801 | 0.757 | 0.762 | 0.796 |

The Human Development Index (HDI) is a summary measure of average achievement in key dimensions of human development: a long and healthy life, being knowledgeable, and having a decent standard of living. The HDI is the geometric *mean* of normalized indices for each of the three dimensions ... The IHDI combines the HDI with how those achievements are distributed among a country's population by "discounting" each dimension's average value according to its level of inequality. Thus, the IHDI is the distribution-sensitive average level of human development. Two countries with different distributions of achievements can have the same average HDI value. Under perfect equality the IHDI is equal to the HDI but falls below the

HDI when inequality rises. The difference between the IHDI and HDI is the human development cost of inequality, also termed "the loss to human development due to inequality."[1] The inequality-adjusted HDI has been in use only since 2010. The "values" recorded are difficult to interpret – on the face of it they are meaningless to the layman. The significant thing is the ranking, which gives some idea of the relative quality of life in various countries. Countries ranked 1–50 are considered to have "very high human development" – and that includes Russia; Canada has dropped from fourth place in the IHDI index in the 1990s to tenth in the most recent iteration. The next group have a "high human development" rank between 51 and 105, and the medium group comes after that. Pakistan sits at the bottom of that third group, but it is worth noting that Pakistan suffers from widespread malnutrition, so talking about "medium human development" is a rather bad joke. (Source: United Nations.)

## INTERPRETATION OF DATA

The greatest problem of such data sets is that because they present a summary of information, and one that is derived from disparate data collecting agencies, they quite often hide the very details that can most illuminate the economic, social, and political changes experienced in individual countries. Nor does such data take into account the effect of factors considered extraneous – such as the levels of money laundering, political corruption, or even the delayed but inevitable costs of pollution and climate change. I have highlighted some of the issues and problems to be borne in mind when interpreting data presented at these levels of generalization:

1 There is a frequent assumption that a healthy per capita growth would be around at least 3 per cent per year. Yet in reality, 1 per cent annual per capita growth is nearer the norm. Thomas Picketty writes, "[T]here is no historical example of a country at the world technological frontier whose growth in per capita output exceeded 1.5% over a lengthy period of time."[2] Overall GDP growth can look higher, but that may be due to changes in population size rather than output.
2 Thomas Picketty points out that between 1990 and 2010 *global* growth exceeded 2 per cent per annum due to the economic catch up of Asian countries, notably China, whose growth rates, according to official data exceeded 9 per cent per annum – "a level never before observed."[3]
3 Population size and growth rate are critical to interpreting data on economic growth: slow growth allows for gradual social and economic change. For example, France's population took more than two hundred years to double from 30 million to 60 million between 1790 and 2010. In roughly the same time period America's population increased a hundredfold from 3 million to 300 million – and is reflected in rapid economic and social change.
4 Statistical information is more reliably compiled in some jurisdictions than in others. Much of it is deemed almost guesswork in some African countries.[4] Or there can be arbitrary government interference in the collection and presentation of statistics, as happened in Canada in 2010 in relation to the data compiled from the long-form census.

5 When looking at GDP growth – either in general or on a per capita basis – any changes in the *distribution* of income are hidden. Thus if we consult more detailed analyses such as those conducted by Milanovic, we find that between the early 1980s and 2010 there has been a palpable decline in the size of the middle class in some Western countries and relatively little in others. Among Western (OECD) countries, the greatest decline has been in the United States and the UK. In America the middle-class population has fallen from around 32 per cent to almost 26 per cent in 2010; in the UK the decline is even starker: the middle class shrank from 41 per cent to 31 per cent.[5]

# Notes

## PREFACE

1 Joan Robinson, professor of economics at Cambridge University, writing in 1971 and quoted in Glyn, *Capitalism Unleashed*, 129. Robinson was a leading British Keynesian who sympathized with the revolution in China.
2 Krugman, "Voodoo."
3 Austria declared war on Serbia on 28 July 1914 and thus launched World War One, also known as "the Great War." The Russian flag was hoisted to the top of the Kremlin, the Russian parliament, on Christmas Day 1991, thus signaling the end of the Soviet Union and of communism, the greatest of the twentieth century's original ideologies.
4 Krugman, "Impossible Dream."
5 Runciman, *Confidence Trap*, 355, n.1; Evans-Pritchard, "Nouriel Roubini"; Jarausch, *Ashes*, 787.

## CHAPTER ONE

1 Huntington cited in Lieven, *America*, 49; for Romney, Tumulty, "American exceptionalism."
2 Quoted in Johnson, *Blowback*, 217, but widely cited as an example of high noon triumphalism.
3 Eichengreen. *Exorbitant Privilege*.
4 For comparative GDP growth, see appendix "World Development Indicators." Discussion of the crisis of the 1970s may be found in Kotz, *Rise and Fall*, 63–7. The term "leadership" was employed by the British when

they appealed to the Americans to take over from them during the Greek civil war in 1947.

5 Helleiner, *Bretton Woods*, 132. Italics in original.

6 Offer and Söderberg, *Nobel Factor*, 233–6, 253–8.

7 "Economism" is the neologism coined by James Kwak to describe the simplistic and highly ideological tenets of what in North America we refer to as "Economics 101." "[Economism] rests on the premise that people, companies and markets behave according to the abstract, two-dimensional illustrations of an Economics 101 textbook, even though the assumptions behind those diagrams virtually never hold true in the real world" (Kwak, *Economism*, 6–7).

8 De Grazia, *Empire*, 5.

9 Bakewell, *Existentalist Café*, 167–8. Bakewell may err in not distinguishing the different views of popular and elite France. Howard (*Power*, 10) argues that de Gaulle and other postwar French leaders were acutely conscious of rising international menace of *les Anglo-Saxons* whose intention it was to diminish the role of France.

10 Crews, *Afghan Modern*, 198.

11 Offer and Söderberg, *Nobel Factor*, 185

12 For Deutsche Bank, Fichtner et al., "German Banking."

13 Samuel, *Island Stories*, 177, 181.

14 Gordon, *American Growth*, 642–3.

15 "Keynesianism" was the economic theory of J.M. Keynes, which called for the intervention of the state in the economy especially to guide it in times of recession.

16 Frieden, *Capitalism*, 262.

17 Helleiner, *Bretton Woods*, 15.

18 Hobsbawm, *Extremes*, 258–9, 263.

19 Augar, "Barclays."

20 Mead (*Providence*, 127) quotes J.M. Keynes' biographer, Robert Skidelsky, who "goes so far as to say that the United States had three principal war aims in World War II; the defeat of Japan, the defeat of Germany, and the defeat of Great Britain." Mead adds, "The last is only slightly hyperbolic."

21 Gindin and Panich, *Global Capitalism*, 235.

22 The bond rating agencies are Standard & Poor's, Moody's, and Fitch. They grade bonds from AAA downward to BB. Standard & Poor's was fined $1.4 billion "to settle charges of grade inflation" (Kwak, *Economism*, 150).

23 None more than the sometime Greek finance minister, Yanis Varoufakis. See his *Minotaur*.

24 Kotz, *Rise and Fall*, 11 and "End of the Golden Age: The Crisis of the 1970s," 63–7.

25 Ibid., 166–75. For Harvard Business School (HBS), McDonald, *Golden Passport*. McDonald writes of the US, "Here's a case of government being successfully operated by business. The claim that we live in a free market is a crock" (7).

26 De Grazia, *Empire*, chapter 1, "The Service Ethic." George Babbitt was a fictional American businessman, the eponymous subject of Sinclair Lewis's withering 1922 novel.

27 Kotz, *Rise and Fall*, 68, for declining profits after 1966, 63–4.

28 Stedman Jones, *Masters*, 180.

29 Ibid.

30 The main think tanks that supported conservatism and neoliberalism were the ancient Hoover Institution (est. 1919), the American Enterprise Institute (est. 1975), the Heritage Institute (est. 1973) and the Cato Institute (est. 1977). Kotz, *Rise and Fall*, 74, Kwak, *Economism*, 44, Meyer, *Dark Money*, 77–9.

31 Offer and Söderberg, *Nobel Factor*, 35.

32 Cited in Kwak, *Economism*, 130.

33 For a succinct contemporary account, largely exonerating Bernanke from any blame, see Cassidy, "Meltdown."

34 For the explanation to the Queen, Stewart, "Credit Crunch."

35 The head of NATO was called the "Supreme Allied Commander, Europe" (SACEUR). The first supreme commander was Dwight D. Eisenhower, who later became the 34th president of the United States (1953–61).

36 Bacevich, *America's War*, 169.

37 Lears, "We came," 8.

38 Chase, "Canadian airstrikes"; Puglese, "Canadian Navy." The absurdity of the Canadian Navy patrolling the Black Sea seems not to have drawn the attention it deserved.

39 Cockburn, *Kill Chain*. For other doubts about the morality of drones, Junod, "Lethal Presidency." For totals, Bacevich, *America's War*, 334. The president and his advisors called the "kill list" a "disposition matrix," ibid.).

40 "Having been seen to have failed in Iraq had dealt a great blow to the [British] army's self image – and, just as important, the image it had enjoyed in US eyes" (Ledwidge, *Investment*, 21); Ascherson, "Painful lessons."

41 Cartoon, *The Globe and Mail*, 7 September 2013, F9. The British prime minister, Cameron, advocated the use of the RAF in air strikes in Syria in 2013 but was defeated in a House of Commons vote. Afterwards, he

noted that the vote reflected public opinion: "I get that," he claimed (Rachman, "Transatlantic").

42 Jarausch, *Ashes*, 761.

43 Ibid., 422; Thatcher's phone call was revealed in the opening of British archives in late 2016. See Mance, "Thatcher."

44 My argument here comes from Layne, *Peace*, chapter 5 "The Containment of Europe"; for de Gaulle's counterbalancing policy, 97; the quote is on 49. In 2013, the French, in particular, yearned for American involvement in Syria. When it failed to happen, Paris was embarrassed; further evidence that America and Europe were "falling apart" (Stevens, "Falling Apart"); Robin Porter ("Why America?") dismisses the "special relationship" summarily.

45 Cited in Judt, *Postwar*, 150–1.

46 Reynolds, *Brittania*, 218.

47 Sanger, *Confront*, 418.

48 For the Baghdad embassy, Langewiesche "Mega-Bunker."

49 Anderson, "American Foreign Policy," 231.

50 Kovach and Carter, "US–Japan deal."

51 Cockburn, *Kill Chain*, 105. The author refers to the Predator drone as "the weapon that in the eyes of large parts of the world would one day come to define America" (50). "Reaper" drones were a snip at $20 million apiece (254). Unlike Friedman, not all military analysts admired the hidden fist. See Sluka, discussing the article in *The New York Times* (17 May 2009), entitled, tellingly, "Death from Above. Outrage Down Below."

52 McCarrather, "Heavenly" in Bacevich (ed.), *Short American Century*, 187. Elsewhere Friedman goes on in the same blathering vein: "In so many ways, globalization is us." It "wears Mickey Mouse ears, eats Big Macs, drinks Coca-Cola or Pepsi and does its computing on an IBM PC" (223) (McCarrather, ibid., 221). There is no mention in Friedman of the "disposition matrix," that is, the "kill list."

53 The invasion of Grenada (called "Operation Urgent Fury") took place on 25 October 1983. It was the first major operation conducted by the US military since the war in Vietnam. As a courtesy, President Reagan apologized to British Prime Minister Margaret Thatcher for not warning her that it was being planned. Grenada, being a member of the Commonwealth, was assumed to be a British "responsibility."

54 Mason, *Globalization*, 11.

55 Bacevich (*America's War*, 352) notes that the political right in America "suspected the president [Obama] of nefariously plotting to get out of Iraq by allowing Iran in."

56 For arms, SIPRI "China" and "United States."

57 For a summary version of Fukayama's ideas, Runciman, *Confidence*, especially chapter 6, "1989. The End of History" and chapter 7, "2008. Back to the Future," especially 240–1.

58 Kurbjuweit, "America."

59 This is the theme of Kruse's *One Nation*, the subtitle of which is "How Corporate America Invented Christian America."

60 Kruse, *Nation*, 67. According to a 2014 Gallup poll, 42 per cent of Americans shared the creationist view, i.e. that God created humans in the present form 10,000 years ago.

61 Ibid., 275, 281, 287; McLannahan, "Goldman Sachs."

62 Sheffield, "Irreligion."

63 Piketty, *Capital*, 98.

64 Huntington (*Civilizations*, 184) concerned himself with "the declining relative power of the West." He made it clear that "the West" was "primarily the United States."

65 Nye, *Paradox*; Bacevich, *America's War*, 173.

66 For the continuing hangover of Vietnam in America, Marlantes, "Vietnam." Auslin (*Asian Century*) argues for the rehabilitation of the West (read: America), and, *per contra*, the growing crises in Asia.

67 Harvey, *Seventeen Contradictions*.

68 Piketty, *Capital*, 99–100."Between 1913 and 2012, the growth rate of world GDP was 3.0 percent per year on average."

69 Cockburn, *Islamic State*, 1–2.

70 Ibid.; Meek, "After the Vote," 8. For Boko Haram and the American pivot to Africa, Turse, *Battlefield*, esp. 79: "From 2008 to 2013, the number of missions, exercises, operations and other activities under AFRICOM' s purview skyrocketed from 172 to 546." AFRICOM is the US Army's Africa Command. For the eight wars, Cockburn, *Jihad*, Afterward,"Eight Wars." For the resurrection of al-Qaida see chapter 7.

71 Denyer, "Island-Building"; Osnos, "Parading." For China in Djibouti, Perlez and Buckley, "China Retools"; in the Middle East, Nasr, "The China Challenge" in *Dispensable*, 215–49: "Unlike China," explained Secretary Clinton to a Senegalese audience, "America will stand up for democracy and universal human rights even when it might be easier to look the other way and keep the resources flowing" (ibid., 217).

72 Even advocates of American leadership recognized American limitations here. Barnett (*Great Powers*, 7): "The Bush-Cheney administration came into power seeking to realign the strategic relationships among the great powers; whipping NATO *into shape*; putting rising China,

India, and Russia *in their place*; and reasserting American leadership. [The Bush-Cheney strategy] achieved the exact opposite across the board."

73 Ascherson, "Russia."

74 Jones, "Dmitry Medvedev"; Goldberg, "Obama Doctrine."

75 Koczanowicz, "Polish Case," 77.

76 Kwak, *Economism*, 167.

77 For China's defence spending and sabre rattling, Clover, "China."

78 Yuan Yang, "China GDP."

79 Dyer, "Global crisis."

## CHAPTER TWO

1 Milward, *Rescue*, 4.

2 Spain and Portugal, neither of which had been involved in World War Two, remained retarded right-wing dictatorships, not unsympathetic to fascism, until the 1970s. Greece joined them briefly in 1967 and then in 1974 saw democracy regained.

3 Populations (2012): European Union: 507,890,191 of which Germany 80.5 m., France 66 m., UK 63.5 m. Italy 60 m., Spain 47 m., Portugal 10 m., Scandinavia (Denmark, Norway, Sweden, and Finland) 25 m., Benelux 28 m., Baltic states 6.5 m., periphery (Ireland, Iceland, Malta, Cyprus) 6.5 m., Balkans (Slovenia, Croatia, Greece) 17.5 m. EU per capita GDP (2010) ranged from $9,615 for Romania through about $35,000 for both the UK and Italy, $40,875 for Germany, $44,747 for France to $54,640 for the Netherlands, with the EU average being $32,400. Canada's score was $43,472.

4 For the deaths in the region of Poland and the western Soviet Union, Snyder, *Bloodlands*.

5 For Berlin, "the world metropolis of the 1920s" and the "capital of the Third Reich" a decade later (6), Schneider, *Berlin Now*.

6 The Scottish independence referendum was held on 17 September 2014. On the question as to whether Scotland should stay in the United Kingdom, the "Yes" vote got 50 per cent, the "No" vote 45 per cent and the "Don't Knows" 5 per cent. That was before the price of oil, a major prop for any independent economy, tanked.

7 Nairn, *Break-Up* (1977). Sequel: Nairn, *After Britain* (2000).

8 The *Frankfurter Allgemein Zeitung* referred to the Front National as "Camembert fascism" on account of the Breton origins of its leaders. The rightwing populist "Alternative for Germany" (AfD) was the schnitzel version of Camembert fascism.

9 Wolf, "Next recession."
10 The Six – France, Germany, Italy, the Netherlands, Belgium, and Luxembourg – came together as the "European Coal, Iron and Steel Community" as a consequence of agreement in 1950 and the 1951 Treaty of Paris. Note that all but Luxembourg had had colonies; Germany, Italy, and the Netherlands had lost theirs while France and Belgium would follow within the decade.
11 Frieden (*Capitalism*, 268–71) stresses American support for European reconstruction and Washington's political leadership. The different view is that of Milward, *Reconstruction*, especially chapter 3, Milward's view is summarized in Anderson, "Interim."
12 Gilpin, *Political Economy*, 5.
13 The assistant secretary of the US Treasury, Marc Leland, admitted in 1984 that the IMF was a "convenient conduit for US influence" (Gindin and Panich, *Capitalism*, 235).
14 Frieden, *Capitalism*, 268–9.
15 Judt, *Postwar*, 361; Berend, *Europe*, 20.
16 Berend, ibid., 23.
17 For the effects of the Plaza Accord on Japan and its investment in Asia, see chapter 4.
18 Frieden, *Capitalism*, 293.
19 Ibid.
20 Glyn, *Capitalism*, 187; Jackson, "U.S. Direct Investments," 1.
21 De Grazia, *Empire*, 165–9, 460–1.
22 For INSEAD, financed by the Ford Foundation, which opened in 1959. The London and Manchester business schools were also founded on the HBS model (McDonald, *Golden Passport*, 126, 232).
23 Frieden, *Global Capitalism*, 295.
24 Cited in Smith, *France*, 1, 43. Smith notes that in late 2013, Todd expressed concern about German influence in the EU. Also Gailbraith et al., "Germany Reconquered Europe."
25 Gildea, *France*, 9; Frieden, *Global Capitalism*, 293, 349. For Todd, Smith, *France*, 1, for hamburgers, Bhagwati, *Globalization*, 106.
26 Jarausch, *Hitler*, 121, 126.
27 Ibid., 198.
28 Ibid., 57, 100, 121–7.
29 Guilbaut, *New York*.
30 De Grazia, *Empire*, 284; Jarausch, ibid., 122.
31 Berend, *Europe*, 144.
32 Jarausch, *Ashes*, 748. Jarausch adds: "When U.S. neoconservatives aimed

for imperial hegemony, many [European] leaders balked at following their lead and chose to assert their independence."

33 Short, *Mitterand*, 247.

34 Milward, *Rescue*, 30.

35 Smith, *France*, 2.

36 For measures of inequality, see appendix, table 4.

37 BBC News, "Corruption"; Anderson, "Italian Disaster." Note that in star-struck works on the EU like that of Van Middelaar (*Passage*), there is no mention of corruption at any level nor of oligarchies or have-nots.

38 Shaxson (*Treasure Islands*) investigates the role of British-protected money laundering.

39 Judt, *Postwar*, 335.

40 The Muslim population of Norway was about 1.5 per cent; 150,000 out of 4.8 m.; it was 6.5 per cent of the population of Sweden. It is anticipated that by 2030 the Muslim population of Europe will be seven per cent of the total. In the same year, the Muslim population of Canada should reach 6.6 per cent of the total. Saunders, *Myth*, 42–3.

41 Two and a half million Indian volunteers fought for the British in World War Two.

42 Berend, *Europe*, 192. Irish prosperity was in part dependent on "tax dumping," that is attracting foreign investment through low taxes. Luxembourg and countries in Eastern Europe followed the same practice that was deplored by the larger economies of Europe. Thomas Piketty wrote in 2010, "First, Ireland was a miracle. Then it was a disaster. Now it looks set to become a scandal" (Piketty, *Bankers*, 95).

43 Berend, *Europe*, 13. It was the decision of the Arab oil ministers in October 1973 to raise the price of oil (to draw attention to the question of Palestine) that cut the ground from under this wonderful growth; after 1974 growth dropped to between two and three per cent in most countries. By 1975, the year Franco died, Spanish GNP growth had fallen from 5.4 to 1.1 per cent (Mitchell, *Carbon Democracy*, 184; ibid., 190).

44 For the threat to the social model, Giddens, *Turbulent*, 99.

45 Cited in Berend, *Europe*, 279–80.

46 IKEA was the European answer to American chains. In business since 1958, it had thirty-seven stores in Scandinavia, fifty in Germany, thirty-two in France, eighteen in the UK, and twenty-one in Italy. Wikipedia, "List of Countries with IKEA stores."

47 O'Brien cited in Anderson, *New Old World*, 34.

48 Beck, *German Europe*, xii.

49 Schmidt, "Germany."

50 The debt was held by French and German banks, about €75 and €53 billion, respectively.
51 Pisani-Ferry, *Euro Crisis*, 17.
52 Spiegel, "Euro."
53 Nardelli, "IMF"; Krugman, "Killing."
54 Evans-Pritchard, "Europe."
55 Piketty "Germany"; Piketty et al., "Austerity." Criticism of Piketty's interpretation of the restructuring of Germany's 1953 debt is in Cotterill "Let's talk …."
56 An insightful sketch of Schäuble is to be found in Rahtz, "*Zuchtmeister* Schäubel."
57 Münchau, "Greece's Brutal Creditors"; *Guardian*, "Greek crisis"; Krugman, "Killing"; Foy, "Greek tragedy"; Pgiaitsis, "Greeks."
58 Connor, "Refugees"; Sherwood et al., "Catastrophe."
59 Piketty, "New Deal." Similar warnings: Anna Sauerbrey's "Merkel Era" and *Spiegel's* "Hate Preachers."
60 Rahtz, "Motor."
61 Watkins, "Casting Off?"
62 Ibid., 27.
63 Tooze, "Logic of Crisis," 8.

## CHAPTER THREE

1 In the elections of June 1981, the French communists polled 14 million votes in the first round and in the end won forty-four seats (out of 491) in the National Assembly. Four communists joined the Mitterand cabinet. In the first round of the French departmental elections of 2015 the communists won nearly 270,000 votes and 121 seats across the country.
2 The speech was given at Fulton, Missouri on 5 March 1946 and is usually seen as the opening rhetorical shot of the Cold War. It is mentioned in most international relations and postwar histories up to the present, for instance Gaddis, *Cold War*, 95, Applebaum, *Iron Curtain*, xix.
3 For Atlanticism, Van der Pijl, *Atlantic*.
4 Strictly speaking this was "Cold War I." "Cold War II" was proclaimed (by some authors) in the 1980s and "Cold War III" in 2015. For Cold War II, see Fred Halliday, *The Second Cold War* (1983) and for Cold War III, Robert Legvold, *Return to the Cold War* (2016).
5 "Containment" was a Cold War doctrine that advocated the isolation of the Soviet Union by means both military and economic. Thus postwar America undertook a policy of simultaneous globalization of capitalism

and containment of communism. The term has also been used for America's "pivot" policy towards China.

6 The exception here was Yugoslavia where a communist regime under Joseph Broz Tito (1945–80) existed independently of Moscow. This independent communism was called "Titoism." While in cultural terms it flourished, by the early 1980s Yugoslavia was paying out 23 per cent of export earnings to foreign banks and the IMF. When it exploded at the end of the 1980s, a bloodbath followed with Serbs, Croats, Kosovars, and Albanians murdering one another at a rate unseen in Europe since the end of World War Two.

7 Applebaum, *Iron Curtain*, 424. *Neues Deutschland* was a communist party propaganda sheet posing as a newspaper.

8 Taubman, *Khrushchev*, 448.

9 Brown, *Rise and Fall*, 472.

10 Taubman, *Khrushchev*, chapter 11. The secret speech didn't stay hushed up for very long. At first, the Polish Politboro let privileged members read copies in a special room at party headquarters. Then some fifteen thousand copies were printed without authorization and one of them reached Israeli intelligence, which gave a copy to the CIA. The CIA slipped a copy to *The New York Times*, which published it on 4 June 1956 (ibid., 284).

11 On American culture, Figes, *Russia*, 255–6.

12 In some interpretations the Brezhnev Era lasted from the advent of Brezhnev in 1964 to the rise of Gorbachev in 1982. For writers on international relations, the era was marked by the Second Cold War.

13 Figes, *Russia*, 261, 263.

14 Goldman, *Piratization*, 43.

15 Andropov had been the head of the KGB, the Committee on State Security, the Soviet Union's main spy organization, between 1967 and 1982. His immediate successor was the Stalinist throwback, Konstantin Chernenko ("a professional clerk, an average bureaucrat") (Arbatov, *System*, 287) who lasted only thirteen months, dying in March 1985. It was under Andropov, who sought to turn the KGB into a kind of political elite, that Vladimir Putin and a number of his homologues, who later formed the *siliviki*, was hired. The KGB became the FSB.

16 Judt, *Postwar*, 632.

17 The Russian population in 2012 was just over 143 million, compared to Germany at 82 million and the United Kingdom with just over 62 million. The population of Ukraine was about 45.5 million, 10 million more than Canada.

18 Berend, *Europe*, 59. Alas, as Berend points out (60), this New World Order seemed in key respects to resemble its predecessor. In December 1989, just a few weeks after the Berlin Wall was brought down, the US invaded Panama.
19 Ostrovsky, *Invention*, 134; Gustafson, *Fortune*, 13.
20 Dawisha, *Kleptocracy*, esp. 316. For Putin's place in the kleptocracy, as leaked in the Panama papers, see Harding, "Revealed."
21 Klein and Pomer, *New Russia*, 17; Cohen, *Failed Crusade*, 154.
22 Offer and Söderberg, *Nobel Factor*, 253.
23 "The shock therapy approach to economic transition has been characterized as an expression of the 'mood of mindless anti-governmentalism' that prevailed worldwide in the early 1990s." Ostrovsky (ibid., 193) writes: "[T]he [Russian] privatization ... was the worst example of an insider deal and outright sham that the world has ever seen."
24 Cohen, *Soviet Fates*, 155.
25 Cohen, ibid., 13.
26 This account is given by Hollingsworth and Lansley, *Londongrad*, 49.
27 Roxburgh, *Strongman*, 24; Dawisha (*Kleptocracy*, 237–56) comes to the same conclusion.
28 Dawisha (*Kleptocracy*, 6) gives his wealth as about $40 billion. For the cost and photos of his palace, see 296–7. While writers like Dawisha make an issue of Putin's wealth, Hill and Gaddy (*Mr. Putin*, 10–11) point out that, "there is little hard documentary evidence to back up even the most credible reporting."
29 Gessen, *Putin*, 233–4, 246–8.
30 Ostrovsky, *Invention*, 80–1.
31 The quote is from Sakwa, *Crisis*, 123. For Berezovsky's fate, Spitznagel, "Mysterious Death."
32 Ostrovsky, *Inventing*, 265. Elsewhere (267) Ostrovsky notes that after the first IKEA store opened in Moscow "middle-class Russians, like everyone else in Europe, were too busy assembling their Scandinavian-style homes to care about politics."
33 Roxburgh, *Strongman*, 32; Gustafson, *Fortune*, 359. For Dresdner Bank and Siemens, Dawisha, *Kleptocracy*, 53–5, 48.
34 Anderson, "Russia," 7.
35 This term belongs to Gustafson, *Fortune*, 275.
36 Sakwa, *Democracy*, 144; Dawisha (*Kleptocracy*, 55) points out how the takeover of Yukos was facilitated by the German Dresdner Bank, at some profit to the Germans who, at least until 2014, had a soft spot for Putin.

37 Judah, *Empire*, 125.
38 Gustafson, *Fortune*, 317.
39 Ibid., 20; Cohen, *Russia*, 6.
40 Cohen, *Soviet Fates*, 164; Cohen, "Distorting Russia."
41 Sakwa, *Democracy*, 145.
42 Ibid., 146.
43 Ibid., 29–37. This author quotes (36) the annual Freedom House rankings, which contend that Russian democracy had been declining since 1999. Dawisha (*Kleptocracy*, 320) also quotes Freedom House.
44 Gessen, *Putin*, 142.
45 Ibid., 248; Sakwa, *Democracy*, 173.
46 Gel'man, *Authoritarian Russia*, 18, 96.
47 This view is Judah's (*Empire*, 326–7). Gel'man (ibid., 106) says that in the aftermath of the 4 December 2011 parliamentary elections "the scope of ... mass mobilization was unprecedented for the country; no antisystemic political protests since the Soviet collapse had so many participants."
48 Anderson, "Russia," 30; Hill and Gaddy, *Mr. Putin*, 249–51.
49 Wood, *Chechnya*, especially chapters 3 and 5.
50 Layne, *Peace*, 2, citing LaFeber, *Illusions*, 354–5.
51 On leaving office Schroder, a social democrat, took up a position with the North European Gas Pipeline consortium, a joint venture involving the Russian Gazprom. (Wood, ibid., 114–15).
52 For the Ukrainian purges and Khrushchev's role in them, Taubman, *Khrushchev*, 118–20.
53 Wilson, *Ukrainian Crisis*, 93. On 12 Wilson refers to rumours of this sum as "defying credibility."
54 Hill and Gaddy, *Mr. Putin*, 3. "European security" is State Department-speak. Most Europeans were hardly aware of the Russian annexation.
55 Wilson, *Ukrainian Crisis*, 118.
56 For the Donbas imbroglio, Wilson, ibid., 118–43. For fighting around Luhansk and Donetsk in August 2014 and late January 2015, Tavernise, "Ukrainian Military" and Lyman and Kremer, "War."
57 Wilson, *Ukrainian Crisis*, 1, 10. Contrary to the claim that a new Cold War had broken out by 2008, Wilson points to the cupboard love between certain European leaders and Putin, notably "the frankly bizarre romance between Putin and Berlusconi." Later, the relationship between Putin and Donald Trump was highlighted.
58 Ibid., 185.

59 Hill and Gaddy, *Mr. Putin*, 368–9.
60 Shevtsova ("Sanctions") discusses the question from a decidedly "Great Power" point of view.
61 Lieven, "Ukraine," 76.
62 Wilson, *Ukrainian Crisis*, 205; Mazower, "European democracy"; Anderson, "Russia."

## CHAPTER FOUR

1 Populations of major states (all 2014 or 2015) except North Korea (2008): Japan, 127 m., South Korea 49 m., North Korea 26 m., Vietnam 92 m., Indonesia 255 m., Taiwan 23 m., Singapore, 5.5 m., Hong Kong 7 m., Thailand 67.5 m., Malaysia 30 m. (Recall that Germany, Western Europe's most populous state, had 81 m.)
2 Harvey, *Contradictions*, 124. For a confident assertion of the end of the American Century, Bacevich, *Limits*; Madrick, "Too Little"; Gordon, *American Growth*. On the theme of global shift, Prestowitz, *New Capitalists*; Mahbubani, *Asian Hemisphere*; Subramanian, *Eclipse*; and Mason, *Global Shift*. A contrary view from an American think tank is Auslin, *Asian Century*.
3 *Japan Times*, "OECD warns." The IMF prediction for 2014 was 1.6 per cent. Catastrophe for China, it was warned, would come with a GDP rate of less than 7 per cent per annum. At 6.8 per cent China's growth rate in 2016 was the slowest in twenty-five years. Japan's 2016 rate was 0.8 per cent.
4 Wang Hui, *China's Twentieth Century*, 285–8.
5 Dower, *Embracing Defeat*, 19
6 Utley, *Feet of Clay*, 9.
7 The heyday of the shogun was the period known as the Tokugawa Shogunate, which lasted from 1603 to 1868. With the return to power of the emperor in the mid-nineteenth century, Japan moved from feudalism to the first stages of industrial capitalism. *American Caesar* was the title of a 1978 biography of MacArthur by William Manchester.
8 Woo, *Race*, 55–6.
9 AFTA is the world's third largest free trade organization after the EU and NAFTA.
10 Woo, ibid., 90.
11 Ibid., 92.
12 Kennedy, *Great Powers*.
13 Piketty (*Capital*, 93) points out that "in the last few decades" Japanese

per capita output grew at a rate of 0.7 per cent, American at double that; for sex, Haworth, "Young People".

14 Garside, *Stagnation*, 4.

15 In October 1967, before he had become president, Richard Nixon wrote an article in *Foreign Affairs* entitled "Asia after Vietnam" in which he explained that the exclusion of China from world affairs couldn't continue (Jager, *Brothers*, 190).

16 In March 1987 a world record for the purchase of a painting was broken when a Japanese buyer paid $49 million for a version of Van Gogh's "Sunflowers." Two years earlier another Japanese buyer had paid $40 million for the same painter's "Still Life: Vase." Sony sold its New York headquarters in the Rockefeller Centre in early 2013 although Japanese investors held on to Columbia Pictures.

17 Bruce Cumings (*Korean War*, 39) suggests that Japan be called a "hereditary democracy" on the basis that "often 70 to 80 percent of their parliamentarians have inherited seats from their fathers or come from political prominent families."

18 Mason, *Global Shift*, 46–7 quoting McCormack, *Emptiness*, 6–7.

19 In 1985 the US, Japan, and Germany signed the Plaza Accord that depreciated the US dollar in relation to the yen and Deutschmark. The appreciation of the yen made Japanese exports more expensive, and as a consequence Japanese capital flowed to Thailand, which became a cheap labour platform. Japanese public debt as a percentage of GDP was 214 (2012), Canada's 84 (2012), Germany's 80 (2013).

20 This indictment of Japanese racism is central to the McCormack's arguments in *Client State* (esp. chapter 2, 9).

21 McCormack, *Emptiness*, 4. One leading functionary of the LDP, Kyuma Fumio, sometime minister of defence, said, concerning Japan's support of Washington on the eve of the invasion of Iraq, "I think [Japan] has no choice. After all, it is like an American state" (ibid.,3) . Here is a sense of prostration that even outdoes the British "special relationship."

22 "Comfort women" were sex slaves. By the time that the system was fully established there were between 50,000 and 200,000 women in the system. The South Korean (ROK) Army set up similar military brothels during the Korean War (Cumings, *Korean War*, 41–2).

23 Dyer, "China and US"; Dyer and McGregor, "US shifts policy."

24 McCormack says a lot about Abe in his 2007 book (*Client State*) and in his "Abe Days are Here Again" in *The Asia-Pacific Journal*. Narusawa Muneo exposes him in "Abe Shinzo," also in *The Asia-Pacific Journal*.

Dyer refers in "China training" to a US navy officer's claim that China is preparing for "short, sharp war."

25 *Business Week*, December 1985, cited in Woo, *Race*, 1.

26 Eckert, *Offspring*, 5; Amsden, *Giant*, 33; Woo, *Race*, 28–30, points to the access by Korean capitalists of bank loans for the nascent Korean entrepreneurs and the role of Koreans in colonial financial institutions.

27 Hwang, *Korean Economies*, 15–17.

28 Ibid.

29 Cumings, *Origins*, 86.

30 Ibid., 136.

31 Wang Hui, *Twentieth Century*, 110–52.

32 Cumings, *North Korea*, 21–42.

33 Cumings, *Korean War*, 151.

34 Halliday and Cumings, *Korea*, 115. Jager (*Brothers*, 527, n.18): "By the fall of 1951 eighteen of twenty-two major cities in North Korea had already been at least half obliterated. In early 1952, the [US] Far East Air Force ... began to target power plants and dams along the Yalu River. The Chasan Reservoirs in South Pyongan province were destroyed in May 1953, causing huge floods that destroyed hundreds of villages and much livestock and food."

35 Woo, *Race*, 45–6, 59; Rodrik ("Economic Convergence") gives 7.3 per cent over the period 1965–95.

36 Woo, *Race*, 80, 87.

37 Ibid., 93.

38 Ibid., 95–6.

39 In what has been called the "Big Push" towards industrialization in the 1970s, massive investments were made in steel, shipping, machine building, metals, and chemicals. Ibid., 119–20.

40 The East Asian Economic Crisis of 1997–98 engulfed states from Thailand to South Korea as well as Russia. The cost to the economies of Thailand, Malaysia, South Korea, Indonesian, and the Philippines is estimated at $2 trillion. The crisis led to South Korea opening its domestic finance services sector to the US. At the behest of the US Treasury the IMF blocked Japanese attempts to create a bailout fund. The effect of the IMF in the crisis was, according to one US trade representative, as a "battering ram" used to open Asian markets to US products (Subramanian, *Eclipse*, 34). In the view of many, the intervention of the IMF exacerbated the crisis and its reputation was seriously damaged.

41 Amsden, *Giant*, 17. Woo (*Race*, 81) characterizes the members of the Ko-

rean junta as viewing capitalism as a conspiracy of the rich: "when they awakened to the need for domestic resource mobilization, they [the junta] badgered the rich and forced citizens, through campaigns and edicts, to salt away chunks of their salaries."

42 Chibber, "Miracle," 122–38.
43 *The Economist*, "South Korea" in Mason, *Development*, 397.
44 Anderson quoted in Lie, *Han Unbound*, vii–viii.
45 Chibber, "Miracle," 134.
46 Woo, *Race*, 193.
47 Ibid., 187, 190–1.
48 Armstrong, *Revolution*, 117.
49 The normal term of office for South Korean presidents is from 25 February of any year to 25 February five years later.
50 In return for the IMF's $57 billion rescue package, known as a "bailout," Kim was forced to accept a number of policy changes than benefited the US financial service industry and US multinationals; labour deregulation, fiscal austerity, the lifting of ceilings on foreign investment, and the opening of domestic markets. See Armstrong, "Contesting," 122; Blustein, *Chastening*, 140–3; and Rodrik, *Globalization*.
51 Blustein, *Chastening*, 143.
52 By 2002 the unpopularity of America was ascending rapidly, in large part because of the 37,000 US troops remaining on South Korean territory. One newspaper poll in 2002 disclosed that only 13 per cent of South Koreans viewed the US favourably while 36 per cent viewed it unfavourably, and 50 per cent were neutral (Ibid., 125).
53 Fifield, "Corruption," 11.

## CHAPTER FIVE

1 Pomerantz, *Divergence*, 111. By "core regions" is meant areas like the Yangtze and Pearl River valleys where industry and commerce had advanced to Western levels. More than anyone else, Pomerantz popularized the idea that some regions within China had been as advanced as the west up to c.1800 and then had fallen behind (for less than two centuries). Note that the "divergence" in Pomerantz' title took place from the Treaty of Nanjing and was followed, in just over a century, by the "convergence" of Baldwin's title and Rodrik's article.
2 Spence, *Modern China*, 389–90.
3 Heads of the communist parties in the Soviet Union and, from 1982, in China, following the Soviet example, were called "General Secretary."

Mao appointed all of the senior officials of the CPC, including Deng Xiaoping. Deng selected his successors up to Wen Jiabao (2003–13) who preceded Xi Jinping (2012–present). Xi Jinping was only the second General Secretary after Mao to be chosen by his peers (MacFarquhar, "China," n.1).

4 The Americans provided Jiang with more military aid than they had to any country of Western Europe after World Two, besides selling him $1.2 billion worth of weapons (Pantsov et al., *Deng*, 125).

5 Fairbank, cited in Mason, *Development*, 353.

6 Bowles and Rusk, quoted in Perlstein, "Chinese Mirrors," 30.

7 Pantsov, *Deng*, 145–6. Land ownership in China was anything but simple. Spence (*Modern China*, 463, 480) refers to surveys that indicate the following categories: landlord, rich peasant, middle peasant, poor peasant, tenant, and hired peasant.

8 Cited in Mason, *Development*, 355.

9 Spence, *Modern China*, 572.

10 Pantsov, *Deng*, 195–7.

11 In his long and careful study, Frank Dikotter (*Famine*, 325–34) argues that the total was more than 45 million, perhaps eight times as many as had died in the Ukraine under Stalin. Others put the figure at between 20 and 40 million over the period 1959–62 (Link, "China"). The estimate for the Sino Japanese war is 9 million Chinese killed, a figure that increases to 11–15 million if loss of life due to famine and similar causes is included.

12 Most official accounts attribute the famine to the weather while party officials have yet to reveal the official casualty rate (Lam, *Chinese Politics*, 285).

13 Lardy, "Economic Recovery."

14 The butchery in 1965 of somewhere between two hundred thousand and two million communists in Indonesia by forces loyal to the pro-American dictator General Suharto may have been the largest political massacre in history (Mason, *Global Shift*, 92–4).

15 Mitter "Mao" in Guha (ed.), *Asia*, 108–9.

16 Deng Pufang became head of China's Disabled Persons Federation. His brother, Deng Zhi Fang, changed his name to David Zhou and got a job on Wall Street after studying in the US.

17 See MacMillan, *Nixon*. This source is particularly valuable for the global reactions to Nixon's visit. Enver Hoxha of Albania, for instance, opined that "[T]he Chinese have made a major opportunist mistake, have shown themselves to be rightists and their action is revisionist and to be condemned" (200).

18 Spence, *Modern China*, 617.

19 Liu Shaoqui (1898–1969) was one of the most prominent victims of the Cultural Revolution. Author of *How to Be a Good Communist*, in 1969 he was accused, like Deng Xiaoping, of being a "revisionist" and "bourgeois" and was purged from his office as vice president of the PRC. Humiliated together with all of his family, he was expelled from the Communist Party to die miserably in 1969, the year Lin Biao was anointed as Mao's successor. Later Liu was rehabilitated to be referred to as a "great proletarian revolutionary" admired among Party members (Lam, *Chinese Politics*, 103).

20 Osnos, *Ambition*, 357–8.

21 Hobsbawm, *Extremes*, 470.

22 Gates, *Motor*, 250–1.

23 Lin, *Demystifying*, 3, 274. Justin Yifu Lin, a.k.a. Lin Yifu, was a captain in the army of Taiwan who defected by swimming to mainland China. He was the first Chinese student to study for an American PhD in economics and the cofounder of China's first MBA program. His remarkable story is in Osnos, *Ambition*, 149–58. Wang Hui (*Revolution*, 42) explains that after 1978 China aligned its policy with the US and other developed countries. Chun (*Transformation*, 5) puts the advent of neoliberalism a little later: "The neoliberal turn after the Tiananmen event in 1989 was confirmed by the Fourteenth Party Congress in 1992 and then boosted by the Fifteenth Party Congress of 1997." Shambaugh (*China*, 51) notes that Deng Xiaoping reignited economic reforms with his famous "Southern Sojourn" of 1992 that we will mention below. "Economic reforms" equal neoliberal reforms, presumably. Wang Hui (ibid.) calls his chapter 2 "The Year 1989 and the Historical Roots of Neoliberalism in China"; Roach, *Unbalanced*, 21.

24 Schell, *Glorious*, 115.

25 Roach, *Unbalanced*, 16, 27. Overseas Chinese from Taiwan, Hong Kong, Singapore, and elsewhere were called *huaqiao*. They were essential to the industrial development of the hinterland of Hong Kong, especially Shenzen, Zhuhai, and Shantou as well as Xiamen in Fujian province.

26 Nolan, *China*, 57–8.

27 I have discussed the *keiretsu* and *chaebols* in the previous chapter. For *yangqi*, Lam, *Chinese Politics*, 153.

28 Nolan, *China*, 57–60; Hung, *Global Capitalism*, 78, table 4.1.

29 CNPC = China National Petroleum Corporation; CNOOC = China National Offshore Oil Company. Of the C$36.7 billion invested in Canada by China since 2005, about three-quarters has gone into the energy

sector. With the drop in oil prices came buyer's remorse (Jones, "Buyers remorse").

30 For this term, see Anderson, "Sino-America," 20–2. "Chinamerica" is another, similar, confection usually referring to the codependency of the two leading economic powers.

31 The PLA had already involved itself in the global arms trade, having signed arms deals between 1984 and 1987 with both Iraq and Iran. By 1988 Iraq and Iran were bombarding one another's cities with computer-guided, short-range Silkworm missiles made in China (Spence, *Modern China*, 731).

32 Wang Hui, *Revolution*, 17, 105.

33 Louisa Lim (*Amnesia*, chapter 8) has written about the protest in Chengdu in Sichuan province where large-scale demonstrations resulted in under a dozen deaths and as many as one hundred seriously injured.

34 Wang Hui, ibid., 22.

35 Brook, *Quelling*, 42; Osnos, *Ambition*, 117, 120.

36 Goldman, *Sowing*, 336–7; Brook, ibid., 42.

37 Schell and Lappin, "Market," 743.

38 Lim, *Amnesia*, 211; Osnos, *Ambition*, 119.

39 Ibid., 366–7.

40 He Qinglian in Chaohua Wang (ed.), *One China*, 166–71. The World Bank considers people living on less than $3.10 a day as paupers.

41 Schell and Lappin, "Market."

42 Lam, *Chinese Politics*, 155.

43 Wang Hui, *Revolution*, viii and chapter 2. But Lin Chun, *Transformation*, "introduction," esp. 1–2, insists on the "socialist market" alternative to capitalist integration and on "the Chinese nation's great rejuvenation"; Schell and Lappin, "China." Madeiros ("Asset-Stripping," 117) compares privatizations in Latin America and Asia and concludes that "Privatization has not so far changed *this significant feature* of Asian capitalism" (my italics). The "significant feature" in question is public, that is, state, ownership. Large state enterprises, he writes, "still occupy the commanding heights of the economy."

44 Wang Hui, *Revolution*, 33.

45 Medeiros and Fravel, "China's New Diplomacy." 1; Gilboy, "Myth," 36–7 comments on China's readiness to accept foreign investment, pointing out that China has absorbed ten times as much foreign direct investment as Japan had in the period 1945–2000. For ownership of exporting firms, Palley, *Financial Crisis*, table 7.1, 109.

46 Roach, *Unbalanced*, 30. Total US debt reached $14.3 trillion during the "debt crisis" of 2011. Most US debt is not foreign owned.

47 Coy, "Yuan." Comparisons: the Canadian national pension fund (CPP) is worth $207.8 billion, Quebec's Caisse de dépôt, $190.6 billion; Blackstone, the leading American investment outfit, controls $210.2 bn. CIC owns Smithfield Foods, its largest US asset. It is also invested in Morgan Stanley and Blackstone, Heathrow airport and Thames Water in the UK. Its only overseas office is in Toronto.

48 Six RMB = $1.00.

49 The Peterson Institute of International Economics (PIIE) was financed by the billionaire Peter G. Peterson, a right-wing philanthropist. The celebrated Canadian commentator, Conrad Black, is on its board of directors (Offner and Söderberg, *Nobel Factor*).

50 Subramanian, *Eclipse*, 4. Subramanian's 2011 book follows in the footsteps of Gary Shteyngart's comic novel *Super Sad True Love Story* (2010), which has America ruled by the IMF from Singapore or Beijing and Americans clamouring for visas to richer countries. As one of the antagonists in the story explains: "[W]hat *will* happen, and I got this from reliable sources, is that the International Monetary Fund will skedaddle from D.C., possibly to Singapore or Beijing, and then they're going to make an IMF recovery plan for America, divide the country into concessions, and hand them over to the sovereign wealth funds. Norway, China, Saudi Arabia, and all that jazz" (256–7).

51 Subramanian, *Eclipse*.

52 *The Economist*, "Shades."

53 Eichengreen, "Dollar's Days." But see Pettis, *Rebalancing*, chapter 8 "The Exorbitant Burden," for doubts about the decline of the dollar.

54 Ho-Fung Hung (ed.), *Transformations*, 1.

55 Pettis, *Rebalancing*, 181.

56 A reminder: US GDP growth, 1947–2015 was 3.24 per cent; growth for 2015 was 2.4 per cent. In 2015 the Eurozone was stalling at 0.3 per cent and Canada surviving at 1.5 per cent. A "technical recession" was admitted when growth was negative for two consecutive quarters. Although it is often claimed that China fudged its growth figures, it is hard to believe that the statistics from other jurisdictions were entirely scrupulous.

57 Pettis, *Rebalancing*, chapter 4. "The Case of Unbalanced Growth in China," esp. 94, chapter 9, 184, and n. 5 for the overstatement of China's GDP and chapter 5, n. 25 for global optimism. Roach, *Unbalanced*, chapter 13, esp. 250–1.

58 Pettis, *Rebalancing*, 94, 189. Assuming the US and Chinese economies to

be codependent (as suggested in the subtitle of Stephen Roach's book) then this is likely to have unnerving consequences for the growth of the whole of the world.

59 Osnos, *Ambition*, 360.

60 Gillis, "China Crisis"; Hepburn, "Fall of China."

61 Osnos, *Ambition*, 361; Roach, *Unbalanced*, 165; figures from Brown, *Emperors*, 157.

62 Branigan, *China's Wen*.

63 Roach, *Unbalanced*, 165.

64 Rogoff, "Trump."

## CHAPTER SIX

1 The 2014–15 population of India was 1,267 million of which 180 million were Muslim. Pakistan's population was 192 million, and that of Bangladesh 170 million.

2 "Sepoys" were Indian soldiers in the army of the British East India Company.

3 Indian volunteers fought under British officers in Mesopotamia (Iraq), German East Africa (Tanganyika), and Flanders during World War One and in the Far East, Middle East, North Africa, Ethiopia, and Italy during World War Two.

4 An essential component of the BJP was the Rashtriya Swayamsevak Sangh (RSS), the National Volunteer Organization, a mass-based and militant organization of the right, home to the odd assassin but a long way from the terrorist organizations of our time including the IRA and the KKK. It was founded in 1925.

5 Ahmed, "India," 175. The population of Kerala is 39 million, West Bengal, 91 million.

6 Guha, *India*, 683.

7 Ibid., 501. The Tatas were Parsees, originally emigrants to India from Persia (Iran) who settled in Mumbai (Bombay). Ratan Tata, chairman of Tata Sons from 1991–2012, whose fortune reached more than $70 billion, has been considered the world's richest man.

8 Thakur, *Government*, 341.

9 A more distant echo of the struggle between the Indian state and Sikh extremists was the Air India bombing of 22 June 1985 in which 329 were killed on a flight from Toronto. This was the worst terrorist attack in Canadian history, made all the more painful by a bungled investigation by the RCMP.

10 Chibber, *Locked*, 250–1.

11 The "Hindu rate of growth" refers to the trend growth rate of 3.5 per cent that prevailed from the 1950s to the 1980s, that is, before the neoliberal reforms. Of course, many countries would kill for that rate in 2015–16. Japan's 2015 GDP growth rate was 1.2 per cent.

12 Tempest, "Washington's Turn."

13 Sardesai, *2014*, 292; Lal, "Economic Miracle?"; Guha, *India*, 684.

14 For the RSS, see n.10.

15 Ahmad, "India," 172.

16 Mehta, *Rajiv*, 157–60.

17 *The Economist*, cited in Sardesai, *2014*, 340.

18 Guha (*India*, 34) quotes Nehru, writing in 1947, on certain "Sikh and Hindu fascist elements" including the RSS. "Many of these people have been brutal and callous in the extreme. They have functioned as pure terrorists." See also Nussbaum who writes, "The RSS is possibly the most successful fascist movement in any contemporary democracy" (*Clash*, 155).

19 Rachman, "India."

20 The BJP scored only 31 per cent of 550 million votes and returned only 23 Muslim MPs. Sardesai, *2014*, chapter 10.

21 Tamil Nadu, Jayalithaa's bailiwick, had a population of 72 million in 2011, nearly as populous as Germany (81 m.). Gujerat had a population of 63 million, just 3 million fewer than France.

22 Teitumbde, "Saffron Neo-liberalism."

23 Sardesai, *2014*, 339.

24 *Times of India*, "Bihar election results." The Janata Parwar group of six parties won 178 seats and the BJP, 58: 122 seats are needed for a majority. Of the new members, one quarter were members of the Yadav group of the Shudra caste. Some 58 per cent of MPs faced criminal charges.

25 Lal ("Miracle," 13) gives GDP growth between 1900 and 1947 as 0.92.

26 Cohen, "Richest 1%."

27 Amsden, *Escape*, 91.

28 Chibber, *Locked*, 131.

29 For India's GDP growth, see appendix, tables 1–3.

30 Guha, *India*, chapter 29, discusses the era of reforms. His chapter title is "Riches." Drèze and Sen (*Uncertain Glory*, 13) "the so-called 'licence Raj' was a huge promoter of a culture of corruption."

31 Anderson, *Indian Ideology*, 159.

32 Lal, "Economic Miracle," 23; Zakaria's predictions for the future may be found in *The Post-American World* (2008); not a good year for predictions.

33 Guha, *India*, 706–7, Sachs, *Price*, 88, 46. "New India" as in Deb's *Beautiful*.
34 Lal, *Miracle*, 23; Rodrik, "Economic Convergence," 33.
35 *Times of India*, "Indian states"; Singh, "New Poverty Line"; Wikipedia, "Poverty in India." Bhaduri, "Predatory Growth," 12. In 2013, Bihar had the most poor with 61 per cent living below the poverty line and Kerala the fewest with 15.9 per cent below. Drèze and Sen make the point in "An Unfinished Agenda" (*Uncertain Glory*, 8–9) where they write, "Whereas twenty years ago India generally had the second-best social indicators among the six South Asian countries ... it now looks second worst."
36 Ghosh, "Indian Economy," 1042. The most celebrated IT centres were in Bangalore, home of Infosys (founded in the early 1980s), Hyderabad, and Pune.
37 Bhaduri, "Predatory Growth," 12.
38 Forbes "India's 100 Richest."
39 Piketty, *Capital*, 82.
40 Ghosh, "India's Woes."
41 Half to one million were killed in the great exodus that characterized the Partition (Khan, *Partition*, 6).
42 The *muhajirs* were Indian Muslims who migrated to Pakistan at the time of Partition. They settled mainly around Karachi, the largest city and commercial capital of Pakistan.
43 The term originally referred to the elite guards of the Roman Empire. It has come to refer to officers who seize power in the interest of their own clique or of the officer class in general. Almost all praetorians have turned out to be dependent upon military aid from Washington.
44 CENTO was also called the Baghdad Pact and bound together Turkey, Iran, Iraq, and Pakistan as a glacis against Soviet expansion. SEATO had the same function further east and also included Pakistan. See McCormick, *Half-Century*, 120. The US military flew the U2 spy planes, prefigurative drones, from Pakistan over the Soviet Union, China, and Vietnam, but in 1960 the Russians shot one down.
45 The third war between Pakistan and India was over Bangladesh in November 1971.
46 Fair, *Fighting*, 27–31.
47 This quotation is a crib from Lord Palmerston (1784–1865). In the heyday of the British Empire in the mid- nineteenth century he said, "We have no eternal allies, and we have only perpetual interests."

48 Terms referring to political Islam such as jihad, jihadist, *mujahideen*, and Wahhabism will be explained in the next chapter.

49 Gall, *Wrong Enemy*, 187. On 6 December 2015, *Lashkar* operatives were rounded up while planning to assassinate Prime Minister Modi.

50 Zia's gap-toothed smile has led Jalal to compare him with the 1950s comic actor, Terry-Thomas. For his rise and flaming demise ("A pair of dentures was all that survived") Jalal, *Struggle*, 216–58.

51 Ibid., 308–9.

52 Siddiqa, *Military Inc.*, gives details of the privileged role of the military in Pakistan's economy.

53 The Pakistani newspaper, *Dawn*, (3 June 2014) headlined the claim by the finance minister, Ishaq Dar, that half of Pakistan lived under the poverty line.

54 Rashid, *Pakistan*, 13. Pakistan GDP growth in 2015 was 4.5 per cent; in 2016, 4.7 per cent. Still, its rate of growth lagged behind both India and Bangladesh.

55 Chughtai and Hashim in "Tehreek-e-Taliban" indicate that Pakistani forces killed 3,000 jihadists since the beginning of military operations in FATA. The Bureau of Investigative Journalism has estimated that between 2004 and 2014 there have been 2,296 to 3,719 drone deaths in Pakistan of which between 416 and 957 were civilians and 168 to 202 children. Wikipedia "Drone Strikes in Pakistan."

56 Rashid, *Pakistan*, 10–11.

57 The business of the dispatch of bin Laden remains murky. Seymour Hersh ("Killing") has claimed that the official American version is simply propaganda and that bin Laden was actually betrayed by a Pakistani army officer. Hersh's version has been verified by Asad Durrani, former head of the ISI.

58 Fair, *Fighting*, 17.

## CHAPTER SEVEN

1 Kepel, *Muslim Minds*, 94. For the background of Osama bin Laden, Coll, *Bin Ladens*; for al-Zawahiri, Gerges, *Isis*, 90–1.

2 The fullest recent discussion of Salafism is Lauzière, *Salafism* (2016). Other spellings of *mujihadeen* are common.

3 Salafism and Wahhibism are both doctrines that seek to return the Muslim lands (*dar al-islam*) to the time of the Prophet and the ancestors (Arabic = *salaf*) in the seventh century. Both are intolerant of non-Sunni

Muslims, like Shias generally, but even of Sunni Sufis who err on the side of mysticism.

4 Kepel, *Jihad*, 299. The attempt to blow up the WTC in 1993 was masterminded by the blind sheik Omar Abdel-Rahman, an associate of Zawahiri. Until he was arrested for his part in the 1993 bombing, he lived in Jersey City, New Jersey. Kepel (ibid., 17–18): "For sheer mastery of spectacle and symbol, their awesome feat far surpassed Israel's military technology or the U.S. Army's performance during the Gulf War."

5 Roberts, (*Battlefield*, 160, 217) refers to the shift by Algeria to dependence on France in the 1980s.

6 For the Comintern, see chapter 3.

7 *Middle East Report*, "ISIS," 2.

8 Owen, *Arab Presidents*, 21–2.

9 Rogan, *Arabs*, 305.

10 Pfeifer, "Economic Reform," 205. Egypt tied with Chile as a neoliberal pioneer; reforms were not introduced into China or India, for instance, for another decade.

11 Kandil, *Soldiers*, 201–3.

12 Nasr, *Dispensable*, 167, 175.

13 The two evaluations from Mohammed Heikal are in Kandil, *Soldiers*, 164–5 and 171–2.

14 Ibid., 176.

15 Bishara, *Invisible Arab*, 14.

16 Shehata and Stacher, "Muslim Brothers," 160, in Sowers and Toesing (eds.), *Journey*.

17 El-Ghobashy, "Dynamics" in ibid., 145.

18 Hobsbawm, *Extremes*, 454–5. Specifically, "blowback" is a CIA term used to describe the unintended consequences of an American intelligence operation. The original work on the subject is Chalmers Johnson's *Blowback* (2000).

19 Kinzer, *Shah's Men*, 140.

20 Cleveland, *Middle East*, 400.

21 For American fears about neutralism, McCormick, *America*, 119–21.

22 Cole, *Engaging*, 214. Grandin (*Kissinger*, 126–8). Kissinger was installed as President Richard Nixon's Secretary of State in mid-1973. For Kissinger's support of the Chilean and Argentine dictatorship, Grandin, *Kissinger*, 148–53.

23 Munson, *Revolution*, ix.

24 Abrahamian, *Revolutions*, 141–2; Bacevich, *America's War*, 13–14. In

1973 alone, Iran contracted to buy more than $2 billion worth of US arms. Over the next six years, purchases rose to more than $19 billion.

25 Abrahamian, *Modern Iran*, 140.

26 Buchan, *God*, 129.

27 Craig and Logevall, *Cold War*, 295.

28 Bacevich, *America's War*, 12.

29 Abrahamian, *Modern Iran*, 141–2.

30 Buchan, *God*, 298–9.

31 Bacevich, *America's War*, 91.

32 Hiltermann, "Chemical wonders," 5–6.

33 Ehteshami, *After Khomeini*, 121, 140.

34 Abrahamian, *Modern Iran*, 140.

35 Halliday, *Islam*, 48.

36 In his *The New York Times* obituary (8 January 2017), Rafsanjani is described as follows: "Known as pragmatist and centrist inclined toward economic liberalism and political authoritarianism, Mr Rafsanjani was accused by critics of corruption in amassing his fortune and of a readiness for harsh tactics to deal with dissent at home and abroad." It was suggested that as president he authorized a number of political murders. He seems thus to have acquired a reputation not a little like Vladimir Putin.

37 Amanet, *Apocalyptic Islam*, 238–9.

38 De Bellaigue, *Struggle*, 181.

39 Dyer, "Iran."

40 Gardner, "Dangerous Moment." Khamenei's analysis dates from January 2016.

41 Bozorgmehr, "Iran."

42 Since the American occupation of Iraq, the significance of religion difference seems to have been exaggerated. On this, see Muttitt, *Fuel*, 355.

43 Yapp, *Near East*, 70.

44 Cole, *Engaging*, 23.

45 Muttitt, *Fuel*, frontispiece.

46 Cleveland, *Middle East*, 400–1.

47 Joseph E. Stiglitz' chronicle of this time is called *The Roaring Nineties* and subtitled *The World's Most Prosperous Decade*.

48 Cockburn, *Jihad*, 37.

49 Muttitt, *Fuel*, xxi; Gruzalski "USA"; Ahmad, "Iraq invasion."

50 Hiro, *Empire*, 54. General Tommy Franks, who was in charge of the

American forces in the Middle East, did much to secure Feith's reputation. He called him "the dumbest fucking guy on the planet."

51 For the maturing of this isolationism by 2016, Kuper, "America's elections."

52 Nasr, *Dispensable*, 185.

53 Gerges (*ISIS*, 18–19) argues that the Arab Spring came at "an emancipatory moment that could have progressively transformed the Arab Middle East had it not been derailed by an unholy alliance of internal and external counterrevolutionary forces." Alongside other conservative forces, he mentions that the Saudis invested billions of dollars "to prevent revolutionary change and keep its conservative Arab allies in control."

54 The Alawites, the main group of Shi'as, are a sect, like the Zaydis of Yemen, that split off from the mainstream of Shi'ism. The Shi'as comprise only some 13 per cent of the Syrian population. For centuries the Alawis were considered by the Sunnis as apostates, that is, less deserving of tolerance than Christians or Jews. The Druzes, who are highly secretive about their ideology, are not Muslims. Sunnis comprise around 85 per cent of the population of Syria.

55 Littell, *Syrian Notebooks*, 6, 85–6. The "all-powerful Minister of Defence and right hand man, for thirty years, of Hafez al-Assad ," was Mustafa Tlass. "[H]is extended family, present at every level in the Army, remains one of the most powerful clans in the country." They were Sunnis. Glass, *Syria*, 100. Yassin-Kassab and al-Shami (*Burning Country*, 12) refer to an "Alawi/military-Sunni/business ruling class" coalescing under Assad.

56 Goldsmith, *Cycle*, 181, 159. Gerges (*ISIS*, 171–2) is clear on the "accelerated neoliberal reforms' introduced by the al-Assad regime driving nearly 20 per cent of the population to below the poverty line.

57 Hizbollah was created in 1982 after Israel invaded Lebanon in 1982. It introduced the idea of suicide bombing to the region.

58 Manhire (ed.), *Arab Spring*, 141.

59 Cockburn, "Special Relationship," 37; Hersh, *Killing*, 67–8.

60 Lesch, ibid., 171–5; deaths, 187, 190, 204; Daragahi, "Syria"; Littell, *Notebooks*, 13; Cockburn, ibid., 35.

61 His background is given in several references in Gerges, *ISIS*.

62 Bacevich, *America's War*, 272.

63 Gerges, *Obama*, 177–80.

64 The Canadian government budgeted C$1.6 billion for its anti-ISIS mission. It dispatched 650 Special Forces soldiers, ostensibly on a training mission. (CBC, "Canada's mission").

65 For Jean Chrétien's anti-interventionist opinion, Chrétien, "Canada's true role"; for the view of a German journalist, see Todenhofer, "Western bombs," also Juan Cole, "War."

## CHAPTER EIGHT

1 For further discussion of the history of developmentalism, Cowen and Shenton, *Doctrines*.

2 Peck, *Washington's China*, 42–3.

3 A comprehensive summary of French apprehensions regarding the Anglo-Americans is Howard, *Power*. The author stresses that the *leitmotif* of French postwar policy in Africa was the restoration of French glory. At its zenith in 1937 the French empire was second in the world, right behind the British and commanding 65 million subjects.

4 Patronizing and myopic, this memoir of nearly forty years of "colonial administration," paints a glowing picture of a relationship between subject and ruler that was unruffled by dissidence; the last czar of Russia had a similar view of his people.

5 Brittain, "Ben Barka."

6 Freeman (*Champion*, 36) notes that in July 1970, barely a month after the Conservative election victory in Britain, Prime Minister Edward Heath announced the resumption of arms sales to South Africa. "The decision was couched in Cold War terms – that British and Western interests were threatened by the Soviet naval presence in the Indian Ocean and by Russian and Chinese influence in Africa." Too bad for the dreamers of a multiracial Commonwealth. Of the monstrous ruler of Central African Republic in the early 1970s, Michel and Bueret (*Chinafrique*, 157) have this to say: "Bokassa était peut-être cannibale, du moins n'était-il pas communiste." In mitigation of this, Bokassa had fought for the French in Algeria and Indochina.

7 In the jargon of development economics, gatekeepers lived off "rents," that is fees or bribes paid by foreigners to exploit the resources of Africa. Income generated by enrolling in America's "War on Terror" has been called "terrorism rent" by Keenan (*Sahara*, 18–19 ff.).

8 Mason, "Mr Johnson." A film version of the novel was made in 1991.

9 By contemporary standards this sentiment seems unacceptably racist. Yet if Orwell (*Write*, 78–9) meant that it is easier to manipulate illiterate African chiefs than highly literate Asians, he had a point.

10 Angus Deaton (*Escape*, 312–24) lacerates the pretensions of the *developmentistas*. His argument: "When aid fell off, after the end of the Cold

War, growth picked up; the end of Cold War took away one of the main rationales for aid to Africa, and African growth rebounded."

11 Doyle, "Firestone." This is a review of a documentary called "Firestone and the Warlord" made by Frontline and ProPublica for PBS. It discloses the close relationship between the American tire company and the murderous warlord, Charles Taylor, who was indicted by a United Nations tribunal in 2003 on seventeen counts of war crimes and crimes against humanity. Doyle notes that Taylor was found guilty on all counts and sentenced to fifty years in prison. Firestone's grip on Liberia seems to have been unimpaired.

12 Dietrich, *Oil Revolution*, 133. In his study of postwar economic decolonization of the oil-producing states, Dietrich mentions "neocolonialism" a number of times but includes no reference to it in his index.

13 Sartre's introduction is a classic of New Left prose and as such too brilliant to miss (Sartre, "Preface"). Regarding the ubiquitous term "populism," Marco D'Eramo ("They, the People," 129) writes, "In the political-science literature on populism, it has long been a commonplace procedure to begin by declaring that no one knows what it is."

14 Nkrumah, *Neo-colonialism*, Woddis, *Neo-Colonialism*. Woddis argues that neocolonialism "is a strategy of imperialism and not a new stage" (50).

15 Mason, *Development*, 415.

16 Bates, *Things Fell Apart*, 44.

17 Bayart et al. *Criminalization*, xiv. *Heart of Darkness* is the title of an 1899 novel by Joseph Conrad, a bleak portrayal of Belgian colonialism and racism in Africa.

18 Westad, *Cold War*, 91.

19 Meredith, *Africa*, 260.

20 Nugent, "States," 59.

21 Nugent, *Africa*, 34.

22 Mulholland "Ghana"; Canadian aid in 2014 totalled CAD $106 million out of $4.9 billion in 2014.

23 Hallward, *Damming*. The quote follows the author's title page and is applied to Jean-Bertrand Aristide of Haiti, successor to "Papa Doc" Duvalier, (see n. 35), an idealist and reformer and, like Mossadeq in Iran, Nkrumah, and Lumumba, a victim of Western intervention.

24 Victoria Brittain ("Africa") noted that Lumumba was "the second of five leaders of independence movements in African countries to be assassinated in the 1960s by their former colonial masters, or their agents." Following his assassination was the ouster of Kwame Nkrumah "in a western-backed coup" and the assassination of Amilcar Cabral of Guiné in 1973.

25 François "Papa Doc" Duvalier (1957–71) turned Haiti into one of the poorest and most hellish of Third World tyrannies. Like Mobutu, he was sustained in power by the United States and France. Hallward, *Damming*.

26 Hochschild, *Ghost*, 129.

27 Bayart, *Africa*, 87–8.

28 Copper prices (per lb.): 1971: $.52; 1988: $1.65; 2011: $4.12.

29 For Bokassa's life and monstrous times, see Brian Cathcart, "Obituary." Of the rich ironies in the case of this African sociopath is his connection with France. His overthrow came on the orders of the French president, Valéry Giscard d'Estang (1974–81). Bokassa's gift of diamonds to Giscard, when exposed by the satirical weekly *Le Canard Enchainé*, contributed to the French president's downfall.

30 The American role in Central Africa and support for Kabila is spelled out in Howard, *Power*, 255–7. Since the French regarded this area as a zone of their influence they were alarmed by the intervention of Washington. For Mugabe's support for Mobutu's son and successor, Joseph, Southall, *Liberation Movements*, 168–9, 253–4.

31 Howard (*Power*, 256) refers to "[t]he American-owned Barrick [sic] Gold Corporation" forming close links with General Kpama Baramoto "one of the most powerful people in the land."

32 Braid, "Mobutu."

33 Prunier, *World War*; Hochschild, "Rape."

34 Van Reybrouck, *Congo*, 440–2.

35 Hoschschild, "Rape."

36 Enough Project, "Conflict Minerals."

37 Van Reybrouck, *Congo*, 456–7.

38 Liberti, *Land Grabbing*, 78. Jatropha is a biofuel from the seeds of which motor fuel can be produced. "[T]his crop is considered by many the fuel of the future" (ibid.,169).

39 Observer Editorial, "Congo."

40 The population of South Africa was nearly 52 million (2013) of which about 80 per cent is "black," 9 per cent "white," 9 per cent "coloured" (métis), and 2.5 per cent Asian (mainly Indian and Malay). The most numerous African groups are the Zulus and Sothos.

41 For its origins and meaning, Dubow, *Apartheid*, 10–16.

42 Ibid., 310, n. 25.

43 Ibid., 119. Dubow points out that in 1956 only two in a thousand Africans attended university. In the Belgian Congo there were no universities at all and practically no secondary schools for Africans.

The Catholic Church was complicit in dumbing down its congregants.

44 For summaries of the apartheid economy, O'Meara, *Lost Years* and Dubow, *Apartheid*, 99–103, 177–9.

45 A military coup led by young officers took place on 25 April 1974, overturning nearly half a century of right-wing rule.

46 The South Africans carried out campaigns against the Marxist regimes of Angola and Mozambique from 1975, a year after Portuguese colonialism in Africa was brought to an end. The wars in these formerly Portuguese African colonies were among the hottest of the Cold War and resembled those backed by Washington in Central America in the same period. The South Africans assumed wrongly that the Americans would support their efforts in Angola. The Cubans, however, did send troops to bolster their Angolan comrades and defeated the invading South African forces in a major battle at Cuito Cuanavale in 1987–88, forcing them to retreat.

47 Freeman, *Ambiguous*, 166.

48 Reader, *Africa*, 678.

49 Mason, *Development*, 245–6.

50 Lewis, *Race*, 185.

51 Southall, *Liberation Movements*, 89.

52 Sources on Chinese emigration to Africa are inconsistent but in the first decade of the twenty-first century, alongside the 300,000–500,000 in South Africa there were 100,000 Chinese in Nigeria, 30,000 in Angola, 40,000 in Zambia, and 50,000 in Madagascar. French, *Continent*, provides some figures; his total for Africa is over a million.

53 Lewis, *Race*, 183.

54 Johnson, "R.W, Johnson," Johnson, *South Africa*, 232.

55 Lewis, *Race*, 185.

56 Johnson, ibid.

57 Kuper, "Inequality"; Caplan, "Corruption"; Southall, *Liberation Movements*, 327.

## CHAPTER NINE

1 Bulmer-Thomas, *Latin America*, 27.

2 Dosman, *Prebisch*, 7.

3 For populations, United Nations, "Growth ... 1920–2000." Madrid's population in 1920 was a mere 742,000; London's was ten times greater at 7,236,000.

4 Milanovic, *Haves*, 233.
5 The story of Lebanese and Syrians in Latin America is typically understated. A number of the continent's political and financial leaders were originally known as "Turcos," that is, possessors of Ottoman identity.
6 Galbraith, *Inequality*, 253.
7 The above section I have reproduced from Mason, *Development*, 47–9.
8 Galbraith, *Inequality*, 256–7. "Market reforms" = neoliberal reforms.
9 Dosman, *Prebisch*, and Dietrich, *Oil Revolution*, 42–5, 130–3, 180–4.
10 About a third of the *desaparecidos* were shop stewards or trade union officials.
11 Dosman, *Prebisch*, 482–3.
12 Dinges, *Condor Years*, 155.
13 For Henry Kissinger's "encouragement" of dictatorships, Grandin, *Kissinger*, 151–5.
14 Howard, *Power*, chapter 11.
15 *Economist*, "Galteri."
16 See Wikipedia CONADEP (*Comisión Nacional sobre la Desaparición de Personas*)
17 Madeiros, "Asset-Stripping," 120; Galbraith (*Inequality*, 252, 258) in a chapter on Argentina and Brazil, suggests that from the early 1990s through 2007 was the period of "high neoliberalism."
18 Klein, *Shock Doctrine*, 199.
19 Skidmore and Smith, *Latin America*, 107.
20 Ibid.
21 The Argentine government paid back 93 per cent of the loans from the bondholders. Only a small group of New York hedge funds held out – aiming to get $20 billion.
22 For Kirchner's left populism, Etchemendy and Garay, "Argentina" in Levitsky and Roberts (eds), *Resurgence*.
23 Ibid., 293.
24 Perez and Turner, "Argentina." In Néstor Kirchner's term as president (2003–2010) his personal fortune went from $2.5 million to $17.7 million; hardly dizzying by comparison to the fortunes of Russian oligarchs, Wall Street hedge fund managers, Mexican *narcotraficantes*, or even the wealth of the ex-prime minister of Britain, Tony Blair.
25 Phelan, "Argentina."
26 Svampa, "Kirchnerism," 86.
27 Pheland, "Argentina," 212–13.
28 Mander, "Argentina."
29 *Economist*, "Ebbing"; Weisbrod, "Macri's Win."

30 Drèze and Sen, *Uncertain*, ix. The same volume contains a comparison between Brazil, India, China, and Russia, 65–8 and a section called "The Old and New Brazil," 68–72.

31 Brazilian independence: 1821–24; Indian, 1947.

32 Reid, *Brazil*, 108, 114.

33 Populations 1950: Saõ Paulo 2,423,000; Rio de Janeiro 2,864,000. Populations 2015: Saõ Paulo 20,397,000; Rio 11,905,000.

34 The Alliance for Progress was devised by the regime of President John Kennedy in the 1960s. Designed as an antidote to the Cuban Revolution, it accepted moderate nationalism and even ISI and supported rural reform and the reduction of income inequality.

35 Wagley in Parker and Walker (eds.), *Middle Class*, 73–4.

36 Besides Dilma Rousseff, the victims of the military included José Dirceu, one of the founders of the PT and Lula's chief of staff. Dirceu was captured but released in exchange for the American ambassador whom his fellow militants had kidnapped. Dirceu then fled to Cuba, had plastic surgery, and sneaked back into the country to become the president of the PT in 1995.

37 Reid, *Brazil*, 110.

38 Alves, *Military Brazil*, 125

39 Reid, *Brazil*, 107.

40 Alves, *Military Brazil*, 233.

41 Ibid., 113.

42 The issue of the despoliation of the Brazilian rain forest became the focus of several studies in the 1990s, notably Hecht and Cockburn's classic *Fate of the Forest* (2014 ed.).

43 Cammack, *Brazil*, 54.

44 Reid, *Brazil*, 124–5.

45 Weyland "Left," in Levitsky and Roberts (eds.), *Resurgence*, 85–6; Madeiros, "Latin America," 121.

46 Hecht, "Love and Death," 130; Hecht and Cockburn (*Forest*, 346) puts the neoliberal reforms of Cardoso down to Lula's electoral victory in 2002. She explains that while Lula kept Cardoso's "macroeconomic neoliberal playbook he also implemented strong redistributive practices, a tropical neo-Keynesianism."

47 Gailbraith, *Inequality*, 263.

48 Ibid., 252. Other economists like Drèze and Sen were also enamoured of Brazil's impressive reforms, as was Anderson in "Lula's Brazil."

49 Hunter, "Brazil," 322.

50 *Economist*, "Expanding Middle."

51 Cala and Economides, *Blind Spot*, 11, 14. Here the authors hammer Washington for "grossly misreading the evolution of Latin America."
52 Lemann, "Anointed."
53 *Economist*, "Brazilian Waxing."
54 Pearson, "Shopkeeper"; Leahy and Pearson, "State." But regional growth was stalled at only 1.2 per cent in 2014 (Rathbone, "Party").
55 The rival parties were the Democratic Movement Party (PMDB) and Cardoso's Social Democratic Party (PSDB), which narrowly lost the elections to the PT in 2014. Cunha was a member of the PMDB, a party with no settled ideology, which, having supported the PT, is now running on its own (Watts, "Dilma Rousseff's fate").
56 Watts, "Lula."
57 Brum, "Brazil's political drama."
58 Frieda, "China-Brazil." For the "commodities super-cycle" explanation, ie. that the cycle had ended in 2013, see n. 58. A "commanding analysis" (Anderson's term), is to be found in Anderson, "Crisis in Brazil."

## AFTERWORD

1 Setser, "China's WTO Entry." China joined the WTO in 2002. On the connection between China joining the WTO in 2002 and the loss of jobs in the US, Setser writes, "China's entry was not the only source of the enormous decline in manufacturing jobs between 2000 and 2005. The broad strength of the dollar from 2000 to 2002 mattered."
2 Milanovic, *Inequality*, 34–5. Milanovic (ibid., 130) goes on to point out that from the 1950s to the mid-1970s , US GDP per capita, expressed in international dollars, exceeded the Chinese GDP by a ratio of around 20 to 1. By about 2010 the ratio was less than 4:1. For the shift of power to Asia, Milanovic (213) and authors like Mahbubani mentioned above. But, Milanovic warns (165), the present slowdown in the demand for raw materials, "may again put an end to convergence." For American growth rates, Gordon, *American Growth*, 637 and appendix.
3 Bacevich, "Tearing."
4 Villepin in Bacevich, "Tearing."
5 Milanovic, *Inequality*, 163–4.
6 Ibid., 81.
7 Ibid., 173. The author explains that the GDPs per capita of Madagascar and the Democratic Republic of Congo are lower today than they are estimated to have been before independence. "In terms of development and catch-up with the richer countries, an entire century has been wasted."

8 Consider: "Donald Trump and the New World Order" in *Spiegel OnLine* (20 January 2017).
9 Stiglitz, "Globalization"; Milanovic, *Inequality*, 195.
10 See, perhaps, my *After Midnight: Climate Change in Contemporary History* (forthcoming, possibly 2019).
11 Hobsbawm, *Age of Extremes*, 583.

## APPENDIX

1 www.hdr.undp.org.
2 Picketty, *Capital in the Twenty-First Century*, 93.
3 Ibid., 99.
4 Jerven, *Poor Numbers*.
5 Milanovic, *Global Inequality*, 196.

# Bibliography


Abrahamian, Ervand. *A History of Modern Iran*. Cambridge and New York: Cambridge University Press, 2008.

– *Iran Between Two Revolutions*. Princeton: Princeton University Press, 1982.

Ahmad, Aijaz. "India: Liberal Democracy and the Extreme Right." In *Socialist Register, 2016*, edited by Leo Panich and Gregory Albo, 170–92. London: The Merlin Press, 2015.

Ahmed, Nafeez. "Iraq Invasion was about oil." *The Guardian*, 20 March 2014. Accessed 29 October 2016. https://www.theguardian.com/environment/earth-insight/2014/mar/20/iraq-war-oil-resources-energy-peak-scarcity-economy.

Amanet, Abbas. *Apocalyptic Islam and Iranian Shi'ism*. New York and London: I.B. Taurus, 2009.

Amsden, Alice H. *Asia's Next Giant: South Korea and Late Industrialization*. New York: Oxford University Press, 1989.

Anderson, Perry. *American Foreign Policy and Its Thinkers*. London and New York: Verso, 2015.

– "Crisis in Brazil." *London Review of Books* 38, 8 (21 April 2016): 15–22.

– "Incommensurate Russia." *New Left Review* 2/94 (July–August 2015): 5–43.

– *The Indian Ideology*. London: Verso, 2013.

– "Lula's Brazil." *London Review of Books* 33, 7 (31 March 2011): 3–12.

– *The New Old World*. London: Verso, 2009.

– "Sino-Americana." *London Review of Books* 34, 3 (9 February 2012): 20–2.

Applebaum, Anne. *Iron Curtain. The Crushing of Eastern Europe, 1944–1956*. Toronto: McClelland and Stewart (Random House), 2013.

Arbatov, Georgi. *The System: An Insider's Life in Soviet Politics*. New York: Random House, 1992.

Armstrong, Charles K. "Contesting the Peninsula." *New Left Review* 2, 2/51 (May–June 2008): 115–35.

– *The North Korean Revolution, 1945–1950*. Ithaca: Cornell University Press, 2003.

Ascherson, Neal. "Painful lessons must be learned by Europe: it will always need America to clean up its mess." *The Guardian*, 19 July 2015. Accessed 20 July 2015. https://www.theguardian.com/commentisfree/2015/jul/19/european-union-angela-merkel-greece.

Augar, Philip. "Barclays and Britain wave goodbye to the big time." *Financial Times*, 2 August 2015. Accessed 2 August 2015. https://www.ft.com/content/3d19368a-fa4e-11e4-a41c-00144feab7de.

Auslin, Michael R. *The End of the Asian Century. War, Stagnation, and the Risks to the World's Most Dynamic Region*. New Haven, CT and London: Yale University Press, 2017.

Bacevich, Andrew J. *America's War for the Greater Middle East. A Military History*. New York: Random House, 2016.

– *The Limits of Power: The End of American Exceptionalism*. New York: Henry Holt, 2008.

– *The Short American Century: A Postmortem*. Cambridge, Harvard University Press, 2012.

Bakewell, Sarah. *At the Existentialist Café. Freedom, Being and Apricot Cocktails*. New York: Penguin, 2016.

Baldwin, Richard E. *The Great Convergence: Information Technology and the New Globalization*. Cambridge: Harvard University Press, 2016.

Barnett, Thomas P.M. *Great Powers: America and the World After Bush*. New York: Penguin, 2009.

Bates, Robert H. *When Things Fell Apart: State Failure in Late-Century Africa*. New York: Cambridge University Press, 2008.

Bayart, Jean-François, Stephen Ellis, and Béarice Hibou. *The Criminalization of the State in Africa*. Bloomington: Indiana University Press, 2009.

Bellaigue, de, Christopher. See De Bellaigue.

Berend, Ivan T. *Europe Since 1980*. Cambridge: Cambridge University Press, 2010.

Bhaduri, Amit. "Predatory Growth." *Economic and Political Weekly* 47,16 (19 April 2008): 10–14.

Bhagwati, Jagdesh, *In Defence of Globalization*. Oxford: Oxford University Press, 2007.

Bishara, Marwan. *The Invisible Arab: The Promise and Peril of the Arab Revolution.* New York: Nation Books, 2012.

Blustein, Paul. *The Chastening: Inside the Crisis that Rocked the Global Finan-*

*cial System and Humbled the IMF.* Oxford: Public Affairs, Oxford, 2001.

Bozorgmehr, Najmeh. "Iran: Inside the battle to succeed supreme leader Khamenei." *Financial Times*, 24 October 2016. Accessed 29 October 2016. https://www.ft.com/content/5fbc8192-321a-11e6-bda0-04585c31b153.

Branigan, Tania. "China's Wen Jiabao signs off with growth warning." *The Guardian*, 9 March 2013. Accessed 5 November 2017. https://www.theguardian.com/world/2013/mar/05/china-wen-jiabao-growth-warning.

Brittain, Victoria. "Africa: a continent drenched in the blood of revolutionary heroes." *The Guardian*, 17 January 2011. Accessed 10 February 2017. https://www.theguardian.com/global-development/poverty-matters/2011/jan/17/lumumba-50th-anniversary-african-leaders-assassinations.

– "Ben Barka killed with French help." *The Guardian*, 2 July 2001. Accessed 9 February 2017. https://www.theguardian.com/world/2001/jul/02/victoriabrittain

Brook, Timothy. *Quelling the People: Military Suppression of the Beijing Democracy Movement.* New York: Oxford University Press, 1992.

Brown, Archie. *The Rise and Fall of Communism.* Toronto: Doubleday Canada, 2009.

Brown, Kerry. *The New Emperors: Power and Princelings in China.* London and New York: I.B. Tauris, 2013.

Brum, Eliane. "In Brazil's political drama, all the players are villains." *The Guardian Weekly*, 16–21 October 2015.

Buchan, James. *Days of God: The Revolution in Iran and Its Consequences.* London: John Murray, 2012.

Bulmer-Thomas, Victor. *The Economic History of Latin America Since Independence.* Cambridge: Cambridge University Press, 2003.

Cala, Andrés and Michael J. Economides. *America's Blind Spot: Chávez, Oil, and US Security*. London and New York: Continuum, 2012.

Calvert, John. *Sayyid Qutb and the Origins of Radical Islam*. New York: Columbia University Press, 2010.

Cammack, Paul. "Brazil: The Long March to the New Republic." *New Left Review* 1/190 (November–December 1991) 21–58.

Canadian Broadcasting Corporation (CBC). "Canada's mission to combat ISIS in Syria and the region, by the numbers." 8 February 2016. Accessed 20 June 2016. www.cbc.ca/news/politics/ISIS-by-the-numbers-1.3439313.

Caplan, Gerald. "Corruption, AIDS, inequality – can South Africa fulfill Nelson Mandela's dreams?" *CBC News*, 11 December 2013. Accessed 15 November 2014. http://www.cbc.ca/news/world/corruption-aids-inequality-can-south-africa-fulfil-nelson-mandela-s-dreams-1.2460390.

Cassidy, John. "Anatomy of a Meltdown." *New Yorker*, 1 December 2008. Accessed 21 September 2017. www.newyorker.com/magazine/2008/12/01/anatomy-of-a-meltdown.

Cathcart, Brian. "Obituary: Jean-Bedel Bokassa." *Independent*, 5 November 1996. Accessed 14 October 2016. http://www.independent.co.uk/news/people/obituary-jean-bedel-bokassa-1350837.html

Chaohua Wang, ed. *One China, Many Paths.* London: Verso, 2003.

Chang, Ha-Joon. *23 Things They Don't Tell You About Capitalism.* New York, Berlin, London, Sydney: Bloomsbury Press, 2010.

Chase, Steven. "Only three Canadian airstrikes in Syria since Islamic State mission expanded." *The Globe and Mail*, 9 July 2015. Accessed 15 July 2015. https://beta.theglobeandmail.com/news/politics/military-strikes-about-one-third-of-missions-they-fly-against-is-forces/article25404069/.

Chibber, Vivek. *Locked in Place: State-Building and Late Industrialization in India.* Princeton: Princeton University Press, 2003.

– "The Politics of a Miracle: Class Interests and State Power in Korean Developmentalism." In *Varieties of Approaches*, edited by David Coates, 122–38. Basingstoke: Palgrave Macmillan, 2005.

Chrétien, Jean. "Canada's true role in this conflict." *The Globe and Mail*, 7 October 2014.

Chughtai, Alia and Asad Hashimi. "Breaking Down the Tehreek-e-Taliban Pakistan." *Al-Jazeera*, 18 September 2015. Accessed 6 December 2015. http://www.aljazeera.com/indepth/features/2013/11/breaking-down-tehreek-e-taliban-20131112121349713830.html.

Chun, Lin. *The Transformation of Chinese Socialism*. Durham and London: Duke University Press, 2006.

Cleveland, William L. *A History of the Modern Middle East*. Boulder: Westview, 2000.

Clover, Charles. "China unveils 'Guam Express' advanced anti-ship missile." *Financial Times*, 3 September 2015. Accessed 4 September 2015. https://www.ft.com/search?q=China+unveils+'Guam+Express'+advanced+anti-ship+missile.

Cockburn, Andrew. *Kill Chain. The Rise of the High-Tech Assassins*. New York: Henry Holt, 2005.

– "A Special Relationship." *Harper's Magazine*. January 2016. Accessed 20 January 2016. https://harpers.org/archive/2016/01/a-special-relationship.

Cockburn, Patrick. *The Age of Jihad: Islamic State and the Great War for the Middle East*. London and New York: Verso, 2016.

Cohen, Patricia. "Richest 1% Likely to Control Half of Global Wealth by 2016, Study Finds." *The New York Times.* 19 January 2015. Accessed 19 January 2015. https://www.nytimes.com/2015/01/19/business/richest-1-percent-likely-to-control-half-of-global-wealth-by-2016-study-finds.html.

Cohen, Stephen F. "Distorting Russia." *The Nation* 298, 9 (3 March 2014): 6–11.

– *Soviet Fates and Lost Alternatives: From Stalinism to the New Cold War*. New York: Columbia University Press, 2009.

Cole, Juan. *Engaging the Muslim World*. New York: Palgrave Macmillan, 2009.

– "No Cause for War." *The Nation* 301, 24 (14 December 2015): 3–4.

Coll, Steve. *The Bin Ladens. An Arabian Family in the American Century*. New York: Penguin, 2008.

Connor, Philip. "Number of Refugees to Europe Surges to Record 1.3 Million in 2015." *Pew Research Centre*, 2 August 2016. Accessed 21 January 2017. www.pewglobal.org/2016/08/02/number-of-refugees-to-europe-surges-to-record-1.3-million-in-2015/.

Cotterill, Joseph. "Let's talk about ... the 1953 London agreement on German External Debts." *Financial Times*, 8 July 2015. Accessed 9 July 2015. https://ftalphaville.ft.com/2015/07/08/2133806/lets-talk-about-the-1953-london-agreement-on-german-external-debts/.

Cowen, M. P. and R.W. Shenton. *Doctrines of Development*. London: Routledge, 2006.

Coy, Peter. "'Give Me Your Yuan.' Chinese are Eager for U.S. Assets." *Bloomberg Business*. 1 August 2013. Accessed 11 November 2015. https://www.bloomberg.com/news/articles/2013-08-01/give-me-your-yuan-chinese-are-eager-for-u-dot-s-dot-assets.

Craig, Campbell and Fredrik Logevall. *America's Cold War: The Politics of Insecurity*. Cambridge and London: Harvard University Press, 2009.

Cressey, George B. *Land of the 500 Million: A Geography of China*. New York: McGraw-Hill, 1955.

Crews, Robert. *Afghan Modern: The History of a Global Nation*. Cambridge: Harvard University Press, 2015.

Cumings, Bruce. *North Korea. Another Country*. New York: New Press, 2004.

– *Origins of the Korean War*. Volume 2, *The Roaring of the Cataract, 1947–50*. Princeton: Princeton University Press, 1990.

Danahar, Paul. *The New Middle East: The World after the Arab Spring*. New York and London: Bloomsbury Press, 2013.

Daragahi, Borzou. "Syria: No end in sight." *Financial Times*, 16 March 2014.

Dawisha, Karen. *Putin's Kleptocracy: Who Owns Russia?* New York and London: Simon and Schuster, 2014.

Deaton, Angus. *The Great Escape: Health, Wealth, and the Origins of Inequality*. Princeton and Oxford: Princeton University Press, 2013.

Deb, Siddhartha. *The Beautiful and the Damned: Life in the New India*. Toronto: Anchor Canada, 2014.

De Bellaigue, Christopher. *The Struggle for Iran*. New York: New York Review Books, 2007.

De Grazia, Victoria. *Irresistible Empire: America's Advance Through Twentieth-Century Europe*. Cambridge and London: Harvard University Press, 2005.

Denyer, Simon. "See China's rapid island-building strategy in action." *Washington Post*, 1 July 2015. Accessed 3 August 2015. https://www.washingtonpost.com/news/worldviews/wp/2015/07/01/new-images-show-china-building-military-facilities-in-south-china-sea/?utm_term=.3646b6681f38.

D'Eramo, Marco. "They, the People." *New Left Review* 2/103 (January–February 2017): 129–38.

Dietrich, Christopher R.W. *Oil Revolution: Anticolonial Elites, Sovereign Rights, and the Economic Culture of Decolonization*. Cambridge and London: Cambridge University Press, 2017.

Dikotter, Frank. *Mao's Great Famine: The History of China's Most Devastating Catastrophe, 1958–1962*. New York: Walker & Co., 2010.

Dinges, John. *The Condor Years: How Pinochet and His Allies Brought Terrorism to Three Continents*. New York: New Press, 2004.

Djilas, Milovan. *The New Class: An Analysis of the Communist System*. New York: Praeger, 1957.

Dosman, Edgar J. *The Life and Times of Raúl Prebisch, 1901–1986*. Montreal and Kingston: McGill-Queen's University Press, 2008.

Dower, John W. *Embracing Defeat: Japan in the Wake of World War II*. New York and London: Norton, 1999.

Doyle, John. "What Firestone did in Liberia for 'profit, profit, profit." *The Globe and Mail*, 17 November 2014. Accessed 18 November 2014. https://beta.theglobeandmail.com/arts/television/john-doyle-what-firestone-did-in-liberia-for-profit-profit-profit/article21619367/?ref=http://www.theglobeandmail.com&

Drèze, Jean and Amartya Sen. *An Uncertain Glory: India and Its Contradictions*. Princeton and Oxford: Princeton University Press, 2013.

Dubow, Saul. *Apartheid, 1948–1994*. Oxford: Oxford University Press, 2014.

Dyer, Geoff. "Global crises demand patience, says Obama." *Financial Times*, 6 February 2015. Accessed 6 February 2015. https://www.ft.com/content/3c01105a-ae23-11e4-8d51-00144feab7de.

– "Iran: Implementation Day Explained." *Financial Times*, 17 January 2016.

Accessed 18 January 2016. https://www.ft.com/content/bc7273ee-bbe9-11e5-b151-8e15c9a029fb.

Dyer, Geoff and Richard McGregor. "US shifts policy focus to Asia-Pacific." *Financial Times*, 15 November 2011. Accessed 20 May 2016. https://www.ft.com/content/a930e392-0fa9-11e1-a468-00144feabdc0.

Eckert, Carter. *Offspring of Empire: The Koch'ang Kims and the Colonial Origins of Korean Nationalism*. Seattle: University of Washington Press, 1991.

*Economist, The*. "Brazilian waxing and waning," 2 September 2015. Accessed 22 October 2015. http://www.economist.com/blogs/graphicdetail/2015/09/economic-backgrounder.

– "The ebbing of the pink tide," 28 November 2015. Accessed 20 December 2015. https://www.economist.com/news/leaders/21679192-mauricio-macris-remarkable-victory-will-reverberate-across-south-america-ebbing-pink.

– "The expanding middle," 10 November 2012. Accessed 22 October 2012. https://www.economist.com/news/americas/21565930-decade-social-progress-has-created-bigger-middle-classbut-not-yet-middle-class.

– "Leopoldo Galtieri," 16 January 2003. Accessed 2 February 2017. www.economist.com/node/1534686.

– "Shades of grey. It was right to let china in. Now the world's biggest trader needs to grow up," 10 December 2011. Accessed 6 January 2015. http://www.economist.com/node/21541408/print.

Ehteshami, Anoushiravan. *After Khomeini: The Iranian Second Republic*. New York: Routledge, 1995.

Eichengreen, Barry. *Exorbitant Privilege: The Rise and Fall of the Dollar and the Future of the International Monetary System.* New York: Oxford University Press, 2010.

El-Ghobashy, Mona. "The Praxis of the Egyptian Revolution." In *Journey to Tahrir*, edited by Jeannie Sowers and Chris Toensing, 22–40, London: Verso, 2012.

Enough Project. "Conflict Minerals 101," 6 March 2012. Accessed 30 May 30. https://enoughproject.org/blog/conflict-minerals-101

Etchemendy, Sebastián, and Condelaria Garay. "Argentina: Left Populism in Comparative Perspective, 2003–2009." In *The Resurgence of the Latin American Left*, edited by Steven Levitsky and Kenneth M. Roberts, 283–305. Baltimore: Johns Hopkins University Press, 2011.

Eui-Gek Hwang. See Hwang, Eui-Gak.

Evans-Pritchard, Ambrose. "Europe is blowing itself apart over Greece – and nobody seems able to stop it." *The Telegraph*, 7 July 2015. Accessed 8 July

2015. http://www.telegraph.co.uk/finance/economics/11724924/Europe-is-blowing-itself-apart-over-Greece-and-nobody-can-stop-it.html.

– "Nouriel Roubini dismisses China scare as false alarm, stuns with optimism." *The Telegraph*, 4 September 2015. Accessed 22 May 2017. http://www.telegraph.co.uk/finance/economics/11845194/Nouriel-Roubini-dismisses-China-scare-as-false-alarm-stuns-with-optimism.html.

Fair, C. Christine. *Fighting to the End: The Pakistan Army's Way of War*. New York: Oxford University Press, 2014.

Fichtner, Ullrich, Hauke Goos, and Martin Hesse. "How a Pillar of German Banking Lost Its Way." *Spiegel Online*, 22 October 2016. Accessed 28 October 2016. http://www.spiegel.de/international/business/the-story-of-the-self-destruction-of-deutsche-bank-a-1118157.html.

Fifield, Anna. "Spectre of Corruption Returns to South Korea." *Financial Times*, (London edition), 10 November 2007: 11.

Figes, Orlando. *Revolutionary Russia, 1891–1991. A History*. New York: Metropolitan Books, 2014.

Forbes. "India's 100 Richest People (2014 Ranking)." Accessed 27 July 2015. www.forbes.com/india-billionaires/list/.

Freeman, Linda. *The Ambiguous Champion: Canada and South Africa in the Trudeau and Mulroney Years*. Toronto: University of Toronto Press, 1997.

French, Howard. *China's Second Continent: How a Million Migrants Are Building a New Empire in Africa*. New York: Knopf, 2014.

Frieda, Gene. "China-Brazil link is top threat to global economy." *Financial Times*, 19 October 2015. Accessed 19 October 2015. https://www.ft.com/content/920b2708-6d9d-11e5-8171-ba1968cf791a.

Frieden, Jeffry A. *Global Capitalism: Its Fall and Rise in the Twentieth Century*. New York and London: W.W. Norton, 2006.

Gailbraith, James. *Inequality and Instability. A Study of the World Economy Just Before the Great Crisis.* New York: Oxford University Press, 2012.

Gall, Carlotta. *The Wrong Enemy: America in Afghanistan, 2001–2014*. Boston and New York: Houghton Mifflin Harcourt, 2014.

Gardner, David. "A dangerous moment for Iran's theocrats." *Financial Times*, 3 February 2016. Accessed 3 February 2016.

Garside, W.R. *Japan's Great Stagnation: Forging Ahead, Falling Behind*. Cheltenham and Northampton: Edward Elgar, 2012.

Gates, Hill. *China's Motor: A Thousand Years of Petty Capitalism*. Ithaca: Cornell University Press, 1996.

Gel'man, Vladimir. *Authoritarian Russia*. Pittsburgh: University of Pittsburgh Press, 2014.

Gerges, Fawaz . *A History of Isis*. Princeton and Oxford: Princeton University Press, 2016.

Gessen, Masha. *The Man Without a Face. The Unlikely Rise of Vladimir Putin*. New York: Penguin, 2012.

Ghosh, Jayati. "Economist Joyati Ghosh: India's Woes Foretell 'Chaos and Violence.'" *Spiegel Online International*, 28 August 2013. Accessed 10 April 2014. http://www.spiegel.de/international/world/indian-economist-jayati-ghosh-warns-of-chaos-and-violence-a-919048.html.

– "The Indian Economy (1970–2003)." In *The Cambridge Economic History of India, Volume II, c.1757–2003*, edited by Dharma Kumar, 1027–45. Cambridge: Cambridge University Press, 1983.

Giddens, Anthony. *Turbulent and Mighty Continent. What Future for Europe?* Cambridge and Malden: Polity, 2014.

Gilboy, George J. "The Myth Behind China's Miracle." *Foreign Affairs*, July/August 2004, 33–48.

Gildea, Robert. *France Since 1945*. Oxford and New York: Oxford University Press, 1997.

Gillis, Charlie. "The China Crisis." *Macleans Magazine*, 3 May 2012. Accessed 2 May 2016. www.macleans.ca/news/world/the-china-crisis-2/.

Gilpin, Robert. *Global Political Economy: Understanding the International Economic Order*. Princeton and Oxford: Princeton University Press, 2001.

Gindin, Sam and Panitch, Leo. *The Making of Global Capitalism: The Political Economy of American Empire*. New York: Verso, 2012.

Glyn, Andrew. *Capitalism Unleashed: Finance, Globalization, and Welfare*. Oxford and New York: Oxford University Press, 2006.

Goldberg, Jeffrey. "The Obama Doctrine." *The Atlantic*, April, 2016. Accessed 14 March 2016. www.theatlantic.com/magazine/archive/2016/04/the-obama-doctrine/471525/.

Goldman, Marshall I. *The Piratization of Russia: Russian Reform Goes Awry*. London and New York: Routledge, 2003.

Goldman, Merle. *Sowing the Seeds of Democracy in China: Political Reform in the Deng Xiaoping Era*. Cambridge: Harvard University Press, 1994.

Goldsmith, Leon T. *Cycle of Fear: Syria's Alawites in War and Peace*. London: Hurst, 2015.

Gordon, Robert. *The Rise and Fall of American Growth: The U.S. Standard of Living Since the Civil War*. Princeton and London: Princeton University Press, 2016.

Government of Canada. "HMCS Fredericton Deploys to the Black Sea on NATO-led Maritime Assurance Activities." New release, 5 January 2016. Accessed 30 May 2016. https://www.canada.ca/en/department-national-defence/news/2016/01/hmcs-fredericton-deploys-on-operation-reassurance.html?wbdisable=true.

Grandin, Greg. *Empire's Workshop: Latin America, the United States and the Rise of the New Imperialism*. New York: Metropolitan Books, 2006.

– *Kissinger's Shadow. The Long Reach of America's Most Controversial Statesman*. New York: Metropolitan Books, 2015.

Gruzalski, Bart. "The USA Attacked Iraq Because Saddam had W$D." *Counterpunch*, 22 March 2013. Accessed 29 October 2016. www.counterpunch.org/2013/03/22/the-usa-attacked-iraq-because-saddam-had-w$d/.

*Guardian, The*. "The Guardian view on the Greek crisis: the European project is at stake." 30 June 2015. Accessed 30 June 2015. https://www.theguardian.com/commentisfree/2015/jun/30/the-guardian-view-on-the-greek-crisis-the-european-project-itself-is-at-stake.

Guha, Ramachandra. *India After Gandhi: The History of the World's Largest Democracy*. New York: HarperCollins, 2007.

Guha, Ramachandra (ed.). *Makers of Modern Asia*. Cambridge and London: Harvard University Press, 2014.

Guilbaut, Serge. *How New York Stole the Idea of Modern Art*. Chicago: University of Chicago Press, 1983.

Gustafson, Thane. *Wheel of Fortune: The Battle for Oil and Power in Russia*. Cambridge and London: Harvard University Press, 2012.

Ha-Joon Chang. See Chang Ha-Joon.

Halliday, Fred. *Islam and the Myth of Confrontation: Religion and Politics in the Middle East*. London: I.B. Taurus, 1995.

– *The Making of the Second Cold War*. London: Verso, 1987.

Halliday, Jon and Bruce Cumings. *Korea: The Unknown War*. London: Viking, 1988.

Hallward, Peter. *Damming the Flood: Haiti and the Politics of Containment*. London: Verso, 2007.

Harding, Luke. "Revealed: The $20 bn offshore trail that leads to Vladimir Putin." *The Guardian*, 3 April 2016. Accessed 5 April 2016. https://www.theguardian.com/news/2016/apr/03/panama-papers-money-hidden-offshore.

Harvey, David. *A Brief History of Neoliberalism*. Oxford: Oxford University Press, 2005.

– *Seventeen Contradictions and the End of Capitalism*. Oxford and New York: Oxford University Press, 2014.

Haworth, Abigail. "Why have young people in Japan stopped having sex?" *The Guardian*, 20 October 2013. Accessed 27 April 2015. http://www

.theguardian.com./world/2013/oct/20/young-people-japan-stopped-having-sex.

He Qinglian, "A Listing Social Structure." In *One China, Many Paths*, edited by Chaohua Wang, 163–88. London: Verso, 2003.

Hecht, Susanna B. "Love and Death in Brazil." *New Left Review* 1/204 (March–April 1994): 129–37.

Hecht, Susanna B. and Alexander Cockburn. *The Fate of the Forest: Developers, Destroyers and Defenders of the Amazon*. Chicago: University of Chicago Press, 2014.

Helleiner, Eric. *The Forgotten Foundations of Bretton Woods: International Development and the Making of the Postwar Order*. Ithaca and London: Cornell University Press, 2014.

Hepburn, Andrew. "The great fall of China." *Maclean's Magazine*. 4 May 2015. Accessed 2 May 2016. www.macleans.ca/economy/economicanalysis/the-great-fall-of-China.

Hersh, Seymour M. *The Killing of Osama Bin Laden*. London and New York: Verso, 2015.

Hill, Fiona and Clifford G. Gaddy. *Mr. Putin: Operative in the Kremlin*. Washington: Brookings Institute Press, 2015.

Hiltermann, Joost. "Chemical Wonders." *London Review of Books* 38, 3 (4 February 2016): 3–6.

Hiro, Dilip. *After Empire: The Birth of a Multipolar World.* Washington: Nation Books, 2010.

Hobsbawm, Eric. *The Age of Extremes: The Short Twentieth Century, 1914–1991*. London: Michael Joseph, 1994.

Hochschild, Adam. *King Leopold's Ghost: A Story of Greed, Terrorism and Heroism in Colonial Africa*. Boston: Houghton Mifflin, 1998.

– "Rape of the Congo." *New York Review of Books*, 13 August 2009. Accessed 23 September 2014. http://www.nybooks.com/articles/2009/08/13/rape-of-the-congo/.

Ho-Fung Hung. See Hung, Ho-Fung.

Hollingsworth, Mark and Stewart Lansley. *Londongrad: From Russia with Cash. The Inside Story of the Oligarchs*. London: Fourth Estate, 2010.

Howard, R.T. *Power and Glory: France's Secret Wars with Britain and America, 1945–2016*. London: Biteback Publishing, 2016.

Hung, Ho-Fung. "America's Head Servant?" *New Left Review* 2/60 (November–December 2009): 5–25.

– "Canadianization?" *New Left Review* 2/88 (July–August 2014): 151–8.

– "China's Rise Stalled?" *New Left Review* 2/81 (May–June 2013): 154–60.

– “The Three Transformations of Global Capitalism.” In *China and the Transformation of Global Capitalism* edited by Ho-Fung Hung. Baltimore: Johns Hopkins University Press, 2009.

Hunter, Wendy. “Brazil: the PT in Power.” In *The Resurgence of the Latin American Left*, edited by Steven Levitsky and Kenneth M. Roberts, 306–24. Baltimore: Johns Hopkins University Press, 2011.

Huntington, Samuel P. *The Clash of Civilizations and the Remaking of World Order*. New York: Simon and Schuster, 1996.

Hwang, Eui-Gak. *The Korean Economies: A Comparison of North and South*. Oxford: Oxford University Press, 1993.

Inman, Philip. “Economics students call for shakeup of the way their subject is taught.” *The Guardian*, 4 May 2014. Accessed 8 March 2017. https://www.theguardian.com/education/2014/may/04/economics-students-overhaul-subject-teaching.

– “Mubarak family fortune could reach $70bn, says expert.” *The Guardian*, 4 February 2011. Accessed 25 May 2015. https://www.theguardian.com/world/2011/feb/04/hosni-mubarak-family-fortune.

Jachnow, Joachim. “What’s Become of the German Greens?” *New Left Review* 2/81 (May–June 2013): 95–117.

Jackson, James K. “Foreign Direct Investment in the United States: An economic Analysis.” *Congressional Research Service*, 11 December 2013. Accessed 8 January 2014. http://digitalcommons.ilr.cornell.edu/key_workplace/1201/.

– “U.S. Direct Investment Abroad: Trends and Current Issues.” *Congressional Research Service*, 11 December 2013. Accessed 7 January 2014. http://digitalcommons.ilr.cornell.edu/key_workplace/1202/.

Jacques, Martin. *When China Rules the World: The Rise of the Middle Kingdom and the End of the Western World*. New York: Penguin, 2009.

Jager, Sheila Miyoshi. *Brothers at War: The Unending Conflict in Korea*. New York and London: Norton, 2013.

Jalal, Ayesha. *The Struggle for Pakistan: A Muslim Homeland and Global Politics*. Cambridge and London: Harvard University Press, 2014.

*Japan Times*. “OECD cuts global economic outlook for 2016 amid China slowdown.” 9 November 2015. Accessed 18 May 2016). www.japantimes.co.jp/news/2015/11/09/business/oecd-cuts-global-economic-outlook-2016-amid-China-slowdown.

Jarausch, Konrad H. *After Hitler: Recivilizing Germans, 1945–1995*. Oxford and New York: Oxford University Press, 2006.

– *Out of the Ashes: A New History of Europe in the Twentieth Century*. Princeton: Princeton University Press, 2015.

Jerven, Morten. *Poor Numbers: How We Are Misled by African Development Statistics and What to Do About It*. Ithaca: Cornell University Press, 2013.

Johnson, Chalmers. *Blowback: The Costs and Consequences of American Empire* New York: Metropolitan, 2000.

– *MITI and the Japanese Miracle: The Growth of Industrial Policy, 1925–1975*. Stanford: Stanford University Press, 1982.

Johnson, R.W. *South Africa: The First Man, the Last Nation.* London: Weidenfeld and Nicholson, 2004.

– "R.W. Johnson: In South Africa, the reality is debt and corruption." *Evening Standard*, 10 December 2013. Accessed 23 September 2014. http://standard.co.uk/comment/rwjohnson-in-south-africa-the-reality-is-debt-and-corruption-8994993.html.

Johnson, Simon and James Kwak. *13 Bankers: The Wall Street Takeover and the Next Financial Meltdown*. London: Vintage, 2011.

Jones, Jeffrey. "China faces buyers' remorse in Canada's oil patch." *The Globe and Mail*, 17 August 2014. Accessed 12 November 2015. https://beta.theglobeandmail.com/report-on-business/industry-news/energy-and-resources/china-faces-oil-patch-buyers-remorse/article20090355/?ref=http://www.theglobeandmail.com&.

Jones, Sam. "Dmitry Medvedev warns of a new cold war." *Financial Times*, 13 February 2016. Accessed 13 February 2016.

Judah, Ben. *Fragile Empire: How Russia Fell In and Out of Love with Vladimir Putin*. New Haven: Yale University Press, 2014.

Judt, Tony. *Postwar: A History of Europe since 1945*. New York: Penguin, 2005.

Juhasz, Antonia. "Why the war in Iraq was fought for Big Oil." *CNN*, 19 March 2013. Accessed 29 October 2016. www.cnn.com/2013/03/19/opinion/iraq-war-oil-juhasz.

Kandil, Hazem. *Soldiers, Spies and Statesmen. Egypt's Road to Revolt*. London and New York: Verso, 2012.

Keenan, Jeremy. *The Dying Sahara: US Imperialism and Terror in Africa*. London: Pluto Press, 2013.

Kelley, Colin P., Shahrzad Mohtadi, Mark A. Cane, Richard Seager, and Yochanan Kushnir. "Climate Change in the Fertile Crescent and Implications of the Recent Syrian Drought." *Proceedings of the National Academy of Sciences*, 112, 11. Accessed 11 May 11, 2017. www.pnas.org/content/112/11/3241.

Kennedy, Paul. *The Rise and Fall of the Great Powers: Economic Change and Military Conflict from 1500 to 2000*. New York: Random House, 1987.

Kepel, Gilles. *Jihad. The Trail of Political Islam.* Cambridge: Harvard University Press, 2002.

– *The War for Muslim Minds: Islam and the West.* Cambridge and London: Harvard University Press, 2004.

Khan, Yasmin. *The Great Partition: The Making of India and Pakistan*. New Haven: Yale University Press, 2007.

Kinzer, Stephen. *All the Shah's Men: An American Coup and the Roots of Middle East Terror*. Hoboken: Wiley, 2003.

Klein, Laurence R. and Marshall Pomer (eds.), *The New Russia: Transition Gone Awry*. Stanford: Stanford University Press, 2000.

Klein, Naomi. *The Shock Doctrine: The Rise of Disaster Capitalism*. Toronto: Random House, 2007.

Koczanowicz, Leszek. "The Polish Case. Community and Democracy under the PiS." *New Left Review*, 2/102 (November–December 2016): 77–96.

Kotz, David M. *The Rise and Fall of Neoliberal Capitalism*. Boston: Harvard University Press, 2015.

Kovach, Bob and Carter, Chelsea J. "U.S.-Japan deal withdraws 9,000 Marines from Okinawa." *CNN*, 27 April 2012. Accessed 21 May 2016. www.CNN.com/2012/world/asia/japan/US/ okinawa/.

Krugman, Paul. "Europe's Impossible Dream." *The New York Times*, 20 July 2015. Accessed 20 July 2015. https://www.nytimes.com/2015/07/20/opinion/paul-krugman-europes-impossible-dream.html.

– "Killing the European Project." *The New York Times*, 12 July 2015. Accessed 13 July 2015. http://krugmen.blogs.nytimes.com/?_r=1.

– "Voodoo Never Dies." *New York Times*, 2 October 2015. Accessed 10 October 2015. https://www.nytimes.com/2015/10/02/opinion/voodoo-never-dies.html.

Kruse, Kevin M. *One Nation Under God: How Corporate America Invented Christian America*. New York: Basic Books, 2015.

Kurbjuweit, Dirk. "America Has Abdicated Its Leadership of the West." *Spiegel International*. 14 November 2016. Accessed 21 November 2016. http://www.spiegel.de/international/world/trump-election-means-europe-must-now-lead-west-a-1120929.html

Kuper, Simon. "America's Elections – or the Worlds?" *Financial Times*, 27 October 2016. Accessed 28 October 2016.

Kwak, James. *Economism: Bad Economics and the Rise of Inequality*. New York: Pantheon Books, 2017.

Lal, Deepak. "An Indian Economic Miracle?" *Cato Journal*, 28, 1 (Winter 2008). Accessed 3 May 2014. http://citeseerx.ist.psu.edu/viewdoc/download?doi=10.1.1.562.2375&rep=rep1&type=pdf

Lam, Willy Wo-Lap. *Chinese Politics in the Era of Xi Jinping: Renaissance, Reform, or Retrogression*. New York and London: Routledge, 2015.

Langewiesche, William. "The Mega-Bunker of Baghdad." Letter from Baghdad, *Vanity Fair*, November 2007. Accessed 19 November 2011. https://www.vanityfair.com/news/2007/11/langewiesche200711.

Lardy, Nicholas R. "Economic Recovery and the First Five-Year Plan." In *The Cambridge History of China*, volume 14, *The People's Republic: The Emergence of Revolutionary China, 1949–1965*, edited by Roderick MacFarquhar and John K. Fairbank, 144–84. Cambridge: Cambridge University Press, 1987.

Lauzière, Henri. *The Making of Salafism: Islamic Reform in the Twentieth Century*. New York: Columbia University Press, 2016.

Layne, Christopher. *The Peace of Illusions: American Grand Strategy from 1940 to the Present*. Ithaca: Cornell University Press, 2006.

Leahy, Joe and Samantha Pearson. "Brazil wealthy set to double in 11 years." *Financial Times*, 18 May 2012. Accessed 31 October 2014.

Lears, Jackson. "We came, we saw, he died." *London Review of Books* 37, 3 (5 February 2015): 8–11.

Ledwidge, Frank. *Investment in Blood: The True Cost of Britain's Afghan War*. New Haven: Yale University Press, 2013.

Legvold, Robert. *Return to Cold War*. Cambridge and Malden: Polity, 2016.

Lemann, Nicholas. "The Anointed. Can a former political radical lead Brazil through its economic boom?" *The New Yorker*, 5 December 2011. Accessed 18 October 2015. https://www.newyorker.com/magazine/2011/12/05/the-anointed.

Lesch, David W. *Syria: The Fall of the House of Assad*. New Haven and London: Yale University Press, 2013.

Levitsky, Steven and Kenneth M. Roberts (eds.). *The Resurgence of the Latin American Left*. Baltimore: Johns Hopkins University Press, 2011.

Lewin, Moshe. *The Soviet Century*. London and New York: Verso, 2005.

Lewis, Stephen. *Race Against Time*. Toronto: House of Anansi, 2005.

Liberti, Stefano. *Land Grabbing: Journeys in the New Colonialism*. London and New York: Verso, 2013.

Lie, John. *Han Unbound: The Political Economy of South Korea*. Stanford: Stanford University Press, 1998.

Lieven, Anatol. *America, Right or Wrong: An Anatomy of American Nationalism*. New York: Oxford University Press, 2012.

Lieven, Dominic. "Ukraine–The Way Out." *New York Review of Books* 61, 10 (15 June 2014): 75–6.

Lim, Louisa. *The People's' Republic of Amnesia. Tiananmen Revisited*. New York: Oxford University Press, 2014.

Lin, Chun. *The Transformation of Chinese Socialism*. Durham and London: Duke University Press, 2006.

Lin, Justin Yifu. *Demystifying the Chinese Economy*. New York: Cambridge University Press, 2012.

Littell, Jonathan. *Syrian Notebooks: Inside the Homs Uprising*. London and New York: Verso, 2015.

Luce, Edward. *The Retreat of Western Liberalism*. New York: Atlantic Monthly Press, 2017.

Lyman, Rick and Andrew E. Kremer. "War is Exploding Anew in Ukraine; Rebels Vow More." *New York* Times, 23 January 2015. Accessed 31 January 2015. https://www.nytimes.com/2015/01/24/world/europe/ukraine-violence.html.

MacFarquhar, Rodrick. "China: The Superpower of Mr. Xi." *The New York Review of Books* 62, 13, (13 August 2015): 32–4.

MacMillan, Margaret. *Nixon in China: The Week that Changed the World*. Toronto: Viking Canada, 2006.

Madeiros, Carlos Aguiar de. "Asset-Stripping the State: Political Economy of Privatization in Latin America." *New Left Review* 2/55 (January–February 2009): 109–32.

Madrick, Jeff. "Too Little, Too Late: Why?" *New York Review of Books* 60, 4 (7 March 2013): 14–16.

Mahbubani, Kishore. *The New Asian Hemisphere: The Irresistible Shift of Global Power to the East*. New York: Public Affairs, 2008.

Mance, Henry. "Thatcher saw Soviets as allies against Germany." *Financial Times*, 29 December 2016.

Mander, Benedict. "Argentina: Handover fears." *Financial Times*, 18 October 2015.

Manhire, Toby (ed.). *The Arab Spring: Rebellion, Revolution and a New World Order*. London: Guardian Books, 2012.

Marlantes, Karl. "Vietnam: The War That Killed Trust." *The New York Times*, 7 January 2017. Accessed 8 January 2017. http://www.nytimes.com/2017/01/07/opinion/sunday/vietnam-the-war-that-killed-trust.html.

Mason, Mike. *Development and Disorder: A History of the Third World Since 1945*. Toronto and Dartmouth: Between the Lines/University Press of New England, 1997.

– *Global Shift: Asia, Africa and Latin America, 1945–2007*. Montreal and Kingston: McGill-Queen's University Press, 2013.

– "History of Mr. Johnson. Progress and Protest in Northern Nigeria." *Canadian Journal of African Studies* 27, 2 (1993): 196–217.

Mayer, Jane. *Dark Money: The Hidden History of the Billionaires Behind the*

*Rise of the Radical Right*. New York, London, and Toronto: Doubleday, 2016.

Mazower, Mark. "European democracy enters dangerous times." *Financial Times*, 30 January 2015.

McCarrather, Eugene, "Heavenly City." In *Short American Century*, edited by Andrew J. Bacevich, 220–30. Cambridge: Harvard University Press, 2012.

McCormack, Gavin. "Abe Days Are Here Again: Japan in the World." *The Asia-Pacific Journal: Japan Focus* 10, 52, 1 (12 December 2012).

– *Client State: Japan in America's Embrace.* London: Verso, 2007.

– *The Emptiness of Japanese Affluence*. Armonk: M.E. Sharpe, 2001.

McCormick, Thomas J. *America's Half Century: United States Foreign Policy in the Cold War and After*. Baltimore: Johns Hopkins University Press, 1995.

McDonald, Duff. *The Golden Passport: Harvard Business School, the Limits of Capitalism, and the Moral Failure of the MBA Elite*. New York: HarperCollins, 2017.

Mead, Walter Russell. *Special Providence. American Foreign Policy and How It Changed the World*. New York: Knopf, 2002.

Medeiros, Evan S. and M. Taylor Fravel. "China's New Diplomacy." *Foreign Affairs*, November/December 2010. Accessed 19 May 2010. https:www.foreignaffairs.com/articles/asia/2003-11-01/chinas-new-diplomacy.

Meek, James. "After the Vote." *London Review of Books* 37, 24 (17 December 2015): 5–8.

Mehta, Ved. *Rajiv Gandhi and Rama's Kingdom*. New Haven: Yale University Press, 1996.

Meredith, Martin. *The Fate of Africa: From the Hopes of Freedom to the Heart of Despair: A History of Fifty Years of Independence*. New York: Public Affairs, 2005.

Michel, Serge and Michel Beuret. *La Chinafrique: Pékin á La Conquête Du Continent Noir*. Paris: Bernard Grasset, 2008.

*Middle East Report*. "ISIS" 276, 45, 3 (Fall 2015).

Milanovic, Branko. *Global Inequality: A New Approach for the Age of Globalization*. Cambridge and London: Harvard University Press, 2016.

– *The Haves and the Have-Nots: A Brief and Idiosyncratic History of Global Inequality*. New York: Basic Books, 2011.

Milward, Alan S. *The European Rescue of the Nation State.* 2nd edition. London and New York: Routledge, 2000.

– *The Reconstruction of Western Europe, 1945–51*. London: Methuen, 1984.

Mitchell. Timothy. *Carbon Democracy: Political Power in the Age of Oil*. London and New York: Verso, 2013.

Mitter, Rana. "Mao Zedong and Charismatic Maoism." In *Makers of Modern*

*Asia*, edited by Ramachandra Guha, 93–116. Cambridge and London: Harvard University Press, 2014.

Montefiore, Simon Sebag. *Stalin: The Court of the Red Tsar*. New York: Knopf, 2004.

Mulholland, John. "'In 10 years' time, Ghana may not require any aid at all.'" *The Guardian*, 15 January 2012. Accessed 14 November 2014. https://www.theguardian.com/world/2012/jan/15/ghana-aid-10-years

Munchau, Wolfgang. "Greece's brutal creditors have demolished the eurozone project." *Financial Times*, 13 July 2015.

Munson, Henry J. *Islam and Revolution in the Middle East*. New Haven: Yale University Press, 1988.

Murphy, R. Taggart. "On Shinzo Abe's Japan. History and Legitimacy in East Asia." *New Left Review* 2/93 (May–June 2015): 113–27.

– "Japan's Economic Crisis." *New Left Review* 2/1 (January–February 2000): 25–52.

– "A Loyal Retainer? Japan, Capitalism, and the Perpetuation of American Hegemony." *The Asia-Pacific Journal: Japan Focus* 41, 3 (August 2010).

Muttitt, Greg. *Fuel on the Fire: Oil and Politics in Occupied Iran*. London: The Bodley Head, 2011.

Nairn, Tom. *After Britain: New Labour and the Return of Scotland*. London: Granta Books, 2000.

– *Break-Up of Britain*. London: Verso, 1977.

Nardelli, Alberto. "IMF: austerity measures would still leave Greece with unsustainable debt." *The Guardian*, 30 June 2015. Accessed 30 June 2015. https://www.theguardian.com/business/2015/jun/30/greek-debt-troika-analysis-says-significant-concessions-still-needed.

Nasr, Vali. *The Dispensable Nation: American Foreign Policy in Retreat*. New York and London: Doubleday, 2013.

Nkrumah, Kwame. *Dark Days in Ghana*. London: Zed, 1968.

– *Neo-Colonialism: The Last Stage of Imperialism*. London: Thomas Nelson, 1966.

Nolan, Peter. *Is China Buying the World?* Cambridge and Malden: Polity, 2012.

Nooteboom, Cees. *Roads to Berlin: Detours and Riddles in the Lands and History of Germany*. New York and London: MacLehose Press, 2012.

Nugent, Paul. *Africa Since Independence: A Comparative History*. Basingstoke: Palgrave Macmillan, 2004

– "States and Social Contracts in Africa." *New Left Review* 2/63 (May–June 2010): 35–68.

Nussbaum, Martha C. *The Clash Within: Democracy, Religious Violence, and*

*India's Future*. Cambridge and London: Harvard University Press, 2007

Nye, Joseph S. *The Paradox of American Power. Why The World's Only Super Power Can't Go It Alone*. Oxford and New York: Oxford University Press, 2002.

*Observer* Editorial. "The Observer view on Congo and the failure of democracy in Africa." *The Guardian*, 23 October 2016. Accessed 16 January 2016. https://www.theguardian.com/commentisfree/2016/oct/22/observer-view-on-congo-failure-of-democracy-in-africa.

Offer, Avner and Gabriel Söderberg. *The Nobel Factor: The Prize in Economics, Social Democracy, and the Market Turn*. Princeton and Oxford: Princeton University Press, 2016.

OICA. "2015 Production Statistics," n.d. Accessed 21 January 2017. www.oica.net/category/ production-statistics/2015-statistics/.

O'Meara, Dan. *Forty Lost Years: The National Party, the Crisis of Apartheid, and the Politics of the South African State, 1948–1993*. Johannesburg: Ravan Press, 1996.

Orwell, George. *Why I Write*. London: Penguin Books, 2004.

Osnos, Evan. *Age of Ambition: Chasing Fortune, Truth, and Faith in the New China*. New York: Farrar, Straus and Giroux, 2014.

– "Why Is China Parading Missiles on TV?" *The New Yorker*, 4 September 2015. Accessed 6 September 2015. https://www.newyorker.com/news/daily-comment/why-is-china-parading-missiles-on-tv.

Ostrovsky, Arkady. *The Invention of Russia: From Gorbachev's Freedom to Putin's War*. New York: Viking, 2015.

Owen, Roger. *The Rise and Fall of Arab Presidents for Life*. Cambridge: Harvard University Press, 2012.

Palley, Thomas. *From Financial Crisis to Stagnation: The Destruction of Shared Property and the Role of Economics*. New York: Cambridge University Press, 2012.

Pantsov, Alexander V. and Steven I. Levine. *Deng Xiaoping. A Revolutionary Life*. Oxford and New York: Oxford University Press, 2013.

Parker, David S. and Louise F. Walker (eds.). *Latin America's Middle Class: Unsettled Debates and New Histories*. Lanham: Lexington Books, 2013.

Pearson, Samantha. "Shopkeeper turned president is dividing voters." *Financial Times*, 25–26 October 2014, 3.

Peck, James. *Washington's China: The National Security World, the Cold War, and the Origins of Globalism*. Boston: Massachusetts University Press, 2006.

Pérez, Santiago and Taos Turner. "In Argentina, Mix of Money and Politics Stirs Intrigue Around Kirchner." *Wall Street Journal*, 28 July 2014. Accessed 15 October 2014. https://www.wsj.com/articles/in-argentina-mix-of-money-and-politics-stirs-intrigue-around-kirchner-1406601002.

Perlez, Jane and Buckley, Chris. "China Retools Its Military With a First Overseas Outpost in Djibouti." *New York Times*, 26 November 2015. Accessed 17 May 2016. https://www.nytimes.com/2015/11/27/world/asia/china-military-presence-djibouti-africa.html.

Perlstein, Rick. "Chinese Mirrors." *The Nation*, 25 June 2007, 25–34.

Pettis, Michael. *The Great Rebalancing: Trade, Conflict and the Perilous Road Ahead for the World Economy*. Princeton and Oxford: Princeton University Press, 2013.

Pfeifer, Karen. "Parameters of Economic Reform in North Africa." *Review of African Political Economy* 82 (1999): 441–54. Accessed 21 May 2016. http://www.jstor.org/stable/4006477.

Pgiaitsis. "Four out of ten Greeks Live in Poverty and Face Social Exclusion." *Chania Post*, 24 June 2016. Accessed 21 January 2017. www.chaniapost.eu/2016/06/24/four-out-of-ten-greeks-live-in-poverty-and-face-social-exclusion.

Phelan, Stephen. "Argentina in latest debt default crisis pits 'motherland' against 'vultures.'" *The Guardian*, 20 August 2014. Accessed 14 October 2014. https://www.theguardian.com/world/2014/aug/20/argentina-kirchner-debts-crisis-bond-holders-economics.

Piketty, Thomas. *Capital in the Twenty-First Century*. Cambridge and London: Harvard University Press, 2014.

– "Germany Has Never Repaid its Debts: It Has No Right to Lecture." *Die Zeit*, translated and published in *The Wire*, 8 July 2015. Accessed 9 July 2015. https://thewire.in/5851/thomas-piketty-germany-has-never-repaid-its-debts-it-has-no-right-to-lecture-greece/.

– "A New Deal for Europe." *The New York Review of Books* 63, 3 (25 February 2016): 4.

– *Why Save the Bankers?* Boston and New York: Hoghton Mifflin Harcourt, 2017.

Piketty, Thomas, Jeffrey Sachs, Hemer Flassbeck, Dani Rodrik, and Simon Wren-Lewis. "Austerity Has Failed: An Open Letter from Thomas Piketty to Angela Merkel." *The Nation*, 7 July 2015.

Pisani-Ferry, Jean. *The Euro Crisis and Its Aftermath*. Oxford and New York: Oxford University Press, 2013.

Pomeranz, Kenneth. *The Great Divergence: Europe, China, and the Making of the Modern World Economy*. Princeton: Princeton University Press, 2000.

Porter, Robin. "Why America?" In *British Foreign Policy and National Interest*, edited by Timothy Edmunds, Jamie Gaskarth and Robin Porter, 120–34. London: Polity Press, 2014.

Prestowitz, Clyde. *The Three Billion New Capitalists: The Great Shift of Wealth and Power to the East*. New York: Basic Books, 2006.

Prunier, Gérard. *Africa's World War: Congo, the Rwanda Genocide and the Making of a Continental Catastrophe*. New York: Oxford University Press, 2009.

Pugliese, David. "Canadian Navy finds 'heavy' Russian presence in Black Sea. Who would have thought?" *Ottawa Citizen*, 14 June 2016. Accessed 17 June 2016. http://ottawacitizen.com/news/national/defence-watch/canadian-navy-finds-heavy-russian-presence-in-black-sea-who-would-have-thought.

Rabe, Stephen G. *The Killing Zone: The United States Wages Cold War in Latin America*. New York and Oxford: Oxford University Press, 2012.

Rachman, Gideon. "India needs a jolt–and Modi is a risk worth taking." *Financial Times*, 28 April 2014.

– "Transatlantic spat exposes deeper cracks." *Financial Times*, 13 March 2015.

Rahtz, Joshua. "Germany's Faltering Motor." *New Left Review* 2/93 (May–June 2015): 129–38.

– "*Zuchtmeister* Schäuble." *New Left Review* 2/104 (March–April 2017): 107–31.

Rashid, Ahmed. *Pakistan on the Brink: The Future of America, Pakistan, and Afghanistan*. London: Viking, 2012.

Rathbone, John Paul. "The Party is ending for Latin America." *Financial Times*, 30 October 2014.

Reader, John. *Africa: A Biography of the Continent*. New York: Knopf, 1998.

Reid, Michael. *Brazil: The Troubled Rise of a Global Power*. New Haven and London: Yale University Press, 2014.

Reynolds, David. *Brittania Overruled: British Policy and World Power in the 20th Century*. Harlow and New York: Longman, 2000.

Roach, Stephen. *Unbalanced: The Codependency of America and China*. New Haven and London: Yale University Press, 2014.

Roberts, Hugh. *The Battlefield: Algeria, 1988–2002, Studies in a Broken Polity*. London: Verso, 2002.

Rodrik, Dani. "The Future of Economic Convergence." 2011 Jackson Hole Symposium of the Federal Reserve Bank of Kansas City, 25–27 August 2011. Accessed 11 January 2017. drodrik.scholar.harvard.edu/files/future-economic-convergence.pdf?m=1435006479.

Rogan, Eugene. *The Arabs. A History*. New York: Basic Books, 2009

Rogoff, Kenneth. "Why Trump Can't Bully China." *Project Syndicate*, 13 February 2017. Accessed 13 February 2017. http://www.nacion.com/opinion/internacional/why-trump-cant-bully-china/2OXKCGYTQVFSRIW-JBGPAP4S37Y/story/.

Rosen, Andrew. *The Transformation of British Life, 1950–2000*. Manchester and New York: Manchester University Press, 2003.

Roxburgh, Angus. *Strongman: Vladimir Putin and the Struggle for Russia*. London and New York: I.B. Tauris, 2012.

Roy, Olivier. *The Failure of Political Islam*. Cambridge: Harvard University Press, 1994.

Runciman, David. *The Confidence Trap: A History of Democracy in Crisis from World War I to the Present*. Princeton and Oxford: Princeton University Press, 2013.

Sachs, Jeffrey D., Ashutosh Varshney, and Nirupam Baipai (eds.). *India in the Era of Economic Reform*. New Delhi,: Oxford University Press, 1999.

Sakwa, Richard. *The Crisis of Russian Democracy. The Dual State, Factionalism and the Medvedev Succession*. New York: Cambridge University Press, 2011.

Samuel, Raphael. *Island Stories: Unravelling Britain. Theatres of Memory, Volume II*. London and New York: Verso, 1998.

Sardesai, Rajdeep. *2014: The Election That Changed India*. Gurgaon: Penguin, 2014.

Sartre, Jean-Paul. "Preface to Frantz Fanon's 'Wretched of the Earth.'" Accessed 30 August 2017. https://www.marxists.org/reference/archive/sartre/1961/preface.htm.

Sauerbrey, Anna. "The End of the Merkel Era." *The New York Times*, 10 February 2016. Accessed 14 February 2016. https://www.nytimes.com/2016/02/11/opinion/the-end-of-the-merkel-era.html.

Saunders, Doug. *The Myth of the Muslim Tide*. New York: Vintage, 2012.

Schell, Orville. *To Get Rich Is Glorious: China in the Eighties*. London: Robin Clark, 1986.

Schell, Orville and Todd Lappin. "China Plays the Market." *The Nation* 255, 20 (14 December 1992): 727–43.

Schmidt, Helmut. "Germany in and with Europe." Speech at the SDP Party Conference in Berlin. 4 December 2011. *Friedrich-Ebert-Stiftung*. Accessed 3 July 2015. http://library.fes.de/pdf-files/id/ipa/08888.pdf.

Schneider, Peter. *Berlin Now: The City After the Wall*. New York: Farrar, Straus and Giroux, 2014.

Sebag Montefiore, Simon. See Montefiore, Simon Sebag.

Setster, Brad. "China's WTO Entry, 15 Years On." Follow the Money. *Council of Foreign Relations*. 18 January 2017. 23 January 2017. https://www.cfr.org/blog/chinas-wto-entry-15-years.

Shambaugh, David. *China Goes Global: The Partial Power*. New York: Oxford University Press, 2013.

Shaxson, Nicholas. *Treasure Islands: Uncovering the Damage of Offshore Banking and Tax Havens*. New York: Palgrave Macmillan, 2011,

Sheffield, Matthew. "The rise of irreligion is the GOP's real demographic crisis." *Salon*. Accessed 20 August 2016. https://www.salon.com/2016/08/20/the-rise-of-irreligion-is-the-gops-real-demographic-crisis/.

Shehata, Samer and Joshua Stacher. "The Muslim Brothers in Mubarak's Last Decade." In *The Journey to Tahrir: Revolution, Protest, and Social Change in Egypt*, edited by Jeannie Sowers, and Chris Toensing, 160–77. London and New York: Verso, 2012.

Sherwood, Harriet, Helena Smith, Lizzy Davies, and Harriet Grant. "Europe's migrant 'catastrophe.' *The Guardian Weekly* 190, 26 (June 6–12 2014): 1, 13.

Shevtsova, Lilia. "The Sanctions on Russia: How Hard Do They Bite?" *The American Interest*, 4 April 2016. Accessed 2 February 2017. https://www.the-american-interest.com/2016/04/04/the-sanctions-on-russia-how-hard-do-they-bite/.

Short, Philip. *Mitterand: A Study in Ambiguity*. London: Bodley Head, 2013.

Siddiqa, Ayesha. *Military Inc.: Inside Pakistan's Military Economy*. Ann Arbor: Pluto, 2007.

Singh, Mahendra Kumar. "New Poverty Line: Rs 32 in villages, Rs 47 in cities." *Times of India*, 7 July 2014. Accessed 4 December 2015. timesofindia.indiatimes.com/india/new-poverty-line-Rs-32-in-villages-Rs47-om-cities/articleshow/37920441.cms.

Skidmore, Thomas E. and Peter H. Smith. *Modern Latin America*. New York: Oxford University Press, 2005.

Sluka, Jeffrey. "Death from Above." *Monthly Review*, May–June 2011. Accessed 25 May 2016. http://usacac.army.mil/CAC2/MilitaryReview/Archives/English/MilitaryReview_20130430_art013.pdf.

Smith, Timothy B. *France in Crisis: Welfare, Inequality and Globalization since 1980*. Cambridge: Cambridge University Press, 2004.

Snyder, Timothy. *Bloodlands: Europe Between Hitler and Stalin*. New York: Basic Books, 2010.

Southall, Roger. *Liberation Movements in Power: Party and State in Southern Africa*. Pietermaritzburg: James Currey/University of KwaZulu-Natal Press, 2013.

Sowers, Jeannie and Chris Toensing (eds.). *The Journey to Tahrir. Revolution, Protest, and Social Change in Egypt*. London and New York: Verso, 2012.

Spence, Jonathan D. *The Search for Modern China*. New York and London: Norton, 1990.

Spiegel, Der. "Donald Trump and the New World Order." *Spiegel Online International*, 20 January 2017. Accessed 26 January 2017. www.spiegel.de/international/world/trump-inauguration-signals-new-world-order-a-1130916.html.

– "The Hate Preachers: Inside Germany's Dangerous New Populist Party." *Spiegel Online International.* 10 February 2016. Accessed 28 May 2016. www.spiegel.de/international/europe/alternative-for-germany-shows-its-true-right-wing-colors-a-1076259.

Spiegel, Peter. "How the euro was saved." *Financial Times*, 11 May 2014. Accessed 18 May 2016. http://ig-legacy.ft.com/content/f6f4d6b4-ca2e-11e3-ac05-00144feabdc0#axzz4yFKBlCK2.

Spitznagel, Eric. "The Mysterious Death of Russian Oligarch Boris Berezovsky." *Bloomberg News*, 4 April 2013. Accessed 21 May 2016. https://www.bloomberg.com/news/articles/2013-04-04/the-mysterious-death-of-russian-oligarch-boris-berezovsky.

Stedman Jones, Daniel. *Masters of the Universe: Hayek, Friedman, and the Birth of Neoliberal Politics*. Princeton: Princeton University Press, 2012

Stephens, Philip. "Falling apart: America and Europe go their own way." *Financial Times*, 17 October 2013.

Stewart, Heather. "This is how we let the credit crunch happen, Ma'am." *The Guardian*, 26 July 2009. Accessed 2 August 2015. http://www.theguardian.com/uk/2009/jul/26/monarchy-credit-crunch.

Stiglitz, Joseph E. *The Roaring Nineties: A New History of the World's Most Prosperous Decade*. New York and London: Norton, 2003.

Stockholm International Peace Research Institute (SIPRI). "SIPRI Military Expenditure Database." Accessed 4 June 2016. www://wipri.org/databases/milex.

Subramanian, Arvind. *Eclipse: Living in the Shadow of China's Economic Dominance*. Washington: Peterson Institute for International Economics, 2011.

Svanpa, Narustekka. "The End of Kirchnerism." *New Left Review* 2/53 (September/October 2008): 79–95.

Taubman, William. *Khrushchev: The Man and His Era*. New York: Norton, 2003.

Tavernise, Sabrina and David M. Herssenhorm. "Ukrainian Military and Rebel Fighters Clash in Donetsk." *New York Times*, 21 July 2014. Accessed 31 January 2015. www.nytimes.com/2014/07/22/world/europe/ukrainian-military-and-rebel-fighters-clash-in-donetsk.html.

Teltumbde, Anand. "Saffron Neo-liberalism." *Economic and Political Weekly*

49, 31 (2 August 2014). Accessed 15 August 2014. http://www.epw.in/journal/2014/31/margin-speak/saffron-neo-liberalism.html.

Tempest, Rone. "Washington's Turn Next in World's Courtship of Rajiv Gandhi." *Los Angeles Times*, 11 June 1985. Accessed 25 September 2015 http://articles.latimes.com/1985-06-11/news/mn-10383_1_rajiv-gandhi.

Thakur, Ramesh. *The Government and Politics of India*. Basingstoke: Macmillan, 1995.

*Times of India.* "In Bihar, BJP fails to win, but tops vote share." 10 November 2015. Accessed 6 November 2017. https://timesofindia.indiatimes.com/elections/bihar-elections-2015/news/Bihar-election-results-2015-BJP-fails-to-win-but-tops-vote-share/articleshow/49738949.cms.

*Times of India.* "8 Indian states have more poor than 26 poorest African nations." 12 July 2010. Accessed 4 December 2015. https://timesofindia.indiatimes.com/india/8-Indian-states-have-more-poor-than-26-poorest-African-nations/articleshow/6158960.cms.

Todenhöfer, Jürgen. "Western bombs will fill Isis with joy." *The Guardian Weekly* 193, 26 (4 December 2015): 19.

Tooze, Adam. "A General Logic of Crisis." *London Review of Books* 39, 1 (5 January 2017): 3–8.

Tumulty, Karen. "American exceptionalism: an old idea and a new political battle." *The Washington Post*, 29 November 2010. Accessed 23 February 2015. http://www.washingtonpost.com/wp-dyn/content/article/2010/11/28/AR2010112804139.html.

Turse, Nick. *Tomorrow's Battlefield: US Proxy Wars and Secret Ops in Africa*. New York: Haymarket Books, 2015.

Utley, Hilda. *Japan's Feet of Clay*. London: Faber and Faber, 1936.

Van der Pijl, Kees. *The Making of an Atlantic Ruling Class*. London: Verso, 2012.

Van Middelaar, Luuk. *The Passage to Europe: How a Continent Became a Union*. New Haven and London: Yale University Press, 2013.

Van Reybrouck, David. *Congo: The Epic History of A People*. New York: Ecco/Harper Collins, 2014.

Varoufakis, Yanis. *The Global Minotaur: America, Europe and the Future of the Global Economy*, London and New York: Zed Books, 2013.

Wagley, Charles. "The Dilemma of the Latin American Middle Class." In *Latin America's Middle Class: Unsettled Debates and New Histories*, edited by David S. Parker and Louise F. Walker, 65–75. Lanham: Lexington Books, 2013.

Wang Hui. *China's Twentieth Century: Revolution, Retreat and the Road to Equality*. London and New York: Verso, 2016.

– *The End of the Revolution: China and the Limits of Modernity*. London and New York: Verso. 2009.

Watkins, Susan. "Casting Off?" *New Left Review* 2/100, (July–August 2016): 5–31.

Watts, Jonathan. "Dilma Rousseff's fate as Brazil president could hinge on her political enemies." *The Guardian*, 9 December 2015. Accessed 20 December 2015. https://www.theguardian.com/world/2015/dec/09/dilma-rousseff-brazil-president-impeachment-pmdb.

– "Former president Lula faces questioning by police over Brazil corruption scandal." *The Guardian*, 11 September 2015. Accessed 18 October 2015. https://www.theguardian.com/world/2015/sep/11/former-president-lula-brazil-corruption-scandal-police-questioning.

Weisbrot, Mark. "Why Macri's Win Is Bad News for Argentina." *Fortune*, 24 November 2015. Accessed 20 December 2015. http://fortune.com/2015/11/24/mauricio-macri-presidential-win-bad-for-argentina/.

Westad, Odd Arne. *The Global Cold War: Third World Interventions and the Making of Our Time*. Cambridge: Cambridge University Press, 2007.

Weyland, Kurt. "The Left. Destroyer or Savior of the Market Model?" In *The Resurgence of the Latin American Left*, edited by Steven Levitsky and Kenneth M. Roberts, 71–92. Baltimore: Johns Hopkins University Press, 2011.

Wikipedia. "Comisión Nacional sobre las Desaparición de Parsonas (CONADEP)." Accessed 19 October 2014. http://en.wikipedia.org/wiki/National_Commission_on_the_Disappearance_of_Persons.

– "List of Drone Strikes in Pakistan." Accessed 20 May 2016. https://en.wikipedia.org/wiki/List_of_drone_strikes_in_Pakistan.

– "List of countries with IKEA stores." Accessed 18 December 2015. https://en.wikipedia.org/wiki/List_of_countries_with_IKEA_stores.

– "Poverty in India." Accessed 5 May 2015. https://en.wikipedia.org/wiki/poverty_in_India.

Williamson, Edwin. *The Penguin History of Latin America*. London: Penguin, 2009.

Wilson, Andrew. *Ukrainian Crisis: What It Means for the West*. New Haven: Yale University Press, 2014.

Woddis, Jack. *Introduction to Neo-Colonialism: The New Imperialism in Asia, Africa and Latin America*. Lawrence and Wishart: London, 1967.

Wolf, Martin. "Why it would be wise to prepare for the next recession." *Financial Times*, 5 February 2016.

Woo, Jung-en. *Race to the Swift: State and Finance in Korean Industrialization*. New York: Columbia University Press, 1991.

Wood, Tony. *Chechnya: The Case for Independence*. London and New York: Verso, 2007.

Yapp, M.E. *The Near East Since the First World War*, Harlow: Longman, 1991.

Yassin-Kassab, Robin and Leila Al-Shami. *Burning Country: Syrians in Revolution and War*. London: Pluto Press, 2016.

Yuan Yang. "China GDP: Out with the Old Economy." *Financial Times*, 15 April 2016.

# Index